MORE ADVANCE PRAISE FOR
Separate and Unequal

"*Separate and Unequal* crystallizes a pivotal moment in American history. At its center is the gripping story of the eclectic team that comprised the Kerner Commission, individuals who confronted the raw realities of a nation torn by racial strife in the wake of historic civil rights victories. In his richly researched history of this infamous report, Steven Gillon captures both the promise still viable in 1968 as well as the emergence of the 'post-civil rights' racial and political order that dominates American life today. It is a timely and essential book."

—**Patricia Sullivan, author of**
Lift Every Voice: The NAACP and the
***Making of the Civil Rights Movement* and**
professor of history, University of South Carolina

SEPARATE AND UNEQUAL

*The Kerner Commission
and the Unraveling
of American Liberalism*

STEVEN M. GILLON

BASIC BOOKS
New York

Basic Books
Hachette Book Group
1290 Avenue of the Americas, New York, NY 10104
www.basicbooks.com

Printed in the United States of America

First Edition: March 2018

Published by Basic Books, an imprint of Perseus Books, LLC, a subsidiary of Hachette Book Group, Inc. The Basic Books name and logo is a trademark of the Hachette Book Group.

The Hachette Speakers Bureau provides a wide range of authors for speaking events. To find out more, go to www.hachettespeakersbureau.com or call (866) 376-6591.

The publisher is not responsible for websites (or their content) that are not owned by the publisher.

Print book interior design by Timm Bryson, em em design, LLC

Library of Congress Cataloging-in-Publication Data
Names: Gillon, Steven M., author.
Title: Separate and unequal : the Kerner Commission and the unraveling of American liberalism / Steven M. Gillon.
Description: New York : Basic Books, 2018. | Includes bibliographical references and index.
Identifiers: LCCN 2017035839| ISBN 9780465096084 (hardback) | ISBN 9780465096091 (ebook)
Subjects: LCSH: United States. National Advisory Commission on Civil Disorders—History. | United States. National Advisory Commission on Civil Disorders. Report. | Riots—Political aspects—United States. | United States—Race relations—Political aspects. | Urban poor—Social conditions—United States. | African Americans—Social conditions—United States. | United States—Politics and government—1963–1969. | Johnson, Lyndon B. (Lyndon Baines), 1908–1973. | Liberalism—United States—20th century. | United States—Social policy—20th century. | BISAC: HISTORY / United States / 20th Century. | HISTORY / United States / 21st Century. | POLITICAL SCIENCE / Political Freedom & Security / Civil Rights. | POLITICAL SCIENCE / Government / General. | POLITICAL SCIENCE / Government / National. | POLITICAL SCIENCE / Public Policy / City Planning & Urban Development. | SOCIAL SCIENCE / Discrimination & Race Relations.
Classification: LCC HV6477 .G56 2018 | DDC 363.32/31097309046—dc23
LC record available at https://lccn.loc.gov/2017035839

ISBNs: 978-0-465-09608-4 (hardcover), 978-0-465-09609-1 (ebook)
LSC-C
10 9 8 7 6 5 4 3 2 1

To Vantuir Luiz Borges

CONTENTS

Introduction ix

PROLOGUE "It Looks Like Berlin in 1945" 1

CHAPTER 1 "What Do They Want?" 15

CHAPTER 2 "Let Your Search Be Free" 43

CHAPTER 3 "I'll Take Out My Pocketknife
and Cut Your Peter Off" 65

CHAPTER 4 "I Think We Should Avoid Overstatement" 91

CHAPTER 5 "A Straitjacket of Facts" 111

CHAPTER 6 "White Racism" 133

CHAPTER 7 "Can You Really Say This in a
Government Report?" 151

CHAPTER 8 "That's Good and Tell Him I Appreciate That" 177

CHAPTER 9 "Lindsay Has Taken Effective Control
of the Commission" 193

CHAPTER 10 "Two Societies" 227

CHAPTER 11 "I'd Be a Hypocrite" 247

CHAPTER 12 "The Most Courageous Government
Report in the Last Decade" 267

CHAPTER 13 "The 60s and 70s Seem to Have Left Us Exhausted" 293

Acknowledgments 319
Notes 321
A Note on Sources 349
Index 357

Photos appear after page 192.

INTRODUCTION

On July 27, 1967, President Lyndon Johnson stood before a national television audience to announce the creation of the National Advisory Commission on Civil Disorders (NACCD). The speech followed deadly and destructive riots in Newark and Detroit, which marked the culmination of four consecutive summers of racial unrest in American cities. The violence in the summer of 1967 marked an important moment in the evolution of the civil rights movement from peaceful protests in the South and the nonviolent rhetoric of Martin Luther King Jr. to violent confrontations in the North and the angry voices of black nationalists such as Stokely Carmichael. The shift shattered the coalition that had just a few years earlier won passage of two monumental civil rights laws—the Civil Rights Act of 1964 and the Voting Rights Act of 1965—and it created a deep and bitter divide between black and white.

The Newark and Detroit riots came at a difficult time in the Johnson presidency. LBJ had dominated Washington during his first years in office. In 1964, after winning election in a massive landslide, he had pushed Congress to pass an ambitious set of social programs as part of his Great Society agenda. Now, however, he found himself trapped, bogged down in a costly and increasingly unpopular war in Vietnam that threatened to tear apart the Democratic Party. Liberals who had cheered his Great Society legislation now split into rival factions of hawks and doves over the war. While Cold War liberals pushed Johnson to wage a more aggressive war, a small but vocal group of critics attacked LBJ from the left, charging that the war squandered resources that should be spent at home. At the same time, a generation gap eroded support for his administration, as many young people, especially those attending elite private colleges and large state universities, vigorously protested the war and rejected Johnson's establishment liberalism.

While fighting off challenges from the left, LBJ was also facing a potent backlash from Republicans and many conservatives who opposed the expansion of federal power under his administration. Most of all, the right tapped into white suburbanites' growing fear of racial unrest. For many white Americans, urban riots appeared to be part of a crime epidemic that swept the nation in the 1960s. Their fears were justified. Property crime (burglary, larceny, and auto theft) soared 73 percent between 1960 and 1967. The rate of violent crime (murder, robbery, rape, and aggravated assault) doubled. Between 1965 and 1969, the crime rate in America increased by double digits every year. Despite the attention focused on cities, the crime rate grew fastest in rural areas and small towns.[1]

A reenergized Republican Party pounced on the divided Democrats. After being declared dead following Barry Goldwater's humiliating defeat in the 1964 presidential election, Republicans clawed back to relevance by attacking their opponents as soft on crime while winning over many moderates with appeals for "law and order." The GOP made major gains in the 1966 midterm elections, narrowing Democrats' control over Congress and limiting LBJ's policy options. The following year, when Johnson asked Congress for a tax increase to fund his Great Society programs, conservative Democrats and Republicans insisted that the administration reduce expenses before it would consider such a measure.

Then came the "long hot summer" of 1967, when riots ripped through more than one hundred cities. Nearly every week came new violent images of angry confrontations between police and protesters, along with widespread looting and arson that culminated with bloody confrontations in Newark and Detroit. By the end of July, with dozens of dead and whole city blocks burned to the ground, LBJ understood that he needed to assert presidential power and reassure the nation. But what could he do?

Creating a presidential commission seemed like the ideal option: it allowed him to demonstrate leadership without committing his administration to a specific course of action. He planned to kick the issue of urban violence down the road in hopes that by the time his commission issued its report, the crisis would have already passed. It was a strategy many postwar American presidents used to handle vexing political issues. Between 1945 and 1955, there was an average of one and a half presidential commissions appointed every year. Johnson would appoint twenty such commissions during his tenure as president. As the burdens on the presidency increased in postwar America, commissions became a convenient way for presidents to fill the gap between what they could deliver and what was expected of them. The popularity of presidential commissions also reflected the postwar fascination with experts and the belief that social scientists could offer objective solutions to complicated social problems.[2]

Johnson filled the eleven-member commission that he announced that evening with mainstream bipartisan figures. For chairman, he selected Illinois Democratic governor Otto Kerner. Although Kerner would not play a major role, his name would become synonymous with the commission and its work. New York's liberal Republican mayor John Lindsay served as vice chairman. There were two African Americans, two Republican and two Democratic members of Congress, representatives from both business and labor, and one woman. There were no radicals or young people, and there was no spokesman for the black nationalist movement. Johnson assumed that his mainstream commission would produce a mainstream report that would endorse the broad outlines of his existing domestic agenda and insulate him from attacks both from the right and from the left.

The new commission, however, failed to follow the White House script. Determined to assert their independence, commissioners hired a team of investigators, visited riot-torn areas, and held hearings with activists and public officials. Their final report, released in March 1968, used stark language to conclude that the riots occurred because white society had denied opportunity to African Americans living in poor urban areas. The report offered dire warnings that only aggressive federal action could prevent future unrest. It proposed a long list of specific recommendations, including the construction of six million new housing units, greater federal spending on education, and more generous welfare payments to those in need. The report stopped short of what many activists and some liberals might have liked, though. At the same time, the cost of funding the report's proposals was far more than President Lyndon Johnson could afford to spend while fighting a billion-dollar war in Vietnam.

Most observers focused on two lines in the summary of the report. Borrowing language from the landmark Supreme Court decision in *Brown v. Board of Education of Topeka* (1954), which declared that "separate educational facilities are inherently unequal," the Kerner Commission concluded, "Our nation is moving toward two societies, one black, and one white—separate and unequal." It also placed blame for urban ills on "white racism." The report asserted, "What white Americans have never fully understood—but what the Negro can never forget—is that white society is deeply implicated in the ghetto," adding, "White institutions created it, white institutions maintain it, and white society condones it."[3]

In many ways, it was remarkable that this group of establishment figures would point an accusatory finger at white racism. Before joining the commission, most members had only an abstract awareness of the conditions in poor urban areas. They were shocked by what they witnessed in their trips to riot-ravaged neighborhoods and by the willful neglect exhibited by white officials and public institutions. They saw firsthand that African Americans attended poorly funded schools and lacked access to jobs and even to decent sanitation. At the same time, the commission's field teams, sent to conduct intensive research in the riot cities, sent back damning reports that underscored the wretched conditions in many areas and documented a history of discrimination and white indifference to black concerns. As a result, a broad consensus emerged among the commissioners that they needed to use the report to educate the public and to do so by using provocative language that would shake white America from its indifference.

Had the report been written a few years earlier, LBJ might have embraced it and its recommendations. But the commission's independence and ambition came at an inconvenient time for the White House. LBJ's coalition was crumbling, the federal budget was tighter, and the president faced stiff opposition for his party's nomination. Fearing that he had created what domestic policy adviser Joseph Califano called "a Frankenstein monster," Johnson soured on his commission within weeks of announcing its creation and worked behind the scenes to sabotage its investigation. Privately, he had promised to fund most of the commission's work with a December supplemental spending request to Congress. He reneged on that pledge, hoping that cutting the commission's financial lifeline would force it out of business before it could issue a final report. But the gambit failed. In the end, a resentful and angry LBJ refused to accept a copy of the final report, and, in a fit of childish pique, he did not even sign customary letters thanking the commissioners for their service.

The tensions between the commission and the president were dramatic, but the commissioners and their staff were also deeply divided, despite the unanimous report they eventually produced. The debates on the commission exposed the fault lines that were emerging in American society. Generational and ideological differences split the young field team members, many of whom had been radicalized by their service in the Peace Corps or their time spent in the civil rights movement in the South, from the mainstream liberals, who dominated the senior positions on the commission. Deep ideological conflicts among the commissioners themselves reflected the larger public debate over race and riots. The commissioners could not agree on what caused the riots or on what solutions they should offer for preventing future violence. Largely because of John Lindsay's efforts, the final document managed to speak with one voice and to push liberalism to its limits. At just the time that the administration was trimming its sails, the commission issued a report that held LBJ accountable for the bold goals he had set in the early days of his administration.

Although the final report was unanimous, the commissioners had failed to reach consensus on many of their specific recommendations. In fact, the commission serves as a microcosm of the unraveling of postwar American liberalism. LBJ had chosen the commissioners because they each represented a constituency that made up his broad coalition. Their work on the commission, however, pushed members in very different directions and exposed the fragile nature of LBJ's consensus. Lindsay and Oklahoma senator Fred Harris would become increasingly skeptical that the nation could solve problems of race and poverty without fundamental changes that went beyond conventional politics. Within a few years, they would redefine themselves as nonpartisan populists, campaigning against a corrupt political system. Although he lost many of the votes on the commission, businessman Charles "Tex" Thornton's advocacy of law and order, and his professed fears of a white backlash, anticipated the conservative revival building on the horizon of American politics.

The Kerner Report represented the last gasp of 1960s liberalism— the last full-throated declaration that the federal government should play a leading role in solving deeply embedded problems such as racism and poverty. A Democratic Congress would continue to pass progressive legislation for the next decade, but none of it came close to the ambition and scope of the Kerner Commission recommendations.

Nevertheless, the Kerner Commission's legacy is enduring, and its haunting prediction about America becoming two societies, separate and unequal, is as relevant today as it was five decades ago. Certainly, there is no denying that the nation achieved significant progress on some fronts since the commission released its report in 1968. There is now a thriving middle class, African Americans are better represented in the professions, and a majority of Americans twice elected an African American president. The influx of new immigrants since the passage of the Immigration and Naturalization Act of 1965 has also made conversations about race in America more complicated. While the Kerner Commission discussed race solely in terms of black and white, today any meaningful dialogue must include other groups, most notably Hispanics and Asians. Tragically, however, much has remained the same. Those living in the poorest neighborhoods in large cities continue to be segregated from mainstream life and to face many of the same obvious signs of white neglect, even as they confront problems of drugs and gangs that are more acute than they were in the 1960s. Growing inequality, a massive shift of wealth to the rich, and the decline of high-paying manufacturing jobs in urban areas have compounded the misery.

Viewed in this context, the riots in Ferguson, Missouri, that followed the shooting death of Michael Brown in 2014, along with the disorder that followed the 2015 death of Freddie Gray, who died of a spinal cord injury while in the custody of Baltimore police, have reignited the debate about race and unrest in America. Surprisingly, the arguments about the causes of such unrest, and the solutions, have changed little in the past fifty years. Much as they did in the 1960s, liberals blame systemic discrimination in employment, housing, and education, along with racial profiling and aggressive policing in black neighborhoods, for creating the conditions that led to the riots. Similarly, much as they did decades ago, conservative pundits argue that the riots were the result of a breakdown of law and order and an outgrowth of permissive and misguided liberals who had convinced blacks that they were victims of an oppressive society and therefore not responsible for their actions.

Given this stalemate and our deeply polarized politics, it seems unlikely that the nation's political leadership will muster the will to even acknowledge the role of white racism in creating the conditions that caused the riots. Any realistic plan for using federal power to address racial injustice seems even more far-fetched. But in the unlikely event that the window of reform opens in the near future, the Kerner Commission's findings will provide the nation with a useful guide to the depth and persistence of white racism, its recommendations will offer a possible road map for change, and its history will provide a cautionary tale about the limits of American liberalism.

Prologue

"IT LOOKS LIKE BERLIN IN 1945"

O N   T H E   E V E N I N G   O F   J U L Y   12, 1967, police in Newark, New Jersey, pulled over John Smith, a forty-year-old African American taxi driver. According to the police, Smith became belligerent and abusive when they asked for his driver's license, and at one point he punched one of the officers. They took him to the Fourth Precinct station house, where they dragged the 150-pound prisoner from the car and carried him through the front door, placed him in a cell, and charged him with assault and battery, resisting arrest, and loud and abusive language. Smith, however, challenged every aspect of the police account. "There was no resistance on my part," he later told investigators. "That was a cover story by the police. They caved in my ribs, busted a hernia, and put a hole in my head."[1]

There is no dispute, however, about what happened next. The Fourth Precinct sat across the street from the redbrick Hayes Homes, a public housing complex. Because it was a hot, muggy night, many residents were sitting outside, and a few watched as the police dragged Smith into the station. Some cabdrivers used their VHF radio band to spread rumors that white cops had just killed a black driver. An agitated crowd of two hundred, many of them teenagers, gathered outside the precinct and started taunting the police, tossing home-made Molotov cocktails and setting a car on fire. The crowd at the station soon dispersed, but looters ran through the streets, smashing windows and pulling fire alarms. By three in the morning, after pleas from local civil rights leaders, the streets of Newark fell silent. The following afternoon, the city's Democratic mayor, Hugh Addonizio, dismissed the "isolated incidents" and assured residents the city was open for business. The violence, however, was far from over.

The next day, leaflets circulated around central Newark: "Stop Po-lice Brutality. Come Out and Join Us at a Mass Rally Tonight, 7:30 p.m., Fourth Precinct." The flyers attracted hundreds of protesters who, ignoring calls for peaceful protest, began roaming along Spring-field Avenue, the city's central business district, once again breaking windows, looting stores, and setting fires. Early on the morning of July 14, the mayor called New Jersey governor Richard J. Hughes, requesting that he declare Newark a disaster area and order the state police and the New Jersey National Guard to restore order.[2]

Within hours, state troopers along with heavily armed National Guardsmen seized control of the city, turning Newark into an armed camp. The guardsmen, 98 percent of whom were white, arrived in full combat gear, carrying loaded rifles. Unprepared for urban violence, nervous guardsmen and state police often fired indiscriminately at crowds and at apartment buildings where they suspected snipers were hiding. In most cases, they were shooting at shadows and at innocent bystanders. "Down in the Springfield Avenue area it was so bad," po-lice director Dominick Spina recalled, "that, in my opinion, guards-men were firing upon police and police were firing back at them." In some cases, the black-owned stores that had been spared by the loot-ers were riddled with bullets of the police and soldiers.[3]

On the fourth day of rioting, Governor Hughes summoned Tom Hayden, a founding member of the Students for a Democratic So-ciety, who had been organizing in Newark for three years. Hayden told the governor that if he did not withdraw the National Guard, "the troops are gonna massacre more people, and you're going to go down in history as one of the biggest killers of all time." Apparently, Hughes heeded the advice: he withdrew the National Guard a few hours later. By the time the guardsmen left Newark on Monday, July 17, twenty-three people were dead, including six women and two children, and more than one thousand were injured.[4]

Just as the flames abated in Newark, racial tension in other cities exploded. Five more New Jersey cities—Plainfield, Elizabeth, New Brunswick, Jersey City, and Englewood—began to stir. In Cairo, Illinois, firebombs lit up the night sky. In Minneapolis six hundred guardsmen were needed to impose order after two nights of rock throwing. Similar, though smaller, incidents occurred in two Iowa cities, Des Moines and Cedar Rapids. Other cities—West Fresno, California; Durham, North Carolina; Erie, Pennsylvania; and Nyack, New York—all witnessed unrest that required police action. But the most violent outbreak was yet to come.

On July 23, a week after the Newark riots ended, Detroit erupted after police raided five "blind pigs"—a term used to describe illegal after-hours clubs. One of the most popular blind pigs in the city was on the second floor of a printing company on the corner of Twelfth Street and Clairmount, behind a sign that read, "The United Civic League for Community Action." At a quarter to four on the morning of July 23, a black plainclothes officer entered the club. He purchased a beer for fifty cents. Having caught the club selling alcohol illegally, he signaled to a group of fellow officers, who burst through the door. Police had expected to find two dozen patrons. Instead, they found eighty-two. The police herded the customers out on the street below. Even at four in the morning, however, Twelfth Street was bustling, and a crowd of fifty people was standing on the sidewalk in front of the printing company.

After the police left the scene, large crowds continued to mill around the neighborhood. Someone threw a trash can through a store window, and then hundreds of others joined in, tossing rocks and looting stores. The police returned but did nothing to stop the rioting. As word spread that the police were allowing looting, more people poured into the streets. With daybreak, thousands of people from all parts of the surrounding community joined in. The scene had a carnival atmosphere, with women, children, and older residents indulging in merchandise from local stores.

Television coverage of the Detroit riot frightened the nation. "Since Sunday morning, mobs of angry Negroes have paralyzed the city, spreading fire and destruction through large areas," reported David Brinkley, the popular anchor of NBC's *Huntley Brinkley Report*. "The turmoil has forced business to a standstill. Chrysler and General Motors suspended production of new cars." A local correspondent on the scene spoke of the smoke that filled the air and the fires still burning in "a twelve-mile area of the nation's fifth largest city." Michigan Republican governor George Romney spoke directly to the camera, complaining about "uncontrollable arson, looting, and the threat to human life by snipers" in the city.[5]

Between eight and noon, the crowd swelled to eight or nine thousand, many of them angered by rumors that the police had bayoneted a black man and left him to die. Just after four, Governor Romney authorized deployment of the National Guard. Just as in Newark, however, the National Guard's presence inflamed the situation. According to *Newsweek*, the guardsmen were "a ragged, jittery, hair-trigger lot, ill-trained in riot control." It quoted one soldier as saying, "I'm going to shoot anything that moves and is black." In one instance, a "flash from a window" (which turned out to be the lighting of a cigarette) brought a .50-caliber machine-gun burst from a National Guard tank that killed a four-year-old child.[6]

Reluctantly, President Johnson sent battle-hardened combat troops equipped with tanks, machine guns, and helicopters to enforce the peace. By the time it ended, forty-three people had been killed and more than two thousand buildings burned to the ground. "It looks like Berlin in 1945," noted an observer. *Newsweek* called the riots "a symbol of a domestic crisis grown graver than any since the Civil War." Detroit, it wrote, was "an American Tragedy."[7]

Detroit's outbreak was followed by a spate of eruptions in neighboring Michigan cities—Grand Rapids, Kalamazoo, Flint, Muskegon, West Michigan City, and Pontiac. By the end of July, nearly seventy cities had experienced racial disorders, forty in the final week of the month alone. As *Time* noted, "In the summer of 1967, 'it' can happen anywhere, and sometimes seems to be happening everywhere."[8]

DETROIT EFFECTIVELY SERVED AS AN exclamation mark on three consecutive summers of racial discontent in American cities. In 1964 riots in the Harlem and the Bedford-Stuyvesant neighborhoods of New York erupted during five days in July. The Harlem riot left 1 dead, 118 injured, 465 arrested, and millions of dollars in property damage. A few days later, a riot broke out in Rochester, New York, forcing Governor Nelson Rockefeller to mobilize 1,000 National Guardsmen. On August 28, riots erupted in Philadelphia when police arrested an African American woman who was blocking traffic in a busy intersection. For three days the rioting continued, leaving 2 dead, 339 injured, and 308 arrested.[9]

The following year, 1965, the first major riot of the decade exploded in the Watts section of Los Angeles. "If a single event can be picked to mark the dividing line" of the '60s, *Life* later editorialized, "it was Watts."[10]

The unrest began on the evening of August 11, when a white police officer stopped a car driven by a twenty-one-year-old black man. When the man resisted arrest, a crowd gathered, forcing police to summon reinforcements. Within an hour, 1,000 residents of the predominately black suburb were on the street, hurling rocks and bottles at the cops and shouting, "Burn, baby, burn!" For four nights, marauding mobs burned buildings, while 500 policemen and 5,000 National Guardsmen struggled to contain the fury. Before the rioting ended, 34 were dead, nearly 4,000 were arrested, and property damage had reached $45 million. It took 14,000 National Guardsmen and several thousand local police six days to stop the arson, looting, and sniping.

The violence continued the following year, when thirty-eight disorders destroyed ghetto neighborhoods in cities from San Francisco to Providence, Rhode Island, during the summer of 1966. In all, the unrest resulted in 7 deaths, 400 injuries, and $5 million in property damage. Images of young black men looting stores while shouting "Burn, baby, burn!" sent shock waves through white society. None of the individual riots matched the intensity of the Watts riot, but combined they made 1966 the most violent year yet.

Why were the nation's cities exploding? The riots of the 1960s were different from those that had occurred earlier in the century. During World War I–era "race riots" in East St. Louis (1917) and Chicago (1919), whites had invaded African American neighborhoods and assaulted residents. In 1921 a white mob in Tulsa, Oklahoma, destroyed a square mile of a black neighborhood. World War II witnessed more than a dozen such race riots. In Detroit a clash between white and black youths in June 1943 ended with 34 dead, 25 of them African Americans. A disturbance in Harlem three months earlier, however, anticipated features of the 1960s riots. The violence there commenced after a white police officer tried to arrest an African American woman. The situation escalated and resulted in gangs of black youth roaming the streets, looting stores, and attacking white-owned businesses.[11]

In most cases, the official investigations of these earlier riots had blamed criminals and "riffraff," refused to criticize the police for often using excessive force, and downplayed evidence that racism, discrimination, and the unequal treatment of African Americans lay at the heart of the riots. The commission investigating the 1919 Chicago riot blamed the disturbances on "gangs of hoodlums." The official governor's report on the 1943 Detroit riot placed responsibility on black leaders for instigating the violence and on the black news media for spreading false rumors. While these reports dominated the headlines, separate investigations by black groups went largely unnoticed. For instance, Thurgood Marshall, chief counsel of the National Association for the Advancement of Colored People (NAACP), launched his own study of the Detroit riot, which concluded, "Much of the blood spilled in the Detroit riot is on the hands of the Detroit police department."[12]

The same pattern held true for the initial official investigations of the 1960s disturbances. Many Americans took comfort in the findings of the McCone Commission, established by California governor Pat Brown and headed by former Central Intelligence Agency (CIA) director John McCone, which studied the causes of the Watts riot. It had concluded that the riot was a "senseless" act of violence whipped up by a handful of alienated blacks. American society and its institutions were sound, the commission concluded. The violence was the result of a small group of agitators and was not representative of black opinion in America.[13]

Amid the disorders in Newark and Detroit in 1967, most political leaders and police officials continued to explain the riots as irrational acts promoted by a few rabble-rousers. Much of the media coverage similarly highlighted the extent of the violence and the hostility of those who took to the streets. One NBC correspondent asked Isaac Wright, a twenty-seven-year-old African American, why he participated in the Newark riot. "In the country of America, they don't want a black man to have nothing," he said, conveying the intense anger and hostility of many poor urban blacks. When asked what he hoped to accomplish by rioting, he responded, "Try and knock the hell out of any white man I see. Tear up his car, tear up his clothes, anything I could find that would destroy him and get him out of this area."[14]

The police and local officials in 1967 pinned responsibility specifically on two prominent black nationalists, H. Rap Brown and Stokely Carmichael. The two men seemed to be everywhere, exhorting crowds to violence. Their role lent credence to the idea—widely believed, although unsupported by evidence—that there existed a well-organized conspiracy to foment revolution in American cities. Carmichael, a twenty-seven-year-old West Indian who attended Howard University, captured the anger of many urban blacks when he coined the phrase "Black Power" after becoming the chairman of the Student Nonviolent Coordinating Committee (SNCC) in 1966. Perpetually dressed in a camouflage jacket and dark sunglasses, he dismissed integration as "a subterfuge for the maintenance of white supremacy."

In April 1967, Carmichael traveled to Nashville, where he urged students at the all-black Fisk University to "take over" the administration. The next day, a group of black militants seemed to take his advice, pelting police with rocks and pellet guns. In June he repeated his familiar refrain, urging black churchgoers in Atlanta to fight back against the "honky" establishment. Hours later, a group of teens looted a local shopping mall. To some, the incidents suggested that Carmichael had the power to provoke violence with his words or his presence. Shortly after the riot in Newark, Carmichael traveled to Cuba, where he told a gathering of Marxist-Leninists from throughout the Western Hemisphere that the "duty of every Revolutionary is to make revolution!" His remarks made front-page headlines across America.

Another SNCC member, Hubert Gerold Brown, known as "Rap" because of his ability to communicate with disenfranchised African Americans, dismissed whites as "honkies" and police as "pigs." In July, while Detroit was still burning, Brown stood on top of a car in Cambridge, Maryland, encouraging a crowd of three hundred African Americans to take their violence to the streets. "Look what the brothers did in Plainfield," he said, referring to the brutal murder of a white police officer. "They stomped a cop to death. Good. He's dead. They stomped him to death. They threw a shopping basket on his head and took his pistol and shot and then cut him." Amid cheers he concluded, "Harlem exploded. Dayton exploded. Cincinnati exploded. It's time for Cambridge to explode." Four hours later, the business district in Cambridge was in flames. Governor Spiro Agnew blamed Brown for the violence. The citizens of Cambridge, he told newsmen, had been victimized "by this man Brown [who] came in from out of town intent on sowing trouble." Police issued a warrant for his arrest.[15]

Brown fled to Alexandria, Virginia, where he was arrested and charged with inciting people to riot and commit arson. As he left the jail on bail, he condemned Lyndon Johnson, calling him "a wild mad dog and outlaw from Texas." Later he held a press conference, telling supporters that "violence is necessary. Violence is a part of American culture. It is as American as cherry pie. Americans taught the black people to be violent. We will use that violence to rid ourselves of oppression if necessary. We will be free by any means necessary." He told his supporters that if they gave him a gun, he "might just shoot Lady Bird."[16]

The riots of the mid-1960s, and the emergence of a new generation of African American leaders, including Brown and Carmichael, marked an important shift in the black civil rights struggle. Since the Montgomery bus boycott in 1954, the modern civil rights movement had focused on confronting a southern political and legal system that systematically prevented African Americans from exercising rights that most Americans of all races considered essential—the right to vote, the right of access to public facilities, and equal educational opportunity. This de jure discrimination was written into law and enforced by the state. The collision of an intransigent white power structure with the nonviolent strategy of civil rights leader Martin Luther King Jr. created a sharp moral contrast between the black struggle for rights and the harsh reality of an oppressive, dominant southern society.

King's policy of nonviolence failed to gain traction in the North, where blacks suffered from less formal but no less pernicious de facto discrimination. Although not officially sanctioned by law, overt discrimination in hiring, housing, and education produced the same result. In 1960 nearly half of all black families in the United States lived below the poverty line of $3,000 for a family of four. Median black family income was only 55 percent of white income, and the unemployment rate stood at twice the rate for whites. While European immigrants to northern cities benefited from high-paying union jobs, African Americans were excluded from training programs and rejected for high-paying positions in the construction industry. Blacks also faced discrimination in housing, which often confined them to living in the poorest areas of a city.[17]

For more than a century, civil rights leaders had debated whether the best way to improve the lives of African Americans was by altering white attitudes or by overhauling American institutions. At the turn of the twentieth century, W. E. B. DuBois had called upon African Americans to forge a sense of class solidarity with poor whites to produce a redistribution of wealth and power in America. More recently, Bayard Rustin had argued that American capitalism itself needed to be changed. Many middle-class black reformers, especially those connected with churches, focused instead on changing white attitudes. Martin Luther King's campaign for civil rights in the South in the 1950s and early 1960s used this approach. By 1967, however, King had grown frustrated by the intense white resistance and slow progress in the North and had moved closer to the positions of DuBois and Rustin.

The 1960s also witnessed the reemergence of another powerful tradition—black nationalism. In the 1920s, Marcus Garvey had promoted what he called "the spirit of race pride and love," telling Africans to put aside their differences and embrace their shared history. "We have a beautiful history," he declared, "and we shall create another one in the future." He established the Negro Factories Corporation, which operated grocery stores, restaurants, and a clothing factory. By the early 1960s, Malcolm X, a leader of the Black Muslims, had emerged as the most forceful and charismatic spokesman of black nationalism. Dismissing the aspirations of white civil rights leaders, he said that black nationalists did not want "to integrate into this corrupt society, but to separate from it, to a land of our own, where we can reform ourselves, lift up our moral standards, and try to be godly." In February 1965, Malcolm X was gunned down at a Harlem rally.

After Malcolm X's death, many black nationalists rallied around Carmichael's plea for "Black Power." Those who embraced the new message were frustrated by the slow pace of change and dissatisfied with liberal pleas for moderation, and they were willing to employ more militant rhetoric and tactics to achieve their goals. According to historian Thomas J. Sugrue, Black Power was not a coherent ideology but instead a "series of impulses." One of these was a rejection of gradualism. Many African Americans had also grown weary of pursuing the integration and assimilation of black citizens into mainstream white society. They rejected established civil rights organizations for having lost touch with the concerns of everyday African Americans. Many saw the struggle for civil rights at home as part of a larger international anticolonial movement in Asia and Africa. For that reason, they drew connections between America spending billions of dollars to fight an unnecessary a war in Vietnam while refusing to confront systemic racism at home. Finally, adherents of Black Power drew on popular postwar social psychology that stressed the importance of self-esteem and racial pride.[18]

The rhetoric of Black Power agitators like Carmichael and Brown, and the spasm of violence that engulfed many cities in the middle years of the 1960s, caused widespread fear. Most of white America had never been comfortable with African American appeals for racial justice, but now whites grew more openly hostile. During the 1940s and 1950s, for example, urban whites in cities such as Detroit had split their ballots. They voted for pro–civil rights candidates for president, but in local elections that directly impacted their communities, they consistently rejected any effort to end residential segregation. In 1963 a *Newsweek* survey found that 55 percent of whites objected to having a black family living next door to them; 90 percent would object to having their daughters date a black man. "I don't like to touch them. It just makes me squeamish," said one northerner. In 1964 voters in California, who elected Lyndon Johnson in a landslide, also passed, by a two-to-one margin, a referendum, Proposition 14, that repealed the state's new fair housing act. "The essence of freedom is the right to discriminate," observed a leader of the repeal movement.[19]

By 1967 the upsurge in urban violence hardened the attitudes of many white Americans. That spring, even before the unrest in Newark and Detroit, 82 percent of white Americans had an unfavorable opinion of civil rights demonstrations. For many whites, the riots altered the image of African Americans from victims to aggressors. The riot cost them the moral high ground. As sociologist and Labor Department official Daniel Patrick Moynihan said, at just the time that the federal government was making progress and demonstrating the need for integration, rioters were giving whites an excuse for saying, "Those monkeys, those savages, all Negroes are rioters. To hell with them." Georgia governor Lester Maddox was more direct, declaring, "You can't say 'please' to a bunch of savages, rapists and murderers."[20]

A poll taken during the Newark riot exposed the deep racial divide in America. A majority of blacks and whites supported LBJ's Great Society federal programs that helped the unemployed and improved conditions in urban areas. They sharply disagreed, however, on the causes of the riots. Blacks identified a lack of progress in housing, jobs, and education, along with police brutality. Whites disagreed. Only one white American in one hundred thought blacks were being treated "badly." Seventy-five percent thought that "Negroes are treated the same as whites." Whites blamed the violence on "outside agitators" and on "Negroes demanding too much." A clear majority of whites, 70 percent, did not think there was any danger of rioting in their cities in the next six months.[21]

Many people, black and white, spoke about the possibility of a bloody race war in America. One newspaper speculated that the summer of 1967 may be "the point in time when the American Negro finally lost all hope in the white man." Others expected that a white backlash to the unrest could produce open warfare on the streets of most American cities. New Jersey senator Clifford Case warned that the riots could split the nation "for all time into two warring camps."[22]

How should the nation respond to this danger? "In every national emergency," the *Washington Post* observed at the end of July 1967, "the country's attention automatically swings to Washington." The public, however, would soon discover that the federal government was divided over the causes of the riots and split on how to respond.[23]

Chapter 1

"WHAT DO THEY WANT?"

H AVING ASCENDED TO THE PRESIDENCY by the whim of an
assassin's bullet, Lyndon Johnson was determined to make
his mark on the office. After winning election in 1964 in a massive
electoral landslide against Republican Barry Goldwater, LBJ pushed
Congress to pass the most ambitious reform agenda since the days
of Franklin Roosevelt's New Deal. By the time of the Newark and
Detroit riots in 1967, however, Johnson and his administration were
under siege. Largely because of the Vietnam War, the most liberal
president in modern times found himself under assault by the left
wing of his own party. At the same time, a resurgent Republican
Party joined forces with conservative Democrats to block funding
for much of the president's domestic agenda. With his legislative options limited, and his political influence diminished, Johnson decided
the best course for dealing with the riots was to set up a presidential
commission to look into the causes of the unrest and to offer possible
solutions.

ON NOVEMBER 26, 1963, FOUR days after John F. Kennedy was
gunned down while riding in an open motorcade in Dallas, LBJ had

stood before a hushed and solemn joint session of Congress and committed himself to fulfilling the slain president's agenda. "We would be untrue to the trust he reposed in us," he said in his distinctive Texas drawl, "if we did not remain true to the tasks he relinquished when God summoned him." Always the political tactician, Johnson realized that Kennedy's death provided him with a powerful symbol to build political support for an expansive liberal agenda. "Everything I had ever learned in the history books taught me that martyrs have to die for causes," he later reflected. "John Kennedy had died. But his 'cause' was not really clear. That was my job. I had to take the dead man's program and turn it into a martyr's cause."

The "martyr's cause" that LBJ created consisted of an ambitious set of new federal programs to aid the poor and to expand the rights of African Americans. In 1964 he outlined his utopian vision for America's future in a twenty-minute commencement address at the University of Michigan. Americans, he told an appreciative audience of eighty thousand who interrupted him for applause twenty-nine times, had conquered a continent and achieved unprecedented prosperity. Now it was time for the nation to address the problems of poverty and racial injustice. The challenge for the future, he charged, was "to move not only toward the rich society and the powerful society, but upward to the Great Society." In this "Great Society," people would be "more concerned with the quality of their goals than with the quantity of their goods."

As part of his Great Society, LBJ launched an "unconditional war on poverty." The Economic Opportunity Act of 1964 authorized almost $1 billion for a wide range of antipoverty programs, including Head Start for preschoolers and the Job Corps for inner-city youth. The law also authorized creation of the Office of Economic Opportunity (OEO) to coordinate the antipoverty battle. And attacking poverty was only the beginning. That November he won a landslide victory over Arizona senator Barry Goldwater, attracting votes from all areas of the country—from labor and business, young and old, black and white—and from across the political spectrum. Johnson now had a mandate to support an ambitious agenda and the congressional majorities to pass it.

His massive victory, however, would prove both a benefit and a burden. It allowed him to push through Congress nearly two hundred major pieces of legislation addressing a wide range of social needs—medical insurance for the elderly, education funding for the young, immigration reform, consumer protection, aid for mass transit, urban development, and slum clearance. "The legislation rolled through the House and Senate in such profusion and so methodically," according to one White House official, "that you seemed part of some vast, overpowering machinery, oiled to purr." Yet the magnitude of his victory convinced LBJ that he could dramatically expand government spending without raising taxes, that he could help the poor while retaining the loyalty of business interests, and that he could fight both poverty at home and communism abroad. The president was convinced that he had constructed an enduring consensus and that the deep divisions that had characterized American politics since World War II were fading in the wake of unprecedented prosperity. He would soon learn, however, that deep cracks existed beneath his superficial consensus and that his ambitious agenda rested on the back of a fragile coalition.

No issues threatened his coalition more than civil rights. Improving the conditions of African Americans was at the core of Johnson's vision of a Great Society. His predecessor had been a reluctant convert to the civil rights cause. By the summer of 1963, however, sit-in demonstrations, freedom riders, and recalcitrant southern politicians had pushed Kennedy to embrace race equality. On June 11, JFK told the nation that civil rights was a moral issue, one that was, he said, "as old as the scriptures and as clear as the American Constitution." Eight days after his speech, Kennedy asked Congress for laws to support voting rights, to aid school districts that were desegregating, to ban segregation of public facilities, and to empower the attorney general to initiate proceedings against segregated schools. But Kennedy's legislation was stalled in Congress when he traveled to Dallas in November 1963.

Unlike Kennedy, LBJ knew how to get legislation through Congress. After his election to the Senate in 1948, Johnson had impressed powerful Democrats with his energy and ambition. As minority leader and then as majority leader, he became a master of parliamentary maneuver and a skillful behind-the-scenes negotiator. A tall, physically imposing man, Johnson was not afraid to twist arms to bend recalcitrant senators to his will. His technique became known as "the Johnson Treatment." "He moved in close, his face a scant millimeter from his target, his eyes widening and narrowing, his eyebrows rising and falling." Vice President Hubert Humphrey once described an encounter with Johnson as "an almost hypnotic experience. I came out of that session covered with blood, sweat, tears, spit—and sperm."[1]

A few days after Kennedy's funeral, Johnson called Martin Luther King Jr. and told him, "I'm going to try to be all of your hopes." At the same time, he informed Congress that he would not accept any compromise. "I don't intend to cavil or compromise," he told Georgia Democrat and close friend Senator Richard Russell. "I'm going to pass [the civil rights bill] just as it is, Dick, and if you get in my way I'm going to run you down."

The president was true to his word. He stood firm against entrenched conservative opposition, most of it from the leadership of his own party, and applied enough pressure to get a strong civil rights bill through Congress. On July 2, President Johnson signed the measure into law. The Civil Rights Act of 1964 was the most far-reaching law of its kind since Reconstruction. The *Congressional Quarterly* called it "the most sweeping civil rights measure to clear either House of Congress in the 20th century."[2]

LBJ did not stop there. In March 1965, sixty state policemen brutally assaulted a group of peaceful African Americans as they marched over the Edmund Pettus Bridge on their way from Selma, Alabama, to the state capital, Montgomery. White spectators cheered the police on, while Sheriff Jim Clark bellowed, "Get those God Damn niggers!" The vicious confrontation, seen on the evening news on all the networks, horrified the nation and pushed the administration into action. A few days later, Johnson went before Congress to make his case for a powerful new voting rights bill. Selma, he told the hushed chambers, marked a turning point in American history equal to Lexington and Concord. "Because it is not just Negroes, but really all of us who must overcome the crippling legacy of bigotry and injustice. And," he concluded, "we shall . . . overcome." Martin Luther King Jr. called Johnson's speech one of "the most eloquent, unequivocal and passionate pleas for human rights ever made by a President of the United States."[3]

In June LBJ told an audience at Howard University that the problems facing African Americans developed "from centuries of oppression and persecution" and flowed from "the long years of segregation and discrimination." He declared that "freedom alone was not enough," arguing that the next phase of the civil rights movement must bring about true equality in all areas of American life. "You do not take a person who, for years, has been hobbled by chains and liberate them, bring him to the starting line of a race and then say, 'you are free to compete with all the others,' and still justly believe that you have been completely fair."[4]

Two months later, on August 6, in the President's Room of the Capitol, where 104 years earlier Abraham Lincoln had signed the Emancipation Proclamation, Johnson signed into law the Voting Rights Act of 1965. With a statue of Lincoln to his right, Johnson spoke of when blacks had first come to Jamestown in 1619: "They came in darkness and chains. Today we strike away the last major shackles of those fierce and ancient bonds."

FIVE DAYS AFTER THE VOTING Rights Act was signed into law, Watts exploded. LBJ could not understand how despite all the progress he had made, the new initiatives launched, and the political capital spent, young African Americans could turn against him. According to White House domestic policy adviser Joseph Califano, during the Watts riots the typically hands-on LBJ had refused to answer the phone or respond to his domestic advisers for guidance on handling the crisis. "He just wouldn't accept it," Califano recalled. When he finally decided to confront the situation, Johnson wallowed in self-pity. "How is it possible? After all we've accomplished? How can it be?" According to NAACP director Roy Wilkins, LBJ "seemed to take the riot as a personal affront, a rejection of all he had done for black Americans." "What do they want?" Johnson asked of his critics. "I'm giving them boom times and more good legislation than anybody else did, and what do they do? Attack and sneer. Could FDR do better? Could anybody do better? What do they want?"[5]

Two years and dozens of riots later, LBJ remained puzzled by the violence. In private conversations, he sometimes referred to the rioters as "hoodlums" and "commie agitators." At other times, he expressed sympathy for their cause and acknowledged that despite all that he had done, it would not be enough. "God knows how little we really moved on this issue," he said. "As I see it, I've moved the Negro from D+ to C-. He's still nowhere. He knows it. And that's why he's out in the streets. Hell, I'd be there too." LBJ further suggested that his Great Society programs may have inadvertently contributed to the riots by giving blacks hope—hope they had never experienced before. "When someone is kept as a slave," Johnson said, "there is a minimum of trouble. As suppressed people begin to rise from prejudice and discrimination there is naturally going to be more problems."[6]

Johnson also understood the frustrations of working-class whites, many of whom had labored hard to achieve only a minimum level of security and then watched blacks rioting on television. "There are thousands of people . . . who've worked hard every day to save up for a week's vacation or a new stove," he said, "and they look around and think they see their tax dollars going to finance a bunch of ungrateful rioters."[7]

After Watts LBJ assumed that his Great Society programs, when fully implemented, would help alleviate some of the anger and frustration that caused the riots. By 1967 he had no such hope. Johnson's cherished consensus was unraveling, he had already spent his political capital to get his ambitious legislative agenda passed, and he had fewer resources available to deal with the many problems at home due to the war abroad in Southeast Asia.

President Kennedy had committed the United States to preventing a communist victory in Vietnam, where rebels backed by China were threatening to overthrow a corrupt American ally in the South. Over the next few years, the situation in the South deteriorated, and the United States faced the real possibility that the government it favored would fall. Johnson had been reluctant to commit American ground troops to Asia, but he was also determined to prevent the communists from gaining ground in the global struggle for power. In July 1965, LBJ sent American troops to Vietnam, convinced that the show of force would convince the enemy to back down. The strategy failed. The North Vietnamese attacks escalated, and so did the American troop commitment. By 1967 there were more than 450,000 American combat troops in Vietnam, and US war planes were dropping thousands of bombs on North Vietnam. Despite the increased American presence, the military situation continued to deteriorate, and American casualties continued to mount.

The war was a constant source of frustration for the president, monopolizing his time and energy and shattering his fragile coalition and cherished consensus. It divided liberals into rival camps of hawks and doves, and it forged a gap between older Americans who were convinced that winning was necessary to preserve American prestige and stem the tide of communism and younger ones who questioned the Cold War assumptions of their parents. As the war dragged on, the number of protesters swelled and the vehemence of their dissent intensified. By 1966 students at leading research universities and elite private colleges were holding mass demonstrations, burning draft cards, and chanting derisive slogans like, "Hey, hey, LBJ, how many kids did you kill today?" Many establishment figures also began raising questions about American involvement in Vietnam. In January 1966, Arkansas senator J. William Fulbright, the powerful chairman of the Senate Foreign Relations Committee, held a series of nationally televised hearings that subjected American Vietnam policy to penetrating, sometimes caustic, analysis. Following the hearings, Fulbright declared that the United States was "in danger of losing its perspective on what exactly is within the realm of its power and what is beyond." Martin Luther King Jr., who had muted his public criticism of the war for fear of dividing the civil rights movement, now complained that "the promises of the Great Society topped the casualty list of the conflict."

The war also eroded public faith in Johnson's presidency. The phrase "credibility gap" found its way into the American vocabulary, as journalists began questioning the truthfulness of Johnson's statements on a whole range of issues, especially the war. The *Los Angeles Times* defined the term as "a phrase invented by Washington news men who didn't want to come out and call any public official a liar."[8]

LBJ repeatedly offered unrealistic estimates of how long the war would go on and how much it would cost. While confidently predicting victory in public, he privately feared defeat. LBJ's penchant for bending the truth to suit his purposes raised doubts about his integrity and began to undermine public trust in his presidency. Harry McPherson, a fellow Texan who served as a presidential speechwriter and adviser, noted at a meeting discussing the 1967 State of the Union message, "The President is simply not believed."[9]

In addition to dividing Johnson's supporters and casting doubts on his truthfulness, the war in Vietnam cost money and drained resources that LBJ had hoped would fund his domestic agenda. By 1967, confronting a growing budget deficit, LBJ recognized that he would need to ask the American people to make sacrifices if they intended to wage wars at home against poverty and abroad against communism. In his 1967 State of the Union address, Johnson asked Congress for a 6 percent surcharge on individual and corporate income taxes. Most members of Congress, however, preferred reductions in domestic spending to increases in taxes. Republicans and many Democrats, including powerful House Ways and Means chairman Wilbur Mills, expressed doubts about Johnson's tax surcharge. Mills said that any tax increase would have to be accompanied by deep cuts in domestic spending.[10]

Although LBJ refused to acknowledge the contradiction between his efforts to fight a war in Vietnam and reform society at home, this tension was obvious to many critics. As he had for the past five decades, syndicated political columnist Walter Lippmann captured the anguish of American liberalism. There was, he wrote in 1967, a disparity between the American ideals of opportunity and the reality of racism. This "ominous gap" had kindled the riots in American cities. Some of the older generation of black leaders accepted the gap and were willing, if not eager, to accept modest steps and gradual progress. Not so young black citizens and activists who demanded immediate reform and rejected the counsel of established civil rights leaders.

Lippmann believed that closing the fissure would require the full attention and all the resources of the federal government. "A general movement of reform and reconstruction can exist only if its objectives are the main preoccupation of the great masses of the nation," he wrote. In 1964 it had seemed possible that fulfilling the promises of the Great Society "would become the main American preoccupation for generations to come." But when LBJ decided to send troops to Vietnam, it became impossible, he wrote, "to expect people to be preoccupied at one and the same time with two dramatically opposite and contradicting commitments: with a war on the other side of the world and with the rebuilding of their own society at home." After LBJ went to war, Lippmann concluded, "the Great Society lost its momentum and its soul and became nothing more than a complex series of political handouts to the poor."[11]

ANOTHER FACTOR TYING LBJ'S HANDS as he confronted the unrest in Newark and Detroit was a white backlash and growing opposition in Congress to his Great Society policies. In 1966 Republicans had tapped into fear of crime and protest by campaigning on a tough "law-and-order" platform. They gained forty-seven House seats and three in the Senate. The Democrats lost more seats in 1966 than they had added in 1964. Republicans were giddy with the results, seeing the victory as a mandate to roll back the Great Society. "I view this election as a repudiation of the President's domestic policies," declared House Republican leader Gerald Ford. Even leading Democrats saw the political writing on the wall. Senate majority leader Mike Mansfield said the watchwords of the new Congress were "stop, look and listen."[12]

Nevertheless, some liberals pushed LBJ to continue to launch new social programs. The president found himself trapped between a liberal wing of his party that demanded he do more and voters who complained that he was doing too much. In the wake of the unrest in July 1967, many liberals argued that the riots were a spontaneous expression of desperation by people who felt excluded from the mainstream of American society. They wanted to address what they believed were the riots' root causes: poverty, lack of opportunity, a growing gap between rich and poor. Senator Robert F. Kennedy compared the riots to the "Bonus Army," a group of World War I veterans and their families who had camped out in Washington, DC, in 1932 to demand immediate payment of bonuses that were not redeemable until 1945. "Today the army of the dispossessed and disenchanted sits, not just in Washington, but in every major city, in every region and section of the country," he told a Senate committee. Liberals demanded renewed federal action to help the disadvantaged. "If we can spend billions of dollars rebuilding Germany and revitalizing the people of Europe, with more billions for arms for Southeast Asia, we can afford to spend a few billions putting our Negro people back on their feet," declared Martin Luther King Jr. The *New York Times* editorialized that cracking down on lawlessness was only part of the answer. "Cities will smolder until the walls that block Negro opportunity come tumbling down," it pronounced. "Anti-riot police will not prevent riots; pro-job, pro-education, pro-housing measures—in the long run—will."[13]

Johnson had developed a different understanding of the riots. Frustrated by the political deadlock in Washington, feeling constrained by a lack of resources, and lacking fresh ideas for preventing future unrest, LBJ resorted to conspiracy theories. Convinced that most blacks supported him and his policies, he became certain the riots were the result of a handful of communist agitators who were part of a well-orchestrated plot to foment violence in the nation's cities. According to Califano, Federal Bureau of Investigation (FBI) director J. Edgar Hoover had been providing the president with "reports of communist involvement, rumors of Chinese communist funding, and ominous predictions of even more dreadful disturbances to come." Speechwriter Harry McPherson noted that Hoover "served up a lot of raw evidence" to support Johnson's belief there was a conspiracy. The explanation was easier to accept than the alternative: that the riots were indeed the result of deep social problems. McPherson summed up the logic this way: "Good Negroes simply don't go around shooting the people unless they are inspired by bad Negroes or bad white people . . . Communists."[14]

The evidence suggests, however, that the White House willfully twisted Hoover's actual assessment of the riots to support its own preconceived view that the disturbances were the result of a conspiracy. Hoover and Johnson were engaged in a dance of mutual self-interest. The two men had been neighbors and friends, and they knew how to manipulate each other. Hoover, who had been a fixture in Washington since he organized Attorney General A. Mitchell Palmer's infamous raids in 1919–1920, saw the riots as an opportunity to enlarge his fiefdom and expand the FBI's surveillance efforts. Over the previous decades, Hoover had instituted a series of administrative reforms that refurbished the FBI's professional image even as it used illegal tactics—break-ins, telephone wiretaps, and electronic bugs—to smear its critics and keep politicians in line. LBJ needed Hoover's credibility as the most respected law enforcement officer in the nation to send a message that the White House was tough on issues of law and order. LBJ called on the FBI so often that he had a direct-line telephone placed in the bedroom of the FBI's liaison with the White House. Johnson also kept Hoover close because he was fearful of what information the FBI had collected on him over the years; he once said that he would rather have Hoover "inside the tent pissing out than outside pissing in."[15]

The FBI's official position was that local incidents instigated the riots in Newark and Detroit and that there was no national coordination or conspiracy. But Hoover could not pass up the opportunity to feed LBJ's paranoia by railing against radicals, communists, the New Left, and even establishment civil rights leaders. On July 26, Hoover sent LBJ a memo about the causes of the riots. Most of its thirty-three pages consisted of a detailed description of how "Black Power" advocates Stokely Carmichael and H. Rap Brown aggravated racial tensions. Although Martin Luther King Jr. opposed violence and had spoken out against the riots, Hoover discussed him alongside Carmichael and Brown, arguing that "certain individuals who have been prominent in civil rights activities must bear a major burden of the guilt and responsibility for the turmoil created by the riots." King, he wrote, "openly professed abhorrence for violence but his views and public observations have actually set the stage for its eruption." Yet buried in his rambling, tendentious diatribe against anyone who challenged the status quo was recognition that the riots "have been characterized by spontaneous outbursts of mob violence."

Hoover skimmed over the central fact that "there is no evidence to date indicating prior organization, planning, conspiracy, or subversive influence in the Newark riot." Nearly all the riots were instigated by an "initial minor incident involving police action," which quickly escalated into an "explosion of blind, irrational mob fury and action." It was at this point, Hoover suggested, that "several subversive organizations injected themselves into the situation."[16]

But Johnson likely never saw the key lines where Hoover, however begrudgingly, acknowledged there was no conspiracy. Certainly, White House aide Sherwin Markham did not highlight the finding in his two-page summary of the FBI director's report. Markham told the president that the riots were characterized "by murder, arson, looting, and wanton destruction." He made vague mention of the riots being "marked by a single incident," before moving on to describe how the "volatile situations were intensified by the efforts of 'Black Power' advocates." In keeping with Hoover's approach, Markham's memo underplayed the FBI finding that there was no evidence of a conspiracy and instead provided a detailed accounting of the various subversive groups that were involved in the riots.[17]

Despite his frustration and his sense of paranoia, however, LBJ had never abandoned his commitment to improving conditions in America's inner cities. He remained convinced that he could end the war in Vietnam and refocus the nation on the issues about which he cared most. Beginning in 1966, LBJ had sent White House aides on secret missions to fifteen American cities to assess conditions there and suggest short-term measures he could take to prevent future outbreaks. The reports coming back to the White House were not reassuring. In Washington, DC, residents complained about rats, exorbitant rents, and poor enforcement of building codes. A report from Chicago observed that many blacks were alienated and angry and predicted that "riots would come and be intensified." In Cleveland everyone believed that riots were "inevitable." A report from the Bedford-Stuyvesant section of New York City described residents as "hard and bitter" and observed that "all the conditions for another riot were present." In

Philadelphia staff members found "frustration and anguish" among urban blacks, many of whom lived in "filthy, rundown, rat and roach infested" apartments.[18]

To demonstrate that he had not abandoned the cities, and that he still believed that the nation could have both guns and butter, LBJ returned to Howard University in 1966 to publicly renew his commitment to the civil rights cause. He was fully aware of the political price he was paying for the promise he had made in his last appearance at Howard. In 1966 McPherson had warned him that Americans believed in the "equality of opportunity" but not in the equality of the "result," which LBJ seemed to be championing. Most people, LBJ's aide argued, believed that ending legal discrimination was enough. They saw a moral clarity in the civil rights struggle in the South, where African Americans were fighting against white racists who forced them to sit in the back of the bus. But now, McPherson noted, "there were no villains—at least none that strangers could identify—in the broken homes of the northern cities where men 'chose' to be unemployed, women chose welfare, and young people chose heroin."[19]

McPherson's sobering message did little to dampen Johnson's genuine commitment to the civil rights cause. He promised the audience that he would never "retract or retreat or amend" the promises he had made in 1965. He listed his impressive contributions to the cause of civil rights. "Because we have come so far," he declared, "I know and you know that we have the power to go further; to make the past 10 years only a prologue, and the next 10 years the time when the Negro in America can say at last, 'I am a free man.' I believe it will be so, I shall bend my will to make it so." By the summer of 1967, however, it was unclear how much further Johnson's will could bend.[20]

PRESIDENT JOHNSON'S IMMEDIATE TASK IN July 1967 was to stop the riots. He had to walk a fine line. If he appeared too sympathetic to the demands of the protesters, he would alienate many middle-class whites; if he took a hard "law-and-order" line, he would anger liberals.

According to McPherson, every time there was a new outbreak of unrest, the administration worried whether increased federal aid to the affected city would be perceived as "rewarding the rioters." LBJ feared the prospect of a white backlash that could turn back the clock on many of the gains that had been made since he entered office. Most of all, LBJ wanted to avoid sending federal troops into American cities to quell the violence. Not only did he fear the political backlash if federal troops accidentally killed innocent civilians, but he also worried that the images of hardened troops patrolling the streets of major American cities would signal the failure of his domestic agenda.

Despite the destruction and deaths, quelling the unrest in Newark was made easier for the White House because New Jersey governor Richard Hughes was a close Johnson ally. On July 14, two days after the Newark riot started, the governor called the White House to let the president know that he would not be asking for federal help, but he wanted LBJ to know that the city was experiencing "a very dangerous riot." White House chief of staff Marvin Watson scribbled on the bottom of the memorandum: "Do Not Think President Should Get into It." Johnson later spoke with Hughes by phone. "Well I just wanted you to know that the President, the Attorney General and everyone here wants to support you and give you any aid," he said, while stopping short of promising anything specific.[21]

While monitoring the riot, LBJ searched for some symbolic gesture to show the public he was taking the unrest seriously. At a July 19 cabinet meeting, LBJ urged officials "to do more on the problems with minority groups and with the cities." The problem, he suggested, was optics. "We are not getting our story over," he said. He also announced that he was setting up a cabinet task force headed by Vice President Hubert Humphrey.

After the meeting, LBJ held a private gathering with NAACP executive director Roy Wilkins and the Urban League's executive director, Whitney Young. Califano, who attended the meeting, was struck by the two African American leaders' "despair." Wilkins had reason to feel despondent. A few days earlier, at the annual NAACP convention in Boston, he fought back an insurgent movement of Black Power advocates demanding more seats on the board. Their goal was to change the "middle-class" image of the storied organization and push it toward more direct action to challenge the white power structure in America. Although Wilkins successfully defeated the insurrection, the affair left him deeply shaken. And both men seemed helpless and confused by the violence in Newark. "They had led so many successful battles for civil rights in the courts and Congress," Califano reflected. "Now they were at bay, numbed by their lack of influence."[22]

During his meeting with Wilkins and Young, LBJ proceeded to recite the many accomplishments of his Great Society, before launching into an attack on white liberals. LBJ never trusted liberals, and they reciprocated the sentiment. He had always believed that people from distinguished families, with old money and Ivy League educations, scorned a self-made Texan like himself. Although he had developed a close relationship with President Kennedy during his years as vice president, he remained resentful of the "Kennedy people," most of whom saw him as a caretaker president and anticipated Robert Kennedy returning the White House to the family. Liberals viewed Johnson as a slick wheeler-dealer devoid of any real principle. "We are now divided. We've got liberal, progressive forces going down different roads. . . . I am a progressive. I'm not a liberal," Johnson told Wilkins and Young. "A liberal is intolerant of other views. He wants to control your thoughts and actions." According to Califano, Johnson leaned forward on the arm of his rocker and asked, "You know the difference between cannibals and liberals? Cannibals eat only their enemies."[23]

LBJ viewed the problem largely as one of messaging. Poor blacks, he reasoned, were simply not aware of all the things his administration was doing for them. The vice presidential task force would help to get the word out, but Johnson never had any intention of giving it real power. LBJ was already steaming over a July 15 United Press International news ticker reporting that Humphrey had called Governor Hughes to offer federal aid. The offer had infuriated Johnson, who told Califano to inform the vice president that he had "no authority, spell it out N-O-N-E, to provide any federal aid to Newark or any other city, town or county in America." But Humphrey kept talking and making promises. On July 16, the Associated Press reported that the vice president had offered to send US marshals to Newark. LBJ told Califano he wanted the vice president "gagged for good," before he "brings down the Administration."[24]

Johnson expected Humphrey's task force to serve two purposes: to give the public the impression that the administration was taking the disturbances seriously and to keep Humphrey busy and out of the way. LBJ gave the new group clear instructions. It should focus largely on public relations. He wanted to make sure people knew that the nation was making progress under his leadership. Blame for the wretched conditions in urban areas rested not with his Great Society, but with members of Congress who refused to provide appropriate funding for Johnson's programs.

Dealing with the violence in Detroit was trickier for the Johnson administration because Michigan's governor, Republican George Romney, was a potential rival for the presidency. While Detroit burned, the two men engaged in a very public blame game. Romney criticized LBJ for hesitating to send in federal troops. LBJ, suspicious that Romney would try to blame the administration for the riots, insisted that the governor publicly state that he had lost control of the situation and specifically request federal troops. Johnson was worried about falling into a Republican trap, but he was also genuinely fearful of the consequences of federal troops killing American civilians. LBJ told aides that he was concerned "about the charge that we cannot kill enough people in Vietnam, so we go out and shoot civilians in Detroit." Despite his reservations, LBJ ordered troops from the 82nd Airborne and 101st Airborne to nearby Selfridge Air Force Base on

July 24 in the event they were needed. At the same time, he sent for-mer deputy secretary of defense Cyrus Vance, who was in Washing-ton to attend his mother's funeral, to Detroit to report on conditions there.[25]

Arriving that same day, Vance initially determined that the sit-uation was under control, but later that evening, when conditions deteriorated, he recommended sending in federal troops. Later that evening, a reluctant LBJ signed the executive order dispatching fed-eral troops to Detroit. According to Roger Wilkins, an African Amer-ican civil rights activist who served as the director of the Community Relations Service in the administration, Johnson shouted, "I don't want my troops shooting some ni . . . ," before realizing that Wilkins was in the room. He quickly substituted "pregnant woman." Deputy Attorney General Warren Christopher claimed that Johnson refused to "be stampeded into committing federal troops until he was sat-isfied that the situation was beyond the control of local resources." Even Califano, however, admitted that LBJ was being "overly legalis-tic." "Johnson could have ignored Romney's vacillation and political maneuvering," he wrote later. "He had the constitutional and legal authority to deploy troops."[26]

Shortly before midnight, LBJ went on national television to ex-plain his decision to send troops into an American city. J. Edgar Hoover, Attorney General Ramsey Clark, Defense Secretary Robert McNamara, and two other Pentagon officials stood on camera be-hind him. The image was designed to send a clear message regarding Johnson's commitment to law and order. Supreme Court justice Abe Fortas, who helped write the speech, convinced LBJ that Romney was trying to draw the White House into the mess in Detroit so he could then turn around and scream about federal intervention. Thus, the seven-minute statement mentioned Romney fourteen times and emphasized the "undisputed evidence that Governor Romney of Michigan and the local officials in Detroit have been unable to bring the situation under control." The not-so-subtle attacks on Romney caught the attention of the *New York Times*. "The President's midnight speech was devoted mainly to saying, with lawyerish repetition, that Governor Romney had lost control of events. He could not avoid taking a shot at Romney."[27]

Throughout the night, the president also badgered Hoover for information that would prove that the disturbances were communist inspired. "The President stated that he had been of the opinion that there was a concerted action and a pattern about all of these riots," Hoover wrote in a memorandum the following day. LBJ, he noted, wanted "evidence which would indicate that there has been a concerted action to bring about these riots." Hoover promised to comply with the request, but he pointed out that "at the present time from the information we have received from our field offices, there has not been any concerted action in the riots which have occurred." The FBI director reiterated its position that the riots had "been triggered by some individual incident," and while "outsiders" did not initiate the event, they rushed in after the riot "was in full force." He emphasized that the FBI also "had no information indicating that the communists initiated the riots."[28]

THE RIOTS IN NEWARK AND Detroit poisoned an already bitter well in Washington. Reflecting a widespread fear among white America, Congress responded to the unrest by pushing for tough law-and-order measures. Senator Robert Byrd of West Virginia said that the riots should be "put down with brutal force" and that looters should be "shot on the spot." Like the president, many members of Congress, Democrats and Republicans, assumed the riots were the result of a well-orchestrated conspiracy. "I can't help but believe that there is in the background some national plan," declared Michigan's Gerald Ford. Senate minority leader Everett Dirksen of Illinois claimed there was "mounting evidence" that the riots may be "the result of organized planning and execution on a national scale." At one point, he suggested that Molotov cocktails were being manufactured in factories in New York and other cities. South Carolina's Strom Thurmond pointed to a range of culprits, blaming the riots on "communism, false compassion, civil disobedience, court decisions and criminal instinct."[29]

Anger and frustration boiled over in the House of Representatives, where members tripped over each other to condemn the rioters and brandish their law-and-order credentials. Conservative Democrats were among the most vocal. Arkansas Democrat John L. McClellan, for instance, saw the riots as an opportunity to undermine civil rights legislation and recent Supreme Court decisions that guaranteed accused lawbreakers the right to an attorney and required officers to inform criminal suspects of their rights. At the same time, the Senate Judiciary Committee, headed by James Eastland of Mississippi, opened hearings on a tough crime bill. The first witnesses were police chiefs from around the country. North Carolina Democratic senator Sam Ervin, chairman of the Senate Subcommittee on Constitutional Rights, complained that Congress had adopted civil rights legislation in 1964 and 1965, under the expectation that the new laws, which he had opposed, would move protests from the streets to the courts. "In both years," he now said, "Congress yielded to this political blackmail. We legislated at gunpoint. If the mindless destruction of our cities has proven anything, I would hope it has now put this myth to rest forever."[30]

Sensing blood in the political waters, the Republican Coordinating Committee, the party's highest policy-making body, placed blame for the riots squarely on LBJ's shoulders. How many more people must die, it asked, "before the president will support or approve legislation to restore order and protect the people of this country?" A weekly House Republican newsletter accused LBJ of responding to the riots with "unpardonable vacillation, indecision and even indifference." Dirksen, the Republican Senate leader, was even more direct. "Today no one is safe on the streets, in his home, or in his property," he declared. "How many millions of people must be made homeless? How many thousands wounded, maimed or killed over the years before the president will support or approve legislation to restore order and protect the people of this country?"[31]

Democratic leaders, meanwhile, rushed to LBJ's defense. House majority leader Carl Albert said the Republican attempt to blame Johnson was "irresponsible and ridiculous." Senate majority leader Mike Mansfield argued that the best way to stop rioting was to approve LBJ's proposals for poverty and controlling the sale of guns.[32]

The hardening of attitudes destroyed any hope of bipartisan cooperation. After Newark Congress scuttled a plan to approve $2 billion for the War on Poverty. The administration believed that if the bill came to a vote on the House floor, it would face certain defeat. Another White House initiative met a similar fate in the wake of the riots. Earlier in the year, Johnson had proposed the Rat Extermination Act, which was designed to protect poor children from being bitten by rats. The measure would have created a two-year, $40 million program to exterminate rats and attack the conditions that breed them. When it came up for a House vote three days after the Newark riots, southern Democrats and Republicans ridiculed the bill and joined forces to defeat it, calling it a "civil rats bill." Florida representative James Haley got a laugh when he said, "Why not just buy some cats and turn them loose on the rats?" The next day, Congress overwhelmingly passed a crime bill that imposed a $10,000 fine and five years in jail on anyone who crossed state lines with the intent to incite a riot.[33]

Unable to agree on a response to the riots, the two parties in Congress punted and called for the creation of a "special" commission. Even here they could not agree on its purpose. The Republican Coordinating Committee called for a joint congressional committee "to investigate on an emergency basis" the "planning, organization, method of operation" of the rioters and to recommend steps to end the "rioting and civil disorder." Dirksen had his own ideas, declaring that he wanted a commission "to see if there is a touch of red behind" the riots. He sponsored a Republican resolution in the Senate that called for a committee not only to investigate the causes of the riots but also to examine any evidence that would "indicate the existence of any conspiracy to provoke such civil disorders and evidence which may indicate that such civil disorders have been or may be organized, instigated or encouraged by any communist or other subversive organization." Senate Democrats, in an effort to derail the Republican proposals, supported a bill by Maryland's Joseph Tydings and Utah's Frank Moss calling for a joint committee of Congress to examine the "crime problem."[34]

Liberals pleaded with LBJ to preempt these investigations by appointing a high-profile White House panel made up of people who would be more sympathetic to the administration's agenda. Even before Detroit, civil rights leader A. Philip Randolph recommended that LBJ assemble "a small group of responsible national leadership, including civil rights leaders." On July 25, two days after the Detroit riot began, Mike Mansfield, the Senate Democratic leader, said he wanted to avoid turning the riots into a "political football" and recommended a blue-ribbon committee appointed by the president.[35]

Later that same day, Oklahoma senator Fred Harris introduced a bill calling for the president to appoint a "Special Commission on Civil Strife." His proposal was similar to Randolph's—and distinct from those coming from his colleagues—because he wanted a panel that included officials from federal, state, and local governments. He suggested that the commission be empowered to produce a short-term report in one month and a fuller report in six months. Harris convinced his fellow senator and friend Minnesota's Walter Mondale to cosign the resolution.[36]

But instead of waiting for the Senate to consider his plan, Harris messengered a copy of the resolution to the White House with a cover note asking the president "by Executive Order [to] appoint such a Commission and set it to work." White House aide Douglass

Cater forwarded the memo to the president, highlighting that Harris believed an executive commission would be preferable to "any kind of Congressional or Joint Committee investigation." Harris's lobbying effort did not stop there. Learning that Mansfield had a regularly scheduled meeting at the White House that evening, Harris asked the Senate leader to discuss with the president his idea for a blue-ribbon commission.[37]

Not all liberals believed a special commission was necessary, however. Connecticut senator Abraham Ribicoff, whose subcommittee on urban unrest had heard a hundred witnesses and compiled more than four thousand pages of testimony, claimed the nation already knew the cause of the riots. What it lacked was the will to act. "We must end the eternal search for consensus and exercise real leadership," he told a meeting of Jewish war veterans. Ribicoff, who called for a "massive, over-all commitment addressed to the basic pressure points in the cities of America," proposed a ten-year, $50 billion program to eliminate substandard urban housing. He estimated that the nation needed to invest as much as $1.3 trillion to develop new schools, health centers, and community facilities. "This is just the answer that Congress does not want to hear," Ribicoff pointed out.[38]

Ribicoff's plan called for massive federal investment in jobs, housing, and education, but it also took another step that made many liberals uncomfortable: it linked the problems in the cities with spending on the Vietnam War. "The cost of eliminating America's slums and giving everybody a guaranteed minimum annual income would probably run to about half the present cost of Vietnam," Ribicoff said. "To put it another way, can a nation that is spending about $300,000 to kill each Vietcong afford to give $500 a year, say, to poor parents for family allowances?"[39]

Ribicoff raised good points that the leadership of his own party chose to ignore. For now, the only consensus in Congress was that the discussion of the riots was too polarized to be handled through traditional means and that only a special commission could address the topic. Even here, though, they disagreed on both the composition and the mandate of the proposed new group.

MOST OF LBJ'S CLOSEST ADVISERS believed that he should make some gesture to reassure the public. White House aide Douglass Cater recognized "the need for action" and suggested "a calm, reasoned act" by the president as soon as the fires stopped burning. A few wanted the president to travel to a riot-torn city to demonstrate his compassion. Cater and White House speechwriter Harry McPherson lobbied LBJ to give a nationally televised address to the nation. Late in the evening of Monday, July 24, McPherson sent the president a draft speech. It contained "few promises of Federal action," he wrote, but it allowed the president to establish "moral leadership at a time of crisis." He said that "the riots are becoming a national problem, and people may begin looking anxiously to the national leader—for perspective, if not for solutions." McPherson's draft made no mention of establishing a commission to investigate the causes of the riots, however.[40]

Initially, Johnson resisted giving a television address to the nation. He worried that giving a speech about the riots would force him to assume responsibility for a situation over which he had little control. He also feared that addressing the nation during a spasm of violence would make him look weak and ineffectual.[41]

Apparently, a call from Supreme Court justice Abe Fortas later Wednesday afternoon changed his mind. McPherson sent a memo to the president, summarizing Fortas's position. "He feels the time has come for you to go on television and address the country—preferably Friday or Saturday," McPherson wrote. "He believes you should ask the nation to observe Sunday as a day of reflection on the racial torment our country is suffering." It was important, the justice said, that the president "speak as teacher and moral leader." Fortas, however, made no mention of a commission to investigate the riots. LBJ scribbled on the McPherson memorandum: "I rather agree—see what you can develop."[42]

The next morning, Thursday, July 27, Johnson informed aides that he had decided to give a speech on national television, and he planned to give it that evening. His staff scrambled to prepare. Now that the president had signed off on giving a national address, the question became: What should he say? LBJ agreed that he needed to establish his moral leadership, and he liked Fortas's suggestion that he designate Sunday as a day of healing and reflection. The president added another ingredient, however: he wanted to announce the formation of a national commission to investigate the causes of the riots and to make recommendations for preventing them from happening again.

To many of his closest aides, this idea seemed to come from nowhere. In all the conversations and memos circulating among aides in the White House in the days after Newark and Detroit, no one had suggested that the president create a commission. There is no evidence that LBJ paid much attention to the proposals along these lines offered by members of Congress. Johnson later claimed that the commission was Whitney Young's idea.[43]

For LBJ, creating a high-profile commission was an attractive course of action. It allowed him to tell the nation that he was taking concrete steps to address the problem of urban racial unrest. Calling for a commission also allowed the president to demonstrate leadership without pinning himself down to specific and possibly controversial positions. According to Califano, LBJ wanted a commission to "help whites understand the plight of black ghetto dwellers" and to demonstrate to blacks that "he was working to alleviate their plight." Just as important, Johnson hoped the announcement would preempt the many proposed congressional investigations and allow LBJ to maintain control over the public's understanding of the riots. He feared that the competing congressional investigations would simply attack him from the right for pandering to rioters and from the left for not doing enough to aid the cities. By contrast, Johnson planned to pack his commission with loyal liberals who could help convince Congress to pass his stalled domestic agenda.[44]

The decision surprised members of Humphrey's cabinet task force, which thought it would be responsible for developing the administration's response to the riots. Humphrey was clearly out of the loop. On the same day that LBJ decided to create the commission, Humphrey provided an update on the task force, writing LBJ that the nation needed "a major televised appeal to the nation by the president to repair these deep wounds in our society." A few hours later, they learned of LBJ's plans for just such an address—and for the announcement of a new commission. Only Health, Education, and Welfare secretary John Gardner had seen the draft of the president's speech. "Several members asked themselves and then the staff just what their role was supposed to be," an aide wrote the vice president. "There was an attitude of chagrin" at the meeting, he noted. The aide had the sense that "the group almost felt that they were asked to meet together to be kept out of the way."[45]

Many of LBJ's advisers, meanwhile, opposed the idea of creating a commission. Califano feared the press reaction to his speech would be "The cities are aflame, the country's coming apart, LBJ can't get a tax bill, so what does he do? Set up a commission and say a prayer." Califano also worried that the commission could easily go astray and end up embarrassing the administration. "To me," Califano wrote in his memoirs, "the commission had the potential to be a political Frankenstein's monster and it was almost inevitable that Lyndon Johnson would sour on his hasty creation." Former White House aide George Reedy voiced similar concerns, telling the president that the commission "could easily wind up creating almost as many problems as the riots themselves." He suggested that the commission would be "most effective if it is somewhat aloof, somewhat detached, and very judicial in all of its aspects." Cater warned that the commission "may try to brainstorm big new government programs of its own."

He suggested that the president limit the commission's mandate to investigating whether the riots were the product of a conspiracy. He believed that Humphrey's task force was better equipped to address the larger questions associated with the riots and to do so on terms favorable to the administration.[46]

Johnson overruled his aides and rejected their suggestions, pushing ahead with his plan to address the nation that evening and announce a commission to examine the riots. But no one in the White House, including the president, had any idea who would serve on the commission, how it would be structured, or what its mandate would be. The White House had approximately twelve hours to figure out the answers to those questions.

Chapter 2

"LET YOUR
SEARCH BE FREE"

L BJ ORDERED HIS WHITE HOUSE staff to set up the commission early on the morning of July 27, 1967. After a frantic day of
activity, they chose eleven members, all of them well-respected, established figures, including representatives from business and labor,
Democrats and moderate Republicans, two African Americans, and
one woman. There were no representatives from local communities
plagued by riots or younger, more militant African Americans.

LBJ charged the commission with answering three questions:
What happened? Why did it happen? And how could it be prevented
from happening again? He promised full cooperation from the White
House and urged the commissioners to follow the facts wherever they
may lead. What he did not provide, however, was any guidance on
how precisely the commission should go about conducting its investigation. The first meetings of the new commission revealed serious
disagreements over both how the commission should function and
what it should investigate. Those fault lines, evident from the start,
would only widen over the next few months.

ALTHOUGH HE HAD OPPOSED THE idea, Joseph Califano, LBJ's domestic policy adviser, took charge of setting up the commission. Brooklyn born and Harvard educated, Califano had joined the White House staff in July 1965 after serving as a special assistant to Defense Secretary Robert McNamara. Even before he was officially hired, Califano traveled to the president's ranch, where he was exposed to LBJ's unique style of leadership. While consuming large quantities of Cutty Sark and soda, the president took the shell-shocked Califano on a whirlwind two-day tour of his property. At one point, LBJ pulled down his pants and asked Califano to examine a boil on his buttocks. Over the next three years, Califano would spend more time, and eat more meals, with LBJ than he did with his own family. He wrote in his memoirs that he saw LBJ "early in the morning in his bedroom and late at night as he fell asleep." LBJ, he noted, "barked orders at me over the phone at dawn and after midnight, in the formal setting of the Oval Office and as he stood stark naked brushing his teeth in his bathroom."[1]

Califano analyzed the congressional proposals for riot-related commissions and discovered that three of the four were appointed by Congress, not the president, and were made up only of congressional representatives. That approach was a nonstarter for LBJ. The proposal that Fred Harris and Walter Mondale had submitted came closest to meeting the White House desires. It called for nine members from both the public and the private sectors, including members of both houses of Congress and some local officials. Harris had suggested that the commission include a chairman and vice chairman, who would be elected by the commissioners themselves. Califano probably knew that LBJ would never accept that arrangement, either. Ultimately, Califano and his team decided that their commission would have eleven members, including a chairman and vice chairman, along with an executive director. The president would have the power to make all the appointments.[2]

While Califano led the effort to shape the commission's structure, White House speechwriters worked frantically to finish a draft of a speech. At four thirty in the afternoon, Douglass Cater sent LBJ the latest version. The president made some minor changes, including toughening the language about his use of federal troops in order to get in another dig at Romney.[3]

Hours before the scheduled speech, the White House had still not settled on whom they would ask to serve on the commission. Attorney General Ramsey Clark played the key role in picking the members. The president made clear that he wanted a diverse group that would include business leaders, organized labor, moderate Republicans, liberals, and representatives from law enforcement. It appears that LBJ also imposed a litmus test on prospective members. They all needed to support, or at least not to have spoken publicly against, his Vietnam policy, and they needed to support his major civil rights initiatives. Clark lobbied hard for LBJ to choose Illinois governor Otto Kerner to serve as the chair of the commission and for New York's liberal Republican mayor, John Lindsay, to be offered the position as vice chairman. Johnson eventually accepted both recommendations.[4]

The impeccably dressed, soft-spoken fifty-eight-year-old Kerner was married to the daughter of Anton Cermak, the Chicago mayor killed in the 1933 assassination attempt against President Franklin Roosevelt. With the help of the powerful Chicago Democratic machine led by Mayor Richard Daley, Kerner ascended the political ladder in Illinois politics, serving seven years as a US attorney before being twice elected as a Cook County judge. In 1960 he won election as governor and was reelected in 1964. During that time, Kerner had earned a reputation as a sound administrator, a strong supporter of civil rights, and a key ally of the Daley machine in Chicago. Clark bragged that Kerner was also a general in the National Guard, which gave him credibility with the "law-and-order" crowd in Congress. Although he would not be a major player in its activities, Kerner's name would become synonymous with the commission's work.[5]

Kerner was a trusted partner, whereas Lindsay was a wild card for the White House. But LBJ's staff felt they needed at least one big-city mayor and, ideally, as many Republicans as possible to establish the commission's bipartisan appeal, and Lindsay was perhaps the most outspoken liberal Republican in the nation. Lindsay grew up in a comfortable Park Avenue apartment, attended Yale as an undergraduate, and after service in World War II returned there to get his law degree. In 1958 he won election to Congress from a section of Manhattan that was dubbed the "Silk Stocking District" because it included wealthy residential areas along Fifth and Park Avenues. Lindsay had displayed a strong independent streak in the House, breaking with his party to support most of the social legislation of the Kennedy and Johnson administrations. In 1965, increasingly isolated in Congress, the forty-three-year-old Lindsay decided to run for mayor in the heavily Democratic city of New York. His victory, and his movie-star looks, propelled him onto the national stage. Once in office, he reached out to the city's poorest residents, walking the streets of Harlem during times of unrest. The gesture worked, keeping New York calm while other cities exploded in violence. The walks were important, a civil rights leader told the *New York Times*, because they showed that "he cares about us."[6]

LBJ was reluctant to appoint Lindsay. "There was no love lost" between the two men, according to Califano. Lindsay had infuriated the president the previous year when he had settled a transit dispute with a wage increase that was far above the White House's wage and price guidelines. In the midst of the Newark and Detroit riots, however, the New York mayor had earned points by dismissing Republican attacks against the president. "I don't think this is the time for partisan statements," he told reporters in response to questions about the Republican Coordinating Committee's criticism. LBJ, however, remained suspicious of Lindsay's intentions, fearing that he had presidential ambitions and would use the commission to increase his public profile. But if that were the case, Lindsay gave no hint of it when LBJ called to ask him to serve. "Mister President," the mayor said, "the country is in trouble, and when you call for help you are entitled to receive it."[7]

It is unclear how LBJ settled on the rest of the commission members. Under normal circumstances, the White House staff would have circulated lists of names of prospective members, crossed out some, and added others, before making final recommendations to the president. The process could take weeks, even months. But in July 1967, the staff had hours, not days, to make the selections. The only list that aides produced included names of people who were *not* selected, including George Meany, the powerful head of the American Federation of Labor and Congress of Industrial Organizations (AFL-CIO); Charles Litton, the chief executive officer (CEO) of Litton Industries; and Julia Stewart, who remains something of a mystery since the LBJ Presidential Library has no record of her. Other names were also floated and dismissed. Cater recommended "a distinguished Negro . . . such as Judge William Hastie," who was the first African American to serve as a federal judge. LBJ would later claim that his top choice to represent African Americans was Whitney Young. It is likely that the White House reached out to at least some of these people only to be turned down. White House telephone records show that LBJ personally called George Meany and Charles Litton. Since every person selected served as a representative for a larger interest group, Clark probably asked those who declined to participate to suggest alternatives.[8]

In the end, with time running out, LBJ settled on his choices. He picked two African Americans for the commission. The staff debated whether to appoint a younger, more militant black voice to the commission, but that was never an option for LBJ, who preferred older, established civil rights leaders. Accordingly, Johnson appointed Roy Wilkins, who had led the NAACP in the two decades following the Supreme Court's *Brown v. Board of Education of Topeka* decision in 1954, because he was "better-known and older and more recognized in the civil rights field."[9]

The grandson of a Mississippi slave, Wilkins had been the first civil rights leader LBJ called after he became president in November

1963. Wilkins was the kind of black leader that LBJ liked: he supported the Vietnam War, and he had sharply criticized Martin Luther King Jr. for linking the lack of progress at home to spending on the war. His critics dismissed him as "Roy Weak-knees" for his unwillingness to break with the administration, and he in turn attacked the "revolutionary fantasies" of young militants. He believed it was foolish to lead 10 percent of the population into conflict with the majority. Progress required patience and compromise, Wilkins argued.[10]

In his nationally syndicated weekly column, Wilkins attacked white racism, but he often reserved his harshest words for black militants like Stokely Carmichael. His trip to Cuba, he wrote, proved that the Black Power movement was "but a tail to another's kite," and that kite was communism. As his comments suggested, Wilkins ticked another box for Johnson: he shared LBJ's belief that a handful of agitators and communists were behind the riots.[11]

The other black commissioner was Edward Brooke, a Republican senator from Massachusetts and the first African American to serve in the Senate since Reconstruction. A graduate of Howard University and a decorated veteran of World War II, Brooke first won election as Massachusetts attorney general in 1962. Over the next few years, he won indictments against more than a hundred public officials, private citizens, and corporations. His success earned him election to the Senate in 1966. Brooke often referred to himself as "a liberal with the conservative bent." He supported the goals of LBJ's Great Society but felt they relied too much on handouts and not enough on self-help. Brooke, like Wilkins, was an outspoken critic of Black Power advocates and a proponent of federal action to aid the cities. Brooke appealed to LBJ for another reason, too. Just four months earlier, in his maiden speech on the Senate floor, Brooke vigorously defended the administration's Vietnam policy, calling the war "necessary." Although he accepted the appointment, Brooke was never seriously engaged in the commission's work. In the middle of the commission's life, he went on a twenty-eight-day tour of Africa. As a result, he would miss a majority of the commission meetings.[12]

Although he was not on the original staff list, Oklahoma's Democratic senator Fred Harris was a natural choice for the commission. Not only was Harris the first Democrat to submit legislation calling for a bipartisan White House–appointed commission, but he and LBJ hailed from neighboring states and enjoyed a warm relationship. Harris was one of the few members of the Washington establishment who could match LBJ when it came to telling tales of his impoverished youth. Harris grew up in the small southwestern Oklahoma town of Walters during the Great Depression. He spent summers "bare-headed and bare-backed," working in the hay fields for a dime a day. In 1956, after graduating from the University of Oklahoma College of Law, Harris won election to the state senate. In 1964 he won a contested US Senate race against the University of Oklahoma's popular football coach Bud Wilkinson. Harris later joked that he won by "hanging on President Lyndon Johnson like a cheap suit." His bumper stickers read "Harris/LBJ." "We literally talked the same language," Harris said of LBJ, "and I truly became a Johnson man."[13]

During his early years in the Senate, Harris had been a cautious middle-of-the-road politician who got along well in an institution that valued conformity. *Time* noted that Harris was the only person in Washington who could have breakfast with Lyndon Johnson, lunch with Vice President Hubert Humphrey, and dinner with Robert Kennedy. Of all the commission members, Harris had the most to lose by serving. He represented a rural state with few African Americans. Most of his constituents took a tough law-and-order approach to the riots and expected him to do the same.[14]

After Harris's appointment, constituents flooded his mailbox with letters offering advice. The clear majority wanted him to crack down on rioters. One wrote that blacks were instinctively inclined toward "stealing, murder, rape, and burning." Another said that these "stupid people" had intentionally destroyed their neighborhoods, "and now we are being asked for money to reward them in their lawlessness and their disregard for law, right and order." A University of Oklahoma professor offered his solution to the riots: "disfranchise" everyone on welfare. "Without the vote they would not be coddled by gutless officials as they are now." A local preacher handed out flyers saying that the riots were part of "the Communist revolution for world domination."[15]

In addition to the two senators, LBJ also tapped two members from the House, one Democrat and one Republican, both strong supporters of his civil rights legislation and both consensus builders who had proved willing to reach across party lines to reach compromise and get legislation passed. William McCulloch, a courtly, fiscally conservative Ohio Republican, first won election to the House in 1947. McCulloch was liberal on race issues but conservative on just about everything else. Although the African American population in his district was small, he had bucked local opinion and played a key role in passage of the Civil Rights Act of 1964. Johnson publicly recognized McCulloch at the time as "the most important and powerful force" in the enactment of the legislation. He was joined on the commission by James Corman, a Democratic congressman who represented the affluent San Fernando Valley in California. As a member of the influential House Judiciary Committee, Corman supported LBJ's Great Society, but he was facing growing political pressure at home. His district, which was 96 percent white and only 2 percent African American, was a stronghold of the archconservative John Birch Society. In 1964 his constituents had voted three to one in favor of Proposition 14, a state constitutional amendment that would allow businesses to discriminate against African Americans.[16]

For a business representative, LBJ selected Charles "Tex" Thornton. He was most likely recommended by his business partner, Charles Litton, who had been on the original list of names under consideration by the White House staff. The fifty-four-year-old Thornton was at the time one of the most celebrated businessmen in America. In 1963 *Time* put Thornton on its cover, calling him the best manager in American business. He was, it noted, "a dreamer and a visionary" who was also "an intensely practical man."[17]

He was also self-made. Born in the tiny Texas town of Haskell, Thornton was just five years old when his father abandoned the family, leaving them dirt poor. (Years later, a pair of hitchhikers murdered his father.) As a child, Tex worked odd jobs to support his mother. "Even before the Depression," he said, "I had to work on Saturdays, picking cotton, making deliveries, working in a store. It didn't matter what other kids were doing, I was expected to work and put aside money." In addition to helping his mother, Tex managed to save enough money to buy forty acres of land by his twelfth birthday. His childhood and early business success instilled in young Tex confidence, strength, and a fierce competitive ambition. It also taught him to question authority, especially since his father, the first authority figure in his life, had abandoned him at such an early age.[18]

In 1931 Thornton dropped out of college to travel to Washington, where he worked various low-level jobs in FDR's expanding government bureaucracy. By the time the United States entered World War II, he was working for the US Army Air Force, where he had established a solid record for using statistics to keep track of planes, parts, and pilots. Realizing that he needed other people like him to oversee the boom in military production, Thornton set up a program at the Harvard Business School to train an elite corps of officers. It was there that he met a young instructor named Robert McNamara. Together they would be the original "Whiz Kids"—a group of World War II army officers who used management systems and quantitative analysis to help win the war. At one point, Thornton had twenty-eight hundred officers under his command. But not all of those who worked for him appreciated his management style. His imperious manner and fierce ambition earned him the nickname "Young Napoleon."[19]

After World War II, Thornton offered his services to Ford Motor Company before going on to run Litton Industries, transforming it from a tiny microwave-tube company into one of the largest and most profitable conglomerates in America. In 1953, when he took over, Litton was a small company with annual sales of $3 million. By 1966 company sales reached $1 billion. The husky, owl-faced, chain-smoking Thornton built the business by buying small, struggling companies and turning them around. Politically, Thornton considered himself an independent, but he did support many of LBJ's Great Society programs.[20]

LBJ also wanted a commissioner who worked in law enforcement to insulate him against charges that his commission was soft on crime. The White House turned to Herbert Jenkins, who had led the Atlanta Police Department since 1947. Jenkins was a rare find: a white southern police chief who supported civil rights. When he joined the force in 1931, Jenkins had been required to join the Ku Klux Klan and once stood with new recruits at Stone Mountain to swear an oath of allegiance before a flaming cross. Subsequently, however, he ended his relationship with the Klan, led a drive to integrate the police force, and initiated programs to educate officers about racial issues. He hired the city's first eight black police officers and spearheaded a special commission to hire officers who offered protection and social services to poor communities. Many observers credited Jenkins with playing a key role in the relatively smooth integration of Atlanta's buses, schools, and restaurants.[21]

Katherine Graham Peden, a commissioner of Kentucky's Department of Commerce, was the only woman on the commission. The president knew her from the radio business. LBJ and his wife, Lady Bird, owned a station in Texas; Peden had worked for a CBS affiliate in Kentucky. In the summer of 1967, Peden was preparing for a Senate run in Kentucky, and LBJ likely put his fellow Democrat on the commission to bolster her thin résumé. Just a few days earlier, Peden had met with LBJ at the White House to discuss the possibility of her taking on a role in the administration. "I really would like for you to consider coming on board here in Washington with us," he told her then.[22]

It's likely that the AFL-CIO's George Meany recommended I. W. Abel for the commission. Abel had established a good record on race issues as the grandfatherly leader of the United Steelworkers of America. He started working in the mills near his hometown of Canton, Ohio, where he got his first job in 1925 making sixteen cents an hour, working twelve-hour days, seven days a week. "That miserable job helped straighten out my social thinking," he reflected, "and pointed me in the direction I was to travel the rest of my life." By 1937 he was organizing wildcat strikes. Over the next three decades, he emerged as one of the nation's most powerful and respected union leaders and won election as president of the union in 1965. A few months after his appointment to the commission, Abel was named a delegate to the United Nations General Assembly. He chose to stay on the commission, but his UN responsibilities meant that he would miss many commission meetings, and he was not an active member.[23]

LBJ started calling candidates just hours before he was scheduled to deliver his address. The first call went to Lindsay at 5:02 p.m. That was followed a few minutes later with a call to Wilkins. It appears that even this late in the day, he was still soliciting advice. At 5:32 p.m. he contacted George Meany. At 5:40 p.m. he reached out to Everett Dirksen, likely asking the top Senate Republican to make a recommendation. Five minutes later, he was on the phone with Brooke. After a meeting with a group of House committee chairmen, the president continued working the phone. He contacted Harris at 8:10 p.m. and McCulloch six minutes later. He then placed a call to Corman, who was on a plane flying back to California. LBJ was told that the congressman would not land until after LBJ had delivered his speech. Johnson decided to announce him anyway. LBJ reached Kerner about thirty minutes before the speech while the governor was traveling down the Mississippi on a riverboat. Having spoken to just

six of the commission's eleven members, the president then delegated
to Clark the job of contacting the others.[24]

The eleven names Johnson announced that evening represented
the groups that made up LBJ's liberal coalition. There were no radicals, either on the right or the left. There were no young people. At
thirty-seven, Harris was the youngest of the commissioners. In addition to appointing only one woman, there was also no one of Spanish
descent, a fact that did not go unnoticed. "We hold that there are
close to 15 or 30 million Spanish-speaking people in the US," a Hispanic spokesman wrote the White House shortly after the president's
speech. "The Negroes claim 20 to 25 million. So we are not very far
behind them. Also, next to them we make up the other large part of
ghetto dwellers." While the commissioners would likely disagree over
precisely how much of a role Washington should play in improving
American race relations, it was unlikely they would engage in heated
ideological clashes over whether government should have any role in
addressing the riots. Nor would they question the liberal emphasis on
slow, incremental change or depart from an understanding of America's racial dilemma as primarily a problem of black and white.[25]

At 10:30 p.m., with fires still smoldering in Detroit, a weary LBJ
delivered his much-anticipated speech to the nation. He made a plea
for moderation in immoderate times. "We have endured a week such
as no nation should live through," he said. It had been "a time of
violence and tragedy." After announcing the creation of a National
Advisory Commission on Civil Disorders and listing its eleven distinguished members, the president warned that "anyone who participated in a riot would be dealt with forcefully, and swiftly, and
certainly—under the law." Violence, he said, "must be stopped,
quickly, finally, and permanently." But police force alone would not
solve the problem. After delivering his tough law-and-order message,
Johnson added that the nation "needed to launch an attack upon the
conditions that breed despair and violence." He listed a "roll call of
laws" that had already been enacted under his administration to help

the urban poor, and, invoking the language of the Howard University speech, he noted, "Our work has just begun." He called again on Congress to pass his $40 million request to fight rats. "A strong government that has spent millions to protect baby calves from worms can surely afford to show as much concern for baby boys and girls," Johnson declared. He concluded with a call for a day of prayer "for order and reconciliation among men."[26]

ON SATURDAY MORNING, JULY 29, less than forty-eight hours after Johnson announced the creation of the commission, its members gathered in the White House Cabinet Room. All eleven were in attendance, along with Vice President Hubert Humphrey, advisers Joe Califano and Harry McPherson, Attorney General Ramsey Clark, and a small number of other White House aides. The president also invited Cyrus Vance, the former deputy secretary of defense, who had advised the president on the situation in Detroit.

Fred Harris later remembered that the atmosphere in the Cabinet Room was almost "like a crisis meeting in the situation room in the White House after multiple invasions." It was, he reflected, "somber, serious, and sober. It was like you're going to a funeral and when you greet old friends you sort of smile and then quickly correct yourself." Even the perpetually ebullient Humphrey appeared worried and subdued. The two great unspoken questions on everyone's mind were "How big is this thing?" and "How long is it going to go on?"[27]

No one knew whether the nation was experiencing another brief spasm of violence or the beginning of a civil war. The night before the meeting, violence had erupted in six cities. In Brooklyn more than five hundred angry black residents confronted police after seven young people were arrested for smashing windows and looting. More than a dozen businesses were vandalized. The crowd taunted a black policeman, telling him to "take off your black mask and show us your white face." In Wilmington, Delaware, police intervened to stop a mob of whites from invading an African American neighborhood after three white men had been shot. In Memphis four thousand National Guardsmen stood ready in the event of trouble after rumors spread that protesters planned an all-night march. In Poughkeepsie, New York, small gangs broke windows, looted stores, and exchanged gunfire with police. In South Bend, Indiana, two white homes in an integrated neighborhood were firebombed.[28]

Johnson entered at 11:40 a.m. and made his way around the room, shaking hands. After five minutes, he took his seat in the designated president's chair at the center of the table. "I welcome you to the White House," he said, reading from a prepared text. "And I commend you for what you have agreed to do for your country. You are undertaking a responsibility as great as any in our society." He gave the panel a broad mandate to examine both the short-term steps necessary to prevent and control riots and "long term measures that will make them only a sordid page in our history." He could have been describing his own feelings when he said that the public was "baffled and dismayed" by the rioting and looting. He asked the commission to address three basic questions: "What happened? Why did it happen? What can be done to prevent it from happening again and again?"[29]

Johnson followed those broad questions with a series of more specific ones: "Why riots occur in some cities and not in others? Why one man breaks the law, while another, living in the same circumstances, does not? To what extent, if any, there has been planning and organization in any of the riots?" He wanted the commissioners to probe for better ways of controlling and containing the violence. "Why have some riots been contained before they got out of hand and others not? How well equipped and trained are the local and state police, and the state guard units, to handle riots?" He asked them to explore how police relations with the local community impacted the "likelihood of a riot" or the ability to keep it from spreading into other areas. Johnson was especially interested in knowing who the rioters were and what their motivations for participating in the unrest were. Was there a common denominator linking the rioters—age, education, work history? "What we are really asking for is a profile of the riots—of the rioters, their environment, their victims, their causes and effects," the president said. Finally, LBJ asked the commissioners to explore the role of the media in fomenting the violence.

LBJ promised the commissioners that he was asking them "not to approve our own notions, but to guide us." He reassured them they would have free rein to follow the evidence wherever it led. "Let your search be free," he proclaimed. "Let it be untrammeled by what has been called the 'conventional wisdom.' As best you can, find the truth and express it in your report." LBJ guaranteed the commissioners "all the support and cooperation" they needed from the White House. "I can assure you of that," he said.

After reading this formal statement, LBJ added that he appreciated the commissioners' willingness to serve, telling them that racial rioting was a "matter of most concern" to the public and pointing to polls showing that 80 percent of Americans said it was the top issue. "I want you to find the truth and express it in your report," he stated. He flattered the commissioners by saying that he had "looked over a nation of 200 million people and selected only 11."

The president then introduced Cyrus Vance to give a detailed report on the circumstances in Detroit that had led him to recommend that LBJ send federal troops to quell the violence. Johnson was still feuding with Michigan governor George Romney over the decision to commit federal troops. After Vance gave a minute-by-minute account of the events in Detroit, LBJ read a list of times when presidents had been asked by governors to supply federal troops. LBJ impressed upon the commissioners how difficult it was for a president to commit troops to patrol American cities. "None of you will ever know how it feels to send federal troops into the cities until you yourself send them in," he said. "It makes chill bumps," he said, to think of federal troops "shooting citizens and citizens shooting back at them." Vance added that it was "imperative" that the administration retrain the National

Guard for riot-control duties. He was shocked at how unprepared they were for urban uprisings and felt they aggravated the situation on the ground.

Shortly after noon, LBJ read aloud Executive Order 11365, which officially established the commission, before using eleven commemorative pens to sign it and distributing one to each commissioner. The executive order called for the commission to make an interim report by March 1, 1968, and to issue a final report and recommendations within exactly one year's time, by July 29, 1968. The seven members of the commission who were not senators or congressmen would be paid one hundred dollars daily when working on official business. Members of the Senate and House would not be paid any additional salary, but they would be reimbursed for travel and expenses.[30]

At 12:18 p.m., LBJ allowed photographers and a newsreel cameraman into the room for carefully choreographed pictures. He made a brief statement for the press, making sure that he had Kerner on one side and Lindsay on the other. Press secretary George Christian thought the photo op "would be good for the evening programs and the special shows which are scheduled for Sunday." The president joked that Humphrey, who stood next to Peden for the official photo, "always gets next to the good-looking women." The comment produced the only laugh of the day. At this point, the photographers and reporters were ushered out of the Cabinet Room. The president again urged all the members and the congressional representatives to give the commission's work top priority. "All too often," he said, "commissions are appointed, pictures taken, and then the members never go to any more meetings." He claimed that he wanted this commission to be different.[31]

He then turned the floor over to Kerner, who acknowledged that expectations for the commission where high and that they would inevitably disappoint some people. But the nation was "anxious and disturbed" and needed direction. He suggested that the commission hold its first meeting after lunch. The president then called on

Lindsay, who agreed that the commission faced an impossible job. He promised the president there was "no room for partisanship" and that LBJ was "entitled to all the support he can get." He believed the top priority was "to find the very best to serve" on the commission's staff. Lindsay then framed the question that would dominate debate for the life of the commission: "Should we seek short-term solutions or should we examine the virus and the decay which exist in our cities?" Picking up on Vance's comments, he suggested that the commission begin by reforming the National Guard.

The commissioners then broke for lunch. According to Peden, Johnson brought the commissioners to the family living room and then escorted them out to the Truman Balcony before accompanying them to the White House mess.[32]

EVEN AS THEY MET FOR the first time that afternoon, it was unclear how the commission would function. LBJ had established broad guidelines and posed specific questions, but he had given no direction as to how the commission would answer them. Would it simply mine existing government reports for the answers, or would it launch its own investigation of the riots? The answer to that question would determine how many staff members would be required. While the president asked them to propose ways to prevent future riots, it was not clear if he wanted specific policy recommendations.

These issues dominated the first formal meeting of the commission and exposed major differences among the commissioners that would shape their debates over the next few months. Lindsay and Harris pushed the commission to assume a wide-ranging mandate "to take on the broad problems that lie behind the riots." Lindsay urged the other commissioners to see the riots as the product of poverty and hopelessness in urban areas—poverty that was, in many cases, created by racism and enforced by discrimination. He claimed that slums entrapped African Americans, isolated them from the rest of society, and denied them economic opportunities. The challenge was to break down the walls separating black ghettos and white suburbs. Harris cheered Lindsay on. "Lindsay and I shared the same sense of urgency about urban problems," Harris wrote in his 2008 memoir. "We both felt deeply and cared deeply about the despair, frustration, and hostility that characterized black communities throughout the country."[33]

Lindsay and Harris seized control of the commission on the first day and never let go. Often Lindsay would lead the charge and set the agenda, while Harris offered moral and political support. The two men were a study in contrasts. Lindsay, a handsome six foot four and leader of the largest city in America, was among the first celebrity politicians. He was a regular on *The Tonight Show* with Johnny Carson, and his face graced the cover of major national newsmagazines. Harris, short and stocky with leathered skin from his days working the wheat fields of Oklahoma, represented one of the most rural states in the nation and one of its smallest African American populations. Yet growing up poor instilled in him a passion for helping the underprivileged.

They possessed different styles, each effective in its own way. Harris was amiable and down-to-earth, using his folksy manner and sharp wit to build coalitions. Lindsay could at times be preachy and aristocratic, but he won converts with his passion and commitment to helping the poor. Harris would be the favorite of the commission's staff, always treating them with courtesy and respect, while Lindsay remained aloof, rarely engaging anyone other than his peers on the commission or the executive director.

Their chief adversary for the next few months would be Tex Thornton, who that first afternoon immediately dissented from the Lindsay-Harris suggestion that the commission focus on the underlying conditions that gave rise to the unrest. Their top priority, Thornton said, "was to support the president's commitment to stop the riots—for the riots, in addition to the problems they cause at home, add to our problems abroad." Thornton viewed the riots as a law enforcement issue, seeing them as representative of a broader break-down of authority in society. The commission report, he would say repeatedly in his distinctive West Texas drawl, must state that the cause of the riots was "an increasing lack of respect for the law." He feared that linking the riots to poverty gave people permission to loot and destroy property. People have always been poor, he argued, but they have never used it as an excuse to burn down cities.

Harris was wary of Thornton from the beginning. Using the terms commonly applied at the time to describe attitudes toward the Vietnam War, Harris divided the commissioners into "hawks" (who favored tough law enforcement) and "doves" (who supported address-ing issues of poverty and racism). Thornton stood out as the leading hawk. "I thought of him right away as a guy who would not be very progressive in his views," Harris stated in 2015. The other obvious doves, besides Lindsay, were Abel, who Harris believed understood the problems facing the working class, and Wilkins, who was a pas-sionate supporter of civil rights. The others did not fit neatly into either category. McCulloch supported civil rights but was a fiscal conservative. Brooke, a moderate Republican, could be counted on to support measures to prevent discrimination, but Harris worried whether he would approve of costly programs needed to rebuild the nation's cities. Peden seemed sensitive to questions of discrimination and racism, but she was running for a Senate seat in Kentucky and was unlikely to support any recommendation that might be contro-versial. Kerner was clearly a dove, but since he announced on the first day that he would vote only in case of a tie, Harris considered him "largely irrelevant."[34]

The ideological fault line that emerged at the first meeting with Lindsay and Harris on one side and Thornton on the other would animate debates for the rest of the commission's life. Still, Kerner put a positive spin on the first meeting, telling reporters afterward that the commissioners were "all of one mind."[35]

THE STAKES FOR THE NEW commission were high. The nation was reeling from the bloody riots in Newark and Detroit and fearful that more disturbances were to come. "No groups of American citizens have ever been given such a crucial assignment since the constitutional convention," declared syndicated *Christian Science Monitor* columnist Roscoe Drummond.[36]

Most observers, however, were skeptical of both LBJ's intentions in setting up the commission and the commissioners' willingness to criticize the administration. The commission appeared too moderate and too mainstream to offer new insight or perspective. "From the chairman, Governor Otto Kerner of Illinois, on down the commission members have obvious vested interests in what has been done, how it was done and the potential of present programs," observed the *Washington Post*. "They are in a position to protect themselves and in turn, the president, from a political backlash and a blunt finding that what has been done, however well intended, has not in practice worked." The *St. Louis Post-Dispatch* reported "murmurs" that the commission was "just a White House front, with the president pulling the strings to get the kind of report he wants, when he wants it." The *Los Angeles Times* noted, "The chief purpose of the commission, one suspects, is to buy the time necessary to give the White House a clearer view of the nation's reaction to the ghetto uprisings." A commission staff member described the "general attitude" of the Congress toward the commission as "one of friendly skepticism."[37]

Many civil rights leaders doubted anything of substance would come from the commission, and other African Americans objected to the lack of younger militant voices. Many black leaders recalled the futile 1966 White House Conference on Civil Rights, which had proposed many costly and sweeping changes to help African Americans. According to journalist John Herbers, who covered the White House for the *New York Times*, the report "dropped from sound and sight, like a heavy stone cast into a deep-sea." Two weeks after the president announced the creation of the commission, Harry McPherson visited

Harlem to talk with local black leaders. He reported back that they were disappointed that LBJ appointed two "establishment" African Americans, whom they dismissed as "office" leaders who had "no following on the streets." Brooke and Wilkins, they said, "neither understand nor are understood by people on the streets."[38]

The biggest challenge facing the commission was to find common ground in an increasingly polarized debate over race and the riots. What could a group of establishment figures say after a few months of study that would change the narrative about race in America? The commission had to produce a report that would be bold enough to inspire blacks and restore their trust in American institutions while not alienating whites, most of whom assumed that society was sound and stable. It had to satisfy an insecure president who demanded loyalty even as he publicly praised the commission's independence. The commission's job was to explore the roots of urban riots, but they would also be testing how far mainstream liberalism could stretch before braking.

Most of all, the commission had to navigate the complicated politics in Washington and find some middle ground between liberals and conservatives. That would be no easy task. A few days after LBJ announced the creation of the commission, the *New York Times* claimed that white Americans "must share the greater burden of responsibility" for the riots. It went on to say that "it is white men's sins of omission and commission that are at the root of much of this summer's turmoil." While recognizing the importance of law and order, it contended that white America needed to acknowledge "the legitimate grievances and brutal injustices that pose the fundamental threat to civil peace and national unity." The *Times* editorial board argued that the federal government had a responsibility to provide jobs, education, housing, and health services that would make equality a reality for African Americans. Because "white people of this country command and create most of its wealth," it argued, "they must be willing to bear the greater part of the economic burden required to realize this program. And that burden is one that will be measured in tens of billions of dollars annually." It also criticized the "paranoid rabble-rousers who play into the hands of those who would make a fascist America."[39]

The editorial incurred the wrath of Patrick Buchanan, a combative speechwriter who had recently joined the staff of former vice president Richard Nixon. The 1960 Republican nominee, after losing to JFK and then failing to win a California gubernatorial race in 1962, had promised to leave politics. Now Nixon was monitoring the political situation, looking for an opening to launch a new campaign for the presidency. After reading the *New York Times* editorial, Buchanan fired off a memo to his boss. Johnson's new commission, he wrote, can "go on Home. Liberals already knew the answer to who was responsible for the riots: white men." He complained that the *Times* failed to mention that "the colored folks has [*sic*] a responsibility too." He went on to say that that the editorial left readers with the impression that if "some black kids" burn down Harlem and Watts "and shoot up a few more cities," the *Times* would have an editorial "tearing the living hide off the white community," telling them they needed to spend billions to prevent more rioting. Buchanan noted that the editorial said that the riots played into the hands of "white fascist[s]"—and "I have an uneasy hunch whom the *Times* has in mind," he wrote.[40]

Chapter 3

"I'LL TAKE OUT MY
POCKETKNIFE AND
CUT YOUR PETER OFF"

D ESPITE PROFESSING THAT HE WANTED the commission
to be independent, President Johnson planned to keep tight
control over its activities. Not only did he choose every commissioner,
but he also reserved to himself the power to pick the commission's
executive director. For that position, he selected David Ginsburg,
an attorney whose loyalties to the Democratic Party extended back
to Franklin Roosevelt's New Deal and who had been a trusted and
reliable friend of the Johnson administration. The White House also
chose Ginsburg's deputy, businessman Victor Palmieri. Over the next
few weeks, Ginsburg and Palmieri assembled a first-rate senior staff.
As was typical of federal policy making in this period, all were men,
and many were well-connected Washington insiders. A large number
were graduates of Harvard Law School.

LBJ had much less success controlling the ambitions of John Lindsay and Fred Harris. As they set to work, both men insisted that the
commission demonstrate its independence from the White House

while also examining the underlying causes of the riots, which they identified from the start as poverty, discrimination, and a lack of opportunity. Not all the commissioners, however, were willing to go along with their agenda. As he had done at the first meeting, Tex Thornton continued to argue that the commission should focus solely on recommending measures that would help the police control and contain riots. An early flash point was the question of whether the riots were spontaneous eruptions or part of a well-coordinated conspiracy. The commissioners hoped that FBI director J. Edgar Hoover would settle the issue, but he provided ammunition to both sides of the debate. Frustrated by Hoover's deliberate obfuscation and Thornton's obstructions, Harris and Lindsay became determined to make a clear statement that the commission would have an independent voice. Their target: the National Guard.

ALTHOUGH AWARE OF THE DAUNTING task in front of them, the commissioners began their efforts in high spirits. They were unanimous in their desire to produce something better than "just another government report" and naively assumed that they could change the narrative about race in America. They were also reassured by LBJ's words. He had asked the right questions, provided them with an expansive mandate, and, most of all, promised White House cooperation. The commissioners were relieved to hear LBJ state unequivocally that they would have free rein to follow the evidence wherever it led them. He seemed to be begging for them to come up with new ideas that challenged the conventional wisdom—including, if necessary, the assumptions that informed his own Great Society.

Over the next few months, however, the commissioners would learn that none of it was true. LBJ planned to control every aspect of the commission by manipulating the levers of power, the same way he had once done so successfully in the Senate. It began with the appointment of the chairman who would become the commission's namesake—Otto Kerner. The administration publicly claimed it picked Kerner because he was a popular midwestern governor with National Guard experience. In fact, domestic policy adviser Joe Califano later wrote, LBJ knew that Kerner was a loyal political operative who once worked behind the scenes "counting" ballots to make sure that JFK carried Illinois in the 1960 presidential election. And if loyalty did not work, Johnson planned to use patronage to control Kerner. It was no secret in the White House that Kerner wanted to be appointed a federal judge.[1]

Johnson's control also extended to the commission's staff. The executive order that the president signed gave him, not the commissioners, the authority to hire an executive director. This would be the most important position on the commission. Since the commissioners all had regular jobs, and thus could be involved with commission work only part-time, they would all depend on the executive director to make the day-to-day decisions that would shape the final report. For that job, LBJ selected the talented Washington insider David Ginsburg.

The fifty-five-year-old Ginsburg was a former New Deal lawyer with close ties to the liberal wing of the Democratic Party. Born into a comfortable middle-class family in Huntington, West Virginia, he had a lifelong ambition to become a lawyer. In 1928, after winning a debating contest, he won a four-year scholarship to West Virginia University. While he was at college, the stock market crashed and the nation plummeted into a deep depression. Morgantown, the home of the university, which bordered the coal fields of Appalachia, exposed him to the other side of America. He and his Pi Lambda Phi fraternity brothers would climb into his Model T Ford and travel to see the poverty that afflicted rural West Virginia. "What got me was the children," he recalled in 1997. "They were literally starving to death." He and his fraternity brothers would buy cases of milk bottles and drive around looking for children. "We would make them drink it right there to be sure they wouldn't take it home and have it sold for something else. But there were always more kids than the bottles."[2]

In 1932 Ginsburg graduated Phi Beta Kappa with majors in economics and philosophy and won a scholarship to Harvard Law
School. Ginsburg had never been very political, but it was at Harvard
that he heard FDR's voice on the radio for the first time. "I remember being struck with the vigor in his voice," he reflected. Roosevelt
gave him a sense that "he cared about average people and understood
their problems." He would come to admire Roosevelt and embrace
his optimistic belief that government could make a difference in people's lives. More important, he felt society had a responsibility to help
those who could not help themselves. "There was a respect for idealism in the Washington of the 1930s. But it was a practical idealism,"
he told the *Washington Post* in 1997. "We weren't dogmatists."

After law school, he took a job with a law firm in Cincinnati. Soon
afterward, Felix Frankfurter, one of his law professors at Harvard
and a future Supreme Court justice, suggested that Ginsburg relo-
cate to Washington to be part of the New Deal intellectual ferment.
Ginsburg jumped at the idea and found a job at the Securities and
Exchange Commission. After a few years, he found himself on the
White House staff, researching and writing speech drafts for FDR.
In 1939 he moved to the Supreme Court, where he clerked for the
Court's newest member, William O. Douglas.

The war in Europe cut short his clerkship. In April 1941, he joined
the Office of Price Administration, which was a key wartime agency
that FDR created to control inflation. The OPA's aggressive efforts,
designed to ration resources and control prices, made it an easy target for conservatives, and Ginsburg was often in the bull's-eye. FDR
came to his defense, but in 1943 he resigned his position and joined
the army, where he rose through the ranks from driving trucks to
serving on the staff of General Lucius Clay. Ginsburg assumed responsibility for developing economic policy and controls in the occupied areas of Germany.

When the war ended, he decided to enter private practice. "I'd
been a lawyer 11 years and never had a client," he explained. But

his heart was always in government. In 1947 he became a founding member of the Americans for Democratic Action, an anticommunist liberal group that included Minneapolis mayor Hubert Humphrey, former first lady Eleanor Roosevelt, and many New Dealers who were concerned about the communist infiltration of liberal organizations in America. Over the next few decades, he would become the consummate Washington insider, traveling in Washington's elite social circles and serving as an informal adviser to Democratic presidents. LBJ elevated Ginsburg's already high profile when he asked him to serve on several presidential commissions and boards that were created to prevent a railroad and airline strike as well as a potential strike among postal workers. "We used Ginsburg a lot," commented White House domestic policy adviser Joseph Califano.[3]

There was a reason LBJ turned to Ginsburg so often, particularly when the stakes were high. He had a well-earned reputation for being able to analyze situations, get people to work together, listen attentively to competing points of view, and use his considerable legal skills to find common ground. He also understood that his job was to find solutions that pleased the president. From LBJ's point of view, Ginsburg was ideal for the job at the Kerner Commission because he was loyal. He assumed that Ginsburg would make sure that the commission followed White House directives and did not stray too far afield. On this score, LBJ would soon be disappointed.

Ginsburg would be the unheralded leader of the commission. Most members did not know or necessarily trust each other, but nearly all trusted and respected Ginsburg. That trust would prove essential in the months ahead. Fred Harris summed up the view of most members of the commission when he described Ginsburg as "a brilliant Jewish boy from the backwater of West Virginia who, after a great legal education, became a superb lawyer," widely respected "for his keen wisdom and flawless honesty."[4]

Ginsburg had been traveling on the West Coast with his family when he received a call from Supreme Court justice Abe Fortas, who offered him the top administrative position on the commission. Although a little surprised that a Supreme Court justice was calling to offer him a job in the White House, Ginsburg agreed. He took a night flight to Washington, went home to take a quick shower, and then hurried over to the White House for a private meeting with the president on Monday, July 31. "Mister President," he said, "you know that I have no background in this area." Johnson waved his hand and ignored the comment.[5]

Having worked closely with the Johnson White House, Ginsburg knew intuitively what the president expected from his "independent" commission: a report that celebrated his Great Society and defended the administration from critics on the right and left. LBJ also made clear to Ginsburg that he wanted his commission to find evidence to buttress his conviction that a handful of agitators were fomenting the discontent. "I remember the scene," Ginsburg recalled of his first meeting in the Oval Office with LBJ after his appointment to the commission. "He was seated at the large desk back in the Oval Office, and I was seated to his side. He then said that it was not possible, in his view, for there to have been so many outbreaks in so many cities simultaneously unless someone had pressed the button, unless someone had made a decision that this was to go." The president, Ginsburg affirmed, "was very clear in his mind that there was a conspiracy."[6]

Ginsburg had no illusions about the task that lay before him. He was supposed to set up a commission that would examine sweeping questions that touched on nearly every aspect of American life. The president directed him to be comprehensive, careful, and fast and to have an interim report ready within six months. "I remember," he said, "the very first afternoon sitting in an empty office, empty desk, alone, and [thinking] how does one begin this?" Ginsburg realized that the work ahead would require money—and a lot of it—but LBJ assured him that he would have the full support of the White House and all the resources that he would need to complete his work. The president's emergency fund provided $100,000 to get the commission off the ground, and Ginsburg was told that the White House would later ask Congress for a supplemental appropriation to keep the commission going. Although he did not know it at the time, squeezing money out of the White House would become a time-consuming and frustrating part of his job.[7]

The White House provided the commission with three floors of an old office building at 1016 Sixteenth Street, not far from the White House and directly across from the Russian Embassy. The commission occupied three of the eight floors in the building. Ginsburg had to decide how to fill those offices and how they would go about organizing the staff to answer LBJ's queries efficiently but convincingly. He was starting from scratch. Over a matter of days, weeks at the most, he had to hire stenographers, lawyers, archivists, researchers, and analysts. He also had to decide whether the commission should create its own independent research staff or instead depend on existing studies and the expertise of executive agencies. And he had to determine whether to follow the lead of the Warren Commission, where the commissioners were figureheads while the staff did most of the work, or instead involve them more closely in the commission's labors.

Ginsburg believed that the president had set the agenda for the commission with his three questions. Answering the first question—"What happened?"—would involve some factual investigation to reconstruct the events and their chronology. It also required an effort to answer the conspiracy questions. Ginsburg felt that explaining "why" the riots occurred would entail hiring social scientists who could discern some common threads that would allow reasonable speculation about the basic causes of the disturbances. The third question, how to prevent future riots, would be perhaps the most difficult. Ginsburg anticipated having to consult with experts, local public officials, private citizens, and community organizations.

Answering this question would also be the commission's most deli-cate task because it would necessitate building consensus among the commissioners while managing White House expectations.[8]

Ginsburg's first priority was to hire a deputy executive director who could help him address these issues. This position would be es-pecially crucial, since Ginsburg decided not to give up his law prac-tice even while he served as executive director. He would begin his days at Ginsburg, Feldman, and Bress and end them at the commis-sion offices. "My first concern," Ginsburg noted, "was to get some-body on the staff with whom I could speak to ventilate these matters." Ginsburg's deputy would hire and manage the staff, scholars, and consultants who would oversee the commission's various research programs. While Ginsburg would be involved in these decisions, he reserved for himself the role of liaison between the commission and the White House.[9]

A few days after the commission first assembled, Kerner invited the director of revenue in Illinois, Theodore Jones, to serve as the dep-uty executive director. Jones was competent, experienced, and black. In their first meeting, LBJ had told Ginsburg that he wanted the commission to include African Americans on the senior staff. Jones seemed to tick all the boxes, so Ginsburg accepted Kerner's suggestion and made the appointment official on August 1. The White House followed up with a statement at a news conference later that day.

Eight days later, however, Jones was gone. It is unclear what prompted the change or what role, if any, LBJ played in pushing Jones out. The move certainly would have sent a clear signal to Kerner that Johnson, and not the chairman, would be making key staff appoint-ments. It was also clear, however, that Ginsburg was unhappy with Jones. In an oral history, Ginsburg said that Jones's "parameters were even more limited than my own." It is likely that Ginsburg regis-tered his discontent with the White House, which set out looking for a replacement. In his resignation letter, Jones wrote that when he accepted the position, he thought he could work for the commission while continuing to work as Illinois director of revenue. But he said that after "careful examination," he realized that he could not "handle both positions with a level of performance meeting the president's, the governor's, or your expectations."[10]

While it is unclear whether LBJ played a part in removing Jones, it is very clear that he picked his successor. Johnson wanted Victor Palmieri, a thirty-five-year-old graduate of Stanford Law School and president of Janss Corporation, one of the largest real estate development firms in the western United States, to take the job. Palmieri was a successful businessman, a strong supporter of LBJ's Great Society, and a forceful proponent of increased federal spending to aid American cities. Surprisingly, he had been on Johnson's radar for a few years. In January 1966, Palmieri had been in Sun Valley, Idaho, when he received a call from Califano, saying that the president wanted to see him in Washington. The White House sent a private plane into a raging blizzard to pick Palmieri up and transport him to Washington, where he was rushed into a meeting with what he later referred to as "the three stooges"—Califano, press secretary Bill Moyers, and White House aide Jack Valenti. They told him that LBJ planned to name him the first secretary of Housing and Urban Development, leading the new federal department created in 1965. Palmieri made clear he would not accept the appointment, but the aides, sometimes together and sometimes one on one, badgered him for three hours. Finally, they whisked him into the Oval Office. "Nobody says no to the president," he was told. LBJ stepped up the pressure. Employing the classic "Johnson Treatment," the president leaned in so close to Palmieri that their faces were only inches apart. But Palmieri held his ground. Clearly not used to being turned down, the president grabbed Palmieri by the arm and pushed him out the door.[11]

Apparently, however, LBJ did not hold a grudge. Even before Jones had officially resigned, Palmieri received a call from Deputy Attorney General Warren Christopher, offering him the position of deputy executive director. This time he said yes. Ginsburg then asked Califano if he could present Palmieri "as his own idea." Given the public skepticism about how independent the commission would be, Ginsburg likely feared a backlash if it leaked to the press that the White House had selected his deputy. "Unless you disagree," Califano wrote LBJ on August 7, "I would propose to tell David in the morning to present Palmieri to the commission as his own suggestion." Ginsburg, it seems, passed his first loyalty test.[12]

Ginsburg and Palmieri would develop a close working relationship. As an old Washington hand, Ginsburg was good at managing White House expectations; as a skilled lawyer, he knew how to negotiate differences and find common ground. Palmieri brought with him considerable management skills and experience dealing with large and complicated ventures. Over the next few weeks, as Palmieri raced to fill dozens of staff positions, the commission relied on an "old-boys" network of well-connected Washington insiders. Nearly everyone in high levels of the commission knew each other or was connected to some high-level government official. Many of those contacts were originally made at Harvard Law School.[13]

Both Ginsburg and Palmieri were assigned executive assistants, who served as gatekeepers to their bosses and the funnels through which information flowed to the top. Their roles would evolve with the changing fortunes of the commission, but they would be involved with most major decisions and would later help to write its final report.

Like Palmieri, his assistant, John Koskinen, hailed from Los Angeles. In 1965, after graduating from Yale Law School and spending a year studying international law at Cambridge University, Koskinen clerked for the chief justice of the US Federal Court of Appeals in Washington, DC. When his clerkship ended the following year, he considered staying in Washington. In 1966 he met with Congressman James Corman in regards to serving as a legislative assistant. Koskinen, however, decided instead to return to Los Angeles, but in August 1967 he traveled back to DC for another meeting with the congressman. Corman told Koskinen about the commission and sent him to see David Ginsburg. After a brief conversation, Ginsburg hired him to serve as the assistant to the deputy executive director. (The conversation took place about a week before Palmieri joined the commission.) Koskinen returned to Los Angeles that weekend, handed off his cases to other lawyers, and took the red-eye back to New York on Monday night to start his new job. "It was a little bizarre," he admitted, "to pack up and move from Los Angeles to Washington in the course of a weekend."[14]

David Chambers, who served as Ginsburg's assistant, followed a similar path. After graduating from Harvard Law School, he spent a short time as an associate in a large Washington, DC, law firm, but he felt a calling to public service. Although he had grown up in a well-off family and had been sheltered from many of the issues that would consume the commission, Chambers had always possessed an instinctive empathy for those who felt like outsiders and faced discrimination. As a closeted gay man living in a straight world, Chambers himself felt like an outsider. Empathy turned to action in July 1967 when he took leave from his firm and traveled to Mississippi, where he provided legal assistance to poor African Americans. The experience changed his life. He recalled sitting with a bunch of young lawyers in Mississippi watching LBJ announce that he was creating a commission to investigate the riots. "We all laughed that LBJ was going to deal with this crisis by appointing another commission," he later said. "Commissions were a way of making problems go away, not to solve them." But the day after he returned home, he received a call from Matt Nimitz, an aide to Joe Califano and a Harvard Law School classmate. Nimitz wondered if he would be interested in working for David Ginsburg. A few hours later, Ginsburg called and asked if they could meet at his office. He offered him the job, Chambers accepted, and he started work the next day.[15]

The position of deputy director of operations went to Stephen Kurzman, another Harvard Law School graduate who had worked

for New York's liberal Republican senator Jacob Javitz. Both Javitz
and John Lindsay were part of a larger group in Congress that pushed
for passage of the Civil Rights Act of 1964. It was Lindsay who helped
recruit Kurzman to join the commission. "I got a call out of the blue
from John Lindsay," he recalled. Kurzman, in turn, reached out to a
fellow Harvard classmate, Charles Nelson, who had been working for
the US Agency for International Development. After living in Brazil
for the previous six years, Nelson had returned to the United States,
looking for a new challenge. He was hired to oversee the field teams
that would be sent into the riot areas to gather data.[16]

Ginsburg and Palmieri were determined to hire a high-profile African American to serve on the senior staff. Thus, Ginsburg offered
the job of general counsel to Merle McCurdy, who had served as a
public defender in Cleveland and had been appointed US attorney
for the Northern District of Ohio by President Kennedy in 1961. Mc-
Curdy brought on another African American, Nathaniel R. Jones, an
assistant US attorney in his office, to serve as deputy general counsel.
Tragically, the fifty-five-year-old McCurdy would die two months
after completing his work on the commission.[17]

While the commission recruited two African Americans for senior
positions, they made no effort to find qualified women. Although it
was typical of the times, Ginsburg and Palmieri clearly saw the commission as a man's job for which no women need apply. When they
talked about creating a "diverse staff," they were only interested in
finding qualified African Americans. "Sad to say," David Chambers
stated in 2016, "I do not remember thinking at the time that there
was anything odd at all about an all-male senior staff. How much the
world has changed."[18]

By Labor Day, Ginsburg and Palmieri had filled most of the senior
staff positions. Ginsburg had planned to recruit the "best and bright-
est" experts and researchers on urban affairs, with the expectation
that money would not be a problem. "I think on the salary business
we will just have to pay what is necessary," he told his staff. "I don't

understand that there is any lack of funds available." He soon discovered, however, that money would not be as plentiful as he had been led to believe and that the funds available were not enough to get the top talent that he had hoped. He ran into other obstacles, too. Since the commission was gearing up at the end of the summer, he had difficulty recruiting experts from universities, as they were already committed to teaching in the fall. Many others, moreover, were skeptical that the commission would produce a meaningful report and did not want to be associated with it.[19]

Despite the hurdles, Ginsburg and Palmieri managed to attract prominent professionals. Arnold Sagalyn had decades of experience training law enforcement on the proper use of force. He had started his career in 1939 as a special assistant to Eliot Ness, the former head of the Prohibition-era "Untouchables," who was now working for the Cleveland, Ohio, police department. In 1961 President Kennedy appointed Sagalyn to coordinate all the law enforcement agencies in the Treasury Department, including the Secret Service. At the time the commission was formed, he was serving as the director of public safety at the Department of Housing and Urban Development. Sagalyn also had another key qualification for service on the commission. He was close friends with David Ginsburg, who called and asked him to assume the role of associate director for public safety.[20]

Ginsburg charged Sagalyn with developing answers to questions about effective riot control and police behavior. Sagalyn held strong views on many of these issues and had lectured around the world, warning police departments to limit the use of excessive force, which he believed was "counterproductive" in a riot situation. "I saw my new position on the Kerner Commission as offering a chance to play a significant role in developing a realistic, effective nonlethal police and military response for the control of racial civil disorders and violence," he wrote in his 2010 memoir.[21]

Shortly after joining the commission, Sagalyn attended the annual meeting of the International Association of Chiefs of Police, where police departments from across the country gathered to discuss new strategies and tactics while also showing off their latest hardware. He was shocked when he saw displays of "intimidating and frightening military-type vehicles and weapons," including army tanks. Sagalyn pulled some of the displays off the wall and brought them back to Washington, where he taped them on the walls of the commission conference room. The senior staff was stunned by the images and appalled when they learned that police departments across the country were being told to prepare for war. "I could almost feel their shocked reaction," he recalled.[22]

Gradually, the once-empty offices filled up with new faces. Journalist Robert Conot, who had authored a highly acclaimed book about the Watts riots, *Rivers of Blood, Years of Darkness*, joined the commission to write the first section of its report, which would answer the question "What happened?" Ronald Goldfarb, a Washington attorney, examined how the administration of justice led to grievances and tensions. Milan Miskovsky, a former CIA analyst who, in 1960, had helped negotiate for the release of Francis Gary Powers after his U-2 spy plane crashed in the Soviet Union, led the commission's investigation of conspiracy. Robert Shellow, a social scientist at the National Institute of Public Health, headed the team investigating the causes behind the riots. Richard Nathan, a fellow at the Brookings Institution and a former adviser to Nelson Rockefeller, was responsible for developing short-term solutions for the interim report. The White House assigned staff member Norman McKenzie as the executive officer responsible for keeping the commission on budget.[23]

Although they were able to quickly design a research plan and hire people to staff key positions, neither Ginsburg nor Palmieri had any illusions regarding the challenges that still confronted them. "So far as my work with the commission is concerned," Palmieri wrote to friends in September, "I can report with some confidence now that the job we are trying to do is completely impossible. Somehow during the next few months, we are supposed to investigate the riots

and find out precisely what occurred in cities throughout the country, hold hearings on an unrelenting schedule both in Washington
and on a regional basis in the right areas, and direct massive research
study culminating—I am told—in a superbly written report which
will lay out the great domestic questions of our time for the American people." He realized that "no matter how good a job we do," the
report will be "satisfying to very few people." After only a few weeks
on the job, he appreciated the conflict the commission faced. "The
problem," he wrote, "is the classic equation of the democratic society
in which law and order rest on one side of the scale and the need for
change on the other. The emphasis in Washington, particularly in
Congress, is all on the side of law and order. The desperate concern
of the black communities, on the other hand, is change."[24]

EVEN BEFORE GINSBURG AND PALMIERI had filled many of the staff
positions, the commissioners began holding hearings. Most of the
commissioners refused to serve as figureheads, and they made clear
their intent to play an active role in gathering information and reaching their own conclusions about the causes of the riots and possible
solutions. The commissioners, along with Ginsburg and Palmieri,
believed that the best way to learn about the urban unrest was to hold
hearings with public officials and local citizens from areas impacted
by the riots and to listen to testimony from experts in urban affairs.
They planned to supplement these hearings with field trips to impacted cities to get a firsthand look at local conditions.

On August 1, the commission held the first of many hearings in the
Indian Treaty Room in the old State, War, and Navy Building, which
would later be renamed the Eisenhower Executive Office Building.
The Indian Treaty Room, with its marble-wall panels and tiled floors,
once served as the navy's library and reception room. Before hearing
from their first witnesses, the commissioners needed to settle important questions: Should they open the hearings to the public? Should
members of the press be permitted to attend the sessions? The lessons

of the Warren Commission hung over their deliberations. Only three
years had passed since the commission released its report that a lone
gunman had killed the president. By 1967 critics had savaged the
report and eroded public support for its findings. Some of the commissioners believed the Warren Commission had done a bad job of
dealing with the press and that its failure to educate the public as the
investigation progressed helped undermine its credibility. To avoid
making similar mistakes, Palmieri hired a respected journalist, Al
Spivak, to serve as its press secretary.

Spivak lobbied for open hearings, including radio and television
coverage, but he ran into stiff resistance from most of the commissioners. Lindsay, Harris, and Kerner believed that public education
was an important part of the commission's work and therefore argued
in favor of holding some public hearings and admitting print journalists. They were less enthusiastic about allowing television cameras.
Most of their colleagues opposed holding public hearings, and they
insisted on holding all sessions in private. Thornton worried that the
press would distort the proceedings and give a platform to militants,
and Corman complained that the public's presence "minimizes rather
than maximizes the information we can get." He said that he did not
"see the role of this commission as one of public education at this
point." Brooke, ignoring the positions of Lindsay, Harris, and Kerner,
declared that a "consensus" had formed against public sessions. While
there was no agreement, a majority of commissioners clearly wanted
to work in private. The commissioners agreed, however, to publish
excerpts from the testimony.[25]

The first witnesses that day were two men with experience leading
large investigations—Lee Rankin, who served as the executive director of the Warren Commission, and Warren Christopher, deputy attorney general, who served as vice chair of the McCone Commission,
which investigated the Watts riot in 1965. Both men talked mainly
about housekeeping details: What types of hearings to hold? How
to deal with the press? "I think you can do much better than we did

with the press," Rankin said, pointing out that the Warren Commission did not even have a press secretary.

But the key witness that day was FBI director J. Edgar Hoover, a sign that the commission wanted to tackle the conspiracy question head-on. Hoover, for his part, was glad to stoke suspicions that the riots had not been completely spontaneous. He personally worked on his presentation and asked aides to include "vicious" quotes from some of the radicals. He also insisted on having a quote from Martin Luther King Jr. that could be seen to condone the violence. Using King's own words, he argued, "would tie him down."[26]

In a long-winded and meandering presentation, Hoover flailed at all his many enemies: King, the media, and anyone who advocated "disrespect for law and order." He did not distinguish between peaceful civil rights protests, legitimate antiwar activity, and rioters who tossed Molotov cocktails. They were all lawbreakers and deserved to be punished. On the specific issue of whether the riots were the result of a conspiracy, Hoover placed charts around the room that tried to show a link between the dates of provocative public appearances by Stokely Carmichael and H. Rap Brown and the racial unrest that followed. He pointed out that one or the other man spoke in nine cities within a short time before disturbances occurred. Their rhetoric about racial conflict attracted support from "subversive and extremist organizations, groups, and individuals," he argued, including the Communist Party. "Communists do not begin trouble," he declared, but they "take advantage of it." Hoover also sought to use the question of conspiracy to attack Martin Luther King Jr., whom he accused of promoting the "communist tactic of linking the civil rights movement with the anti–Vietnam War protest movement."[27]

Mayor Lindsay sat through Hoover's two-hour testimony, waiting his turn to ask questions. When it came, he began with polite and respectful inquiries about the FBI's intelligence operations. Eventually, however, Lindsay confronted Hoover with the central issue: "I gather" from your testimony "that the explosions at Detroit and Newark were not the result as far as we know of any general conspiracy." Hoover, who answered most queries with long-winded responses, uttered one word: "Right." Lindsay continued: "Yet at the same time it appears that once it was triggered off by some relatively minor incident that there was a very rapid mobilization of skills and planning ability." Hoover: "That is correct."

Lindsay nudged Hoover to speculate about the causes of the riots. If they were not the product of conspiracy, then what had prompted them? Hoover's answers, apart from the Cold War rhetoric, sounded a lot like the views articulated by Lindsay and Harris. He blamed the unrest on the horrible conditions in the ghettos that led those living there to be "thoroughly justified" in their anger toward the rest of society. All they needed, he said, was "some incident to arise" to rush out and "begin to protest and charge police brutality." Communists would then take advantage of the incident to incite more unrest. But, he conceded, the FBI had "never found . . . any pattern which shows the thing is planned days" in advance or that it was scheduled "to happen and at a certain time." The riots were always instigated by a spark that "occurs accidentally where there is a large Negro population living in maybe deplorable areas."[28]

Thornton, perhaps realizing that Lindsay had gently led the FBI director to admit that poverty and not a communist conspiracy produced the riots, jumped in to challenge the notion that the commission should recommend additional spending on social programs to attack the underlying conditions in urban areas. There were those, he declared—obviously referring to Lindsay and Harris—who argued that "what we have to do is open the gates and spend lots of money." Thornton pushed Hoover to return to his original message of condemning lawbreakers and demanding that law and order be restored. Hoover, who had responded curtly to Lindsay's questions, was back in his comfort zone, attacking civil rights leaders, rioters, and antiwar protesters.[29]

The commission released excerpts of Hoover's testimony to the press, highlighting his statement that the FBI had no evidence of a conspiracy behind the riots. But the press reports did little to change opinions.

The conspiracy hypothesis was loaded with meaning for both its advocates and its detractors. Many conservatives, and some liberals, had convinced themselves that the riots were an aberration, fomented by a handful of agitators who did not reflect majority opinion in the black community. Like whites in the South in the era of Jim Crow, those who took this view convinced themselves that most blacks were content with their lot. For Republicans, political calculation reinforced their faith that the riots were the product of a conspiracy. They planned to rebuild their party by playing to the fears of white suburbanites who worried about rising crime rates and diminishing respect for law and order. By suggesting that a handful of agitators were behind the violence, they absolved the larger society of any responsibility for it. LBJ's lenient policies toward crime and his civil rights agenda, they argued, gave blacks license to riot. Underlying social problems, many of them created and enforced by discrimination and racism, had nothing to do with the violence. For many on the left, however, the conspiracy argument oversimplified a far more complicated reality. Poverty and despair lay behind the riots, and the anger and hostility of African Americans toward white society were both pervasive and justified. For advocates of the conspiracy interpretation, the unrest was largely a law enforcement issue; for civil rights activists and their allies on the left, this explanation only distracted from the measures that might actually stem future riots: rigorous enforcement of existing civil rights laws and some form of redistribution of resources.

LBJ found himself trapped between the two viewpoints. Intellectually, he appreciated that his policies had made only a dent in the suffering in black communities, and he recognized that he may have inadvertently contributed to the uprisings by raising expectations in the black community. For a complicated variety of personal and political reasons, LBJ clung to the conspiracy theory. Politically, LBJ did not want Republicans to outflank him on the law-and-order issue.

Personally, conspiracy helped soothe his inflated ego. After sacrificing so much political capital in support of civil rights, he could not accept that the black community was rewarding him by taking to the streets and undermining support for his presidency.

Apparently, Johnson had little faith that the commission would confirm his suspicion of a conspiracy. The next day, White House chief of staff Marvin Watson called Hoover's assistant Cartha D. DeLoach and asked the FBI to conduct a parallel investigation of the conspiracy issue. Hoover refused the president's request, and he told his staff to prepare a letter for the White House that made clear that "we have checked with all the offices and the only information available is that which I gave yesterday." The trouble with LBJ, Hoover wrote in a memorandum the same day, was that he "asks two, three, or four people to do the same thing."[30]

In his dealings with both Johnson and the commission, Hoover was playing a delicate game. There was no evidence of a conspiracy, but he wanted to use the riots as an excuse to attack his many enemies and potentially expand his surveillance efforts; stirring fears of an organized plot could be useful on both fronts. When asked directly, Hoover admitted there was no conspiracy to riot, but he preferred to feed fears of insurrection while pointing an accusatory finger at anyone who advocated for social change. His strategy allowed everyone to hear what they wanted to hear. In the wake of Hoover's testimony, Lindsay focused on the FBI director's clear statement that no conspiracy existed. Thornton, however, accepted Hoover's charge that Stokely Carmichael and H. Rap Brown helped provoke the riots. "I don't think we can possibly say it doesn't exist," he told fellow commissioners about the possibility of a conspiracy, and he insisted that the commission focus on the "degree [to which] it exists." Everyone knew, Thornton said during the commission's August 1 discussion, that "Carmichael and some of his cohorts" were holding meetings where they discussed "how do we start riots, how can we organize to do so." He feared that if the commission flatly declared there was "no conspiracy," they would be tagged "as being a bunch of liberals."[31]

The debate over conspiracy during the commission's first session made for some strange bedfellows. Roy Wilkins suggested that the commission embrace a broader interpretation of the meaning of conspiracy than the FBI had. "It was not as if Stokely Carmichael sat around the table and told people to go out and riot," Wilkins admitted, but he was reluctant to abandon the idea that the militants possessed "some informal but effective" way to instigate the violence.

Thornton and Wilkins's defense of the conspiracy theory troubled Fred Harris, who chastised them for offering "rather simplistic solutions." If the commission believed "one or two people in the country can cause riots," he responded, "I think we really missed the boat." He insisted that the group examine the social conditions that made "Black Power" a "siren call" for many African Americans. The commission needed to get to the root of the problem and not delude itself into believing that a handful of people were responsible for the riots. Harris offered a psychosocial interpretation of the violence that was popular among liberals. Discrimination, poor public facilities, along with a lack of education and opportunity, he argued, created "sadness and desperation." Preventing riots required addressing the "pervasive feeling," especially among young people, "that they have not really any voice or any control in the destinations that govern their lives."

Thornton did not stop at lending credence to the idea that the riots were the product of a conspiracy. Clearly agitated by Lindsay's insistence that the commission look at the roots of the violence and consider new social programs, Thornton articulated his own alternative theory about what caused the disorder: the rioters were opportunists who were using violence to extract more benefits from government. In response to LBJ's request that the commission provide a profile of the rioters, Thornton believed it was important to examine whether they were southern migrants who came north to liberal cities like New York because they "pay more relief [there] than they do down in Mississippi." Had they come north now, not as many liberals suggested, for better jobs and new opportunities, but rather "because that is where the action is?" Did they, he asked, "see on TV that there is liquor and guns that are being taken from stores and broken into" and want to get a piece of the action?

Thornton believed the commission should limit its focus to identifying specific measures that would help local police and National Guard units enforce the law and contain future disturbances—what he called "action recommendations." He predicted a "white backlash" if the commission did not actively pursue a law-and-order agenda and the riots continued. There was, he said, "a short fuse in the white population," and he foresaw the possibility of "riots against the rioters." Thornton's warnings about a white backlash would prove prescient in the coming years, but on this day he had a very specific concern in mind. The wealthy white neighbors in the exclusive area of Los Angeles in which he lived, he pointed out, depended on "black servants," who would come to their houses a few times a week to clean and perform various chores. Now, having listened to H. Rap Brown exhort blacks to burn down "their homes" and "their factories," his neighbors would no longer hire blacks. "They are fearful," he told his colleagues.

Meanwhile, Thornton also drew a line in the sand, making clear that he would be skeptical, at best, of any new social programs the commission might support. In an obvious dig at Lindsay and Harris, he suggested that liberal politicians who promised too much and delivered too little deserved some of the blame for the riots. Black agitators, he charged, fed on the dashed expectations of African Americans who had been told by liberal politicians that they deserved the benefits of middle-class life but had never been asked to make the sacrifices necessary to achieve them.

Tex Thornton's interventions throughout the first hearing—from his interest in the conspiracy hypothesis to his preoccupation with "action recommendations" and his suggestion that urban blacks were lazy—made clear that Lyndon Johnson's liberal coalition hardly spoke with one voice when it came to race. Indeed, this was evident in

Thornton's very language. Throughout the day, Thornton repeatedly referred to African Americans as "colored people." After the meeting, Roy Wilkins pulled him aside. "Despite the fact that I run the National Association for the Advancement of Colored People," he said, "it's more appropriate today to use the terms Negro or black." Thornton listened sympathetically, and at the next meeting he repeatedly pronounced "Negroes" as "Nigras." Whether Thornton knew it or not, the term was deeply offensive and commonly used by southern white racists. "We could see Roy Wilkins cringe every time he said it," recalled David Ginsburg's executive assistant, David Chambers.[32]

WHILE MANY OF THE COMMISSIONERS disagreed with Thornton's views, they all shared his desire to write a report that would have a meaningful impact. For all the debates and disagreements that would characterize their work, the commissioners and staff were united in their desire to shape public attitudes and influence policy makers. They differed, though, on the best way to accomplish that goal. Lindsay and Harris advocated a policy of "shock and awe": shock the public with strong language and then awe them with statistics, figures, and a list of new social programs designed to address the problem. Thornton and the two House members, James Corman and William McCulloch, shared the belief that the report needed to paint a vivid portrait of life in the ghettos, while stopping short of endorsing specific social programs. They opposed raising expectations by recommending new programs that stood no chance of passing Congress. Lindsay and Harris understood these short-term political challenges, but they nevertheless wanted to use the report to look over the horizon and set long-term goals for the nation. This dispute, too, would shape the commission's work in the months to come.

Harris and Lindsay also believed that the commission needed to quickly establish its credibility and its independence from the administration. An obvious target was the National Guard. In the commission's first meeting at the White House, Cyrus Vance told them that the Guard had not only been ineffective in Detroit, but it may have made conditions worse. In his testimony before the commission, Deputy Attorney General Warren Christopher made the case that the Guard was ineffective because it was not racially integrated. Michigan, for example, had only 120 blacks out of a force of 10,000. Nationally, blacks made up only 1.5 percent of all Guard troops. The airborne troops that LBJ sent to the area performed much better, Christopher suggested, in part because of their superior training but also because 20 percent of the paratroopers were black. "I will just tell you," Christopher said, "there was a tremendous difference on the streets of Detroit in areas where the airborne troopers were every third or fourth man was Negro. They understood the problem."[33]

From the early days of the commission, Harris led the charge for requiring the National Guard to be more aggressive in attracting and promoting African Americans. The demands, so early in the life of the commission, put Ginsburg in an awkward position. As Califano later reported to Johnson, Ginsburg complained that he was getting "pressure from commission members (particularly from Senator Fred Harris) to 'do something' within the next few days." But Califano assured the president that Ginsburg "believed the commission should focus its attention both publicly and privately on a thorough study of riots—that is what you asked for." He urged Ginsburg to stop Harris from making any public comments about the National Guard. "David will do everything he can with Tex Thornton and perhaps others to keep the commission from shooting from the hip, which we both believed would be damaging," Califano told Johnson.[34]

Apparently, Ginsburg's efforts failed. On August 10, after a second meeting with Cyrus Vance, the commission sent a letter to Johnson, recommending that the National Guard recruit more African Americans and receive improved riot-control training; they also advocated a careful review to guarantee the quality of officers appointed in the Guard. The commission's letter noted that members "believe strongly that this deficiency must be corrected as soon as possible."[35]

LBJ accepted the recommendation with public equanimity, while privately seething. Johnson informed the press that he had passed on the recommendations to Defense Secretary McNamara with instructions that "this is a matter of highest urgency and I know you will give it your immediate attention." Shortly after the commission issued its recommendation, however, Johnson made a phone call to Fred Harris. "I want you to remember that you're a Johnson man," he told Harris. "I'm your friend, Mr. President, and I won't forget," the junior senator responded. "If you do, Fred," Johnson said, "I'll take out my pocketknife and cut your peter off."[36]

Johnson was not the only person in Washington upset by the commission's proposal. The recommendation brought a swift response from conservative lawmakers and the National Guard itself. Congressman F. Edward Herbert declared that the commission had "indicted" the Guard "without one scintilla of evidence." Those who made the recommendation, he said, "are people who probably never heard of the National Guard before they were put on the commission." When reminded that Kerner was a commander of the Illinois National Guard, Herbert insisted, "That doesn't mean he knows anything about the National Guard." Major General James Cantwell, president of the National Guard Association of the United States, accused the commission of casting "a slur" on the "competent, dedicated National Guard officers, and without good cause." A constituent let Harris know what he felt about recruiting more African Americans into the Guard. "Will the black boys you want to train in the National Guard be better snipers in the next riots?" he asked.[37]

The move may have angered the president, but many in the press applauded it, confirming Harris's hopes that taking quick action to suggest changes to the National Guard would establish the commission's independence. The *Washington Post* noted that the letter "is encouraging, both because the proposal has merit and because it indicates that the commission intends to make appropriate recommendations whenever it reaches a mature judgment on a problem." The

New York Times called the recommendations "refreshingly swift and perceptive." The American Veterans Committee, a liberal alternative to the American Legion and Veterans of Foreign Wars, applauded the commission's recommendation. "The commission is to be commended at the prompt and perceptive pinpointing of one of the most disturbing aspects of the handling of the urban riots this summer—the role of the National Guard." The conservative *Chicago Tribune*, however, called it ironic that "the first recommendations of the presidential commission were critical not of the rioters, snipers, and looters," but of the Guard, who risked their lives "to restore peace."[38]

In its first few weeks, Ginsburg and Palmieri managed to fill key positions on the commission, and the commissioners started holding hearings to investigate the causes of the riots. Although everyone agreed that they wanted to have an impact on the discussion of urban unrest, they disagreed on many basic questions: Were the riots the product of a conspiracy among a handful of militants? Was a tough law-and-order approach necessary to end the riots, or did the commission need to examine the underlying social and economic causes of the disorders? Ironically, the debate over the National Guard proposal accentuated these differences. The warm press reception to the recommendations emboldened Harris and Lindsay, who became even more aggressive in their efforts to push their colleagues to support a more liberal agenda. At the same time, however, the move angered Thornton, who feared that the commission was straying from its original mission, which he viewed as largely a law enforcement issue. Some of the commissioners hoped that traveling to the riot areas and seeing conditions there might help break the ideological stalemate.

Chapter 4

"I THINK WE SHOULD
AVOID OVERSTATEMENT"

WITHIN WEEKS OF PRESIDENT JOHNSON'S July 28 announcement, the commission was charging forward on many different fronts. It was fully staffed and took on the shape of a giant octopus, with arms flaying in many different directions. David Ginsburg and Victor Palmieri created a small in-house group of social scientists, and they also convened meetings with outside consultants who were leaders in the field of race relations and urban unrest. They solicited academic papers relevant to their investigation and sent field teams into riot-torn areas to conduct in-depth investigations.

Simultaneously, between hearings in Washington, the commissioners traveled in small groups to riot-ravaged cities to get a personal look at the devastation, talk with residents, and meet with local officials. Some of the more moderate commissioners—especially James Corman, William McCulloch, Edward Brooke, Herbert Jenkins, and Katherine Peden—had only a vague intellectual understanding of the deplorable conditions in poor urban areas. The poor schools, inadequate housing and sanitation, and scarcity of jobs they found there shocked them, as did the often callous indifference and arrogance of local governments. Their travels made some of the moderates believe that Lindsay and Harris were right: it would be impossible to prevent future riots without address the underlying conditions that fed black anger toward white society.

Meanwhile, the White House monitored these developments with growing concern that the president's high-profile commission was going off the rails.

ON AUGUST 15, MAYOR LINDSAY and David Ginsburg traveled to Newark, where they walked along Springfield Avenue, past storefronts that were still boarded up from the violence a few weeks earlier. The commissioners had agreed that their trips would be unannounced, but the media-conscious mayor nevertheless tipped off the press. Most residents stood on the sidelines and watched silently as Lindsay, quickly surrounded by a swarm of newsmen and photographers, walked past. A woman who recognized Lindsay hugged him. "I'm going to ask my mayor why he doesn't come up here," she said. Another woman told him that jobs were the biggest need. "Jobs, jobs—that's it—that sums it up," Lindsay said in response. Later, the two men toured the city streets in a fire engine–red convertible and viewed the damage by air in a helicopter.[1]

Many Democratic mayors were angry that the president had given Lindsay, a Republican, a platform he could use to criticize them. They already felt under attack from activists on the left who ran community-action programs funded by the administration's War on Poverty and by angry white voters worried about crime. Lindsay did not help matters when he toured neighboring Newark without paying a courtesy call on its powerful mayor, Hugh Addonizio. "We can have some very serious political controversy if Lindsay and other members of the commission move in on some of the cities where mayoralty [*sic*] elections are scheduled this fall," New York Democratic congressman Hugh Carey wrote the White House.[2]

Brooklyn, where the New York mayor traveled next, was safer ground. He and Ginsburg visited Brownsville in East New York. In the early part of the twentieth century, Brownsville had been a haven for first-generation immigrants, especially Russian Jews. By 1920 it had earned the nickname "Little Jerusalem." In the 1950s, however, when the New York City Housing Authority decided to build new public housing projects in the neighborhood, many Jews fled and were replaced by low-income black and Latino residents. By 1967 Brownsville's unemployment rate was 17 percent, which was double the average for the city, and crime had become rampant. Lindsay later recalled that he and Ginsburg entered a dilapidated house where a young, unemployed woman greeted them. Lindsay asked where she grew up. "I came from Mississippi," she responded. When the mayor inquired as to why she came to Brownsville, she replied, "To find a better life." Had she found one? Yes, she answered, this was a better life than what she had left behind. Her answer, Lindsay asserted, "completely stunned David Ginsburg and me."[3]

The following week, more commission members traveled to Newark: Roy Wilkins, Katherine Peden, I. W. Abel, Tex Thornton, and Herbert Jenkins. Unlike Lindsay and Ginsburg, they stopped by the mayor's office before heading out on their tour. The group attracted much less attention than Lindsay had the previous week. A few older African Americans recognized Wilkins, but to younger residents he was just another black man in a suit. The commissioners visited a middle-class African American neighborhood and stopped by a black-owned barbershop, where the owners were angrier with the police than with the rioters. They told the commissioners that when the riots began, they closed shop and hung a "soul brother" sign on the outside. The rioters passed the building without inflicting damage, but the state police needlessly fired into their shop.[4]

On August 21, Herbert Jenkins, William McCulloch, and James Corman met with the leaders of a dozen grassroots organizations and

other community leaders in some of Detroit's riot-ravaged neighborhoods. Corman recalled later that the black leaders were trying "to
assault and demean us, and they were really angry." When asked
what the greatest problem facing the community was, one of the
local leaders declared without hesitation: "Opportunity." Although
the community representatives discussed the specific issues that
plagued poor areas, especially dilapidated housing, unemployment,
and underfunded schools, they told the commissioners that the underlying reason for the riot was that "Negroes are systematically excluded from the mainstream of life." The commissioners asked about
the differences between discrimination in the North and the South,
but their interlocutors saw little distinction. "The difference is purely
an intellectual exercise," said one. "Being black in the United States
is the same anywhere; you feel the same way." One activist revealed
that every black man in the room had been in jail at some point in
their lives. They pointed out the gap between what the nation spent
on urban problems and what it spent on the Vietnam War. At one
point, Corman asked if the Mafia existed in Detroit, suggesting that
it may have been responsible for the riots. The room erupted in laugh-
ter. "The riots are completely the responsibility of the white society,"
the commissioners were told. "Until they are willing to indict themselves, we will live in guerrilla warfare." And residents were tired of
liberal platitudes about helping them: "You talk about bringing up
the Negro; you are not going to bring me up anymore. You're going
to get your foot off my back or I'm going to break your leg." The assembled leaders were not impressed by the Kerner Commission, and
most, according to a summary of the visit, "felt this was just another
talk session and that nothing would come out of it."[5]

When the meeting ended, Corman asked one of the more militant participants if he could suggest a nearby drugstore where the
congressman could pick up a souvenir for his daughter. The young
man, who had been angrily denouncing him a few minutes earlier,
responded, "I'll walk over there with you so you won't get lost." The

act of kindness left a deep impression on Corman, who recalled it nearly twenty-five years later. "I thought," he stated in a 1994 oral history, "underneath all this sort of surface hatred, we can reach each other." Still, the meeting had made clear that bridging that divide would not be easy.[6]

A few days later, Fred Harris traveled to Milwaukee accompanied by Katherine Peden, Roy Wilkins, and Herbert Jenkins. Although it received less attention than disturbances in Detroit and Newark, the Milwaukee unrest, which started on the same day that the Kerner Commission held its first White House meeting, ended with four deaths and 1,740 arrests. The commissioners arrived for an evening meeting with city officials, including Mayor Henry Maier and the chief of police, that lasted well past midnight. The mayor, and his aides, painted a rosy picture of the city, claiming that it was largely free of racial tensions. Oblivious to the frustration in the black community, Maier blamed the riots on "outside agitators" and claimed they were attempting "to embarrass him politically." He also expressed satisfaction that local law enforcement had crushed the rebellion, concluding that the city was "healthier now than before, having developed pride in being able to successfully combat violence." The director of the Milwaukee Commission on Community Relations parroted the mayor's position, stating that only "a small percentage of Milwaukee Negroes were involved in the riot" and that the clear majority approved of the mayor's tough response to the disturbance.[7]

However, an excursion through the riot-torn area the next day exposed the gap between the official account of race relations in the city and the harsh reality. The commissioners were shocked by the level of segregation. They noticed that in a large department store, there were no black clerks and only two black tellers at a local bank. "Several ghetto residents remarked that the only people in Milwaukee who rioted were the police," staff member Henry Taliaferro wrote in a report about the trip. The commissioners were told there was no riot; just a handful of teenagers "on a destructive lark" were responsible for the damage. Residents accused the mayor of overreacting, most likely to shore up support from white voters. Harris broke away from the group to talk with people in a black barbershop. "Where are you from?" Harris asked one man, who was from Alabama. Harris wanted to know if Milwaukee was more segregated than Alabama, but the men in the shop seemed puzzled by the question. "It turned out in Milwaukee," Harris recalled, "they didn't see any white people."[8]

The commissioners had lunch with Father James Groppi, a radical Catholic priest who was leading the campaign for open housing. The perpetually haggard, chain-smoking Groppi refused to condemn the riots. "The black man has a right to use violence if other techniques don't work," he declared. Also in attendance at the luncheon was a small group of "burly teenage boys" who wore sweatshirts with *NAACP* on the front and *COMMANDOS* on the back. They were all African American and well educated, and they worked with local organizations in the slums. "They are quite bitter about the resistance of city government and of the white majority to Negro demands," Taliaferro observed. They listed as their top priorities open housing, improving inner-city schools, and more jobs. Several in the group stated that matters were beyond the talking stage. "Given the hostility of the city government, they had lost hope that they could solve urban problems working through established means," Taliaferro concluded. Mayor Maier was an "energetic" and "hard-working" liberal, the commission staffer wrote, but like many white liberals, he was out of touch with the reality on the streets. Making matters worse, Maier appeared "to resent the fact that his best efforts have not been rewarded by content among Negroes."[9]

After Harris and other commissioners visited Milwaukee, he and Mayor Lindsay traveled together to Cincinnati, where one person was killed and sixty-three injured during nearly two weeks of unrest in June 1967. What they heard and saw left both men deeply shaken. The day began with a meeting with city leaders and representatives of the local Community Action Program. Afterward, Harris and Lindsay toured the riot area. The first stop was a public housing project. "I remembered the smell of the Negro slums I had walked through that day," Harris wrote in a book published in 1968, "the garbage in the streets, the terribly overcrowded housing conditions, three and four families living where one had been intended."[10]

As they continued their tour, the two commissioners encountered fifteen young African Americans shooting craps by the side of one of the units. Suspicious of the group of white men in suits, the young men asked if they were FBI agents. When they said no, the youths turned back to their craps game. Harris and Lindsay tried to engage them in conversation, asking them how the government could help them. "We want a job, man," Harris recalled them saying. "Get us a job, baby. Can't you get us a job? Get us a job. We want a job." Lindsay and Harris learned that two men in the group lost their jobs after being arrested in the riots. Another had been employed by a federal summer jobs program, but that initiative had ended.[11]

The most dramatic encounter took place when they met secretly with a group of black militants. "We went into a room where we were all asked to identify ourselves and our job," Taliaferro wrote in a memo. "When we entered the room, everyone refused to shake hands with us." A young Presbyterian minister, who had a degree in theology and a master's in sociology from Columbia University, was the principal speaker. "He is intensely bitter," Taliaferro wrote. Except for the minister, all the men were dressed in African shirts, some with amulets around their necks, and "generally in such fashion as to deny any identification with the white man's conventions." They were all college graduates; most either had a graduate degree or were working toward getting one. They had all been involved in the nonviolent civil rights movement and had worked helping poor families in the slums. But now they had given up on nonviolence and on the white establishment.[12]

The minister began with a twenty-minute monologue delivered with passionate intensity, but in a very calm, low-key manner. "He would not look at me while he talked," Harris recalled. The preacher insisted that Harris refer to the riots as a rebellion, and, he warned, "it's just the beginning. . . . Look, man, we're hip to you white people. We know, now, it's no good trying to appeal to your morals; you've shown you don't have any morals. The only thing you believe in is your property—that's what this country is all about, baby—so we are going to burn it down." Another young African American reinforced the message, saying, "It is ludicrous for you white people to be here asking black people what's wrong, what our grievances are. You made this system, and you must change it," he lectured them. His bitterness and anger were palpable. "We tried marching and begging 'whitey,' but now we found out that you white people ain't going to give a black man nothing; we got to take it away from you."[13]

Taliaferro wrote later that the meeting "was a dramatic experience for all of us." The commissioners "were the personal targets of deep bitterness, hopelessness and frustration and hate." Harris admitted that he had known these feelings of anger and frustration existed, but he had never been confronted by them so directly. As the commissioners and staff members drove away from the encounter in silence, Harris thought to himself, "This is a long way from Walters, Oklahoma."[14]

The group ended the day at city hall, meeting with a new group of city officials who regaled them with stories of all the progress being made in the city. Lindsay and Harris were stunned. Had any of these local leaders ever ventured into a public housing project or met with young militants? They proceeded to describe in detail what they had seen and heard that day. According to Taliaferro, the officials "appeared to listen" and looked "somewhat stunned." It was unclear to Taliaferro whether they were reacting to the description of conditions in the projects or were shocked that Lindsay, a Republican, was dressing them down for their failures.[15]

It was not only white commissioners who were getting an earful from young militants. Around the same time, Senator Edward

Brooke held a secret meeting with H. Rap Brown in a "shabby basement apartment on 7th Avenue in Harlem." Brown had insisted that
Brooke come alone. When the senator arrived wearing his customary blue suit, Brown sat him down in a wooden chair facing about
a dozen young male militants dressed in blue jeans. "I listened attentively to bitter, profane criticism of me and the American system
of government," Brooke stated. "You're not black," Brown lectured
him. "You are not one of us. In the Senate, you are part of the white
establishment. You are what's wrong with America." Brooke pushed
back, arguing that working within the system was the only way to
make change. In response to their cries of "Black Power," Brooke
asked, "What is power but the ability to change the basic conditions of life?" He told Brown that his advocacy for Black Power was
"self-defeating," because minorities needed to build coalitions with
the majority to enact meaningful reforms. Neither side conceded any
ground, and after two hours Brown escorted the senator out of the
room. "No one shook my hand or thanked me, nor did I expect it,"
he reflected.[16]

The commissioners' trips to cities that experienced riots continued
through September. On September 27, Kerner traveled to Newark,
where he walked down Prince Street, which had been devastated by
the uproar. He visited a partially completed public housing project
with "some of the dreariest most depressing housing units" he had
ever seen. All day he engaged residents in conversations about race.
They all spoke about the same issues: "extreme" police brutality, the
need for jobs and public transportation, and a better way to find
homes for people displaced by urban renewal projects. At the office of the United Afro-American Association, a local support group,
the organization's president, Willie Wright, told the governor that
"unless Negroes were admitted into the mainstream of American
society and particularly the economic portion of the society, more
and bigger riots would be forthcoming." Kerner also met with city
officials, who seemed oblivious to the issues that mattered most to

poor African Americans. The police commissioner told Kerner that before the riot, he had believed that the police had an "almost ideal rapport" with residents and that "he was astonished that a riot occurred in Newark."[17]

Kerner also made a quick twenty-four-hour tour of Detroit, accompanied by Peden and Thornton, where they visited the riot area and met with individuals impacted by the violence. Kerner broke away from the formal tour and tried to start a conversation with a young mother who was sitting on the curb. Without identifying himself, he simply said that he was working with a group to improve conditions for blacks living in urban areas. The woman was not impressed. "You don't live here," she said, "so what do you know about it? You sit in a big office in Washington and you draw up some plans and tell us what to do." She told him what residents needed most was more police protection. Her plea underscored the complexity of the relationship between the police and the communities they served. Residents complained about police brutality, but they also charged that officers avoided their neighborhoods and were slow to respond when called.[18]

THE COMMISSIONERS' EXPLORATIONS OF URBAN areas, combined with the testimony of a parade of witnesses at hearings held throughout August and September, impressed upon the commissioners the deep and profound sense of rejection and alienation felt by many African Americans. They saw firsthand how in "the ghetto," the garbage was the last to be collected, the police were more aggressive and less respectful, schools were falling apart, and housing was dilapidated. "All of us knew these things intellectually," Harris said after touring Cleveland. "Now we feel them." Kerner's response was similar. "I thought I knew the problem fairly well," he asserted, "but I certainly was not aware of the depth and breadth of it." Congressman McCulloch echoed the same refrain. "I would say that while I have been generally familiar with some of the cities, I was shocked to see conditions in one or two that I visited," he told a local Ohio reporter.

"I mean that. I was shocked. I am now convinced it is the most difficult, deep-seated problem of our century so far." Even Tex Thornton was moved by what he saw. "I'll be a son-of-a-gun," he said. The tours and testimony "brought me 99 miles further to the left than I thought I would be."[19]

For both commissioners and staff, the trips highlighted the desperate conditions in the urban areas, the gap between the way poor blacks and white suburbanites lived, the limited reach of many Great Society programs, and the failure of local governments, and their Democratic mayors, to come to grips with the nature of the problem. The discussions with residents, and those who participated in the riots, also substantiated what FBI director J. Edgar Hoover had told the commissioners on the first day of hearings. There was no organized conspiracy behind the riots. Instead, what they found in city after city was that the riots were caused by a spark, usually a quarrel between a policeman and a local resident, which ignited a firestorm of unrest. Kerner told a conference in Springfield, Illinois, that the riots start with "a dry-grass situation in a congested area full of frustration and broken promises."[20]

Harris later said that soon after the tours, all the commissioners "came to feel that America was in the midst of its greatest domestic crisis since the days of the Civil War" and that "racism, poverty and powerlessness" had created an explosive mix that the nation needed to defuse or "face the unacceptable choices of anarchic violence or unprecedented repression." Harris had been advocating for aggressive federal action to address urban needs, but he was shocked by the depth of the problems and the amount of resources that would be necessary to have any hope of successfully addressing them. Before the tours, Harris suggested to local Oklahoma reporters that the commission's recommendations would be modest, saying on August 20 that spending $20–$25 billion was "just not a practical solution" when the nation was already spending $25 billion a year in Vietnam. A month later, however, when asked a similar question about the feasibility of a $30 billion program for the cities, he said the figure was "not as alarming as you might think," claiming that "we have got to make political, economic and social equality real for all Americans."[21]

For other commissioners, meanwhile, the in-person visits to cities that had experienced unrest reinforced the basic message that Lindsay and Harris had been delivering—that it was impossible to stop future riots without addressing the conditions that led to them. Kerner said that after all his discussions with unemployed young people, he found only one who did not want a job. "It was clear to us, as we walked in the ghettos," he wrote a few months after the tours, that "the people who live there want some very simple things: more police protection against crime in their own communities; more and better jobs, schools and housing; improved public facilities and service such as street lighting and garbage collection; an opportunity to elect people of their own choosing to public office; a decisive voice in the planning of their own communities—and an end to disrespectful treatment from white Americans."[22]

Brooke had a similar awakening. After touring Detroit's riot-torn areas, he told reporters that it would "take a massive effort similar to the Marshall plan after World War II to make a dent" in urban problems. Brooke was not the first person to advocate for a Marshall Plan for the cities. Urban League director Whitney Young had raised the idea at his organization's 1963 national convention, arguing that the history of slavery and racial prejudice had left African Americans unprepared to take advantages of the benefits of postwar economic growth. Young had advocated then for a "special effort" by the federal government and private industry to provide job training and education for blacks in the rural South and urban cities. But having a Republican senator endorse the same notion gave it greater visibility and bipartisan credibility.[23]

Perhaps no one involved with the commission was more shocked by the conditions they witnessed than the director, David Ginsburg. "David began his work in August 1967 with no more than an average white upper-class liberal's understanding about race and the riots," his assistant, David Chambers, wrote in 2016. "His views were shaped by living in the segregated worlds of West Virginia and Washington, DC, by working in white elite institutions, by having highly placed Democratic friends and by reading the *New York Times* and the *Washington Post*." He had an abstract awareness of racism, but he had never seen it up close or understood the tangle of problems that it caused. The first few months on the commission changed all that. "David underwent a profound education," Chambers wrote. "He visited Newark with a couple of commissioners and walked around in the damaged areas, he attended a half dozen days of often passionate testimony in the hearings before the Commission," and he "spent a great deal of time talking with people he respected, all of whom believed in the centrality of racism to the current situation." Ginsburg quickly became determined to ensure that the report highlighted the theme of white racism and forced all Americans to confront the shameful legacy of racism.[24]

Indeed, like Ginsburg, many commissioners and staff were coming around to the position that it would be impossible to ignore the ultimate cause of the conditions that had led to the riots—racism. Poverty, unemployment, poor schools, and inadequate medical care all contributed to the misery of urban life. The common thread was that African Americans were always at the bottom of the ladder, with little chance to move up. And the chief reason was that they were black in a white-dominated society.

BETWEEN VISITS TO THE RIOT areas, the commissioners returned to the musty and ornate Indian Treaty Room to listen to more witnesses. Most of the testimony they heard reinforced what they were observing in the field. The commissioners listened patiently as Newark mayor Hugh Addonizio, a bulky, balding liberal Democrat, testified about the conditions that led to the riots, accompanied by twenty aides. Addonizio told the commission that it was the "cruelest of

myths . . . that middle class America has an interest in saving cities."
He said that wealthy Americans "are gripped more by the need to
buy a vacation home, a sports car for their college-bound son and a
second television set than they are with sharing their affluence with
the poor." The suburbs, he declared, were indifferent to the problems
plaguing cities. He insisted that most Americans "would vote the cities out of existence if they could." Local civic leaders, who followed
Addonizio, painted a picture of a dysfunctional city plagued by poor
funding and an indifferent municipal government.[25]

Addonizio had a dual mission: he wanted the federal government
to pour millions of new dollars into Newark, but he also wanted to
make sure the funds came directly to city hall and not to the local citizen groups. While advocating for a Marshall Plan for the cities, Addonizio vehemently opposed the underlying premise of the Johnson
administration's "War on Poverty," which provided resources directly
to local communities, bypassing city hall. The Office of Economic
Opportunity had required that the local community-action agencies
that received federal funding be "developed, conducted, and admin-
istered with the maximum feasible participation of residents of the
areas and members of the groups served." Addonizio lashed out at
the OEO for "bypassing city governments and dealing directly with
neighborhood groups."[26]

He was not alone. The poverty program had from the start incurred
the wrath of many other Democratic mayors who could not understand why a president of their own party would be funding groups
that challenged their authority. While some community-action initiatives were unthreatening—summer day camps for poor children,
a health center in Boston—many others organized local citizens to
protest city hall. In New York, local organizers complained to city
hall about poor public facilities and demanded better garbage collection and enforcement of housing codes. Mayors and governors complained to the president that he was funding organizations that were
undermining their power and authority. "What in the hell are you

people doing?" Chicago's mayor Richard Daley asked Johnson press secretary Bill Moyers. "Does the president know he's putting money in the hands of subversives?"[27]

The early testimony, covered widely in the press, challenged the very foundation of LBJ's Great Society, dismissing his programs as either misconceived or grossly underfunded. The presentations made clear that potential solutions—if there were any—were beyond the fiscal reach of the administration.

Mayors and other local officials were just one source of information for the commission. The commissioners also heard from high-profile sociologists and economists. Most of these experts confirmed what Addonizio had said—Johnson's Great Society and his much-heralded "War on Poverty" offered little help to people who needed it most. "We cannot mishandle a social problem for 350 years and assume that palliatives, retraining programs, and so on are going to change it," said Professor Eli Ginzberg of Columbia University. Paul Bullock of the University of California–Los Angeles (UCLA) said that the civil rights successes in the South "had no impact whatsoever, and had been almost totally irrelevant" for African Americans living in big cities in the North. Herbert Gans, a Columbia University sociologist, called the War on Poverty a failure, largely because it was underfunded. It looked good on paper, he said, but most programs had little or no impact on the lives of poor urban residents. The only way to avoid future riots, he asserted, was to provide services at the same level that Americans supplied arms to fight the war in Vietnam. William Taylor, staff director of the United States Civil Rights Commission, piled on, telling the commission that current federal antidiscrimination policy had been unsuccessful in ending bias in the workplace. He also used the example of urban renewal to highlight the unintended consequences of some federal programs. These projects, he declared, produced "nothing in the ghetto except houses which have been condemned, but are still standing," providing a refuge for vandals and illegal activity.[28]

Testimony of this sort was not what LBJ wanted to hear from his blue-ribbon panel. After attending the hearing about Newark, White House aide Fred Bohen told Joseph Califano that the testimony highlighted a central point: Johnson's Great Society programs had barely made a dent in dealing with the problems of big cities. Bohen was shocked by the "electricity" of the testimony from "indigenous" witnesses, especially young people. He discovered that the unemployment rate in Newark was 37 percent. Youth unemployment was a staggering 40 percent. There had been no new private housing development in fifty years, and public housing in low-income areas "only scratches the surface" of what was needed. Young African Americans "were alleged to be *fearless* of police and state troops and willing to risk their lives wantonly because they had lost faith in progress by any other route." Bohen concluded that the "magnitude of the problem, the scale of the effort required to make any impact at all was manifest." Great Society programs represented only a "modest effort." He warned that as the commission made public conditions in urban areas, "*it is going to be immensely difficult, if not impossible, to cut much ice with the strides made in the last few years.*" He suggested that the White House avoid bragging about its accomplishments because the testimony before the commission revealed that its programs were having little impact on the lives of urban residents. Bohen concluded, "I think we should avoid overstatement."[29]

As dramatic as some of the early testimony was, it provided little new evidence to help the commission respond to the questions they were charged with answering. The meetings with the mayors produced good theater but not very good information. The senior staff was especially disappointed by Addonizio and his aides, who simply repeated their official position that the federal government and white suburbanites were to blame for the unrest in their cities. The commissioners' trips to Newark had already made them skeptical of that claim. Palmieri described the presentation as "time-consuming and not very productive in terms of evidence, but necessary, nonetheless."

The commission decided that in the future, it would meet with elected officials on their home turf and reserve official hearings in Washington primarily for scholars, local officials, and grassroots organizations that could help them achieve their three major goals: gathering information that would help in re-creating the riots' scenarios, producing an analysis that would explain the causes of the violence, and offering recommendations that would prevent future riots.[30]

Ginsburg was also growing impatient. While he was focused on producing a report on time, the commissioners seemed to prefer a more discursive approach. Ginsburg found the hearings cumbersome, complaining about the "relaxed atmosphere" that allowed commissioners to waste valuable time asking questions that were irrelevant to their mission. The hearings, he said, were "time-consuming and unwieldy" and threatened the staff's ability "to produce a timely report." He asked Kerner whether they should adopt new procedures, suggesting that the staff prepare questions ahead of time for the commissioners or simply call fewer witnesses. The commissioners, however, balked at any effort to limit their role.[31]

EVEN AS GINSBURG WORRIED THAT the unwieldy hearings threatened the commission's ability to report its findings in a timely fashion, the commissioners decided to speed up the release of the interim report. The executive order creating the commission had called for an interim report in March 1968 and a final one in July. In early October, Lindsay led a drive to push up the release date for the interim report from March to December 1967. The mayor, along with Harris and Wilkins, felt it necessary to produce an initial statement of findings as quickly as possible to reassure the nation and suggest steps that could be taken immediately to head off further unrest. Lindsay also wanted the commission to be able to shape LBJ's 1968 legislative agenda. Most of his fellow commissioners, genuinely shaken by what they had seen on the tours and heard in testimony, agreed to the schedule change. Kerner made the announcement at an October 6

press conference, telling reporters they would produce an interim report by December that would concentrate on short-range steps that
private industry, foundations, universities, communities, and states
could take immediately to prevent future riots, without requiring
any legislation.[32]

There was one major obstacle to producing a report three months
ahead of schedule: the commission had thus far made little progress
in actually answering any of the questions that LBJ had posed back
in July. Despite the investigations the commissioners had undertaken
and the many witnesses they had heard from, the answers seemed
more elusive and far more complicated than anyone had anticipated.
Furthermore, there were still deep divisions among the commissioners about how to answer the president's questions and even about how
to define their mandate.

The commission's change of plans did not sit well with LBJ, who
became increasingly worried that Lindsay was using the commission
as a platform for his own political ambitions. LBJ's handpicked chairman turned out to be a weak leader, and the hard-charging Lindsay
quickly filled the leadership gap. Ginsburg affirmed that Kerner was
"never passionately involved with the detail and the substance of the
effort," and Palmieri has declared that Lindsay "was the real leader
of the commission." In a 1993 speech, he said that tensions between
the commission and the White House "resulted from the fact that
President Johnson awoke to realize that while it might be called the
Kerner Commission, it was very much in danger of being the Lindsay
Commission!"[33]

Johnson had been leery of Lindsay from the beginning. On August
2, the day after Hoover testified at the commission's first hearings,
the *New York Times* carried a front-page photo of Ginsburg walking
to the session with Lindsay. That afternoon Ginsburg received a call
from Califano: "The president saw your picture in the paper this
morning and really doesn't think you ought to have too many of those
taken with Lindsay."[34] As the fall wore on, Johnson became obsessed

with Lindsay. "It pained Johnson to see that he had elevated Lindsay," according to Palmieri. LBJ exploded when Lindsay announced that he was trying to shape the president's legislative agenda by moving the interim report from March to December. LBJ told Califano to send a message to the media-hungry mayor: "Tell Lindsay that there's something I've learned from a long life and politics: it's a darn sight easier to slip on bullshit than it is to slip on gravel. If he doesn't stop the bullshit, he's going to slip and break his ass."[35]

In September Harris went to the White House to introduce an Oklahoma native who had been named Miss America. Not even the presence of a beauty queen could distract Johnson from his focus on the charismatic New York mayor. "I'm surprised to see you up, Fred," LBJ said sarcastically. "Sir?" a puzzled Harris responded. "I'm surprised to see you up," the president repeated. "I heard old John Lindsay had you down and had his foot on your neck."[36]

Johnson asked Harris to stick around after the others left. He picked up a copy of that day's *New York Times* with a headline announcing that Lindsay had released federal poverty funds to his own ailing city. "Now look at this shit, Fred," Johnson exclaimed. "[B]y God, you've got to read all the way down to the bottom of the damn page before you find out it's *my* program." A few weeks later, while drinking brandy and smoking cigars at the White House with a handful of senators, Johnson returned to his new obsession. He opened the conversation by glaring at Harris. "Fred," he said in a mocking voice, "tell us about your friend Lindsay's campaign for president."[37]

Chapter 5

"A STRAITJACKET
OF FACTS"

URING THE FIRST FEW MONTHS of the commission's work,
while the commissioners were listening to witnesses and traveling to riot-torn areas, David Ginsburg and Victor Palmieri organized
the staff to conduct their own more systematic fact-finding missions.
They sent teams of investigators swarming into cities. The teams sent
back to Washington thick, detailed reports that combined impressionistic evidence gleaned from interviews with residents, community
leaders, and city officials and a mountain of statistics assembled from
local records and census reports. The evidence they gathered of persistent racial discrimination, and a growing gap between blacks and
whites, was both overwhelming and irrefutable.

Through the work of these field teams, the commission's staff created what John Lindsay aide Jay Kriegel called "a straitjacket of facts."
They proved that African Americans living in urban areas confronted
overt discrimination from real estate agents and local authorities, who
refused to allow them to move into white neighborhoods; they faced
a lack of jobs because manufacturers had fled to the suburbs; and
they were forced to attend poor, underfunded schools because the

white middle class, and their tax dollars, had escaped to the suburbs. Those indisputable facts would ultimately leave the commissioners, whatever their ideological predilections, with scant room to maneuver, offering them little choice but to endorse the new social programs the staff recommended for addressing the problems they documented so conclusively.[1]

GINSBURG AND PALMIERI HAD ORIGINALLY planned to gather "masses of data" about the political and economic characteristics of urban areas and then dump it into a computer in the hopes of finding revealing patterns. But the short time frame for the commission's work, and the primitive state of the technology, prevented that type of statistical analysis. Instead, the staff opted to create their own field teams that would travel to a handful of riot areas to gather data as well as talk with residents, community leaders, local business owners, and public officials. These field teams provided the information that served as the lifeblood of the commission. Robert Conot used it to craft his narrative of events, and the commission's social scientists analyzed it for patterns that could help explain why the riots occurred. Since the commission could not afford to send field teams to all the riot areas, they choose cities that offered a representative sample of the variety of disturbances. From an FBI list of fifty-two cities that had experienced major violence, they chose a representative sample of twenty-six, including Milwaukee, Minneapolis, Spanish Harlem in New York, Nashville, Detroit, and Newark.[2]

Many of the men—they were all men—hired for the field teams were young and idealistic, and they viewed working on the commission as a way of contributing to solving America's racial problems. Many had been hired through TransCentury Associates, a consulting firm that catered to returning Peace Corps volunteers. "This is a group of people, almost entirely liberal, with extensive international experience that now gravitated toward the commission," said Bruce

Thomas, one of the field-team leaders. Their experiences working with the poor and disenfranchised in other countries provided them with empathy for those left out of the system. Field-team members with such backgrounds also tended to be instinctively more skeptical of the liberal emphasis on gradualism and moderation. For those who grew up in middle-class families and attended elite universities, their experience on the commission would expose them to a part of America they had only read about in books.[3]

Bruce Thomas was one of those recruits. Thomas, who was white, graduated from Harvard and spent three years at Oxford University as a Rhodes scholar before joining the commission. Having grown up in a small town in New Hampshire and then attended elite universities, Thomas had never seen the "other America." He was shocked by what he saw and heard from residents of poor urban areas. "I came to see an America I've never known before," he asserted nearly five decades later. "I had a sense of America's original sin."[4]

The commission hired forty investigators who worked in teams of six. Each team was divided into pairs of two that would take responsibility for interviewing different groups: the official sector, residents in the riot area, and business leaders. They would take notes as discreetly as possible, but they did not tape their interviews. Each team of six had at least one African American member. The assumption was that African Americans would be more comfortable talking to a black team member. "We'd go into the city with a racially mixed team and would divvy up assignments to go out and interview people," according to Thomas. "The black staff guys talk to blacks, and whites to whites." Isaac Hunt, one of the African American field investigators, recalled that a black activist in Atlanta told him that when he contacted people, he needed to tell them that he was black, "because," he was told, "you don't sound black."[5]

The staff had prepared a "checklist" for the field teams to follow. It started with a pretrip briefing, where the team received official letters of authorization and an information kit on the city they were going to visit. The commission's social scientists prepared a list of questions the teams were required to ask: What was the chronology of events? What precipitated the riot, and how did it evolve over time? How and why did it end? They also needed to examine the grievances of residents: Were their complaints justified, and how did local officials respond? Were there adequate channels of communication between the African American community and city government? What was the relationship between residents and the police? The commission staff believed that these microscopic studies of individual cities would reveal general themes and patterns within the disorders, the ways that they developed, and how authorities responded. After spending the day gathering information, the team members would return to their hotel rooms, compare notes, and swap stories over a meal. They would record that conversation, using the notes to jog their memories. The tapes were then sent back to Washington for transcription, and the investigators returned to the Washington offices often to brief the staff and social scientists there about their findings.[6]

The field teams' experiences in poor black neighborhoods and their conversations with local activists and community leaders, as well as elected officials, underscored the depth of the racial problems in America. Many of the field-team members began to question the tenets of mainstream liberalism, convinced that Johnson's Great Society programs had little meaningful impact on the daily lives of poor blacks. Instead, they became enamored of more radical approaches to addressing urban ills. Thomas remembered meeting with a group of black parents who were trying to create an alternative to the Boston public schools. "I listened to this tale of what was happening to black kids in the Boston public schools," he recalled. "It was shocking." Hunt, who grew up in an upper-middle-class family in Virginia, was deeply troubled by the stories of police brutality he heard. He quickly came to believe that most "police systems" were run by "ill-educated, racist people with absolutely manifestly no judgment."[7]

Whether they began their work on the commission with experience and empathy for the poor and marginalized or were seeing poverty and racism for the first time, many field-team members would become deeply distrustful of the Johnson administration and the liberal approach to addressing race issues and urban poverty. Even as liberals congratulated themselves for all the progress that had been made, they seemed to many field-workers oblivious to the ongoing plight of the urban poor and the limited reach of their programs. Many team members believed that the nation needed to go further than piecemeal social programs and consider more radical alternatives, including a redistribution of wealth and power in America. Many also came to distrust the commission's senior leadership, who, they feared, would water down some of their most disturbing findings to placate LBJ.

Over time, a mutual wariness developed between the senior staff and the field teams. Ginsburg and Palmieri, who were just as concerned about America's racial crisis as the younger representatives, tended to view America's racial problems through the lens of conventional liberalism. They were also more sensitive to the delicate politics of the commission. The senior staff and all the commissioners agreed on the need to produce a unanimous report, and that meant authoring a document that both John Lindsay and Tex Thornton could sign. The field teams, on the other hand, saw their job as channeling the anger and frustration of poor urban blacks, regardless of the political consequences. That gap in outlooks, small at first, would widen and eventually become unbridgeable.

There was also a racial dimension to the mistrust. According to journalist Andrew Kopkind, who published an article about the commission shortly after publication of the final report, many of the black investigators became suspicious that their interviews would be rewritten and misrepresented by the commission staff. He quoted a field investigator who was convinced that "the whole thing was a racist operation." African American field investigators complained that all of the commission's senior staffers except for one, general counsel

Merle McCurdy, were white. Nearly all the consultants were also white. "Overall," Kopkind wrote, "the Report was always thought of as a white document written by white writers and aimed at a white audience—*about* black people." The tension revealed that the commission was not immune to the broader atmosphere of racial mistrust, and it showed the challenges Ginsburg and Palmieri confronted in reconciling black and white staffers to a shared understanding of the commission's aims.[8]

THE REPORTS FROM THE FIELD offered a fresh perspective on the riots, one that often challenged the official narrative from journalists and government reports. They captured the raw sentiment of blacks in poor urban neighborhoods, along with the arrogance and indifference of local officials and the abusive practices that were common in most police departments. They documented wide disparities in income, employment, housing, and education and highlighted how, in many cities, racial tensions were growing, not receding. The reports were relentless in their criticism of local white officials and police departments for ignoring the legitimate complaints of residents and confirmed what many of the commissioners discovered during their tours.

The lack of good-paying jobs was one constant source of frustration for African Americans living in urban areas, especially for young people. The unemployment rate in Newark was double the national average of 4 percent, and among young blacks it stood at 33 percent. While the average unemployment rate for Detroit was 3.3 percent, it was 7.4 percent for nonwhites, and among blacks in their late teens and early twenties it stood at 25 percent.[9]

Newark's riot-torn area suffered from old and obsolete public facilities and substandard housing. The Newark team described public housing facilities as "institutional, penitentiary-like, and shocking in their bareness—no amenities, no grass, and just clay outside."

Housing in Detroit was "quite old and is deteriorating rapidly," the report noted, highlighting how the city's "inattention to housing problems reinforces the widely-shared feeling in the black community that the white power structure is totally disinterested in the welfare of the black man." In Atlanta's black neighborhoods, garbage was sometimes not picked up for two weeks in succession. Garbage cans overflowed, and litter filled the streets and empty lots, providing a breeding ground for rats. Inadequate storm drains led to flooded streets.[10]

Chronic unemployment and poor living conditions led to higher rates of disease and death in poor areas. Newark had the highest maternal mortality and venereal disease rate in the entire country. It also had the highest infant mortality rate and the highest number of tuberculosis cases. It ranked seventh among ten cities in the total number of drug addicts.[11]

Education also ranked among the top complaints of poor African Americans, the field teams found. The reports revealed how recent demographic changes had impacted the quality of urban schools. Over the previous decades, millions of blacks migrated from the South to cities in the North. At the same time, many middle-class whites fled the urban core for the greener suburbs. Cities found themselves with a diminishing tax base and less revenue for education, even as school enrollments grew and student populations became predominately black. Detroit was a good example. During the previous ten years, Detroit lost about twenty to thirty thousand families, while the public school system had gained approximately fifty to sixty thousand children. Blacks made up a majority—56 percent—of students in the public system. The investigators stated that fourteen of the nineteen high schools in the city were racially segregated. In Newark more than 74 percent of public school children were nonwhite. Although enrollment had increased substantially, school buildings were old and poorly maintained. Nearly half of the city schools were built in the nineteenth century. The oldest had been built before the Civil War.

One school had been condemned earlier but was reopened without renovation to handle student overflow.[12]

Most of the grievances in Atlanta focused on the public school system. Until the passage of the Civil Rights Act of 1964, the Atlanta public school system had been segregated. Desegregation was proceeding slowly. By 1967 most of the schools were still divided by race. Blacks made up 60 percent of the total public school population, but they were crammed into only nine predominately black high schools. There were fourteen predominately white schools. Black high schools were so "grossly overcrowded" that students were forced to attend schools in four-and-a-half-hour shifts. There were no split sessions at the white high schools, where students attended classes for six and a half hours per day.[13]

There were also measurable differences in the quality of education between black and white schools. In nearly every city investigated, it was clear that black schools suffered from lax standards and a quality of education inferior to that of white schools. In Detroit statistics showed that achievement levels in black schools were three to five years behind white schools. Some employers refused to accept diplomas from inner-city high schools because it was known that "graduates generally have no better than a sixth-grade education." By another estimate, high school graduates in Detroit had only about a tenth grade education. As a result, African Americans who graduated from high school ended up stuck in low-paid manual-labor positions. A survey of one Detroit high school showed that two years after graduation, 72 percent of black graduates were still unemployed.[14]

Despite their overwhelming majority among students, African Americans were often excluded from well-paying jobs as teachers and school administrators in the cities investigated. Newark had its first black principal in 1960. In Detroit African Americans made up between 75 and 99 percent of the student body at many schools; seven schools were 100 percent black. But white administrators made up between 76 and 96 percent of the supervisory staff. Black leaders accused the Detroit schools of maintaining these white employees' "dominance" by using a biased application process. As evidence, they pointed to the fact that the application for principals was 30 percent written and 70 percent oral. "A system weighed so heavily in favor of a nonobjective or oral test is a ready-made vehicle for racial discrimination and personal abuse," the field team reported.[15]

The grievances the field investigators found went beyond jobs, housing, and schools. Many blacks believed that white landlords, businessmen, and city officials exploited them and that they lacked any power to stop it. They had to contend with high prices on necessities such as food, exorbitant interest rates from loan companies and pawnbrokers, and higher rents than whites living in the same area. "There is general resentment of white owners of ghetto businesses who take their profits back to the suburbs," the field team wrote about Detroit. Many residents they spoke with felt "general indignation about the fact that the black community cannot control its own destiny." They believed that "almost every aspect of their lives is controlled by the white man." African Americans were "no longer satisfied with the white man's anointed black leaders and are demanding a voice in all decisions which affect their lives." In Atlanta field teams discovered a simmering anger about the "poor quality of food sold in ghetto grocery stores, higher prices paid in ghetto stores, poor recreation facilities," and a lack of city services. In Plainfield, New Jersey, investigators noted that the grievances resulted from "a desire for more of the tangible good things of life and a desire for common respect as human beings."[16]

There were also the daily indignities. One informant in Dayton, Ohio, mentioned that white teachers routinely referred to blacks as "boys" or "niggers." In Atlanta one of the daily papers still advertised jobs by race, despite civil rights laws that made the practice illegal. Some factories also still advertised separate "Negro jobs" and "white jobs." The jobs designated for blacks were low-paying janitorial and maintenance positions that offered little chance for advancement into management.[17]

In nearly every city, residents complained of police brutality. The investigators referenced an Urban League study that revealed that the number-one grievance among residents of the riot areas, and the prime cause of the riots in their minds, was "police brutality." The Detroit field team claimed that the police "often performed with no greater professionalism than one might expect from a huge armed force of white civilian extremists." They argued that most African Americans believed that police brutality was "rampant," and there were no effective channels for dealing with their grievances. According to a congressional aide the team interviewed, African Americans viewed the police as "an occupying enemy force, and not as a protector of law-abiding citizens." An interviewee said that the "excessive and unnecessary force used by police were of such a magnitude that they could only be called 'atrocities.'" In Milwaukee African Americans viewed the police department "as brutal, corrupt and segregated." Only in the past few years had police in Plainfield stopped using the word "nigger" when talking over the radio. Nearly all police forces in major cities were overwhelmingly white. The Dayton police force had fifteen black officers in a force of four hundred men.[18]

The apathy, indifference, and outright hostility of police officials and elected leaders, who refused to acknowledge that brutality was an issue, added to the frustration. The Dayton police chief summed up the attitude of many local law enforcement officials to black protests. "Freedom of speech is our greatest problem," he said. Firmness and discipline, he believed, were the best way to prevent unrest. "When you tell a darkie something you have to mean it," he insisted. The Newark field team recited more than a dozen examples of incidents of police brutality that had never been investigated. Many police and city government officials denied any suggestion of brutality. In some cases, those who complained of mistreatment were arrested or sued for making "libelous charges." The City of Newark, for example, filed a $4.5 million lawsuit against John Smith, the cabdriver whose arrest had sparked the riot there. Mayor Addonizio told one black leader, "This is my city. You don't like it, move out, or wait until 1970!" New Haven's police chief told investigators that blacks had "received everything [they] demanded from the city administration." He blamed antagonism toward the police on "the disruptive influence of the Negroes who came up from the south during World War II and the Korean War." Clueless Detroit officials claimed the police had "basically a good relationship" with the African American community.[19]

Similar indifference and unwillingness to acknowledge black concerns were evident in other aspects of local government. An African American in Dayton told investigators that it was "the universal opinion of the Negro community that the white power structure either doesn't or can't communicate with Negroes." In Cambridge, Maryland, they concluded that "a good deal of the difficulty stems from the strong segregationist attitudes held by local officials [who] refuse to believe that Blacks had legitimate grievances."[20]

The investigators discovered that most whites they interviewed either denied that their city had a racial problem or rejected the idea that government had a responsibility to help those living in poverty. The Dayton, Ohio, field team noted that whites there believed the local government was already responsive to black concerns and that many whites complained that blacks were in fact getting "special treatment in order to prevent future riots." City officials denied there were any "legitimate" black grievances and were convinced that "everything was being done for Negroes that was possible." The team believed that government officials viewed the "routine benefits of government for whites as privileges for Negroes—for which they should be grateful." The mayor dismissed civil rights protesters there as "thieves" with no legitimate grievances, and most city leaders believed that further violence was unlikely unless H. Rap Brown or Stokely Carmichael came to town. The underlying cause of the riots, the mayor said, was that "the Negro subculture doesn't espouse white values." In Plainfield, New Jersey, the recreation commissioner refused to build a pool in the black area of the city. "If you give them an inch," he told investigators, "they'll take a mile."[21]

White officials thought they had done everything possible for the black community and felt betrayed by the riots. The white city officials in Newark felt like "its hand was bitten while it was feeding the dog." "Why should I hire them?" a white businessman in Newark said, referring to black employees. "So they can burn down my place from the inside, rather than have to break in?" The team concluded that "Newark is swiftly becoming a city of rival armies, the population in the middle gravitating towards the two opposite camps." They raised the prospect of "a truly terrifying bloodbath." The inaction of local officials to address legitimate grievances was making the situation worse. Phoenix was typical. The investigators noted that city officials refused to address any of the grievances after the riot. "It is pretty much business as usual," they reported. "The most often repeated point of view among officials and the press since the disturbance has been that it is of the utmost importance [to] avoid the appearance of rewarding the rioters."[22]

African Americans had few effective means to address their communities' problems because they lacked political power, the field teams found. In Cincinnati blacks made up 26 percent of the population, but only one of nine city councilmen was black. Blacks made up only 6 percent of the police force. "The city administration seems rather unresponsive and committed to maintaining the status quo," the team reported. "This fact coupled with the absence of more Negroes in positions of power only serves to heighten anger and frustration." In Atlanta local council positions were elected by citywide votes, which limited the political power of blacks. Only one of the six aldermen was black, and a number of black wards were represented by white aldermen. As a result, many blacks "felt they were not being properly represented on the city government."[23]

In many cities, the field teams also observed a generational gap within the black community, as younger, more militant activists replaced an older generation of black leaders. "Younger black men saw no meaningful change taking place and became tired of talking and lost faith in the institutions of the larger society and in the sincerity of the whites who staff the institutions," a field team noted. "For many of these people all other tactics have failed and violence as the alternative no doubt seemed attractive." The investigators were told that the violence in Newark by black residents started because "the young people won't take the same kind of talk [from police] that the old people took." Young blacks had lost faith in their own leaders and in the white power structure. As a result, they had "little or nothing to lose in total racial war," and high unemployment and limited opportunity provided "an abundant source of recruits for the more revolutionary black nationalists." Investigators noted that black leadership in Cincinnati was divided between the leaders recognized by the white community, dismissed by others as "the Negro Republicans," who had been "co-opted by the whites and at best are out of touch with the people in the street." Many younger blacks "feel hostility toward the NAACP and according to one informant the head of the NAACP is about as welcome in the ghetto as is the local police chief."[24]

The investigators also faulted the news media for its coverage of the Cambridge disturbance, in particular. The field teams described the disturbances as "small scale," but newspaper accounts perpetuated the false narrative that H. Rap Brown "incited a riot" and that there was widespread violence immediately following Brown's speech. The facts, they argued, were not so clear-cut. Brown's presence had prompted the city to respond as if a riot were already under way, but the actual riot was provoked more by the police overreaction than by anything Brown had said. "To the extent that Brown encouraged anybody to engage in precipitous or disorderly acts," the report noted, "the city officials are clearly the ones he influenced most." Brown, they concluded, "was more a catalyst of white fears than of Negro

antagonisms" and "the disturbance more a product of white expectations than of Negro initiative."[25]

And perhaps most dismaying of all to the Johnson administration,
the field teams found little evidence that the War on Poverty was
making significant inroads. They called the federal programs in Milwaukee "deplorably uncoordinated." In Detroit the administration's
initiative had "little impact on the daily lives of most people living
in the ghetto." Most poor people they spoke with there felt they had
been "untouched" by federal programs. Even worse, the field teams
observed that the hype surrounding the programs created hope and
then frustration. They concluded that federal programs "have failed
to reach the true poverty class as that class was led to believe they
would." In Atlanta investigators reported that "it must be concluded
that federal programs" had not affected "the problems in the ghettos measurably enough to eliminate or lessen the real causes of civil
disorder." In Phoenix the poverty program was "losing the battle of
being a real meaningful change agent" because of insufficient funds.[26]

ON FRIDAY, OCTOBER 27, AS the field teams' reports started trick-
ling into Washington for processing, Ginsburg and Palmieri organized a meeting at Washington's Statler Hilton Hotel with more than
a dozen of the country's leading social scientists. The commission had
a small team of in-house experts, but Ginsburg also wanted to hear
from the leading lights in the field. Angus Campbell of the University of Michigan's Survey Research Center presided over the meeting.
Ginsburg told the gathering that he called them together "to review
the recent research in the field of race relations" and to guide the
commission's research agenda. All the commissioners were invited to
attend, but only Corman showed up.[27]

By late October, the commission continued to be torn between
two competing explanations of the riots: Thornton's insistence that
the riots resulted from a lack of law and order and Lindsay and

Harris's view that the riots were the result of racial discrimination and the poverty and lack of opportunity that it produced. The tours had certainly tilted the balance on the commission and among staff in favor of Lindsay's perspective, but the staff still lacked hard data to back it up.

Unfortunately, the social scientists' presentation only muddied the water. Using a wealth of new surveys, they demolished the McCone Commission's conclusion that most of the rioters in Watts were disaffected individuals who did not represent the community at large. That conclusion had fed the popular belief that most of the rioters in subsequent disturbances were new migrants from the South, criminals, and alienated high school dropouts. A study of nine poverty areas in Cleveland, however, revealed that up to 26 percent of African Americans approved the use of violence to address their grievances. A survey of Los Angeles showed that one-third of African Americans spoke favorably of the disorders. Many of those surveyed believed that the disorders "brought sympathy and more attention to their problems." The rioters were hardly anomalies.

The researchers, however, also chipped away at the emerging consensus on the Kerner Commission that there was a direct relationship between poverty and rioting. Their studies had found poor African Americans were no more likely to participate in the disorders than their middle-class neighbors. The researchers painted a portrait of riot participants that was unexpected in several ways. The typical rioter was born in the North and was a lifetime resident of the city in which he lived. Those most active in the riots were young, urban, educated men. They were not misfits; instead, they voted, read newspapers, and were generally plugged into the world. Most sympathized with the black Muslim movement. The researchers found that women were angrier than men, and those who considered themselves "very religious" were least likely to protest. Racial integration, although a top priority for white liberals, attracted little interest among most rioters. Integration, surveys from Watts, Houston, and San Francisco suggested, was "not a prime goal in and of itself." Most cared more about "better schools, housing, and jobs."

Rioters were not, by all the evidence, disproportionately poor or disengaged from the communities around them. But the researchers did find one common denominator that determined who rioted and who did not, one neither Thornton nor Lindsay had emphasized. Those most likely to riot shared one characteristic: they had experienced or witnessed an act of police brutality.

Still, the picture the researchers painted was a complicated one. They could not offer a simple explanation for why some cities erupted in violence while others remained largely peaceful. One study created a "dissatisfaction index" that included information on income, education, and housing. Surprisingly, cities ranking highest on the dissatisfaction scale did not experience a riot. The city lowest on the scale, Dayton, did. Their conclusions were clear: "There was absolutely no direct relationship between economic status . . . and participation in street demonstrations."

The social scientists' findings were far from conclusive. They marshaled considerable evidence indicating that many rioters were not poor, but they failed to prove that poverty was *not* an underlying cause of the unrest. The presentation, in short, underscored that there was no simple answer to LBJ's simple question, "What caused the riots?" It was easy to list the many grievances of residents in poor African American neighborhoods where the riots occurred; it was far more challenging to show a direct relationship between those specific grievances and the violence that erupted. Why did some poor people take to the streets and others not? How to explain why some cities where conditions were wretched remained calm, while others with better conditions experienced disturbances? These questions continued to puzzle the social scientists. The lack of definitive answers complicated the commission's task of preparing a convincing response to the president's questions.

OVER THE COURSE OF THE fall, Ginsburg and Palmieri juggled the many different aspects of the commission's work. Even as they were running the research wing of the investigation, hiring consultants, reviewing the information pouring into Washington from the field teams, and reviewing drafts of the interim report, they also organized hearings for commissioners, assuaged their delicate egos, and responded to their requests for information. Ginsburg had decided that each commissioner could have one assistant whose salary would be paid by the commission. Five of the eleven commissioners took him up on the offer, and a few of these assistants insisted on being actively involved, becoming a daily nuisance to the senior staff. Ginsburg was also in regular contact with the White House, keeping Califano up-to-date on the commission's work and hoping to keep his client, the president, content. All the while, the two men were trying to keep the unwieldy commission focused on producing an interim report by December.

By October, with the once empty commission offices jam-packed with staff and consultants, Ginsburg lobbied the White House for more space. Ginsburg said that the commission needed only a few additional offices and a conference room. It was "vital," he wrote, that "we get out of the bedlam of the city teams and task forces." He asked that the White House evict the other executive task forces with whom they shared their Sixteenth Street building. The White House refused, but it did provide offices in a new Executive Office Building at the corner of Seventeenth Street and Pennsylvania Avenue. In October the senior staff, which included Ginsburg, Palmieri, Merle McCurdy, and Milan Miskovsky, along with their assistants, moved into the new offices, while the rest of the staff remained behind.[28]

There was already anxiety among the staff, especially the field teams, that their reports would be edited to please the White House. When the top management of the commission relocated to a separate office away from the rest of the staff, it only added to these worries. Palmieri did not help the situation when he announced that "the

really important people will be moving to the new quarters." Kerner's
assistant, Kyran McGrath, complained that the move widened "the
gap further between the so-called thinkers and the so-called doers."[29]

Unease also grew among the commissioners themselves, who had
little contact with the field teams and were curious about what they
were finding in their investigations. Some of the commissioners were
suspicious that they were intentionally being kept isolated from the
other aspects of the commission's work. Some feared that they were
part of a White House public relations gimmick. The commissioners
worried that Ginsburg and Palmieri were doing the president's bid-
ding and that the two men would write most of the report and then
ask them to rubber-stamp their conclusions. At the same time, all the
commissioners had full-time jobs and knew they would not have time
to write the report themselves.

As early as September 29, McGrath informed Kerner of "grum-
blings" from some of the other commissioners, who feared that they
were "being more entertained in their work," while the staff was
doing "the actual work" of the commission. The commissioners felt
that with a packed schedule of hearings and tours, they had little time
to talk with each other, share ideas, and provide direction to the staff.
A few weeks later, McGrath told Kerner than many of the commissioners had the impression that Ginsburg and Palmieri would write
most of the report "and that it will be presented to the commissioners at the 11th hour," giving "time for them to add a few token paragraphs," but not enough to make "substantial alterations." The real
fear among some of the commissioners was that the White House was
shaping the report behind the scenes. Many felt the staff's approach
to the commissioners was to "keep them busy and out of the way of
writing the report."[30]

In response to the criticism, Palmieri met with the commissioners' assistants and assured them that what the commission produced
"definitely is not to be a White House report." Ginsburg met privately
with Congressman Corman, who seemed to be the person doing most

of the complaining, and told him that the commissioners, not the staff, would set the direction for the report. According to McGrath, "Corman sat through the hand-holding session and concluded that he'll look to the chairman for direction and not especially to Dave [Ginsburg]."[31]

In late October, Palmieri invited one of the Detroit field teams to make an informal presentation to the commission. It was a risky move. Their experiences in the field had radicalized many of the investigators. They were instructed beforehand to stick to the facts and avoid editorializing, reminded that they had been charged with collecting data, and told that explaining what the data meant was supposed to be the job of the staff social scientists. But the commissioners pushed them to give their own views on the causes of the riots, and the investigators had no reservations about sharing them. Drawing on their experiences, they described the horrible conditions in the cities and suggested that the riots were "justified." When pushed to explain how riots that destroyed whole sections of cities and led to dozens of deaths could be justified, the field-team members stated that the conditions in the cities were so horrible, and the white power structure so unresponsive, that taking to the streets was the only rational way for residents to get attention and force officials to address their grievances. The passionate defense of the riots and the rioters did not sit well with many of the commissioners. According to Robert Shellow, one of the staff social scientists, the commissioners seemed puzzled and angry by the presentation and now questioned whether they could trust the staff to provide an objective analysis of the riots.[32]

The commissioners' first exposure to the field teams revealed one of the weaknesses in the commission's methodology for addressing the questions posed by the president. Ginsburg and Palmieri had realized that the roots of unrest were complex and involved a thicket of issues: racism, discrimination, poverty, and other long-simmering grievances. They had hoped that the field teams would untangle that thicket through their in-depth investigation of the riot areas and that the social scientists would then distill that research to present a coherent explanation that would both address the needs of urban residents and satisfy the political expectations of the commissioners. None of that happened. By the end of October, despite the detailed field reports and the feedback from outside social scientists, the commission seemed as far away as ever from articulating a coherent explanation for the cause of the riots.

And now time conspired against them. Ginsburg and Palmieri had assumed initially that the work would unfold in stages, as defined by LBJ's questions. The first phase would involve investigations. The field teams would fan out to various cities, and the commissioners would hold hearings and conduct their own tours, all to gather evidence. Next, the staff would analyze and attempt to answer why the riots occurred, while the commissioners started reviewing drafts of the interim report. Finally, the commissioners would debate and, eventually, vote on proposed recommendations. It proved impossible, however, to move in such a logical progression. The commissioners wanted to hear the staff's explanation for why the riots occurred before the social scientists had analyzed the information generated by the field teams. They also started debating solutions before they had agreed on the riots' cause. The commission staff was focused on socioeconomic problems that could be solved by tangible and politically tenable solutions. The field teams, on the other hand, were exploring the deeper motivations that lay behind the riots and questioning the limits of liberalism to deal with the problem. "It was all very difficult," Palmieri admitted."[33]

The field team presentation unsettled the commissioners, but it shocked Ginsburg and Palmieri. Egged on by the commissioners, the investigators went far beyond their expertise and used the occasion to vent their own political views. Those views were often not significantly different from what many of the senior staff, including Palmieri and Ginsburg, were also beginning to believe—that the conditions in the ghettos were so bad, and the white power structure in

American cities so unresponsive, that there was a rational dimension to the riots. But the staff knew many of the commissioners were not ready for that message, and if it was to be delivered, it had to be done in a more diplomatic manner. Ginsburg, ever the skillful lawyer, decided that he would take the lead in finding a message that would unite the commissioners while doing justice to the painful reality that the field teams unearthed in the cities they visited.

Chapter 6

"WHITE RACISM"

B Y LATE OCTOBER 1967, THE commissioners had toured riot areas and listened to hours of passionate testimony and were gaining a far more intimate understanding of the deep despair in poor, racially segregated urban communities. Yet the commissioners had still not yet arrived at a common answer to the central question: What caused the riots? The field teams had flooded the Washington office with boxes of information about conditions in urban areas, overwhelming the small team of social scientists assigned to review it and formulate their own answer to that question. Some of the nation's leading authorities on race and urban sociology had cast doubt on some common myths without adding much clarity. It was left to David Ginsburg to try to shape a consensus. Like almost everyone else involved with the commission's work, Ginsburg had been shocked by the miserable conditions that he observed during his tours and the powerful testimony that he heard from many of the witnesses who appeared before the committee, which had unsettled some of his own assumptions about the problems confronting America's cities and their residents. As October drew to a close, he had begun speaking privately with the commissioners, feeling them out, probing for points of consensus. The one common theme that emerged in conversations with each of the commissioners was the fact that white society bore the responsibility for the conditions of America's slums.

FROM PRIVATE CONVERSATIONS AS WELL as written communications, Ginsburg knew that most of the commissioners appeared willing to grant that the discriminatory attitudes and actions of white Americans were the most important underlying cause of the riots. It was not clear where Tex Thornton or Katherine Peden stood, but he could likely garner the support of nine commissioners for his proposition. Chief Jenkins told Ginsburg that "the inability of our white society to understand the Negro and failure of the Negro to achieve a place in the community through peaceful means has led too many Negroes to accept the brute force and violence advocated by the black power leaders." William McCulloch, who often sparred with John Lindsay, accepted that discrimination made it impossible for most African Americans to get a quality education and that it "was responsible for high unemployment and the dismal conditions in the ghetto." James Corman insisted that "the report should sharply portray the corrosive effects of slavery and segregation upon democratic institutions." James H. Jones, an African American steelworkers union official from Philadelphia who served as I. W. Abel's representative, noted that the testimony had "repeatedly referred to an appalling ignorance among white Americans" about the plight of poor African Americans. Years later, Roy Wilkins noted in an oral history that most of the commissioners came to realize that they could not compile a history of "pervasive discrimination" in employment, housing, and education and then "fail to say that white racism was the underlying cause."[1]

In a speech delivered the next year, a few weeks after the commission issued its report, Kerner said it took months of "soul-searching" before the commission "fully acknowledged white racism." Some members initially felt that phrase was too shocking and wished to substitute "discrimination" or "intolerance." Harris said that most of the commissioners felt it was important to use the phase to boost the self-esteem of young blacks who often accepted the narrative of the "dominant society" that they were poor because they were lazy. "Now," he said, they could say to themselves, "maybe it's not just me. Maybe I'm not, by myself, at fault. Maybe there's something else going on." Other commissioners, while realizing that it would make people uncomfortable, believed talking directly about white racism was the only intellectually honest way to describe the problem. "We could not back away" from the phrase, Kerner asserted. He admitted that the commissioners never defined the term "racism," but he personally believed that it referred to a constellation of ideas suggesting that "if you are white, you are superior—and if you are black, you are inferior." He called it "astonishing" the number of Americans who clung to "discredited racist beliefs."[2]

Ginsburg believed that in "white racism," he had found an explanation for the causes of the riots that could gain approval of the commission and serve as an organizing theme of the report—something that he desperately needed if he was going to meet the December deadline for the interim report. White racism was broad enough to gain the support of Democrats and Republicans on the commission, yet elusive enough to avoid pointing the finger at specific institutions. Its emphasis on attitudes suggested that minds, not politics or institutions, needed to change. For Ginsburg, who had come to the commission with little understanding of the complex nature of race relations in America, highlighting white attitudes also made perfect sense. While noting that the nation had made significant progress in the one hundred years since the end of the Civil War, the field-team reports and his conversations with experts persuaded Ginsburg that race still mattered and that it mattered much more than most people were willing to admit. He knew there was no simple explanation for the riots, but he genuinely believed that racism created the social and

economic conditions that made the riots possible, and he was determined to make sure the commission's final report used the strongest
language possible to make that point.

Ginsburg had charged the social scientists with formulating a response to the question "Why did the riots happen?" Now he answered the question for them. Emphasizing white racism was not an
approach informed by social science methodology or rigorous analysis. Instead, it was based on the impressionistic, but convincing,
evidence gathered through testimony and city tours combined with
in-depth conversations with experts, filtered through the political
maze of commission politics, and crafted by a skilled lawyer searching for consensus. "And from there on, he considered himself to have
found a theme for the report as a whole and a mandate from the
Commission to find data to back it up," Ginsburg's assistant David
Chambers wrote about his boss in 1970. Chambers concluded that
"scientific accuracy was hardly at the forefront of his intentions."[3]

Ginsburg planned to test the white racism theme at a meeting of
the commission in early November. McCulloch started the discussion
by affirming that white attitudes about race were the most important
factor in creating the conditions that led to the riots. All the other
commissioners, except Thornton, who remained uncharacteristically
quiet, readily agreed. After securing the commissioners' support for
the "white racism" theme, Ginsburg quickly drafted what would become the most important chapter in the final report—Chapter 4—
that laid out the "basic causes" of the riots. The report would go
through many drafts in the weeks and months that followed, but
Ginsburg's chapter remained largely untouched.

In that chapter, Ginsburg blamed the riots on a "massive tangle of
issues and circumstances" that impacted race relations in America.
Although complex, "the most fundamental is the racial attitude and
behavior of white Americans toward black Americans." Race prejudice had shaped the nation's past, and it threatened its future. "White
racism," Ginsburg wrote in an early draft, "is essentially responsible

for the explosive mixture which has been accumulating in our cities since the end of World War II." Racial prejudice had produced what he called "bitter fruits" in the form of discrimination, segregation, a white exodus from the cities to the suburbs, and the creation of black ghettos that lacked basic facilities and opportunities. These historical patterns had intersected with the frustrated hopes of blacks, whose expectations had been raised by the success of the early civil rights movement. Many blacks, he pointed out, believed they were being exploited politically and economically by a white power structure that was indifferent to their needs. Ginsburg stated flatly that police behavior played a significant role in causing the riots. "Almost invariably the incident that ignites disorder arises from police action," he wrote. For many blacks, he observed, "police have come to symbolize white power, white racism and white repression. And the fact is that most police do reflect and express these white attitudes." Ginsburg knew he would have to include some of Thornton's pet themes to gain his approval, so alongside this account centered on white racism he listed "legitimation of violence" and "incitement and encouragement of violence" as subsidiary causes of the riots.[4]

At the next meeting, the commissioners approved Ginsburg's draft chapter with only minor changes. But although Ginsburg had forged a superficial consensus around the idea of white racism, he soon discovered that the commissioners had very different interpretations of what it meant and in what direction it should lead the commission's investigation going forward. Despite agreeing on a basic answer to Johnson's second question, the commissioners were still divided along familiar lines. For the more liberal members of the commission, the focus on white racism set in motion a logical sequence. If racism created social and economic conditions that in turn precipitated the riots, then it was logical that the commission should recommend programs to address those conditions and remedy African Americans' economic disadvantages. The commission's report, in their view, should educate the public about the problem of racism and propose government programs to mitigate the "bitter fruits" of that racism. Although neither the field teams nor the academic consultants hired by the commission had found any direct link between poverty and rioting, the liberal members of the commissioners appeared ready to make the connection nonetheless.

Fred Harris and John Lindsay continued to be the most forceful and powerful advocates of this point of view. They believed that the riots exposed significant structural problems within American institutions, flaws that perpetuated and reinforced racial discrimination. The commission, they argued, needed to shock the public into confronting the legacy of race in America and propose a more aggressive federal program to attack the roots of the unrest—poverty, poor education, limited housing. If the federal government refused to enact meaningful reforms, it would lose further credibility with poor blacks, produce more disillusion, and, likely, lead to more violent riots in the summer of 1968. They thought it imperative that the final report not only confront sensitive issues of race in all aspects of American life, but also propose specific government programs to address the plight of poor urban blacks. The solutions needed to be appropriate to the size of the problem, which meant that only massive, large-scale government programs would suffice. The reason so many urban residents had not benefited from Great Society programs, in their view, was that the initiatives were not ambitious enough. Despite polls showing a growing white backlash against the Great Society, both Harris and Lindsay persisted in believing that if the public saw the "facts," it would rally around their proposed reforms.

Lindsay and Harris knew they could count on a slim majority of the commission to support their agenda, with their most reliable supporters being Roy Wilkins and Herbert Jenkins. "I believe we should give support to those who advocate a massive rebuilding program in our cities financed by the federal government," Jenkins argued. "This would include rehabilitation of the disadvantaged inhabitants, as well as physical reconstruction of the ghettos, a plan like the Marshall

Plan that the United States government financed to rebuild the European cities after World War II." Brooke and Abel also leaned toward the Lindsay-Harris camp, but they rarely attended meetings. Abel, however, made his feelings known through his representative, James Jones. "Let us challenge the federal government to launch massive radical programs to meet the crisis," Jones wrote Ginsburg in December. He did not believe that the commission should worry about whether Congress would approve their proposals. If the commissioners believed that the creation of millions of jobs was necessary, then *"it should say so."*[5]

Just as important, most staff members aligned with Lindsay and Harris, believing that the commission should be willing to propose bold solutions in addition to casting blame on white racism. In November Stephen Kurzman, the deputy director for operations, sent out a draft titled "Final Report Options." Developed by a staff task force and distributed to the commissioners for their consideration, it stated that the goal of the final report was to convince the American public that "the underlying cause of recent urban disorders is embedded in our social system (racial segregation, discrimination and poverty); that the use of force and repression alone is not a feasible solution; and that correction of the underlying cause, through basic change in the social system, is a necessary and feasible solution."[6]

The two congressional members of the commission, Corman and McCulloch, acknowledged that white racism was at the root of the disturbances. But they failed to see a direct connection between poverty and the riots. Corman, who was the only commissioner to attend the all-day session with the outside academic consultants, had listened as they presented a more nuanced view of what caused the riots and had noted their clear statement that they found no connection between poverty and the violence. As a result, Corman possessed far more modest expectations for what the commission could accomplish in a few months. If social scientists who had been studying race relations for years could not divine the full causes of the riots or speculate about possible solutions, how were he and his fellow commissioners to develop answers in six months? Corman, joined by McCulloch, wanted the report to educate the public about the role of racism in American life, but not to propose specific expensive and controversial policies. The two men argued that the commission lacked the expertise to propose solutions to complicated issues and expressed skepticism about the ability of the federal government to solve festering social problems. As members of Congress, Corman and McCulloch saw little possibility of their colleagues passing an ambitious set of new social programs in the short run. "No foreseeable action or combination of action, either public or private, can significantly alter the objective facts of life in Negro ghettos before next summer," Corman wrote Ginsburg on October 17. Corman argued that the commissioners should focus the nation on racial problems but then defer to experts, and to other White House task forces, on particular issues such as jobs, housing, and education. And if the commission was going to propose ideas to improve conditions in the ghetto, he insisted that the commissioners themselves and not the staff take the lead. Especially after the field-team presentation, Corman became critical of the staff, complaining they were too liberal, or radical, and not responsive to his concerns.[7]

As usual, Thornton sat on the right fringe of the emerging consensus around white racism. The trips to ghettos were eye-opening for Thornton because they revealed the awful conditions that existed in many cities and forced him to acknowledge the role that white racism played in creating that environment. But he was not ready to question his own basic assumptions about race or to accept that white society bore the sole responsibility for black urban poverty. He wanted to make sure that the commission did not allow its focus on white racism to justify the riots or to glorify the rioters. He continued to argue that the commission's first and only responsibility was to make suggestions for improving law enforcement as a way of preventing future riots. He insisted that the commission call for tough new sedition and obstruction-of-justice laws to be used against agitators such as H. Rap Brown and Stokely Carmichael. "We can't have these people going around preaching riot," he told his colleagues. Thornton rejected the argument that social and economic conditions were at the heart of the violence and that therefore spending money was the way to prevent future outbreaks. He erupted at a November meeting when Ginsburg read a staff paper that blamed the riots on "bitterness and despair" in urban ghettos. If the commission claimed that poverty was the cause of riots, then "30 million poor people" would have an excuse to riot, he thundered.[8]

Thornton could usually count on Peden to back him up. Although she rarely spoke at meetings and wrote few memorandums that spelled out her thinking, Peden usually explained conditions in poor urban neighborhoods as the product of pathology. She accepted that white racism existed, but she failed to see how it explained the toxic environment that existed in many urban areas. Embracing the argument that poverty was the result of a poor work ethic, she blamed the poor conditions in the slums on the people who lived there. Blacks, she said, did not take enough pride in their homes and in their communities. It was, she suggested, up to civil leaders, churches, and other local institutions to take responsibility for their communities. "People who see an accident and won't stop to help are just as guilty as people throwing gas bombs."[9]

Despite the different interpretations about the meaning of white racism, and how much it should shape later deliberations about programs the commission should recommend for preventing future riots, the commissioners' decision to make it a central theme of the report marked an important step forward. But there were many other issues that still needed to be resolved.

IN NOVEMBER THE COMMISSIONERS BEGAN meeting more often to review draft chapters that would be included as part of the December interim report. The commissioners did not cast votes but instead used the meetings to debate and discuss the proposals before sending the drafts back to the staff for rewriting. Ginsburg began meetings by reading a section of the draft word for word while the commissioners followed along with their own copies. After each section, Ginsburg would pause and invite questions and discussions. Palmieri later said that Ginsburg adopted the strategy to keep the commissioners focused on the specific language in the drafts. But, he confessed, it also served a secondary purpose of limiting debate. Reading the drafts aloud ate up a lot of time, which limited the opportunity for discussion. More important, Ginsburg defused potential conflict by "boring them to death."[10]

First up was Robert Conot, who drafted the chapter addressing LBJ's question about what happened during the riots. Conot based his draft on the detailed chronologies of the riots that the field teams had assembled. He covered the walls of his office with small cards containing nuggets of information from the reports. When it came time to write, he sat behind his typewriter and used binoculars to read the notes. His section of the report, a straightforward narrative, produced the least controversy and the fewest objections. Most commissioners liked his fast-moving narrative that stuck closely to the facts and avoided editorializing. That was exactly what Ginsburg had wanted and needed to reassure the commissioners that the staff was capable of submitting work they could approve.[11]

Roy Wilkins raised the most serious objection to Conot's draft. Wilkins was sensitive to any wording that might "exaggerate" the influence of the young Black Power advocates at the expense of middle-class African Americans and organizations like his own, the NAACP. He complained that Conot made militants "appear as saviors of [the] black race" and that he perpetuated the false narrative that middle-class blacks had abandoned the ghettos. He reminded Conot that it was middle-class blacks who had sponsored the first lawsuits to end segregation and extend voting rights. Militants, he asserted, had made no investment in the ghettos. "Negro militants won't put a dime in Negro banks . . . [or] in Negro insurance companies."

Believing that it was important to place contemporary race problems in a historical context, Ginsburg had asked John Hope Franklin to compose a chapter on the history of race relations in America. Franklin, chairman of the History Department at the University of Chicago, was one of the nation's most accomplished historians. His experience growing up as a black man in the segregated South had inspired him to study race relations and to make sure that colleges and universities incorporated African American history into the narrative of America's past. In 1947 he published *From Slavery to Freedom*, which became the standard textbook about African American history. His long chapter in the report was an abbreviated version of that popular text.

But Franklin's insights did not accord with Tex Thornton's history of the United States. In a blistering eight-page letter sent after Ginsburg circulated the draft, Thornton attacked the history chapter for lacking "moderation and judicial temper." He wanted to see the impact of slavery downplayed, white people positioned in a better light, and greater emphasis placed on the progress that had been made in race relations, especially under LBJ. Instead of blaming white European settlers for slavery, Thornton wanted the chapter to state that "slavery was a well-planted African institution before the opening of America." He thought the history section needed to be more sympathetic to slaveholders. One reason the South had defended slavery for so long, he argued, was that "in all fairness," the slaveholders "were frightened" by the "disorders and uprisings of Colored people in Santo Domingo (Haiti)" that led to the massacre of some whites. He called "highly deplorable" Franklin's statement that the Emancipation Proclamation only "freed Negroes where [the federal government] had no power" and "left them slaves where [it] had power." This observation was, he said, an "old Southern and Copperhead sneer" that was "completely inaccurate."[12]

Thornton was especially aggravated by Franklin's depiction of more recent events. He believed that the chapter's emphasis on the Ku Klux Klan in the 1920s ought to be balanced by discussions of those who fought against them. He thought that the account overemphasized that "various scattered factories had denied jobs to colored people" during World War II and de-emphasized that the president issued an executive order "forbidding improper racial discrimination" in the defense industry. (Thornton neglected to articulate what constituted "proper" discrimination.) He felt that Franklin could have described the groundbreaking *Brown v. Board of Education* decision (1954) in "more generous and appreciative terms." Instead, Franklin emphasized and described in detail the harsh response from white southerners who opposed the decision. "Grudging and hostile pages, partisan in character, are out of place in what should be a scholarly, objective and well-balanced presentation of the subject," Thornton wrote. Overall, he concluded, "the paper deals too much with negative tendencies and too little with constructive steps in race relations."[13]

Most of the commissioners dismissed Thornton's sweeping critique and rejected his effort to downplay slavery, but they did agree on some minor changes. McCulloch asked to strike a claim that Abraham Lincoln held racist beliefs. McCulloch did not assert that Franklin's criticism of Lincoln was untrue. Rather, he believed the commission should not besmirch the reputation of the Great Emancipator, who was revered by so many Americans, black and white. Wilkins resisted the move, but the commission yielded to McCulloch. For Ginsburg, the biggest problem with Franklin's report was not its content but its length. His eighty-page draft required significant editing, and Ginsburg used the paring-down process to tone down some of the language that Thornton found so objectionable while retaining many of the hard-hitting descriptions of white repression.[14]

The commission's discussion of the history of race relations led to a debate about the present conditions. For some of the commissioners, it was impossible to discuss past practices without proposing solutions to address existing injustices. If the black experience had been so terrible, they reasoned, then it was imperative to put forward solutions that matched the problem. Agreeing that now was the time to face the legacy of racism, Wilkins proposed that the commission come out in support of a federal open-housing bill in the report. Not surprisingly, Thornton and Peden took the opposite point of view. Peden repeated her prior comment that blacks, who refused to take proper care of their property, were responsible for the poor housing conditions in the ghettos. Thornton focused on the politics of passing an open-housing law. "Open-housing helps force Negroes onto whites and releases bad and hostile attitudes," he declared. Why, he asked, "butt our heads against the wall, the wall of white attitudes?" He believed that housing was not central to understanding the causes of riots. Such claims, he declared, were a repetition of "old, tired arguments."[15]

Wilkins sat ready to pounce on both Peden and Thornton. "As to Negroes wrecking property and causing slums," he said to Peden, "the fault is really caused by poor code enforcement on overcrowding tenants in housing." He also reminded his colleagues that despite Thornton's dismissive comment, "it happens that the same old tired things . . . still caused riots." He said that if African Americans, who made a middle-class income, were not allowed to move into middle-class neighborhoods, then they were being treated as "second-class" citizens. "What's the use of struggling to make $20,000 a year if you can't spend it on a decent way of life?" he asked. Wilkins felt the need to draw a line in the sand, this time threatening to resign from the commission if its report did not include a recommendation supporting a national open-housing law. Thornton backed down but reminded his colleagues of the strong opposition to such a measure. "Let's not overemphasize it in our report," he said. Wilkins agreed but warned they should also not "gloss over it."[16]

The next draft up for discussion was Arnold Sagalyn's chapter on police and community relations. Reflecting the reports coming in from the field teams, and his own deep understanding of the topic, Sagalyn claimed that police brutality was rampant, officers were poorly trained to deal with racial unrest, and their actions often made disturbances worse. He stressed that the police departments relied too heavily on firepower to control riots when the proper use of nonlethal force represented the best hope for de-escalating racial tension in the cities. Sagalyn called for the creation of community review boards to oversee police practices and investigate complaints of brutality.[17]

His draft set up a clash with some of the commissioners, who viewed it as an extended assault on the police. "Very disappointed in this section," Corman said. "It condemns all police." Thornton backed him up, pointing out that even "ghetto people want police protection, law and order." He said that the paper gave the impression that "if there'd been no police involved this past summer, there'd have been no riots." Violence was a "two-way" street, Thornton declared, and the commission should not forget that rioters "provoke and injure policemen." Surprisingly, Harris sided with Thornton on this point, saying the draft chapter failed to account for the difficult job facing most officers. "Police have human fears, too, and they got cause to be fearful in the ghetto," he declared.[18]

The two African American members of the group strongly disagreed with the criticism of the draft. Roy Wilkins made a passionate plea to highlight the role of the police in mistreating minorities, precipitating the riots, and then often overreacting once the unrest started. Wilkins reminded his colleagues that "every single riot was started with a police incident," and he went on to cite examples of African Americans being subjected to abusive treatment. Something "stinks," he declared, when an officer with numerous complaints against him for using excessive force "shoots a 15-year-old boy." He pointed out that local police had once handcuffed Martin Luther King Jr. for carrying a driver's license that had been expired for only four days. He predicted that African Americans would read this section of the report first, and the commission would lose credibility if it did not take the concerns about police brutality seriously. To underscore the depth of his feelings on the issue, Wilkins once again threatened to break with the commission, declaring that he would write a minority opinion if the commissioners tried to downplay his concerns. Brooke, who was absent at the meeting when this chapter was first discussed, supported Wilkins a few weeks later when they returned to the subject. He declared that there was "overwhelming" evidence that "most incidents [are] caused by police action." He acknowledged Thornton's observation that "ghetto people want law and order," but he pointed out that it was "a big mistake to make police sacrosanct." The report, he insisted, should not treat the police with "kid gloves."[19]

Most of the commissioners naturally deferred to Chief Jenkins on law enforcement issues, and he tried to stake out a middle ground. He disagreed with Wilkins's contention that police brutality was rampant and instead blamed the problem of police relations with black residents on "inefficiency" and "corruption." He agreed, however, that racism permeated many departments. He told the story of getting a phone call late at night from a Ku Klux Klan member after the chief had hired African Americans to serve on the Atlanta force. He asked Jenkins if he would want his wife arrested by a black officer. "No," Jenkins replied, but added he would also not want her to be arrested by a white officer.

Similar divisions emerged over Sagalyn's recommendation that the commission support the creation of civilian review boards. While Sagalyn admitted that "most police commissioners" opposed the boards, "ghetto people want a place" to take their complaints, he wrote. Corman suggested that the commission should avoid addressing the issue. "We'll never see a widespread use of civilian review boards. We can't solve it here." Lindsay, who had been absent for some of the commission's prior discussions about police brutality, spoke up, charging Corman with "copping out." Lindsay understood the political challenges of setting up a civilian review board. In 1966 he had used an executive order to establish one in New York, only to have it soundly defeated in a referendum later that year. Despite that bruising loss, Lindsay remained committed to the idea. "Where," he asked, "does [a] 19-year-old Negro go to complain that he got beat up by police?" Lindsay insisted that the commission "provide some machinery for handling complaints," pointing out that there was "widespread ghetto feeling that we get nowhere with complaints about police." At the end of the heated discussion, the commissioners sent the chapter back to the staff for rethinking and rewriting.[20]

Although the topic was not raised in the early drafts discussed that day, the commissioners also devoted some time to a spirited debate over whether the riots were the result of a conspiracy. Lindsay insisted that the commission's report make emphatically clear that there was no connection between speeches of people like H. Rap Brown and the violence that occurred afterward. Thornton refused to let the issue go. While there may not be an immediate connection between the inflammatory rhetoric and the riots, he said, "the speeches leave fuel to smolder for a later date." He found an unlikely supporter in Wilkins, who wanted to qualify Lindsay's observation: "We must say that we found some organized local and state activity, but it doesn't amount to criminal conspiracy." Thornton added that when some militants brag about being "in touch with North Vietnamese to train us. That implies a group conspiracy right there." Once again, the issue was left unresolved. At some point, the commissioners would need to stop arguing and start voting. For now, however, they chose to kick the topic down the road.[21]

Oddly enough, after their first long, contentious meeting to discuss draft chapters of the report, Kerner summed up the discussion by saying, "We all agree very much, and disagree only in minutia." In fact, there was little real consensus beyond the superficial acknowledgment that white racism lay at the root of the riots. The commissioners could not even agree on the proper tone of the report. Thornton did not want a report that would offend white Americans or prove embarrassing to the White House. Once again, Wilkins challenged him. "If we don't use some abrasive language in our report," he responded, "we won't rock the country."[22]

Despite all their differences, however, the commissioners still agreed they did not want to produce another report that would be quickly forgotten, destined to collect dust on library shelves. That meant producing a unanimous report. How could the commissioners claim any moral authority on such a hot-button topic if they did not speak with one voice? The airing of their differences as they discussed early draft chapters discouraged some of the liberal members of the commission, who realized that it was unlikely they were going to be able to produce a final report that would be both unanimous and appropriately bold. There seemed little chance that either Thornton or Peden would vote to recommend reform of police training and practices. Corman and McCulloch also appeared unwilling to support recommendations of major new federal expenditure to improve housing, education, and employment in urban areas. Lindsay, constantly pushing from the left, warned that they needed to address jobs, housing, and education, "or a final report won't even be worth doing." Wilkins told his colleagues that he was hearing rumors that the commission would not accomplish very much. "I am beginning to believe it myself," he said.[23]

No one was more skeptical than Fred Harris. Having taken the temperature of the commission over the first few months, the senator was convinced they would be unable to build consensus around the kind of hard-hitting report that he and Lindsay wanted to see. So he decided that he would write his own. He secretly contacted the New York publishing house Harper & Row and agreed to write a book about his work on the commission and his suggestions for what needed to be done to solve America's racial crisis. The book, *Alarms and Hopes*, would be published a few months after the release of the official commission report.

Chapter 7

"CAN YOU REALLY SAY THIS IN A GOVERNMENT REPORT?"

B Y EARLY NOVEMBER 1967, THE commission agreed that their report to the president would identify "white racism," and the social and economic disadvantage that it produced, as the root cause of the riots. The commission staff had met with a large group of outside social science consultants, but they had yet to hear from their small in-house team, which was now preoccupied with processing the massive amount of material that was pouring in from the field teams. But by this point, having reached their own answer to the question as to "why" the riots occurred, the senior staff needed the social scientists only to confirm their diagnosis and potentially lay the groundwork for a series of policy solutions that flowed logically from their conclusion.

On November 22, the commission's own social scientists finally weighed in, producing a hard-hitting report titled "The Harvest of American Racism." Both Victor Palmieri and David Ginsburg quickly and angrily dismissed the report as too provocative and out of sync with the commission's needs. Their rejection of the social scientists' conclusions produced a deep split that threatened the future of the commission itself. "Harvest" was supposed to answer LBJ's critical second question, about why the riots occurred, and without it there was now a gaping hole in the center of the commission's overall report. It was not clear if the commission would have the time to recover and write a new chapter in time to meet their December deadline for reporting their interim findings.

THE SOCIAL SCIENTISTS HIRED TO answer why the riots occurred worked under the direction of a young social psychologist, Robert Shellow, the commission's assistant deputy director for research. Unlike many of his professional colleagues, Shellow enjoyed working in nonacademic settings, believing it was important to apply abstract theories to real-life situations. He had spent much of his professional career doing just that. After earning his PhD at the University of Michigan in 1956, he joined the Public Health Service, where he worked with delinquents and youth offenders at the Bureau of Prisons. In 1958 he moved to the National Institute of Mental Health, where he set up a juvenile bureau. That experience exposed him to many of the people and institutions that touched the lives of troubled youths: police, judges, and social workers.

In late August 1967, Victor Palmieri invited the thirty-eight-year-old Shellow to a steak dinner at the Mayflower Hotel in Washington, DC. They were joined by many of the key players on the commission, including John Lindsay, Otto Kerner, and David Ginsburg. "It was a lovely setting with all the cigar smoke and all these big shots," Shellow recalled in a 2015 interview. At the end of the evening, Palmieri pulled Shellow aside. "We'd like you to take the job heading up the social science part of this commission," Palmieri said. "Would you be willing to do that?" Shellow pointed out that he lacked formal training in race relations and that other people were more qualified for the job. "I don't care," Palmieri responded, "as long as you got that PhD."

In retrospect, Shellow realized that comment should have been a red flag, revealing that the commission was looking for a warm body with the right degree. But caught up in the moment, he agreed.[1]

It was not surprising that Palmieri would invite a social psychologist to lead the team of social scientists. Beginning with World War II, and continuing through the 1960s, psychological experts played a key role in assisting the federal government. During World War II, the military turned to psychologists to help them train troops and maintain morale. During the Cold War, the government employed them to study the causes of communist guerrilla movements. Now in the 1960s, the Kerner Commission looked for psychological explanations for the riots. Ginsburg informed the staff that he had directed Shellow and his team to "explain the disorders in social-psychological terms."[2]

Shellow embraced the mission, but he thought the staff was naive in thinking they could reach any definitive answers in the few months that the commission would exist. The commission was formed, he realized, during a time when people were "frightened and confused," and given the time constraints, there would be "little leisure for careful systematic study." Social scientists needed time to gather reliable data, sort through it, and then identify common patterns. That was an impossible task in this case, especially given the complexity of the questions that LBJ had asked them to answer. Social science methodology, he told Ginsburg, "does not allow us to complete a credible investigation. We just don't have the tools to do what the president has asked of us." Shellow also fretted about the lack of social scientists among the senior staff, which meant no one who would be able to educate the commissioners about how such experts went about their work.[3]

Shellow was competent and thoughtful but, by his own admission, "a relatively unknown social psychologist." He learned later that the commission had first offered the position to several well-known scholars, but they declined because they either had teaching commitments or feared that the commission would be little more than a public relations stunt for the Johnson administration, whitewashing the real problems of the inner cities. Shellow nevertheless managed to attract two established scholars to join his team. David Sears, a respected social psychologist at UCLA, was not directly involved in the commission's daily activities, but he had completed extensive research on black and white attitudes following the Watts riot. Shellow borrowed extensively from his work and incorporated it into the report. Gary T. Marx, a young sociologist at Harvard, who had just published a highly regarded book, *Protest and Prejudice*, which studied black attitudes toward civil rights issues, agreed to join the commission as a consultant, even though he was skeptical of its mission. "The goals of the political animal that is the presidential commission and the goals of the scholarly and professional who serves on the commission are antithetical," he stated in 2016. "The social scientists were window dressing. There was no way you could adequately explain the riots in a few months."[4]

Two promising graduate students participated in the daily work of the commission. David Boesel, a bright and soft-spoken political science graduate student at Cornell University, was writing his dissertation on ghetto riots. "I was trying to do a comprehensive theoretical analysis of the riots as a political phenomenon," he recalled in 2016. Boesel described himself as a "polite radical." During the 1960s, he marched in antiwar demonstrations, traveled to Tennessee to register black voters, and attended a conference organized by Students for a Democratic Society. He was joined by Lou Goldberg, a mercurial graduate student in sociology at Johns Hopkins, whom many of his colleagues later described as brilliant but also "unstable." "He was an angry young man who was filled with fire," Marx maintained.[5]

Significantly, the commission had assembled an all-white team of social scientists to study the problems of largely black ghettos. The team worked quietly behind the scenes until the Detroit field team made its disastrous presentation to the commissioners in October, where they volunteered their own theory for the cause of the riots. Afterward, Palmieri rushed over to Shellow's office and asked if he could undo some of the damage. As Shellow recalls the scene, Palmieri said, "you can't believe it"—one of the city teams met with the commissioners, and they "went off." Palmieri said the presentation left the commissioners baffled. "My God, is this what they're coming up with?" they seemed to be saying. From the commissioners' point of view, the staff was identifying "with the miscreants, with the aggressors, with the criminals." He told Shellow that he feared losing their confidence. "What can we do about it?" he asked. "Can you put something together?"

Shellow's group had been circulating drafts of his team's analysis of two riots—Plainfield, New Jersey, and Cambridge, Maryland. Palmieri decided the studies were in good-enough shape to present to the commissioners. In a matter-of-fact manner, the social scientists pointed out that in addition to inequities of income, living conditions, and education, the grievances in the black community grew out of an attitude of superiority within the white community. Most of the social scientists' presentation, however, consisted of an hour-by-hour account of events leading up to the riots and a description of the riots themselves. They kept the number of "interpretive statements" to a minimum and refused, even after prodding by the commissioners, to offer conclusions that went beyond the evidence they had gathered to date.[6]

The presentation succeeded in restoring the confidence of the commissioners. Afterward, both Ginsburg and Palmieri thanked the social scientists for their effort. Shellow and his staff had put out a small fire, but they were about to ignite a far larger one that would threaten the life of the commission.

AFTER THEIR APPEARANCE BEFORE THE commission in late October, Shellow's team went back to work analyzing the reports coming in from the field. Ginsburg and Palmieri were desperate for them to produce a comprehensive report. "Have you got it ready?" Palmieri asked repeatedly. "How much is done? Is there anything we can look at?"

For weeks, they worked long days and nights, often sleeping on cots at the commission offices, to finish a draft of their report. To maximize efficiency, they each took responsibility for specific sections based on their expertise. Marx wrote most of the material that dealt with the interaction between the police and protesters and contributed to the analysis of riot events and their consequences. Boesel authored the parts that documented the growing power of black youth. David Sears does not recall participating in the writing of the draft and speculated that he was listed as an author because Shellow made extensive use of his research. Goldberg wrote the conclusion. Shellow served as the general editor. He offered some suggestions, but his main contribution was to knit the different parts together. By all accounts, he edited with a light hand and allowed each of the authors to speak in their own voice. "I was not an expert in these areas," Shellow acknowledged. He had extensive experience working with police departments and in the prison system, but he had no formal training in the issues that his team was asked to address. "My job was to watch what they were producing and stay out of the way. I don't remember ever intervening in their work."[7]

The various authors were so overwhelmed with preparing their own sections that they had little time to sit down and review each other's work. Not surprisingly, the report lacked a single voice. Instead, it was more a collage of different styles. Shellow either did not read the final report before submitting it to the senior staff or only glanced through it. But he was not worried. He understood that it still needed careful editing and could benefit from thoughtful critiques—but he had every reason to believe this would happen after he submitted it for consideration by the senior staff. On November 22, after many sleepless nights, Shellow handed Palmieri a 176-page draft titled "The Harvest of American Racism: The Political

Meaning of Violence in the Summer of 1967." Palmieri smiled and thanked him for the report. "And that's the last smile I saw on his face," Shellow remembered.[8]

In many places, the report either complicated or challenged the conventional public narrative about the riots. The report began by pointing out that the term "riots" was imprecise and failed to capture the full range of social unrest. They broke riots down into a handful of overlapping categories. First, there was general upheaval that pulled in "all segments of the ghetto population" and included "an extraordinary wide range of activities." These riots were characterized "by widespread, and aggressive action by ghetto Negros," followed by a "harsh" police response. This was the pattern that had emerged in Detroit, Newark, and Watts. Second, there was the riot "as political confrontation," where protesters used violence to "achieve political ends." Cincinnati, where the black community acted in "concert" and revealed "a high degree of coherence in the overall organization of the various protest activities," offered the best example of this type of disorder. The third category, "official anticipation as a cause of disorder," resulted when police and city officials were the aggressors, and the actions of black residents tended to be "defensive, protective, or retaliatory." The most extreme case fitting this description took place in Cambridge, Maryland, where city officials overreacted to an appearance by H. Rap Brown, turning an isolated incident into a racial crisis. The fourth and fifth categories were rare. "Expressive rampage" looked more like a group of drunk college students, what the authors called "a kind of 'Fort Lauderdale' spree" than an organized riot, and the black-against-white "race riot" was "conspicuous for its absence."

While the public, and many officials, tended to see all riots as an irrational expression of pent-up anger by a handful of discontents, "Harvest" argued that many of the riots were rational responses to genuine grievances. "Whether the riots were rational acts was a pervasive discussion while we were writing the report," Boesel said decades later. "My take on it was that at the core the riots were political and rational. It was a rebellion against the white establishment." Many young blacks, finding that traditional forms of political protest did not work, took their objections to the next level. "It was angry but it was rational. The riots were primarily and initially rational acts by oppressed people who could not get redress any other way." Shellow's team used the words "rational" and "political" interchangeably in their writing; both meant that the riots were justified given the oppressive conditions protesters faced.[9]

The report dismissed the notion that "outside agitators" had moved from city to city, spreading violence. In several cases, local black leaders had recruited H. Rap Brown and Stokely Carmichael to address residents to bring attention to issues in their communities, but there was no causal relationship between their presence and the violence that sometimes followed. "Harvest," however, came down hard on the news media, arguing that sensationalized stories of violence presented on television played a much larger role in promoting the disturbances than did black radicals.

In one of the hardest-hitting sections of the report, Marx highlighted how the police either incited violence or overreacted once it occurred. While he commended some police departments for being restrained in the use of force, he pointed out that "in many cities," they "acted in ways to encourage, rather than contain the spread of violence." The report declared that "some 75 percent of the police departments in the country" showed "evidence of strong racist attitudes." Officers' deep personal prejudice, combined with the perception that a crowd of angry blacks was "inherently irrational, anarchic and probably nihilistic," led them to exaggerate the danger they confronted and justify using excessive force. In some cities, the police engaged in daily harassment of ghetto residents with "stop-and-frisk" tactics and verbal abuse. Not surprisingly, Marx concluded that "disruptive police activities" played "a prominent role either in starting the violence or in escalating it once it started." A youth from Watts told investigators that "the police used to be a man with a badge; now he's just a thug with a gun." Once a disturbance erupted, professionalism broke down, and officers turned into "avengers of their personal and departmental pride."[10]

In his section of the report, Boesel underscored the growing power of young blacks as a political force in urban areas. Although young black men between the ages of fifteen and thirty played a significant role in the riots and now constituted "a profound social force in the ghettos," they were cut off from the older middle-class black leaders in their community. Young blacks, he argued, rejected the "compromises and subservience of their elders" and were "developing a racial pride" that was becoming "self-sustaining." Lacking access to traditional levers of political power, this group was "inclined to take matters into its own hands." Any plan to prevent future riots, he claimed, required the nation to grapple with the growing power and legitimate grievances of his group.

In examining the rioters and their motivations, "Harvest" drew heavily on surveys that David Sears had conducted—the same studies that the outside experts had summarized in their earlier meeting with the commission's senior staff. Sears's research directly challenged the most commonly accepted theories about the rioters and their motivations. He had tested various hypotheses regarding who had participated in the riots. The first was the "poverty hypothesis," which maintained that the rioters were mainly poor and uneducated people with nothing to lose. "On this point the evidence from our surveys is very strong and unequivocal in its message," he wrote. "Those who participated in the riots for which we have relevant data were just as likely to be well-educated, employed, of substantial income, of white-collar occupational status, as those who did not riot." Poor people "were no more active in the rioting than those who are better off." He pointed out that a sense of relative economic deprivation relative to whites played an important role in the riots, but poverty alone did not explain riot behavior.

He also tackled and dismissed two other popular explanations. Some observers had claimed that those who rioted were disproportionately recent migrants from the South, but Sears and others studying the background of the rioters discovered that the most active participants in both the Watts and the Detroit uprisings were native born. He also challenged the theory that the riots resulted from the breakup of the traditional family. In 1965 Daniel Patrick Moynihan, who was at the time assistant secretary of labor, wrote a controversial essay, "The Negro Family: The Case for National Action." The report claimed that many of the pathologies found in poor urban areas resulted from the breakup of the nuclear family and the rise in the number of black single-mother families. Sears acknowledged that the breakup of the family might be responsible for many urban problems, but rioting was not one of them. He found that "people raised in mother only households were no more active in the rioting than those raised in father-mother, or father-only households."

There were a few common denominators in explaining who participated in the disturbances. In Detroit, for instance, the "typical rioter" was "a young, northern born male, who is extremely dissatisfied with his current economic situation, particularly when he compares it to that of whites." He possessed a strong sense of "black consciousness" and "thoroughly rejected the old stereotypes of Negro inferiority." He was dissatisfied with the "existing political structure and with the nation as a whole" and claimed that he would refuse to defend it against foreign enemies. The typical participant in the disturbances believed the riots were the result of the "depressed economic conditions of the Negro" and the "failure of the political system to do anything about it."

Sears could discern no clear pattern in how local authorities responded to the violence or regarding whether the riots ultimately produced constructive change or simply added to racial tensions. "The short run consequences of violence for the cities analyzed have been highly varied," he wrote. "Some cities experience a dramatically heightened polarization, some did not; some experienced improved communications and instituted massive remedial programs, some did not." For most cities, however, "it still seems to be business as usual, perhaps with an increase in expenditures for riot control equipment, perhaps with additional programs to create jobs but by and large no major changes in either of the predicted directions." Sears observed that "the view that disturbances led to polarization and a hardening of racial attitudes" was "an oversimplification that does not square with the facts."[11]

Goldberg's conclusion to the social scientists' report, "America on the Brink: White Racism and Black Rebellion," presented a passionate, well-written, and tightly organized summation of the arguments that Black Power advocates had been making for the previous few years. The city teams had captured much of the anger that was boiling over in poor black communities. Now Goldberg distilled that discontent into his concluding chapter. But his section's supercharged rhetoric distorted the tempered and nuanced findings his colleagues had presented in the previous pages, infusing them with his own passionately held radical views. "The extreme radical to revolutionary rhetoric is Lou Goldberg's alone and a reflection of his temperament and his political outlook and motivation," recalled Boesel. Goldberg transformed Boesel's description of the growing power of black youth into a portrait of America on the cusp of a racial war. "Negro youth are in the forefront of a massive urban black movement which will settle for nothing less than complete equality," he wrote. "It would be a grave error to assume that the riots are just a temporary aberration, the product of an anachronistic class of Negro militants which will soon be assimilated to urban life." The evidence "indicates that the impulse to violence is likely to become more common, rather than less, as [blacks'] transition to urban industrial life from rural, agricultural backgrounds is completed."[12]

Goldberg stated that the United States faced three alternatives for dealing with the racial crisis in America. The first would be to continue the current liberal approach of gradualism and moderation, the pursuit of slow, incremental change. In his mind, this was not a viable option. Goldberg dismissed LBJ's Great Society as "tokenism," representing little more than an effort to "get the Negroes out of our hair and no more." Young black men, he wrote, "are just not interested in being moderately discriminated against, moderately free from arbitrary police practice, moderately skilled, moderately unemployed, and moderately unsure of what their future holds in store." With little supporting evidence, he declared that "the moderate, or liberal approach to the race issue, in many areas, has become an intolerable threat to personal freedom and security." At least repressive societies allowed people to know they were being repressed, he observed. "White moderation," he concluded, "is the stuff out of which black rebellion is made."

If the nation continued down the pathway of moderation, the result would be guerrilla warfare on the streets of many American cities, Goldberg declared. He predicted a day in the not too distant future when "20 men, dedicated, committed, willing to risk death, and with intelligence and imagination could paralyze an entire city the size of New York or Chicago." He painted a truly frightening portrait of the future where urban warfare would continue to grow exponentially. "The beginnings of guerrilla warfare of black youth against white power in the major cities of the United States: that is the direction that the present path is taking this country," he wrote. "The history of Algeria or Cyprus could be the future history of America."

Goldberg then described a second possible path forward: "harsh and ruthless repression of the Negro movement." This approach would require the arrest of "major radical leaders," killing "great numbers of people," and military occupation of major American cities. Many blacks would refuse to accept such measures and decide to wage war against white society. "Preferring to die on their feet, then living on their knees they will, ala guerrilla movements in other developing areas, go underground, surfacing periodically to engage in terrorist activities." He pointed out that other repressive states had suppressed "movements by subordinate groups who have revolted against their masters," using the Soviet Union's brutal suppression of the Hungarian Revolution of 1956 as an example. "The choice for white America," he concluded, "thus boils down to a choice as to whether they are willing to act like the Russians did in Hungary."

The final option, and the one Goldberg favored, called for "highly accelerated social change." He described this alternative as "a way to save America." What did "accelerated social change" entail? It meant transferring "power on real decisions about program policies to the young militants in ghetto areas." He acknowledged that this approach would be unacceptable to many "local white politicians" and moderate civil rights leaders, but it was "consistent with the concept of government which places the well-being of the whole community over the best interest of entrenched local power groups." He recommended that the federal government "seriously consider" funding massive social programs and doing so on a level far exceeding anything the Johnson administration had proposed as part of its "War on Poverty." He insisted that the federal government distribute the money directly to militant groups. "All of this," he wrote, "will require an opening of the white power structure." One way of opening that power structure was "to refrain from the temptation to allow white elected officials to exercise veto power over federal government programs." Doing so also required changing the role of the police, so they serviced "the concerns of the poor as well as that of the middle class and the rich."

Despite his ominous warnings, Goldberg claimed there was still time to act. "There is still time for our nation to make a concerted attack on the racism that persists in its midst. If not, the Negro youth will continue to attack white racism on their own. The harvest of racism will be the end of the American dream."

Goldberg was freelancing in his conclusion, hijacking his colleagues' findings and using them to promote his personal political agenda. For example, although he drew on Boesel's analysis of the growing power of young blacks in warning that a racial war was imminent if America did not accept his calls for accelerated change, he went far beyond what Boesel himself had found. Nearly fifty years later, Boesel said that he believed a race war could have happened in 1968, but it was a "remote possibility" and certainly not one that he would have embraced. Goldberg seemed to relish the prospect. In his strident condemnation of LBJ and liberalism, Goldberg failed to mention the strides that had been made the previous decade or to reference survey data elsewhere in the report revealing that most of the rioters had positive feelings toward the federal government and believed most of the obstacles they confronted were local.[13]

Goldberg's proposed solutions represented an assault not only on mainstream liberalism but also on the basic structures of American representative democracy. He recommended that the federal government funnel resources to local militant organizations by bypassing elected white politicians. It was unclear how that could be done. The White House was already dealing with the blowback from its modest community-action programs. Democratic mayors were in open revolt, claiming that the administration was supporting groups that were protesting city hall and undermining their power. Based on that experience alone, it was naive to believe a larger and more ambitious effort that turned key decisions over to young militants had any chance of being enacted.

David Boesel recalled reading the last chapter before it was handed to Shellow. The language shocked him. "I was wide-eyed about [it]," he said. "Can you really say this in a government report?" Although he considered himself a radical, he felt Goldberg's "summary" was "out-of-bounds." He believed that it placed "too much emphasis on one outcome that was only among several possibilities." Marx did not see the section before it was submitted but said in a recent interview that had he read it, he would have suggested toning down the language. Shellow did not read it carefully. When asked in 2015 if he had any regrets about the report, Shellow laughed, admitting that he should have "given a much closer look at the last chapter." He acknowledged that it was "a departure from the rest of the document because it had too much advocacy in it."[14]

"HARVEST" RECEIVED A COLD, ANGRY response from the senior staff. David Chambers, Ginsburg's assistant, recalled that his boss "thought it was a hack job." Ginsburg told Stephen Kurzman, the deputy director for operations, the same thing, dismissing "Harvest" as "unusable." Kurzman agreed. It was, he stated in 2016, "an ultra-left-wing diatribe against the whole country." Nobody, he admitted, "wanted this to be Chapter 2 of the report."[15]

Nearly fifty years later, Palmieri claimed that the social scientists "went rogue." Palmieri quickly rejected the report, refused to circulate it beyond the senior staff, and ordered copies destroyed. He believed that the role of the commission's social scientists was to help analyze the wealth of information collected by the field teams and to work with the staff to develop responsible and politically viable solutions. The final section of "Harvest," with it strident condemnation of LBJ and liberalism, was a nonstarter, and he was angry that the social scientists would be so blind to the complicated politics of the commission. He and Ginsburg were doing their best to write an overall report that was "objective," he maintained in 2016. Some of the conservative commissioners already criticized the staff for being too liberal, and now the social scientists seemed to be suggesting that they were not radical enough.[16]

Not everyone interpreted the report as a "hack job," however. Those staff members who were closest to the field teams—who had read their reports and met with them when they returned to Washington for debriefings—approved of "Harvest." Charles Nelson, who oversaw the field teams, summarized their views in a memorandum. "We wish to emphasize that we view the paper as a whole an excellent piece of work," he wrote. "Both the point of view and most of the content express to a large extent what team members have been thinking for the past several months." Indeed, one of their chief complaints was that the report was not critical enough of the police. "If we sugar-coat these complaints, we have failed in our task of alerting the country to the true state of facts," he told the commission staff.[17]

Shellow was surprised by the senior staff's harsh reaction. He had submitted the report as a draft and had expected that it would produce comments and criticism and that his team would have time to revise it. That opportunity would never come. Not long after he submitted the report, Shellow found himself ostracized. He was no longer invited to attend staff meetings, and while he kept his office, it was made clear that his services were no longer needed.

Why the harsh response? Partly, it was a matter of style. Ginsburg and Palmieri had repeatedly told their staff to avoid provocative statements and keep their reports grounded in facts. They often reminded the academics on the staff that they would be writing for a nonacademic audience and should avoid jargon. They viewed the commission's overall report as a legal brief designed to educate both the White House and the public about the profound problems facing America's urban centers and to persuade them to adopt their recommendations for change. A week before Shellow submitted "Harvest," Palmieri had "requested everyone to avoid unsupported generalities and loose and discursive writing." On the same day that Shellow submitted "Harvest," Ginsburg stressed at another meeting that "the style of the sections being written is as important as the substantive material." He went on to encourage everyone to avoid long sentences and to use short paragraphs. In a 1994 interview, Ginsburg said that he had told the staff that "anyone who had an eight[h] grade education should be able to read and understand" the final report. "There should be no fancy words," he instructed his team.[18]

Clearly, a lack of communication also played a role. It was just weeks before the interim report was due in December, and Palmieri was expecting the social scientists to turn in what could be presented to the commissioners as Chapter 2 of that report. He needed them to submit a document that was comparable to Robert Conot's well-received and polished draft of Chapter 1. It's unclear whether Palmieri failed to communicate his expectations clearly or the social scientists ignored his instructions. Either way, Shellow planned to turn in a rough draft that would be analyzed by the staff and then returned to his team for revision. "If [Palmieri] entertained the belief that we would produce a completely finished product within two weeks under the pressures we were experiencing," Shellow wrote the author in 2017, "he was out of touch with what was likely much less possible."

Shellow had a point. Palmieri's expectation that the social scientists turn in a polished report was unreasonable. Unlike Conot, the social scientists had to analyze the city team reports in light of a large, and sometimes contradictory, body of existing sociological literature on riots. Conot could read and start writing the individual city narratives as soon as the teams filed their reports. The social scientists had to wait for all the reports to be submitted before they could begin identifying patterns. And as Shellow feared all along, Palmieri and Ginsburg did not understand that social scientists could not produce high-quality research under the time constraints imposed by the commission.[19]

But the conflict was not just a matter of tone and timing. There was also a real and substantial philosophical and political gap between what the senior staff expected from the report and what "Harvest" delivered. The commission staff sought to identify a cause of the riots that could be addressed within the context of American liberalism. Even Lindsay, while insisting that the report not shy away from the harsh reality of urban life, argued that those urban problems could be solved by spending more money. The Great Society was not flawed, he reasoned; it just did not go far enough to have an impact. "Harvest" suggested a far more complicated set of problems that likely could not be solved with more resources alone. It found no direct link between poverty, unemployment, welfare, family structure, or educational attainment in the motivations of those who rioted. And Goldberg's summary suggested that future riots could be prevented only by a massive transfer of both wealth and power to young militants, acknowledging them as legitimate political actors.

There were other aspects of the report as well that went far beyond what the commission could possibly accept. It was impossible for Ginsburg to show the commissioners a report that described the riots as justified. There was no way he could build consensus around the need for the federal government to recognize and support the growing militancy of young urban blacks. In addition, the commissioners would never accept a report that was so critical of the police. The criticisms in "Harvest" were based on solid data and supported by other White House task forces, but the report would be a nonstarter for the more conservative commissioners, especially Tex Thornton.

On a most superficial level, "Harvest" confirmed the commission's view that racism lay at the heart of the riots. It was, after all, titled, "The Harvest of American Racism." But in the end, it also highlighted the limited analytical value of the using "white racism" as the organizing theme of the report. Ginsburg had built a fragile consensus around the underlying role that racism played in defining many of the problems plaguing poor urban neighborhoods. But then what? The challenge was to agree on a series of steps to end racism and compensate for the economic disadvantage that it caused. Here there was little agreement, even among the commissioners, about possible next steps. "Harvest" added another powerful voice to the debate, one that went far beyond what even the most liberal members of the commission could accept. Certainly, Lindsay, Harris, and Wilkins, even perhaps Jenkins, might agree to the type of social spending that Goldberg's accelerated change recommendation would require, but no one would support his contention that Washington needed to bypass white officials and funnel resources directly to militant groups.

In the end, the social scientists should have presented a cleaner draft to Palmieri, and Shellow, as the team leader, should have reviewed

Goldberg's contribution and forced him to bring it in line with the rest of the report. Yet had Ginsburg and Palmieri looked beyond Goldberg's incendiary summation, they would have found a report grounded in empirical data, one that made for painful but necessary reading. Bringing the commissioners around to it would still have been a challenge, but it would have been one well worth undertaking.[20]

THE SENIOR STAFF'S REJECTION OF "Harvest" left a gaping hole in the middle of the report. The commission was supposed to produce an interim report in December, and now, with just weeks to go before that self-imposed deadline, it had failed to produce even a tentative answer to one of the three broad questions that LBJ had asked. Ginsburg determined that the staff needed to start from scratch.

Ginsburg assigned operations deputy Stephen Kurzman to take over responsibility for writing the chapter. Kurzman, with field-team chief Charles Nelson assisting, went back to the original field notes. "We discarded 'Harvest,'" Kurzman said. "We never looked at it again." That was unfortunate. By discarding "Harvest" altogether, and relying solely on the field reports, the commission cut itself off from a broader body of social science literature that could have informed its conclusions. They lost Sears's detailed surveys of the Detroit rioters and the extensive scholarship produced in the two years since Watts. By ignoring "Harvest," the commission failed to consider the political nature of the disorders in places like Plainfield and New Brunswick, where the riots led to direct negotiations between city officials and black youths. It failed to grapple with Boesel's discussion of the growing political force of young black youths in the ghettos or with Marx's analysis of how police, by anticipating disorder and massing troops in ghetto areas, helped incite disorder in the first place. "Harvest" may have been overheated, but it also included valuable insight and analysis that deserved to be included in the final report.

After reviewing the original field reports, Kurzman decided that the social scientists had distorted the facts and "imposed theories" that did not match the evidence. He claimed they had oversimplified the riot process and drew too many conclusions that were not supported by the data. He was struck by the many variations and differences among the many riots—differences that the social scientists either glossed over or discarded "if they did not fit some preconceived theory." He was determined to write the chapter so that it did justice to the complexity and uniqueness of the different riots.[21]

Kurzman approached the material in strikingly different ways from the social scientists. As a social psychologist, Shellow believed it was his responsibility to discern the motives behind actions, while also placing the data into some larger theoretical framework. Kurzman, a Harvard-trained lawyer, was just as skilled at discerning patterns, but instead of speculating about motives, he offered careful statistics that underscored the economic disadvantage between blacks and whites while cataloging the grievances of black residents. Following Ginsburg's advice to "stick with the facts," he avoided broad generalizations that were not supported by specific data or sworn testimony. Kurzman was also sensitive to the politics of the commission. At this stage of the game, the commission staff needed evidence to support its conclusion that the economic disadvantage caused by "white racism" produced the riots. "The dominant lawyer methodology values an approach which simply brushed aside that of the social scientist," Shellow wrote in his private journal at the time. "That is: get conclusions first, then build back up for the analysis, interpretations, and implications for action." Shellow's criticism, however, is not entirely fair. Although the commission staff did not rely on the analysis that Shellow's team produced, it did spend a considerable amount of time talking with outside social science consultants and other experts before arriving at his conclusion that "white racism" was at the heart of the riots.[22]

Not surprisingly, Kurzman delivered a draft that toned down the objectionable conclusions in "Harvest." It pointed out that residents listed police practices as one of their grievances in nineteen of twenty cities and "one of the foremost serious complaints" in fourteen of those cities. But he made no judgment about whether those grievances were justified, and he refused to criticize police practices. He claimed that the riots were the result of an "accumulating reservoir of grievances" that were ignited by a "precipitating" event. He provided statistics to show that young men were the driving force in many of the riots, but stopped short of recognizing youth as a new power base in the cities, much less calling for political empowerment. There was no judgment that the riots could be a rational and justified response to the refusal of local white officials to address legitimate grievances.[23]

Kurzman replaced interpretation and generalizations with facts—a lot of them. The chapter noted there were eighty-four deaths and 1,950 injuries in the seventy-six disturbances in sixty-six cities studied. Only 17 percent of the disturbances led to fatalities. Nearly all the deaths, 81 percent, occurred in just two of the cities—Detroit and Newark. In all but twenty-four of the disturbances, officials used force or the threat of force in response to the violence. During the first four hours of a disorder, 98 percent of the rioters were men, 82 percent were under twenty-five years old, and 95 percent were black. During the remaining forty-eight hours, the proportion of blacks declined to 66 percent, as other urban residents joined in the disorders. During the first four hours, 68 percent of the arrestees were charged with disorderly conduct and disturbing the peace. Other charges included arson, malicious destruction, profanity, and resisting arrest. In contrast, 58.6 percent of the arrests made during the final forty-eight hours consisted of curfew violations.

In each disorder, the report pointed out, it was impossible to generalize or to find a single discernible pattern. "A single, clearly defined pattern of violence has not emerged from what we have seen in 24 disturbances," he wrote. There was also no "single, clearly defined pattern of official response" to the riots. The pattern had been "as varied as the disorders themselves." In one of the few definitive statements in his draft, Kurzman dismissed the conspiracy theories, writing, "We have found no evidence of organized direction or control in the 24 cities [surveyed]."

The new draft fell in line with the "white racism" consensus, pointing out that "there was a clear pattern of severe disadvantage experienced by Negroes as compared with whites, whether the Negroes live in the disturbance area or outside." Kurzman highlighted many of the facts that the field teams had unearthed, showing that African American areas of cities had witnessed a dramatic increase in population and that people in these areas were younger than the white population, earned less income, and experienced high unemployment, with those who were employed having lower-paying and lower-status jobs than whites. While focusing on tangible evidence of discrimination that coincided with the commission's focus on housing, employment, and education, the draft offered hope that conditions could be changed, although Kurzman did not make concrete recommendations. The data revealed, he concluded, that "Negroes, like other Americans, respond to opportunity to break out of the pattern of disadvantage."

In many ways, Kurzman's report fell victim to the opposite problem that plagued "Harvest." The commission's research department, which reviewed and analyzed all of the drafts, objected to the chapter, claiming that it was "not an analysis and was not intended to be. It is rather a compilation of facts which might be useful in an analysis." It went on to charge that the "undiscriminating use of gross statistics often obscures more than it reveals." Shellow also had the opportunity to critique the new draft. He agreed that it used statistics to cover up rather than reveal important aspects of the riots and that it downplayed one of the central points in "Harvest": that the police often overreacted and made riots worse. He argued that the best approach was not simply to catalog the riots that took place, but instead to see them as the product of an interaction between rioters and public authorities. Shellow complained that the Kurzman draft simply labeled the rioters as irrational and the police as rational actors. In private notes taken at the time, Shellow observed that "Ginsburg and Palmieri have not been able to produce the scholarly yet readable 'analysis' to support their brief, namely the need for massive infusion of aid to the ghettos."[24]

Stuck between a draft that generalized too much and one that avoided reaching any conclusions, Palmieri asked for an independent opinion. In mid-January, he hired Hans Mattick, the associate director of the Center for Studies in Criminal Justice at the University of Chicago Law School, to "try to make sense of the riot process" and to do so in a way that people could understand. After reviewing the field reports, written summaries, "The Harvest of American Racism," and Kurzman's draft, he largely endorsed Shellow's conclusions. He disagreed with the polemical style in "Harvest" but agreed that the evidence supported two of its central points: that the police contributed to the riot process and that the disorders were often a rational and justified response to legitimate grievances. Unfortunately, these were the two conclusions that the staff could not include in the report that would be presented to the commissioners. Mattick was told the commissioners "wouldn't like" his description of the riots as rational acts. "You can't tell the public that a riot is rational," a senior staff member said. In the end, the commission rejected Mattick's analysis and decided to retain and fine-tune the Kurzman draft.[25]

EVEN AS KURZMAN WORKED ON his draft, the senior staff's angry dismissal of "Harvest" sent shock waves through the field teams. Tensions between the field teams and the senior staff had been building for months, but now the harsh response to "Harvest" seemed to confirm the investigators' nagging fears that the commission was acting under orders from the White House and incapable of producing an independent report.

In late November, Palmieri drew together all the commission staff, including the field teams, to discuss the commission's direction. Team leader Bruce Thomas remembered the meeting as "very tense," with a lot of "tough questions" for Palmieri. Around the same time, Isaac Hunt recalled team members assembling for another contentious meeting with Kurzman. He could not cite the specifics of the meeting, but looking back nearly fifty years later, he remembered Kurzman lecturing them about "their responsibility to the commission." Hunt interpreted that comment as a vague threat and an effort to intimidate them into toning down their reports. "We are not going to do what you want us to do," he told Kurzman. "We're going to do what we think is right, and we will have to fight it out."[26]

For many team members, the senior staff's rejection of "Harvest" was the last straw. They were now convinced that the commission's final report would be a White House whitewash. Beginning in late November, they started coming into the office in the evening when the senior staff was absent, to make copies of the reports they had submitted from the cities they visited. "We felt we might have to write our own report," Thomas stated. "There was already suspicion among certain members of the staff, including me, that it was going to get watered down," he said in 2016.

Some team members shared their concerns with the media and with members of Congress. "We knew some of them were on Capitol Hill looking for sympathetic ears," admitted Palmieri. The result was a flurry of negative stories about the commission. By November rumors were circulating that the commission would put most of the blame on unresponsive city governments for the riots. These rumors, along the modest proposals the commission had already made for reform of the National Guard, led people to suspect that the commission would be a cover-up. Elizabeth Drew, writing in the *Atlantic*, sharply criticized the commission, claiming that its middle-class members had lost credibility with black militants, who dismissed it as "a fink operation." She had little hope that the commission would be willing to challenge LBJ and offer bold proposals for change. "No one here is betting, therefore, that the commission's product will differ radically from one that the president wants."[27]

By the end of November, the commission was in crisis. Ginsburg and Palmieri found themselves in the unenviable position of being distrusted by both the field teams and some of the commissioners. In either case, the complaint was the same. Some of the commissioners and most of the social scientists and field teams worried that the senior staff would write the report to please LBJ. Both, however, misinterpreted miscommunication as conspiracy. Although everyone on the commission knew that LBJ wanted a report that would validate his Great Society programs, Ginsburg's experiences touring riot areas and listening to witnesses made him increasingly skeptical of the status quo. In most cases, the problems resulted from a senior staff that was both overwhelmed and overworked in a chaotic setting with baked-in problems that ensured conflict.

No one anticipated what came next: LBJ was about to register his dissatisfaction with the direction of his blue-ribbon panel by attempting to force it to shut down operations.

Chapter 8

"THAT'S GOOD
AND TELL HIM I
APPRECIATE THAT"

L BJ HAD LAUNCHED THE COMMISSION with great fanfare
in July, but despite promising commissioners that money would
not be an issue, neither he nor any of his top aides had initially given
much thought to how the enterprise would be funded. There was
simply not much time to figure out the finances. After all, only twelve
hours separated the time the president informed his aides of his decision to create the commission and his nationally televised announcement. LBJ may have assumed that, given the commission's short life
span, it would not need much money. He probably never anticipated
that its members and staff would take his charge to heart and attempt
to reach an independent assessment of the state of race relations in
America. Doing so required money—a lot of it—to hire consultants
and support field-team investigations.

Once it became clear that the commission required greater resources, LBJ balked. His top aides urged him to seek a supplemental appropriation from Congress to allow the commission to keep

functioning. LBJ, however, was consumed with anger over the direction of his runaway commission and deeply resentful of the dominant role that John Lindsay played in steering its deliberations. In early December, he rejected the advice of his two top advisers and pulled the financial plug on the commission, forcing it to cut staff and scramble to issue its report.

ALTHOUGH JOHNSON INITIALLY ALLOCATED ONLY $100,000 from the president's emergency fund to get the commission off the ground in July, he made clear that money would not be an issue. Kerner said that Johnson told him when the commission's work began that he would have the full resources of the government at his disposal. When asked at a White House news conference on August 1 about the budget, Ginsburg told reporters, "No limits have been imposed on the commission."[1]

Actually getting money from the White House, however, proved more difficult than had been anticipated. On August 17, Charles Schultze, the budget director, estimated that the commission would require about $1.5 million, which exceeded the $1 million in the president's emergency fund. He suggested that the president release $800,000 immediately, restore the fund with a supplemental appropriation, and then make a second allocation in 1968. If necessary, Schultze wrote, LBJ could make a third allocation from the 1969 emergency fund.[2]

Meanwhile, with the commission staff setting up field teams and hiring scores of consultants to aid in their effort, Ginsburg realized that Schultze's $1.5 million figure would not nearly meet their ambitious agenda. In September he asked John Koskinen to produce a working budget for the commission. Koskinen came up with an initial list of expenses and presented it to his boss. Ginsburg pulled out a pencil and started crossing out figures, switching expense items at random from $40,000 to $40,553 or from $100,000 to $99,421, so that it appeared that careful estimates lay behind the final figures. "The first lesson of budgets in the government is always remember to lie in odd numbers," he said.[3]

The original budget that Ginsburg submitted amounted to $5.7 million, far more than White House expectations. Schultze trimmed Ginsburg's estimate to $4 million, but even that figure did not satisfy the president. As of October, the president had not even allocated the $800,000 that the budget director had previously requested. The commission was living off the fumes of the original $100,000. Since the commission had already spent $275,000, Schultze pointed out that LBJ's high-profile initiative was "in serious financial trouble" and "for all practical purposes" broke.[4]

Realizing that the president was reluctant to provide the needed money, Schultze proposed an alternative. He suggested that the president instruct "the various Departments and agencies whose interests [were] germane to the Commission's assignments" to provide manpower and resources to keep the commission afloat. While departments could not shift money directly from their budgets to the commission, the president could create an "interagency effort" to examine civil disorders. The Departments of Defense and of Health and Human Services, the Office of Economic Opportunity, and others would then contribute money and personnel to that effort, which, in turn, would funnel those resources to the commission. Schultze recommended that the new interagency effort "assume financial responsibilities totaling about $4 million." He pointed out that "agency heads will strongly resist making any substantial contributions unless you direct that they do so." This approach was, the budget director concluded, the "only feasible solution" to the commission's financial woes.[5]

On October 11, Joseph Califano weighed in on the commission's behalf and in support of Schultze's recommendations. Although Califano had recommended against creating the commission in the first place, once it was established he fought hard within the administration to make sure that LBJ at least appeared to be supporting its mission, largely because he feared the political blowback from liberals if the president abandoned it. "We postured it," he noted in a 2017 interview, "so that if there was a fall guy, it would be Congress and not the president." Finally, after weeks of lobbying, LBJ agreed to the proposal to create the interagency effort.[6]

The plan ran into obstacles almost immediately. Congressman George Mahon, chairman of the Appropriations Committee, balked at the plan to have the Defense Department allocate $1 million for commission projects. He insisted that the Department of Defense had to get congressional permission to reallocate funds. Since the administration used this method to fund "countless task forces," Schultze concluded that persisting in this case represented *"too big a risk,"* potentially creating a precedent for congressional intervention every time the executive branch sought to move funds around this way.[7]

The budget director thus switched his recommendation and called for the White House to send a supplemental appropriations request for the commission to Congress, while tapping the agencies "for relatively insignificant amounts sufficient to get the commission through December 1." The supplemental appropriations process provided the administration with the ability to ask Congress for additional funding during the fiscal year. Such requests had become common in the modern presidency, employed to provide added resources to existing agencies or, in the case of the commission, to obtain funding for new administration priorities. The only other alternative, Schultze warned, was "to dismantle the Commission," which the budget director viewed as politically untenable. If, however, Congress rejected Johnson's funding request, they would have to shoulder the blame for the commission's demise.

LBJ approved the proposal. He instructed the other executive departments to keep the commission running until December, when the White House would ask Congress for a $3 million supplemental appropriation thereafter. The White House told Ginsburg that it would send him, along with John Lindsay and Otto Kerner, to

Capitol Hill to ask Congress for the money. The White House made a similar promise to Senator Fred Harris. Ginsburg was confident enough that the money would be forthcoming that in an application for a grant from the Ford Foundation, he wrote that "the president has decided to ask for an appropriation from the Congress covering a substantial portion of the budget of the commission." Members of the press were told the same thing. On November 15, Philip Meyer, a reporter for Knight newspapers, wrote that Budget Bureau spokesman Joseph Laitin acknowledged that the administration planned an appropriation of $2–$3 million.[8]

By the first week in December, the commission had run out of money. But Ginsburg had been picking up signals that approval for the supplemental appropriation was in trouble. On November 27, a Budget Bureau spokesman told him "in passing" that "consideration was being given to excluding" the commission's "appropriation from the final supplemental." Ginsburg fired off a letter to the budget director, asking for clarification. "Before this we had been told that it was highly desirable to wait for the final supplemental," he noted. "Why the change?"[9]

A flurry of decisions during the first week of December decided the commission's financial fate. On Saturday night, December 2, LBJ discussed the supplemental with Schultze and Califano. The president told them that he wanted to send only those items that were "absolutely essential" for immediate congressional approval and could not wait until January. The two aides suggested that Johnson send to Congress a request for $5.7 million to fund necessary government functions, along with the $29.9 million for various programs such as unemployment compensation for former servicemen and federal employees. They also requested money for the administration's top priorities.[10]

One of those priorities was the riot commission. On December 4, Schultze and Califano suggested that LBJ include a trimmed-down

$2.8 million for the commission in the supplemental. Without additional money, they wrote, the commission would have barely enough money to make it through the month. Probably realizing that the president wouldn't mind the commission's fading away, they focused their arguments on something he cared deeply about: politics and the potential blowback if the administration refused to fund the commission. The "political flak would be substantial," they warned. Schultze and Califano fretted the public would perceive it "as a further abandonment of domestic problems because of the Vietnam war." There would be other consequences, too. Both men feared the dislocation, and the stories it would produce, if the commission's staff were suddenly cut loose. They saw little harm in putting the proposal before Congress. If members balked, the administration could blame Congress for refusing to fund the commission. And time was of the essence: LBJ needed to decide by the end of the day.[11]

A few hours later, LBJ met with Schultze and then, briefly, with Califano. There is no record of what was discussed, but most likely it was in these conversations that LBJ revealed that he was not going to include the Kerner Commission in the supplemental. Without the additional money, LBJ had every reason to believe that the commission would be forced to phase out its work before the new year.[12]

LBJ's refusal to request the funding deepened Califano's worries that the president was sacrificing important domestic priorities to appease fiscal conservatives in Congress. Califano thought it was important to spell out his own vision for the administration, its priorities, and the direction he hoped that it would move in the future. Later that evening, he sent the president a three-page memo suggesting that "we should reexamine our over-all strategy." He was convinced that the American economy possessed the productive capability to fight the war in Vietnam while "also meeting the challenge of American life." The task was to "summon the will and determination" of both the people and the Congress. The president needed to call on the American people to make sacrifices to provide the funds needed to fight the war at home and the one in Vietnam. This approach, he argued, would "appeal to the traditional sources of Democratic strength—the cities, the liberals, and the low-income individuals, white and Negro alike." The president should stop trying to pacify powerful House Ways and Means chairman Wilbur Mills, who seemed determined "to force the President to bow down to him in a way that will permit him to indicate he brought you to your knees." Califano feared that both in Vietnam and domestically, LBJ was doing enough to prevent defeat but not enough to declare victory. "I think that in January," he concluded, "the people will be looking for you to show them that you intend to attack these problems and—while recognizing their difficulty—you can give them a sense of hope that they are not impossible of solution. Perhaps most important, that we do not have to wait until the war in Vietnam is over to get at the domestic problems."[13]

The memo failed to change LBJ's mind. He assigned Charles Schultze the unenviable task of informing the commission's senior staff that they would not be receiving the promised appropriation. The budget chief called Ginsburg, Palmieri, and Koskinen to the White House for a meeting. The commission staff assumed that the conversation would involve the budget, most likely a briefing on the strategy for selling the supplemental to Congress. Instead, Schultze explained that "there is not going to be a supplemental so there will be no more money." And there was more bad news. Schultze told them that the president's emergency fund was dry, and while they could continue to draw on the federal agencies for support, he could not promise those agencies' cooperation. Koskinen understood immediately what that meant. "Now all of a sudden we have to shrink the staff and get out a final report as quickly as possible."[14]

Why did LBJ cut the commission's financial lifeline? There was no doubt that by the end of 1967, LBJ was under intense pressure from fiscal conservatives in Congress, especially Wilbur Mills, to make sharp cuts in federal spending. Many of his economic advisers, especially Treasury Secretary Henry Fowler, who fretted about the prospect of a fiscal 1969 deficit of $28 billion, echoed Mills's calls for cuts in domestic spending. But the real reason Johnson refused to ask for money was because he had soured on his commission. Although LBJ told the commission on its first day to follow the truth wherever it led, what he really wanted was an endorsement of his Great Society programs. From the earliest days, the commission made clear that it planned to assert its independence from the White House. By December it was evident that the commission would likely endorse an ambitious set of new social programs. From LBJ's perspective, the commission had become just what Califano had feared from the beginning—a Frankenstein monster. Over the first few months, LBJ did what was necessary financially to prevent the commission from collapsing, likely fearing the public relations maelstrom that would result if he moved against his high-profile commission. But when faced with a choice between letting it go out of business or asking Congress for supplemental funding, he chose the former.

The truth was not lost on members of the commission. Palmieri recalled that LBJ "felt he'd been betrayed by David [Ginsburg] and by the rest of us" and used the cuts as retribution. Fred Harris, who knew Johnson well, never had any doubt about his motives. "On several occasions," he noted in 2015, LBJ "went out of his way to express to me his displeasure with what the commission was doing." Harris was certain that LBJ "personally and purposely" cut the budget as an act of revenge against what he saw as a runaway commission. "Johnson was a micromanager," he continued. "He knew the tiniest detail about what the federal government was doing, and I'm sure he was aware of the minutest item in the federal budget. Nothing under his watch happened by accident. And he could be quite vindictive when anything was being done that was not to his liking."[15]

The same week that LBJ refused to ask for a supplemental, members of Califano's staff began strategizing the best way to justify that decision to the commission and the public. In a two-page memorandum, they suggested that the White House justify severing the commission's financial lifeline by flattering its members, claiming that their work was too important to wait until the spring. The memo proposed that the best argument was to claim there was an "urgent need for basic recommendations," and the commission should produce a single report "to ensure maximum impact." Although the memorandum projected "80 percent" of the commission's work would be phased out by January 1, it also suggested that the administration "avoid the appearance of undue haste" by allowing a skeleton staff to continue working until March 1. As a loyal soldier, Califano protected the president and spouted this new White House rationale. He never told Ginsburg that he and Schultze had indeed fought hard over two months to secure funding for the commission or that he opposed the president's decision not to ask for more funds from Congress.[16]

Now it was up to Ginsburg to decide how to handle the news. He might have threatened to resign in an effort to force the White House into fulfilling its promises to him, or he could have leaked the information to the press to shame the president into asking for funds. But Ginsburg rejected both strategies and, like Califano, chose to regurgitate the White House's disingenuous justification. "David was still protecting the president," remembered David Chambers. "If he had told the commission and certainly Lindsay about the budget cuts, I think Lindsay would have gone public, or at least there was that risk. David considered Lindsay untrustworthy." Ginsburg knew that it would be impossible to complete the investigations and write a report in a few weeks. Many chapters were still in early drafts, and there were whole sections of the report that had not been written at all. At the end of the day, however, Ginsburg was the loyal soldier.[17]

When the commission gathered later that week in Washington, Ginsburg claimed that he now believed that the threat of future unrest was so great, and their recommendations so urgent, they no longer had the luxury of waiting until the next summer to release the final report. He suggested they scrap the interim report planned for

December and issue a final report as quickly as possible in the early months of the new year. He suggested the commissioners explain the decision to the public by claiming they had decided to "expand" the interim report, and therefore there would be some delay, although he was vague on when the final report would be released. "We can't give [a] specific date," he said.[18]

Most of the senior staff, and all the commissioners, accepted this explanation. Ginsburg made no mention of the White House role in cutting the budget. Even the number-three man on the commission staff, Stephen Kurzman, was unaware of the White House intrigue. "It was devastating when we were told that we had to complete the report so quickly," he maintained. "The staff was not told anything about the budget cuts. We were told that the report was urgently needed so they moved up the time frame."[19]

Lindsay, who had pushed for moving up the interim report to December, changed his mind when he realized that the staff only planned to use it to identify short-term solutions. He now complained that these measures would not be equal to the problems they were trying to address. He dismissed these short-term approaches as "Band-Aids." He worried that coming out with an interim report that suggested only minor reforms would reinforce the view that the commission was not taking the problem of racism in America seriously. A commissioner was quoted anonymously as saying that the investigation had brought to light a "situation so critical we cannot afford to waste time writing an interim report." Thus, although for very different reasons than those motivating Ginsburg, he embraced the idea of a single comprehensive report.[20]

In the wake of the White House budget cuts, Ginsburg needed to wrap up the commission's work as quickly as possible. Although he had been vague with the commissioners about possible dates for finishing their work, Ginsburg was more precise with the White House. After the December 9 meeting, he called Califano to inform him that "the riot commission voted unanimously today to consolidate their work into a report that would be submitted either in late December or early January." Califano passed the message on to LBJ, saying that the commissioners "felt the urgency of the situation require that they report to you as promptly as possible." Johnson responded, "That's good and tell him I appreciate that."[21]

But Lindsay—unaware of the budgetary shortfall that was the actual reason for accelerating the final report—continued to press the commission to intensify its work. Two weeks after the commission decided to cancel the interim report, Lindsay wrote Kerner, pleading with him to "multiply significantly our resources in the program area." He insisted that the commission enlarge the research staff and borrow more experts from elsewhere in the government. He hoped the commission would set aside funds in its budget to use mass media to promote the report and its findings. He even suggested they create a documentary based on the report: "It should be ready for distribution by the fall of 1968 with special emphasis on school audiences." Lindsay's insistence that the commission expand its resources apparently rattled Ginsburg, who forwarded a copy of the letter to Califano with a note saying, "I'd appreciate a telephone call as soon as you have read it."[22]

Although Lindsay and the other commissioners went along with issuing a consolidated report earlier than expected, they "agreed that the Commission would continue working" and be "available to the President until July 28." Ginsburg supported the idea and lobbied Schultze, reminding him that the executive order that LBJ signed provided for a one-year life span for the commission. If the White House terminated the commission's life before July 1968, he warned, "some Commissioners are likely to be openly critical and the press would probably regard the decision as confirming reports that the Administration has decided to abort the Commission's effort." He predicted that if the money was not forthcoming, "serious trouble, within and outside the Commission, is almost a certainty." Apparently, the threat of bad publicity managed to pry some money from the White House. After highlighting the need to continue cutting costs, Schultze promised a onetime allotment of $555,000 for "essential" activities. "I see no possibility of any further financial assistance over and above these amounts," he warned.[23]

On December 11, three days after it decided to cancel the interim report, the commission issued a press release saying that the final report would be issued "within the near future" and "not later" than March 1, 1968. The release included a joint statement from Lindsay and Kerner, saying the commission was convinced, based on the evidence already gathered, that "we cannot delay until next summer" their recommendations. "The Commission has found that there is urgent need for public awareness, and widespread action, much sooner than" next summer.

It is unclear where the March 1 date originated. Just two days earlier, Ginsburg told the White House the report would be finished by early January at the latest. Most likely, the reference to March 1 was Ginsburg's effort to square Lindsay's demands for a strong report with the White House's insistence that the commission close shop as soon as possible.[24]

THE COMMISSION HAD NINETY-EIGHT PROFESSIONALS and seventy-one clerical workers at the time the White House decided to defund it. Over the next few weeks, the staff would shed forty-eight professionals and forty clerical staff. Among those let go were all the field-team members. Ginsburg assured the commissioners that the staff dismissals would not impact the commission's ability to produce a final report. Most of those released, he explained, had completed their work and were no longer necessary. He maintained the same position when addressing the press, telling them that the dismissals were "a normal phaseout" and that the field teams had "largely completed" their studies in twenty-three "target cities." This was patently false. The commission had not completed their studies, and they had made plans to send teams back to cities for a second round of research. "We had plans to run more investigations" before the budget cuts, Koskinen recalled.[25]

It was left to Palmieri to announce the firings to the commission's workforce. For the second time in less than three weeks, he pulled the junior staff together and repeated the White House justification for the change of plans. The report, he said, was too important to wait until the next summer, so the commission needed to end its investigation of the riots and begin writing the report. As a result, they would no longer need the junior staff's services. Only senior staff would remain. "It was not a pleasant task to explain to the staff," Koskinen admitted. "Here were a lot of people who had signed up to work for this cause, had made career choices, and had the expectation of being there for a year." It was, he said, "unpleasant" for those who were staying, but especially for those cut loose. Kurzman agreed: "It was devastating."[26]

The announcement, and the matter-of-fact way Palmieri delivered it, infuriated the nearly one hundred people in the room. People leveled angry, pointed questions at him. Most were skeptical of the assertion that the commission had undergone a revelation in the previous days, suddenly becoming convinced that their final report was so urgent that it needed to be published without a moment to spare. The commissioners may have accepted Ginsburg's rationale for canceling the interim account and moving up the final report, but many of the understandably angry young staffers who were about to lose their jobs did not. They correctly guessed that the White House was behind the move, but they misinterpreted the reasons for the staff reductions. Many of the young staffers assumed they were dismissed because of the staff's angry rejection of "The Harvest of American Racism" report. The terminations reinforced a sense that LBJ was a puppet master pulling all the strings and that the commission lacked the will and the White House support to truly tackle the underlying causes of the riots. "I believed that the dismissals were a direct response to the report," said David Boesel, one of the social scientists

who wrote "Harvest." "I assumed we were fired" because of it. Boesel's colleague Gary Marx reviewed the thinking among the social
scientists: "At that point, the conspiratorial story was that we wrote
this report and spilled the beans. It was powerful stuff, and Johnson
was afraid of it politically. He feared he had created a runaway commission, and he moved to end it."[27]

While the fired staff's suspicion that the White House was behind
the cuts was well founded, there is no evidence that "Harvest" inspired the decision. Ginsburg and Palmieri had ordered copies of that
report destroyed and had never circulated it to the commissioners.
Fred Harris learned about "Harvest" only after the Kerner Commission's official report was published. When asked in 2016, Califano
said that he never saw the report. There are no copies in White House
files and no mention of it in any memos. Shellow, who supervised the
writing of the report, was correct when he later claimed there was no
connection between the report and the cuts, but he was alone among
the social scientists and the field-team representatives in believing it
at the time.

Nevertheless, the disgruntled former staffers aired their concerns
in the media. On Tuesday night, December 12, an anonymous caller
contacted the *Washington Star* and the *Washington Daily News*. He
read a statement accusing the White House of cutting off funding
to the commission, leading to the firing of 120 employees. "This action was taken without knowledge of the commission," he said. The
caller speculated that LBJ made the move after reading the "Harvest"
report and its criticism of his administration. Without an independent staff to complete the final report, the informant speculated, the
document "will now be completed much along the lines the White
House wishes it to take."[28]

The phone call produced several stories critical of the commission. On December 14, the *Washington Star* published a lengthy article describing the deep divisions on the commission between young,
more ideological staffers and the older, more practical liberals who

dominated its leadership. According to the *Star*, young staffers be-lieved that the guidelines under which the commission operated were themselves proof of White House meddling. They complained that the commission had been instructed to find solutions that built on existing programs and to avoid spending large sums of money. "If they end up with the same routine time-worn proposals," one of the dismissed staff members told the *Star*, "we will be vindicated next summer" when even more violent riots occurred. The cuts also pro-duced a rebuke by Congressman William Ryan, a liberal Democrat from New York, who charged that the commission was being "cut off in midair."[29]

The commission developed a two-pronged approach to the crit-icism, denying the charges that LBJ was behind the move, while reassuring critics they would produce a bold report. Press secretary Al Spivak told reporters that the commission's decision to change its timetable was not based "on *any* staff or consultant documents." An anonymous source from the commission criticized the dismissed staffers, "who think they're being paid with government funds and working in a government office building in order to plan a revolution against that government." Fred Harris was blunter, calling the allega-tions by former staffers "rash, irresponsible and totally inaccurate."[30]

At the same time, the commission's more liberal members reas-sured the public that the report would tackle difficult questions. A week after the purge, they announced that the commission would make bold recommendations without regard to the political and eco-nomic costs. "We ought to say what it takes to do the job and let the country make a conscious choice," Harris told reporters. "It is the unanimous decision of the commission to say what is needed." Sena-tor Brooks agreed, declaring that if their report was "to be meaning-ful," it will "take a total commitment by the American people, not only by the federal government, but by state and local governments and the private sector. Nothing short of this sort of commitment is going to be successful as a preventative."[31]

In January Kerner held a press conference to respond to the ongoing rumors about White House interference in the writing of the report. A reporter mentioned a former staff member who had described the commission's forthcoming report as a big "sanitary job." Kerner snapped at the comment, saying there was "absolutely not an iota of truth" to the charge. Kerner denied that the White House had read any portion of the commission drafts. "I don't know how the White House could ask us to tone it down or up," he declared, clearly frustrated by the line of questioning. "They have not seen it yet, nor has it been discussed with them." He insisted that the commission report would be "uncomfortable to the people of the United States."[32]

The liberals' public pronouncements regarding the report's boldness surprised some of the more conservative members. The commission had, in fact, not even begun to discuss the recommendations they would make for addressing the urban unrest; furthermore, there was no consensus on endorsing the types of expensive social programs that Harris and Kerner seemed to be suggesting. Meanwhile, the public controversy over whether and why LBJ had refused to continue funding the commission missed a larger point. As a *Newsweek* article commented at the end of 1967, "If the United States cannot afford the millions to pay for the panel survey, how can it afford the billions it will take to remake the cities?"[33]

President Johnson and his advisers tracking developments in Detroit and debating whether to send troops to the area to quell the violence on July 24, 1967. *Left to right*: Ramsey Clark, LBJ, Cyrus Vance, and Robert McNamara.

Credit: White House Photo. LBJ Presidential Library. (A4475-18)

After sending Cyrus Vance to Detroit, LBJ reluctantly decided to order federal troops to Detroit. Here members of either the 82nd or the 101st Airborne Division patrol Detroit's East Side in a tank.

Credit: Tony Spina. Walter Reuther Library. (35779)

The official photograph of the National Advisory Commission on Civil Disorders, taken at its first meeting in the White House Cabinet Room on July 29, 1967. *Standing (left to right)*: Tex Thornton, James Corman, William McCulloch, Fred Harris, Hubert Humphrey, Katherine Peden, Chief Herbert Jenkins, Edward Brooke, Cyrus Vance, and Ramsey Clark. *Seated (left to right)*: Roy Wilkins, Otto Kerner, President Johnson, John Lindsay, and I. W. Abel.

Credit: White House Photo. LBJ Presidential Library. (523-18a)

With President Johnson and Roy Wilkins looking on, chairman Otto Kerner addresses the commission at its first meeting.

Vice chairman John Lindsay speaks to the commission on its first day.

Otto Kerner talks to the media following the August 2, 1967, commission meeting. As the many news cameras suggest, there was enormous public interest in the commission and its deliberations.

Credit: AP Photo/Joe Rosenthal. (670802046)

The commission's field teams fanned out to dozens of riot-torn cities, sending back detailed reports of the horrible conditions in many poor black neighborhoods. Their vivid reports, including photos such as these, helped convince many of the commissioners that they needed to make bold recommendations in order to improve conditions in the nation's cities and prevent future disturbances.

On October 6, 1967, Otto Kerner and John Lindsay inform reporters that the commission is moving up the
deadline for the interim report from March 1968 to December 1967.

Credit: AP Photo/Bob Daughtery. (6710060119)

Beginning in January, the commission held meetings in a basement room at the Statler Hotel in Washington. It was in these meetings that the commission started reviewing drafts of the final report. Executive chairman David Ginsburg is seated next to Kerner at the far end of the table.

Commission members gather for the formal signing ceremony for the report on February 28, 1968. Just a few minutes before this photo was taken, Tex Thornton threatened to issue a minority report and sabotage the carefully choreographed image of consensus.

Credit: Bettmann/Getty Images.

Richard Nixon understood the value of using the report to appeal to white voters and tap into the backlash against urban unrest. On March 6, at a five-hundred-dollar-a-plate GOP congressional dinner, Nixon charged that the report placed too much emphasis on white racism and failed to indict the "perpetrators" of the riots.

Credit: Bettmann/Getty Images.

Chapter 9

"LINDSAY HAS TAKEN EFFECTIVE CONTROL OF THE COMMISSION"

WITH THE COMMISSION'S MONEY RUNNING out, a small team of staff members struggled over the course of January and February to turn out a final report. Although the staff had produced drafts of most of the report's chapters, they had yet to tackle what promised to be the most controversial section of the report—the recommendations for future action. Given the obvious differences in outlook between John Lindsay and Tex Thornton, the senior staff knew it was going to be difficult, if not impossible, to come up with a draft of this section of the report that every member of the commission could accept. For many of the policy recommendations, David Ginsburg turned to an outside economist, Anthony Downs, who emerged as one of the unheralded leaders of the commission. He proposed an outline, which the staff edited and revised through a series of drafts in January and early February. Downs's ideas provided the general framework for the recommendations offered in the final report. As usual, John Lindsay dominated the debates over Downs's proposals, pushing his fellow commissioners to support measures for even greater federal spending to aid American cities. But not everyone embraced Lindsay's suggestions. One commissioner, Congressman James Corman, backed by two staff members, eventually argued that the commission should refrain from making any controversial policy recommendations. Corman and his allies feared the proposals would distract from the heart of the report: the detailed, factual evidence that white racism was at the root of the disorder plaguing many of America's cities. With only weeks before the March 1 deadline for a final report, consensus remained elusive.

WHITE HOUSE AIDES BELIEVED THAT without a supplemental appropriation, the commission would be forced to shut its doors by the end of December 1967 and before it could consider possible program recommendations for preventing future riots. The best the aides expected the commission could do would be to release the more descriptive chapters of the report that had already been drafted. David Ginsburg and Victor Palmieri, however, refused to give up. They were determined to keep working and to complete a final report before the March 1 deadline that they had publicly announced.

To do so, the two men had to revise the draft chapters on which they had already secured feedback from the commissioners and staff, draft additional sections that had not yet been written, and then secure final approval of the document. The first section, describing what happened, was in good shape and needed only minor editing. Most of the response to the second question, why the riots happened, was still in rougher form. The commissioners had provided reactions, but the significantly smaller staff still needed to rework parts of this section in response, especially those that dealt with the role the police played in the disorders. Ginsburg knew that answering the third question Johnson had originally posed to the commission, what could be done to prevent future riots, would be the most challenging task they faced in completing the report. They now had at most about six weeks to spell out all their recommendations and secure approval. And it was obvious from the discussion over the previous weeks that the commissioners were still far apart in their thinking. How could they propose solutions that would satisfy John Lindsay and his demands for more aggressive government intervention, as well as Tex Thornton's insistence that the commission emphasize law and order?

But Ginsburg and Palmieri accepted the challenge. "After the White House cut off the funding, I got five or six staff members, and we locked ourselves in the office to get the report out," Palmieri noted in 2015. In addition to the handful of staffers remaining after December's dismissals, Ginsburg created a "kitchen cabinet" of outside advisers to provide guidance regarding the section of the report that would describe the problems facing cities and the programs that the commission could recommend to address them. Among the members of this ad hoc group were Kermit Gordon, the president of the Brookings Institution; Yale University economist James Tobin; Louis Winnich of the Ford Foundation; and Mitchell Svirdoff, who had previously held a senior position in Lindsay's administration. The group met three times with the staff and commissioners in the final weeks of 1967.[1]

Anthony Downs, an economic analyst of urban affairs, would prove the most influential of the new consultants. Ginsburg observed that it was Downs who "carried the laboring oar" in the final months of the commission. Jack Rosenthal, a former Justice Department official hired to edit the final report, likewise called Downs "one of the seminal figures at the commission." It was Downs who produced the blueprint for the vital final sections of the report. His solutions, rooted in the assumptions and strategies of mainstream liberalism, provided Ginsburg with an approach around which he hoped he could build much-needed consensus among the commissioners without alienating his client in the White House.[2]

After earning his PhD in economics from Stanford University, Downs had served as a consultant to the government, the RAND

Corporation, and the City of Chicago. In the spring of 1967, he spelled out his thinking about the future of American cities in testimony before the Senate Subcommittee on Executive Reorganization. As the commission was getting down to work late that summer, Palmieri had sent Ginsburg a copy of Downs's testimony with a note: "This is a good exposition of Tony Downs thinking—(and mine!) about urban-ghetto problems in terms of national policy." The trends in urban life, Downs pointed out, were all moving in the wrong direction. As many whites fled to the suburbs, cities were becoming poorer and more segregated from the mainstream of American life. He pointed out that in 1950, there were 6.3 million nonwhites in central cities. By 1960 that figure had grown to 10.3 million, with nearly all of this growth occurring in poor, segregated neighborhoods. At the same time, the white population of the largest cities had declined. Although ghettos were growing, white suburbs were growing even faster. He estimated that between 1960 and 1980, America's suburban population would grow twice as fast as the ghetto population. Jobs and power would follow the white population to the suburbs, and over time the suburban population would be less willing to pay taxes to support social programs that disproportionately aided the central cities.[3]

Downs disagreed with critics who claimed that current policy toward the "ghetto" had failed and that a new, more radical approach was necessary. The problem with many Great Society programs, he declared, was not that they were ill-conceived, but that they had not yet been tried on a large-enough scale. Federal programs often foundered because they "suffered from the desire to find a cheap solution to what is an extremely expensive problem." Although he admitted that any effort to eliminate the ghetto would require enormous resources, he rejected claims that the cities were in a state of "crisis." Most urban residents had over the previous few decades "experienced rapidly improving conditions in almost every respect." The problem, he argued, was that aspirations had risen even faster than living standards. "So," he contended, "if there is a crisis in our cities, it should be viewed as resulting from a disparity between aspirations and performance, rather than a complete failure of performance." This was the message that Ginsburg wanted to hear—a mainstream liberal approach that fitted with the general philosophy of the Great Society.[4]

In his congressional testimony, Downs had suggested three possible "antighetto" strategies. The "status quo approach" involved maintaining current policies and the thinking that undergirded them. While he acknowledged that the administration's antipoverty effort had significantly improved conditions in the ghetto, it would not alter the growing trend toward greater inequality and segregation. An alternative line of attack, the "ghetto-improvement strategy," called for increased federal funding of existing programs to improve conditions in the ghetto. Finally, there was the "dispersal strategy," which placed strong emphasis on integration. It recommended implementing policies that would persuade or require whites to interact with blacks. In housing it meant enacting and enforcing a national fair housing law and providing incentives for white residents and businesses to move back to the cities while making sure that blacks could move to the suburbs. Downs considered this approach the most radical and the least feasible.[5]

There was an underlying modesty to the way Downs approached these issues. He recognized the political problems associated with any effort to improve conditions in the ghettos. As an economist, he believed it was his job to spell out the options, without advocating for any specific alternative. He deferred to the politicians, who had to face the potential wrath of white voters, to make the hard choices. Downs saw no easy solutions for the cities, and, in his speeches and testimony before Congress, he was careful to spell out the benefits and risks of each of the strategies he outlined while confessing that he "did not know what the consequences of the various strategies" would be in the "real world." He cautioned against launching large and unproven social programs on a national scale and suggested that the government proceed on an "experimental basis" with new ideas for improving conditions in the cities, testing ideas the same way that companies used market-testing techniques before bringing a new product to market.[6]

Downs cautioned policy makers to be cognizant of the "law of dominance" when it came to implementing new policies to improve conditions for poor urban residents. Except for the status quo strategy, which would simply continue current policies, the most difficult challenge would be gaining the support of a dominant and "relatively well-off white majority." He argued that the government needed to provide this group with good reasons to spend money on urban problems, articulating "arguments and incentives" that would appeal to specific segments of the white community—business, labor, suburbanites, senior citizens, and farmers. Downs believed that a solid majority of whites would be willing to send their kids to integrated schools or to live in integrated neighborhoods, if they were certain those schools and neighborhoods would remain majority white. Whites, he contended, wanted to maintain a degree of "cultural dominance," and public policy, he argued, "cannot ignore this desire if it hopes to be effective." The challenge, then, was to develop programs that meaningfully helped urban minority residents while also reassuring whites that they would remain the dominant group in racially integrated areas.[7]

Downs answered another question that had vexed the commission: Should it propose policies that would benefit all poor people or only those policies that specifically focused on African Americans? Downs argued that policies designed to help both poor blacks and poor whites would disproportionately aid whites. "The critical issue is essentially this: although the social and economic conditions of Negroes have improved in *absolute* terms since 1960, relative to the progress made by whites in this same period of affluence, Negroes have had to run fast just to stay in place." Their relative disadvantage, he contended, would likely increase racial tension and produce more unrest. For that reason, he supported policies directed at improving the lives of African Americans.[8]

Ginsburg welcomed Downs's approach and invited him to meet informally with a few commissioners to test their reactions. On December 20, Downs met with John Lindsay, Katherine Peden, James Corman, and Fred Harris to discuss an outline of his proposals. They were impressed and invited him to make a formal presentation to the entire commission in January.[9]

In preparation for the January presentation, the staff took many of the program recommendations that were part of Downs's "antighetto" strategies and packaged them into a single seventy-page document. As Downs sent material to the commission, John Koskinen and David Chambers, both former law-review editors, discarded what they could not use and edited what they could. As the two men finished the edits, they passed their revised versions on to Ginsburg and Palmieri, who gave final approval of what was sent to the commissioners. The scaled-down staff worked long hours to finish the final report. Koskinen remembered his wife complaining that he was coming home at eleven every night. "Then one night I did not come home at all," he recalled with a chuckle. He worked over the Christmas holidays, even though he had the flu. He took only Christmas Day off.[10]

The document they produced would be tweaked, rewritten, and revised, but its basic thrust would shape the final report when it was issued several months later. While acknowledging there were no programs that could prevent disorder, the staff's summary of Downs's strategies argued that "major social and economic programs were essential to eliminate racial segregation, discrimination, and deprivation which create riot prone citizens in neighborhoods."[11]

Three key elements of Downs's thinking were not included in the document the staff drafted, however. The first was any suggestion that new programs should be launched on an experimental basis or any hint of modesty regarding whether the recommendations would work. The senior staff likely assumed that a high-profile presidential commission could not build enthusiasm around mere pilot projects. Second, the draft made no mention of incentivizing white Americans to accept the need for ambitious programs to promote integration and to spend large amounts of money on poor urban areas. Finally, whereas Downs had previously highlighted the important differences between his three possible strategies for aiding urban areas, and acknowledged that there existed limited political capital to address every urban problem at the same time, the staff's version instead packaged all of Downs's various program suggestions together without any attempt to prioritize them. Downs had aimed to offer politicians a menu of options from which to choose; the staff's draft suggested they ordered every item listed.

The outline the staff prepared for the commissioners adopted the argument favored by Lindsay and his allies that there existed a direct connection between poverty and civil disorder. The recommendations were designed both to expand opportunities for "city-bound blacks" to work and live in the more affluent suburbs and to dramatically increase funding to improve the quality of life for those who remained in poor urban neighborhoods. But the outline suggested that the violence was also rooted in a "feeling of powerlessness and lack of control over one's own destiny." But except for a few ideas for breaking up large bureaucratic public school systems in the urban areas, the document was generally silent on specific initiatives designed to empower poor blacks.

Most of the recommendations prescribed the expansion of existing Great Society programs or promoted ideas that were already popular among liberals. Drawing heavily on the recommendations of the 1966 White House Task Force on Urban Employment Opportunities in its discussion of the job market, the commission's draft emphasized how the federal government could stimulate job growth and increase opportunities for blacks by reducing discrimination in employment and offering wage subsidies to employers to hire minorities. Most of the proposals were conventional: expanding the Neighborhood Youth Corps, which provided programs for school-age children; increasing the minimum wage; launching a large-scale public service program; and passing a federally enforced fair employment–practices bill. The draft advocated for two new initiatives: a program modeled after the GI Bill that would provide disadvantaged individuals with training and job benefits and the creation of a Metropolitan Service Organization comprising government, business, labor, and civic leaders who would oversee all programs related to equal employment in poor urban areas.

When it came to welfare, the draft gestured in several different directions simultaneously. It called for expanding or liberalizing existing federal welfare programs, including by establishing a federally mandated minimum standard of living and abolishing the "absent-father" and the "man-in-the-house" rules, which prohibited welfare payments to mothers and their children when a man was living in the house with the mother. While these reforms were designed to attack the structural roots of poverty, many of the other suggestions focused on changing the habits of poor black women. Perhaps to appease some of the more conservative members of the commission, the draft proposed requiring single mothers to live in YWCA-style dormitories with other women who were not pregnant and to participate in special programs to help them prepare for the workforce. While the mothers were learning new skills and better habits, their babies "would be placed in special institutions (similar to orphanages) or put into the normal adoption and foster-care channels." The stated "purpose of this program" was "to remove these young mothers from the environment which fostered illegitimacy and give them a chance to follow a better life, and to remove their children from the same environment." Other recommendations included converting some public housing projects into "intensive service centers," where families would be "saturated" with counseling and other support services, and others into "maximum stability developments," which would offer a lower level of support to those deemed less in need. In addition, the draft called for the creation of special neighborhood welfare and diagnostic centers that would provide a host of services for people living in poverty.

The housing recommendations, which filled twenty-one pages, called for providing subsidies to allow blacks to move to the suburbs while also improving conditions for those who remained in the city. Most built upon existing programs or were proposals already supported by the Johnson administration: a federal open-housing law, money to expand public housing and provide incentives to builders to construct more units, and federal subsidies to help poor households afford decent housing. This section of the draft also called "grossly unfair" the existing practice of compensating families displaced by urban renewal projects using a fair market value for their current properties. "Compensation should be based upon the cost of adequate substitute housing actually available in the area concerned," it concluded.

The draft's approach to education deviated the most from liberal orthodoxy. Here, in addition to familiar calls to increase spending for schools attended by disadvantaged children and to expand the Head Start program, it recommended that schools develop special programs in the fine arts, including theater, writing, sculpture, music, and painting. The draft called on the federal government to provide funds to restructure teacher education and training to focus on providing instruction to disadvantaged children. To promote integration, it supported magnet schools that would attract students from different parts of the city and approved busing students to "equalize the racial balance" in schools. But—unlike most liberals at the time—the draft acknowledged that notwithstanding integration efforts, there would always be black schools in poor urban areas. Thus, it was necessary make sure urban schools were properly funded and to allow parents of black children more control over those schools. The draft's boldest recommendation was to decentralize large urban school systems, giving local schools greater control of their budgets and educational standards. It also advocated for providing federal grants to private schools that would be "deliberately outside existing school boards," including religious institutions.

Although he had little invested in the specific proposals for preventing future riots, Ginsburg embraced Downs's conventional liberal approach. At this point, his only concern regarding program proposals was to get ideas on the table that could secure the signatures of all eleven commissioners. Downs appeared to offer a road map toward achieving that consensus. "For David, by far the most important message was white racism," according to David Chambers. "Ginsburg certainly had no stake in particular federal programs."[12]

But it would not be easy. Ginsburg knew that even these suggestions would anger conservative members and require significant revision. His small full-time staff, including Chambers, John Koskinen, Stephen Kurzman, and two young attorneys in the general counsel's office, David Birenbaum and Roger Waldman, would need to perform the herculean task of editing and constantly revising the document to incorporate feedback from the commissioners.

Not everyone on the staff agreed that the commission ought to be echoing Downs's recommendation of major new programs designed and run by the federal government. Ever since the earliest days of the commission, the research staff, while agreeing that Washington needed to fund new programs in the cities, had been divided over the types of programs they should endorse and the role the federal government should play in managing them. More radical staff members were convinced that Washington should limits its involvement to providing a basic minimum income, offering training, and rigorously enforcing antidiscrimination laws to create an environment where blacks could create their own organizations to improve their lives. Shorn of its hyperbole, "The Harvest of American Racism" reflected this thinking, although its contention that the federal government should fund militant groups took the argument further than most would accept. But Downs and the more traditionally liberal members of the commission staff argued that the government needed to play a more direct role in creating and managing compensatory programs to improve education, housing, and employment.

Both groups claimed that the riots were the result of "powerlessness." But they proposed different solutions. Radicals wanted to give blacks the resources to make their own decisions, realizing that, initially, there might be considerable waste as the previously powerless tried to set up their own infrastructure. Integration would follow once blacks had established their own institutions and had won the leverage necessary to compete with whites. Liberals found this approach unworkable. They believed that poor blacks needed resources but that they also required expert technical and political advice to rebuild their communities from the ground up. Taxpayers would balk at any hint of waste and fraud, so the rebuilding needed careful supervision. Also, they knew that black grievances revolved around housing, education, and jobs. Once these conditions improved, blacks could get on equal footing with whites and begin to exercise social, economic, and political power.

Back in October, when the staff first started discussing possible long-term solutions that the commission might propose, many of the radicals had opposed the idea of presenting a laundry list of new Washington-based social programs. "Programs should be designed not to do things for people but to organize the system so that things get done by people," they wrote. The federal government should limit its role to "general planning and administration with the detailed decisions being made at the local level." They recommended that programs offer the poor the "tools necessary for some minimum involvement in our society." In addition, the government should provide them with some "minimum say in the institutions relevant to their day-to-day life," including "neighborhood control over education, health and welfare policies," along with mechanisms for addressing their grievances."[13]

The draft produced in December, based on Downs's ideas, seemed to fall into the trap of giving rhetorical support to empowering poor urban residents while offering only a grab bag of federally run programs rather than local control. A few senior staff members pounced on that contradiction. Director of research services Mel Bergheim argued, "One distressing theme that seems to run through the recommendations under study is the tendency [toward] too much bureaucratic management of the lives of the poor." He quoted from both Bayard Rustin, who complained about the "bedlam of community action programs" in the War of Poverty, and Daniel Patrick Moynihan, who observed the irony that blacks were coming to power in cities only to "find direction of city affairs has been transferred to Washington." Bergheim argued that Washington should limit itself to raising incomes of the poor so they could make decisions for themselves. For that reason, he believed the commission should stress income maintenance for the employed poor, family allowances for welfare recipients and those below the poverty line, and providing housing subsidies for poor families.[14]

Roye Lowry, an adviser on loan from the Bureau of the Budget, raised similar concerns, pointing out that the draft could not make up its mind about the best way to help poor blacks. Did the commission "aim to have Negroes become fully free, active participants in an integrated democratic society or do they feel that this goal is so hopeless that many Negroes must be kept more or less wards of the federal government," with only the trappings of freedom? Like Bergheim, Lowry believed that the report should focus on ending discrimination, providing income, and offering training. He objected to the "kind of enlightened paternalism that starts with the notion that the beneficiaries are incompetent or next to it." The document, he charged, assumed "that too many Negroes can't earn their way in this world, that we have to create, in essence, a second world for them to live in—subsidized employment in private enterprise, subsidized employment in public service." He was particularly critical of the Metropolitan Service Organization, claiming that it represented the worst features of paternalistic liberalism: a federally run program over which residents had no say and no influence. He argued that "for developing a sense of powerlessness, this organization has no peer." He concluded by saying that it would "simply ruin the commission if this paper became [part of] the commission's report."[15]

Kyran McGrath, Governor Kerner's special assistant, raised another concern. He worried that the draft was so conventional in its thinking that people might suspect the commission was aiming to appease LBJ with its recommendations. He feared that if the commission accepted the draft without significant changes, it would turn the report "into a vehicle for selling the Great Society programs to Congress." Without major revisions, the report "will become a Christmas tree for Washington bureaucracy," and the public "will discard the report as another sales pitch from the White House."[16]

Ginsburg and Palmieri ignored those concerns, just as they had earlier rejected the social scientists' analysis of the cause of the riots. Their priority was creating a final document that both liberal and conservative commissioners could support unanimously and that the president would embrace. It was going to be difficult enough to get the more fiscally conservative members of the commission to support expanding existing programs; convincing them to spend money with little federal oversight was politically untenable. Just as Ginsburg had rejected the social scientists' recommendations of direct funding to militant groups, so did he disregard some staff members' call for direct income supplements and greater empowerment of local residents.

IN JANUARY 1968, THE COMMISSIONERS began to meet two days a week in a basement conference room at Washington's Statler Hotel to review drafts of the final report. Over the next six weeks, their debates would only heighten the deep differences among the commissioners. But the stakes were higher. Since their first meeting, the commissioners had been discussing recommendations they would make to the president about preventing future riots. Now, for the first time, they had in front of them a catalog of specific suggestions to focus their attention. Time for debate was running out, and they would have to start voting on each of the proposals. Initially, instead of pulling the commissioners closer toward consensus, the document pushed them further apart, making Ginsburg's hopes for a unanimous report appear unattainable.

The more conservative commissioners were shocked when they read the thick document containing the recommendations. "They had been working on the report chapter by chapter, page by page," a staff member told the *New York Times*. "There had been no votes at first, only discussion. But when they began to read the full text, and see the breadth and scope of what they were saying, they began to worry whether they could sign the report." As usual, Thornton took the lead, challenging the underlying premise that poverty and powerlessness caused the riots. Clearly agitated by the tone and substance of the draft recommendations, Thornton insisted that the government should not be in the business of creating jobs. The problem, he said, was "not lack of jobs, but lack of jobs that Negroes will accept." Thornton was convinced that young African American did not have jobs because they "make more hustling off streets than they could at say two dollars per hour." He argued that "more effective law enforcement" would shut down the illegal drug trade and force young people "into lawful employment." He believed the commission should depend more on private enterprise to create jobs, and he objected to the premise that public investment produced better results than tax incentives.[17]

Perhaps anticipating Thornton's objections, Ginsburg had already placed him in charge of an advisory panel on private enterprise and told him to propose ideas about creating economic opportunities in depressed urban areas that could garner the support of big business. It's unclear whether Ginsburg was really interested in hearing from the panel or was just trying to keep Thornton busy. Regardless,

Thornton took the assignment seriously. Now that the commissioners were examining proposals related to jobs and employment, Thornton shared with his colleagues that his panel had surveyed thirty-eight American companies, and all of them said they would participate in a program that would provide them a tax rebate for employing poor people.

Thornton continued this line of attack on the report over the next few weeks. He repeatedly emphasized the role of culture and individual responsibility as causes for unemployment and poverty, stressing that it was important to teach young African Americans the "value of learning discipline and getting out of their environment." And since he did not see a clear relationship between poverty, poor housing, and inadequate schools and social disorder, he was convinced the commission had lost its way. "How did we get into all these recommendations?" he asked at a January 19 meeting. "We're a riot commission."[18]

Although she rarely spoke at meetings, when she did Peden usually backed Thornton, especially when it came to blaming the poor for their own plight. She opposed any programs that would put more money in the hands of the poor, objecting "to handing money to people who can't even fill out the forms." Like Thornton, she believed that conditions in the ghetto were bad, but they were not ready to erupt in violence. "I have a feeling that the tone of the nation is one of a little more tranquility," Peden told the Associated Press. "I don't believe that were going to be sitting on a powder keg that we saw in so many of our major cities last summer."[19]

Lindsay stood on the opposite side of the debate over the draft recommendations. As the most unconventional and provocative thinker on the commission, he often straddled the fence between liberals and radicals on the staff. Because he believed the conditions in the cities were so bad, and the threat of future violence so great, he was willing to experiment with new ideas. More than anything else, he was convinced that the report needed to shock white America into accepting that a national commitment was necessary to prevent future riots.

While he supported the thrust of the staff's recommendations for national action, Lindsay believed that they did not go far enough. He argued that attacking "white racism" was the first step; they also needed to address the poverty, lack of jobs, poor schools, and substandard housing that the racism had caused. "We ought to put it on a wartime basis, five years, to save the country," he told his colleagues. "It's a plain example of national neglect."[20]

Lindsay pushed the limits of liberalism, supporting a guaranteed national income for all Americans and dramatically more federal spending on new housing and better schools than recommended in the draft the staff had prepared. On housing, for instance, Lindsay noted that the draft called for one million new low- and middle-income housing units by the end of ten years, whereas the Urban Coalition, a private group created to study problems in the city, was calling for that many units be built *per year*. Lindsay also complained that the draft's welfare proposals simply added more money to ineffective existing programs. He insisted that they include a strong statement saying flatly that welfare "hasn't worked." He wanted to replace the entire welfare system with a simple guaranteed income for all Americans. Only Harris joined him in supporting this position. "I don't think anything else but a minimum wage will prove feasible," he said at a January 20 meeting.[21]

Lindsay was also the only member of the commission willing to bring the Vietnam War into the discussion of program recommendations, even though it should have been impossible to ignore. The government was spending $30 billion a year on the conflict. That was money, Lindsay believed, that could be better spent building urban communities. Knowing that he was unlikely to get anywhere asking his colleagues to come out against the war, Lindsay instead suggested that his colleagues attach price tags to the programs they were recommending. His goal was to highlight the gap in spending between domestic programs and the war. The administration's last budget had called for spending $4.3 billion on welfare and labor. By contrast, the

Department of Defense budget stood at $60 billion. If the war could end soon, then the "peace dividend" could fund new social programs without additional taxes. Projecting expenses alongside the recommendations would help highlight this possibility.

Lindsay's coalition abandoned him on this issue. Kyran McGrath wrote Kerner that it would be "the height of folly" for the commission to attach spending projections to its recommendations. He feared that the debate and controversy surrounding the specific estimates would distract the report from its real purpose: "to lay before the public the destructive effects of racism in the United States." Moreover, Lindsay's strongest ally, Fred Harris, and all the other commissioners were still on record supporting the war. Harris, who likely knew that even implicit criticism of the war would anger LBJ, told Lindsay that he did not feel it was appropriate for the commission to make decisions that could impact national security. "Somewhere you've got to limit what you do," he recalled saying. Lindsay, however, would keep fighting until the final days before the report's release to get his colleagues to acknowledge the obvious: they could not propose programs that cost billions without offering advice on how to pay for them, and that required at least acknowledging the fact that the nation was engaged in an immensely expensive war.[22]

As Thornton and Peden sought to steer the recommendations to the right and Lindsay tried to push them to the left, a small majority of commissioners—Harris, Chief Jenkins, Otto Kerner, Roy Wilkins, and, when they were present, I. W. Abel and Edward Brooke—supported most of the staff recommendations. During the initial discussion, the commissioners did not cast votes for or against specific proposals, but their responses provided Ginsburg with the feedback that he needed to revise the draft in the hopes of achieving his elusive consensus.

When Thornton announced that he opposed the fair housing provision of the draft, Jenkins called discrimination in housing a "moral problem" that was leading to "more hypocrisy than anything else

since prohibition." But it was Wilkins who was most passionate about
the subject. He threatened that "if this commission doesn't recommend an open housing bill," he would "resign now." Support for fair
housing was "so basically fundamental," he said that it could not be
avoided. "You talk to Negroes fighting in Vietnam," he lectured his
colleagues, "and first thing they ask is that when they get home, will
they be able to buy a house where they want." He told the story of
a young African American who was hired to teach at the University
of Colorado at Boulder, but could not find housing once he arrived
because no one in the city would rent him a room. The university,
he said, congratulated itself on hiring "a Negro professor and gave
itself arthritis patting itself on the back. But he couldn't find a house
near other faculty members." Without mentioning Thornton and
Peden by name, Wilkins also took the opportunity to object to his
two colleagues' repeated references to blacks being lazy and the riots
being irrational. "If whites were treated like Negroes, they'd revolt
tomorrow," he said. "Negroes [have] been remarkably patient. These
kids are crazy as hell, but they shouldn't be sold short. They've got a
point."[23]

The draft recommendation's departures from liberal orthodoxy
on education prompted unusual alliances. Thornton joined Lindsay
in supporting the draft's call for decentralizing big school systems.
Lindsay, as mayor of the nation's largest city, knew a great deal about
urban schools and flatly declared that they "simply don't work." He
and Thornton supported a voucher program that would provide cash
grants to allow parents to shop around for instruction outside of the
public school system. They argued that large public school systems
needed competition from private educators capable of experimenting
with innovative techniques. Rhetorically, they both seemed to agree
that throwing money at education was not the solution. "Money
alone," Lindsay said, "doesn't improve quality of education at least
not in New York." What Lindsay meant, however, was that the nation
needed to spend a lot of money on education, but that money "alone"

would not solve the problem. Thornton was opposed to spending any additional money at all and instead stressed the need for more discipline. "At some age," he said, "a child has to learn discipline and many of them in the ghetto aren't getting it at home."[24]

The debate over education often pitted Lindsay against one of his closest allies, Roy Wilkins. The mayor said that he supported improving the quality of education in urban areas over integration of urban and suburban schools. Most African Americans, he said, were more concerned with quality education than racial integration. "But Negro leadership," he said, "can't say 'quality' rather than 'integration' from a political viewpoint." Wilkins retorted that black parents were stressing quality education because they realized there would be no meaningful integration. He warned that if the nation planned to turn its back on integration, it should "be ready to spend billions on improving Negro schools." Wilkins was not sure what should be done to change the educational system, but he was unimpressed by the draft proposals. Although the recommendations were among the most radical in the document, Wilkins labeled them "pedestrian and ordinary." He did not want to "pussyfoot and split hairs" when it came to recommendations for change. He wanted to point out that the system has failed both blacks and whites. "Don't want to destroy it," he said, "but we can't let it go on as it has in the past."[25]

There was near unanimity among the commissioners that the welfare system was broken, but little consensus on what to do about it. Channeling the Moynihan report, which identified a link between poverty and the breakup of black families, Lindsay pointed out that nearly half of all black children in New York were born to unwed mothers. The mayor suggested that welfare programs contributed to teen pregnancy. Wilkins agreed and added a shocking suggestion. What "if we take [the] first illegitimate child away from mother? Will that reduce further illegitimacy?" A few weeks later, Wilkins changed his tone and suggested that the commission drop any recommendations for preventing out-of-wedlock births. Thornton, ever sensitive to incentives for bad behavior, worried that the welfare section of the draft, which provided financial support for unwed mothers, would encourage them to have more babies. He wanted the report to stress family planning. He was aware of "genocide charges" that the proposal would produce, but he insisted that the "subject is very important." Only Harris spoke out against the argument that welfare produced poverty or encouraged teen pregnancy. He argued that it was poverty, not welfare, that produced bad behavior.[26]

There were lighter moments. When Abel attacked Wilkins for suggesting that the teachers' unions needed to loosen seniority rules, Wilkins joked that the labor leader "was sore because he didn't buy" Thornton's stock "26 years ago." If he had, Wilkins said, "he'd be as conservative as Tex is now." Thornton picked up on the joke, responding that in the business community, "they call me a liberal." Wilkins retorted, "They'll call you a communist for being on this commission." Abel got in the last word, telling Thornton, "That's nothing compared to what they will call you when this report comes out." Another time, when they were engaged in intense discussions about federal aid to promote integration, Corman looked at Wilkins and said he recalled the words of "the great statesman, Richard Nixon," who "wanted to make the ghetto so attractive that you people [Negroes] would want to stay there." Lindsay jumped in, reminding the group that Nixon, who hailed from California, was now a resident of New York City. "Now you be careful what you say about my constituent," he said to Corman. "Just make your area [California] so nice that he'll want to go back."[27]

The occasional humor aside, the initial debates over the staff's program recommendations underscored the challenges that Ginsburg and Palmieri faced in trying to secure a unanimous report. It was clear that many of the commissioners would support most of the proposals, but it was also apparent that it would be nearly impossible to produce a final report that both Thornton and Lindsay would endorse. For now, Ginsburg planned to produce a new draft that responded to the commissioners' objections, trying to strike a balance that would keep open the possibility of consensus. Ginsburg likely realized that he would never convince all the commissioners to support each of the proposals, but he might be able to allay enough fears to get them to endorse the entire report.

IN ADDITION TO DEBATING RECOMMENDATIONS for new social programs, the commissioners struggled with another contentious part of the report during their January meetings: the role of the police in the riots. The commissioners had never read the field reports, which had pointed out that police actions had often precipitated riots and that once the disorder started, police overreaction made matters worse. Nor had they read the rejected "Harvest of American Racism," which drove home these sharp criticisms. Instead, they had reviewed Stephen Kurzman's draft of Chapter 2, on the causes of the riots, which was significantly less critical of the police.

However, there remained Arnold Sagalyn's chapter specifically on police and community relations. Many of the commissioners had strongly opposed an earlier version of the chapter when they reviewed it in November for being too harsh in its criticism of the police. While Sagalyn and the senior staff removed some of the offensive language, the thrust of the chapter remained the same when the commission turned to it again in January. It noted that effective law enforcement required support of the local community, but that support "will not be forthcoming when a substantial segment of the community feels threatened by the police and views them as an occupying force." It called for major changes to eliminate misconduct and abrasive police practices and to provide residents with mechanisms for addressing their grievances. The new draft included a long section on public safety that outlined in detail the types of weapons, equipment, and logistical support that police officers should have during a disturbance, recommending against rifles and carbines that employed high-velocity ammunition; arguing that chemical agents, not bayonets, should be used for riot operations; and calling for banning "weapons of warfare"—like machine guns, flamethrowers, and tanks from urban environments.

For Thornton, the new draft still read as "a general condemnation of all police." The commission was kicking "all the police in the mouth," he insisted. Even recommending that cities hire more black officers was too much for him. But Thornton found himself isolated on this issue. Under pressure from Lindsay and Corman, he backed down while insisting that he did not want to "wave a flag in white faces." It was only a matter of time, he charged, that blacks "will expect 'rapid' promotion and whites will resent it."[28]

Thornton also found himself alone in his objections to restricting certain weapons in urban disturbances, saying the commission should defer to local police in the streets to decide what weapons they wanted to use. "Once you turn loose police with weapons of mass destruction," Lindsay retorted, "you have innocent mothers and children lying all over the streets in pools of blood." The commissioners did not resolve the issues, but the discussion made Ginsburg realize that to satisfy Thornton, he would need to tone down some of the criticism of the police and to remove many of the specific suggestions involving police tactics and weapons.[29]

During the first weeks of January, the commissioners also reviewed drafts of several other chapters of the report for the first time, reacting skeptically to many of them. One was the chapter on the media's role in the disorders. Most of the commissioners were convinced that the media played a major role in whipping up discontent in many cities. The way they saw it, black militants ignited the unrest, and then the media fanned the flames. They were not alone. A poll showed that 99 of 268 members of Congress and 67 of 130 mayors agreed that "irresponsible news media coverage of riots" was of "great importance" in the "build-up of the riots." British journalist Henry Fairlie expressed what some of his own colleagues believed when he said, "However spontaneous the original outbreak of violence, as television cameramen and reporters move into the streets looking—literally looking—for trouble, they add external provocation. The crowds play up to them."[30]

The staff had devoted considerable resources and time to trying to find a connection between news coverage and the riots, but with little success. In November they had organized a two-day conference in Poughkeepsie, New York, to discuss with major media outlets what, if any, responsibility they shared for the riots. A few organizations, most notably the *New York Times*, refused to attend, claiming that the "investigation of news coverage is not really a proper subject for a government inquiry." In his opening comments welcoming the participants, Kerner said they had to answer a basic question: "Has news coverage cause riots to occur or to spread?" The conference ended with no clear answer, but the commission staff felt that they had placed the media on notice that they might be facing tough criticism in their report.[31]

Given the intense public interest in the role of the media in the riot process, Palmieri tasked the Simulmatics Corporation with studying television and newspaper coverage in fifteen American cities. Their preliminary results showed that, for the most part, television and print journalists had acted with editorial restraint in their coverage. When they read the preliminary study, however, the commissioners refused to believe those findings. Peden insisted that "next to [the] U.S. white public," the "media is one of the top causes of riots." When Ginsburg reminded Peden that their contractor had found that criticism invalid, Thornton jumped in: "Why are they in a better position to say no TV abuse than us?" Wilkins agreed with Thornton and Peden. "The main purpose of media is to send info out to whites about Negroes to stir up the confrontation through the news," he declared. Ginsburg again defended the conclusions, saying that since Watts, the media had been "pretty decent about their coverage." He said that the preliminary evidence from three cities had found "little to criticize the newspaper[s]." Ginsburg reminded them that the main purpose of the section of the report was "to put media on notice that [the] public will be looking at them."[32]

The commissioners also discussed the draft of the chapter on conspiracy. Ginsburg invited director of investigations and former CIA agent Milan Miskovsky to attend the meeting. Miskovsky pointed out that there were thousands of reports of people threatening to destroy cities in the United States, and most used the word "we" to suggest they were part of a larger conspiracy. But, he said, the research he had overseen revealed "no conspiracy." The only incident that had occurred in the previous year that resulted from a conspiracy was a threat to blow up a police station in New Haven, Connecticut, in December. That threat, however, came from a white supremacist group. Still, not all of the commissioners were convinced. Wilkins suggested that although there may be no conspiracy when it came to action, black militant groups, and leaders like Stokely Carmichael and H. Rap Brown, still represented "an assault on American society." Thornton took this threat a step further: "We ought to wave [a] red flag that despite small membership in these militant groups [they were still dangerous;] Hitler and Mussolini started small too."[33]

The only new part of the draft that commissioners enthusiastically accepted was the revised section on the future of the city. Written by Jack Rosenthal, it was based on Downs's three strategies for addressing urban problems: status quo, ghetto improvement, and dispersal. The chapter began by reciting the irrefutable statistics showing how all the trends proved that urban blight and racial segregation were destined to intensify without ameliorative action. It produced a rare moment of much-needed unanimity. "Excellent," Jenkins declared. "Put[s the] finger on the problem." Thornton also called the section "excellent," and Wilkins judged it "the best section yet." Corman and even Thornton agreed that it was a strong section, but they wondered why it did not come out and state explicitly that racism was responsible for most urban problems. As they moved through the material page by page, Thornton also objected to calling continuing current policies the "status quo choice." Doing so, he complained, "condemns the president's programs and all past programs, too." Wilkins also demurred when it came to this language, but for different reasons: "It means different things in say Alabama than in Ohio or Pennsylvania." Still, the commissioners agreed that this chapter was close to finished in its current form.[34]

CORMAN LIKED THE "FUTURE OF the cities" chapter, but, overall, he was frustrated as the new year began, feeling caught in the middle of the back-and-forth exchanges between Lindsay and Thornton. Corman, as a member of two powerful House committees, Judiciary and Ways and Means, forged deals between Democrats and Republicans all the time. He was used to brokering compromises, but he saw little hope of finding common ground in the commission debates. "He was very much a centrist," director of operations Stephen Kurzman recalled years later. Soft-spoken and, initially, reluctant to speak out at commission meetings, Corman preferred to work behind the scenes, holding private conversations with his colleagues. He did not share Thornton's unquestioned faith in the healing power of private enterprise. He insisted that public investments, not tax cuts, were necessary to help the poor. He also objected to Thornton's insistence that law and order would solve the riot problem. Yet he directed most of his anger to the left, at John Lindsay and the commission staff.[35]

While Downs had created a politically palatable starting point for the policy recommendations, Corman questioned the strategy of including specific proposals in the final report at all. On January 13, the congressman wrote a long letter to Kerner, spelling out his position. "When the president appointed me to the commission on civil disorders I looked forward to participating in an historic project," he stated. But he claimed that "the potential for significant national service" had "slipped from our grasp," because of the pressure to engage "in an indiscriminate and unstudied attack on every problem of American society." He rejected the notion that blacks were "engaged in widespread armed rebellion" and that the nation stood on the precipice of a new civil war. The riots did not indicate "the need for abandoning fundamental American institutions and principles," but instead demanded redirecting them to include blacks. He complained that the staff regularly bragged about proposing recommendations that were "revolutionary" and "designed to be controversial." The staff "exaggerated the nature of the problem," he wrote, to justify "their preconceived solution of dramatically increased federal involvement in the nation's cities."

The commission, he observed, seemed to be presented with two alternatives: one, championed by conservatives, would use repressive police power to create an "armed camp" in America's cities. Just as bad was the liberals' "ill-considered and totally unrealistic proposal for a radically different America." There was, he argued, a third course. The commission should play an educational role in highlighting how "white racism" had created intolerable conditions for blacks in urban areas. That was as far as he would go. He refused to endorse a "variety of detailed, experimental and, in some cases plain silly programs" for the nation. The effort to impose an ambitious agenda of new social programs on the commission "gravely" impaired "the prospect for the unanimous report so necessary to start national understanding and action."

Corman saw two ways forward for the commission: they could present a brief narrative report, focused on educating the public about "white racism," that would be acceptable to all commissioners, accompanied by a supplemental section where individual commissioners could express their support for specific programs, or they could issue separate minority and majority reports. He preferred a unanimous report, meaning he preferred the "first option to the second." Corman insisted that he came to this conclusion reluctantly, and, although he did not mention him by name, he clearly blamed Lindsay and those pushing for "unrealistic and unrealizable recommendations" for bringing about the crisis. He called on Kerner to assert his leadership and return the commission to the mission that "the president called upon us to perform."[36]

Two days later, Corman raised his objections directly to the White House, calling to tell the president that "John Lindsay has taken effective control of the commission." Corman warned that "a majority now accept Lindsay's thesis that the cities are in a state of war, a $40–$50 billion program is essential, [and that] the city's expenditures should be compared with outlays for space and Vietnam." He warned that there would very likely be a separate minority report, and the commission "is considering such far out proposals as racial quotas for schools, jobs, neighborhoods." The congressman asked the White House if the commission was "headed in the direction desired by the president."[37]

Finally, in a rare outburst, Corman spelled out his concerns at a January 19 meeting of the full commission. He reiterated that he wanted to "defer to these other special commissions" that the president had established in recent years when it came to specific policy recommendations in areas such as housing and welfare that were not "directly related to riots." Corman's comment must have shocked Lindsay. Up to that point, Corman had not offered opinions when these topics were discussed, and Lindsay hadn't counted him among those like Peden and McCulloch who were aligned with Thornton. Lindsay offered to rewrite parts of the report to make clear the connection between poor housing and the riots. Wilkins accused Corman of willfully ignoring the conditions that had led to the disorders. Corman snapped back that it was "not ducking to say I don't agree with details of many of these recommendations and we're not competent to study them here." He reiterated that the commission, which had met for only a few months, lacked the expertise to advocate for an "entire revision of school systems" or for "taking away [a mother's] firstborn illegitimate child." He wanted the commission simply to "point out the horrible failures of [the] system and the need to find more successful methods." Corman worried that "embracing all these programs will divert a great deal of attention from the real purpose of this report."[38]

Corman suggested that they keep focused on the one issue on which they all agreed: that racism was the source of the riots. It was not, as Lindsay and Harris argued, along with many staff members, poverty or poor housing or a lack of educational opportunity. "That's why I hope this report won't dwell on details of how to reduce poverty and improve education," Corman said. "Stress racism." Corman pointed out that "a lot of white people living on less than $3000 a year don't throw firebombs." Poverty, he declared, "does not cause racism." He believed the commission should attack "those rules which are different for whites than they are for Negroes."

Corman's comments produced a spirited response from Lindsay and Wilkins. Lindsay reiterated that it was impossible to address the roots of the riots "without coming back to housing, jobs and education," all of which were affected by racism. Wilkins worried that simply identifying racism as the problem would not improve anything. "We need more wide-ranging changes than in the past," he insisted. "We have to recommend something." Corman held his ground. "I don't want to recommend things in this report like guaranteed minimum wage, that [have] nothing to do with riots," he responded. He also echoed the point that McCulloch had been making all along: Why bother recommending a bunch of programs that Congress would never pass? "It would be harder to get Congress to spend the money to build a new school system than to get a judge to order accessibility to the good ones," he declared. Chief Jenkins listened quietly to the sparring before weighing in on the side of Lindsay and Wilkins. He said that he "cannot agree that poverty is not a cause of the riots." If someone gave an "inflammatory speech in a good neighborhood," he continued, "you'll have no problems. But give it in a poor neighborhood and you might get a riot."[39]

The conversation left Corman exasperated. He realized that Lindsay had the votes to support most of the recommendations that he and his allies advocated and that the best he could do was tweak some of the language. Corman was not the type to present colleagues with an ultimatum, but he gave one now: accept his suggestion to issue a more modest report, or he would refuse to sign the final document and instead write his own minority report. Wilkins had made similar threats in the past, but this one seemed more credible. Corman could likely get at least three other commissioners, Peden, McCulloch, and Thornton, to sign on to his minority report. The threat produced a quick response from Kerner. "I hope you're talking philosophically," he said.[40]

He was not. Instead, Corman's frustration with the direction Lindsay was pushing the commission only intensified over the next few weeks. Ginsburg and Kerner had assumed that Thornton represented the greatest threat to a unanimous report, but now they grew more worried about Corman, who seemed increasingly less willing to reach compromise on important issues. "Something is bothering him," McGrath wrote his boss. "Even Katherine [Peden] and Tex [Thornton] are worried about him."[41]

Corman did not stop at verbal threats. He reached out to staff members who he believed would be sympathetic to his concerns. Robert Conot, who wrote the widely praised first section of the report, recalled getting a phone call asking him to meet with Corman and McCulloch on Capitol Hill. When he arrived, he found two other commissioners, Thornton and Peden, waiting for him. They praised his section of the report but complained that the draft program recommendations were "unbalanced" and politically untenable. When they told him they were considering a minority report, Conot responded that "such an action would undermine the very purpose for which the commission had been created—bridging the rift between black and white America." He told them to share their concerns with Ginsburg.[42]

Still, Conot was the right person for them to contact, because he shared many of their complaints about the program recommendations under consideration. He separately wrote Ginsburg that he feared that issuing a report containing such ambitious recommendations would lead to the "false impressions among ghetto residents" that they would receive immediate relief. Those unfulfilled expectations would only "tend to exacerbate frustrations," he wrote. In addition, he claimed that if the recommendations were implemented, many of the militants would see the growing presence of the federal government in their neighborhoods "as a *plot* to further emasculate the Negro male and prevent him from becoming master of his own fate." He argued that the presentation of facts alone would "lead to a climate conducive to correcting the injustices of the past." Finally, he feared that a highly charged debate over the program recommendations would distract from the commission's mission to educate the public. "Should the American public's image of the commission come to be that of a revolutionary, 'socialistic,' and 'do-gooding' body," he wrote, many of the "more practical and implementable measures" would fall by the wayside. The whole report, he feared, would be dismissed as biased and unusable. Lindsay aide Jay Kriegel forwarded Conot's comments to the mayor with a note: "This is a remarkable letter."[43]

Corman's and Conot's were not the only voices calling into question the liberal strategy. The same week, Jack Rosenthal, whom Ginsburg hired to edit the final report, penned a memo to Ginsburg, questioning the strategy of trying to "shock" the American public and propose programs that were not politically or financially feasible. The nation already knew what steps were necessary to assimilate African Americans into American society, he argued. "What we do not have is the national political will to act on our knowledge." It was a waste of time to agonize "over program details" until the administration could deliver on its existing promises. "Otherwise," he wrote, "new program recommendations merely added to the list of promises so often unmet that by now they may well breed not calming hope, but cynical revolt."[44]

Given the strong feelings of some of the liberal commissioners, however, Rosenthal also recognized that it would be impossible to produce a "program-less report," as Corman preferred. As a compromise, he suggested that the commissioners turn the section recommending programs and solutions into an appendix, which would be presented as "an inventory of all the various thoughtful ideas that are already available." In essence, he declared, this approach would convey the following message: "See, white America, we know a lot of things to do. If you are not racist, if you really mean to keep the American promise, if you really mean to oppose injustice, then here are the *kinds* of remedies you will have to adopt and here is the price you must be willing to pay." For Rosenthal, the most important goal of the commission should be to educate white Americans about the realities of life for many poor blacks. But he strongly opposed the effort by some to shock white America. "I could not think of a worse tactic—[or] one more likely, if publicly believed, to lead to extreme repression," he wrote.

IN RETROSPECT, CORMAN'S AND ROSENTHAL'S proposals to focus on educating white America about their complicity in creating the conditions in urban America while avoiding proposing a host of controversial, unproven reform programs might have offered the commission a way out of the divisions they confronted. LBJ had instructed his commissioners to offer solutions, but he did not say they needed to decide on the number of housing units that needed to be constructed or the number of public service jobs that needed to be created. And in the end, the commission's legacy would be defined by its hard-hitting condemnation of white racism, not by the soon-to-be-forgotten program recommendations that it ultimately did issue.

But instead, those very policy suggestions threatened to split the commission with just weeks remaining before its self-imposed deadline. In those final days, the commissioners fell into rehearsing traditional liberal and conservative arguments over the role of the federal government to aid urban blacks. The new drafts that Ginsburg and Palmieri produced left behind the more provocative proposals, discarding them as too risky and politically untenable. Still, in February, with less than a month left before the final report was due, the commission seemed hopelessly deadlocked. Two commissioners, Wilkins and Corman, had made clear their willingness to file minority reports, and it also seemed unlikely that Thornton or Peden would sign on to the sort of report that a majority of the commission would happily approve.

Chapter 10

"TWO SOCIETIES"

A T THE END OF JANUARY, the commission started holding
its meetings in a small first-floor room of the Capitol beneath
the Senate chamber. The room's location allowed the congressional
members of the commission easy access to the House and Senate floor in the event of a vote. For weeks, they had been reviewing drafts of chapters. Now, with time running out to reach their
March 1 deadline, the commissioners needed to start voting to approve the report, including the controversial drafts of the program
recommendations. In response to the commissioner's feedback, the
staff produced a new draft of the entire report. David Ginsburg
instructed the staff to limit editorializing in the new version and
focus on facts and, with a few exceptions, establish broad goals and
avoid getting tied down in specifics. But the changes did little to
ease the deep divisions, making a unanimous report seem unlikely.
Although John Lindsay, and his coalition, won most of the votes,
the mayor insisted that the report include a hard-hitting summary
at the beginning of the report before he would approve the final
document.

IN MID-JANUARY, THE STAFF PRODUCED a new draft of the full report that incorporated many changes in response to discussions and
feedback to the sections they had discussed over the previous weeks.
Based on comments at an earlier commission meeting, the staff had
hired sociologist Herbert Gans to pen a short new chapter responding
to the idea that blacks should follow the model of the European immigrant experience and lift themselves up without federal intervention. The new draft chapter, only a few pages long, pointed out that
when past generations of immigrants earned more income, they had
migrated out of ethnic neighborhoods and established new clusters
in the suburbs. Discrimination and residential segregation, however,
prevented many blacks from following the same patterns. As a result,
they remained trapped in the inner city, while the suburbs remained
overwhelmingly white. Discrimination also limited blacks to all but
the lowest-paid, lowest-status jobs, and that pattern was both more
profound and persisted far longer than the prejudice experienced by
European ethnic groups that had migrated to America. The commissioners accepted the new chapter with little discussion.[1]

The new draft reflected numerous other revisions to chapters that
the commission had already seen. The introduction of the previous
draft stated that the commission's mandate required them to address
the social and economic ills and injustice of not only the black community, "but also the people of Spanish surname, the American Indian and other minority groups to whom this country owe so much."
The February draft dropped this language, instead emphasizing the
problem "in the black ghettos of our cities." It significantly shortened
John Hope Franklin's section on history, which had run far too long
in its previous form. While removing some of the references that had
disturbed Thornton, the staff kept many of the hard-hitting and powerful descriptions of racism in American history. The new version also
contained a more expansive section on the administration of justice
under emergency conditions, which highlighted many of the ways
the criminal justice system discriminated against the poor. The riots
in the summer of 1967, it pointed out, led to "indiscriminate" mass

arrests that resulted "in inefficient prosecution and severe hardship for defendants."[2]

Given the persuasive, objective data that proved false the charge that the media played a major role in fomenting violence, Ginsburg felt comfortable ignoring the commissioners' objections to the previous iteration of the media chapter. The new draft doubled-down on its earlier conclusions, stating that television and newspaper reports of the riots were balanced. It described the tone of television coverage as "calm" and "factual." It noted that both local and national television stations adopted "a conscious editorial policy of caution and restraint," although the chapter pointed out that coverage devoted little attention to the underlying issues of life in the ghetto. It also rejected the common complaint that television provided a platform for radical leaders, noting that moderate black leaders were featured on television three times more frequently than militants. The same pattern held for newspaper coverage, which it described as "generally calm, factual and restrained, not emotional or inflammatory."

But the chapter did not let the media off the hook. Television coverage, the draft noted, tended to view the riots as a confrontation between whites and blacks, even though most of the deaths and property damage occurred in black neighborhoods. It highlighted a few examples of "gross flaws" in reporting. For example, in Tampa, Florida, the national wire services reported that a sheriff had been killed by rioters. Later, they discovered that he had actually suffered a massive heart attack. Coverage also placed too much emphasis on law enforcement and not enough on the underlying causes of the disturbances. "Far too often, the press acts and talks about Negroes as if Negroes do not read the newspapers or watch television, give birth, marry, die and go to PTA meetings," the report stated. It called on the media to provide a richer portrait of life in urban areas and to hire more African Americans.

The section "The Police and the Community" continued to evolve. Ginsburg refused to back away from the central point that the police contributed to the unrest and needed more training in riot control.

But he toned down some of the language and added mollifying disclaimers to smooth out the edges. Instead of clearly stating what all the evidence proved—that abusive police practices were all too common and a leading cause of the unrest—the draft referred only to "police misconduct," saying that "it cannot be tolerated even if it is infrequent." A subhead reading "Police Misconduct and Abrasive Patrol Practices" became "Police Conduct and Patrol Practices." The new draft continued, however, to cite evidence that many officers assigned to black neighborhoods "expressed prejudice or highly prejudiced attitudes toward Negroes."

David Ginsburg sent the revised chapter to Herman Schwartz, a law professor at the State University of New York at Buffalo. Schwartz bluntly replied that the chapter "does not press the panic button hard enough." He pointed out that the information in the commission's own files made clear that "police-community hostility may well be the most dangerous factor in today's explosive urban crisis." The commission was obligated, he charged, to be explicit that relations would only get worse if the nation imposed "get-tough" policies. He repeated many of the points that the social scientists had made in "The Harvest of American Racism" report about police racism and prejudice. "Perhaps the Commission doesn't feel it can say this, but the policemen—particularly from certain ethnic backgrounds like the Italians in Newark—are really implementing the repressive and prejudiced attitudes of the dominant white society."[3]

In the section on jobs and employment, the new draft reflected the work of Thornton's private-enterprise group. According to Robert Conot, Ginsburg had learned about Conot's Capitol Hill meeting with Thornton, McCulloch, Corman, and Peden and went out of his way to respond to their concerns. The new draft stressed "the role that private enterprise firms" should play in running neighborhood-improvement operations. It criticized unions for engaging in "discriminatory practices" and insisted they should face heavy penalties if they failed to file annual reports identifying their minority membership. Instead of public investment to improve urban areas, the draft emphasized the importance of private-sector economic growth in providing jobs and called for the formation of a "national business leadership group" to "spearhead" business involvement in creating jobs in poor areas. It also added a new section on developing rural areas with high poverty levels. Although most of the staff believed the report should focus only on urban areas that had experienced riots, this was likely a way of securing Thornton's support. He spoke often about how rural areas, like the small town he grew up in Texas, were hemorrhaging jobs and opportunities.[4]

The new draft neutered the staff's bold and hotly debated recommendations for educational reform. The previous draft had proposed decentralizing large urban central school systems and providing federal funds for experimental schools. The new one discouraged talk of "radical" educational innovation and instead called for maintaining centralized control over finances and standards, while ceding local control over unspecified "other aspects of educational policy." It added wording advocating that schools stress basic reading and writing skills, while also "providing better vocational counseling . . . elementary work skills and discipline in school."

Surprisingly, the staff made only minor changes to the controversial welfare provisions. The previous version "required" single mothers to participate in group homes and place their children in "special institutions." Now it made such programs voluntary. "Unmarried girls and women from disadvantaged families experiencing their first pregnancy should be given several voluntary options other than returning with their child to the environment that gave rise to illegitimacy if they choose," it stated.

The new version of the report included more facts and less opinion. The staff lawyers writing much of the report were making a case before the jury of commissioners. Realizing that not only Thornton but also Peden and Corman were sensitive to staff editorializing, they let facts make their arguments. The new draft included detailed statistics on nearly every aspect of urban black life: the number of black female-headed families, incomes compared to whites, ages of rioters, arrest figures, years of education, dropout rates, levels of street crime and narcotic use, and myriad other informative charts and statistics.

The commissioners discussed the new draft of the program recommendation during all-day sessions on January 30 and 31. Kerner, who was back in Illinois tending to state business, asked Kyran McGrath to sit in on the meetings. According to McGrath, the commissioners reached a compromise on the open-housing provision. They agreed to include "a strong, unqualified" recommendation that such a law be passed, but refused to mention the specific steps that would be necessary to enforce it. "The emphasis," he reported, "would rest on strong language for nationwide open-housing." The commissioners rejected Lindsay's call for including specific cost estimates alongside policy recommendations. But McGrath advised Kerner that the new draft still contained many provisions that would alienate whites. Kerner himself had never expressed concern about the impact of the program recommendations on whites, and it seems likely that McGrath's real worry was that the proposals would anger Thornton and his allies on the commission. The section "Recommendations for National Action," he complained, called for "massive Federal expenditures" that would "close off public debate in the white community." The employment recommendations were vastly improved, but the section "still cites too many specific cost estimates." Similarly, the education chapter mentioned "too many specific Federal programs." And the welfare recommendations failed to address the problem that was of most concern to whites: "those welfare recipients able to work who may not nor do not want to work." There were, in his view, still too many particular programs and costs, which, he feared, gave "the section a Christmas tree appearance."[5]

Apparently, McGrath's concerns were shared by other staff members, because on February 1 they produced another revised version of the program recommendations. In this draft, it's possible to see the final report taking form. Ginsburg removed many, but not all, of the dollar figures and detailed recommendations and replaced them with broader goals. "We do not claim competence to chart the details of programs," the newest draft stated. "We do believe it is essential to set forth goals and to recommend strategies to reach these goals." The latest version prefaced its recommendations with long narrative sections that described the problems that the proposed solutions were designed to address and the goals they were trying to achieve. Surprisingly, the staff removed the language that had been inserted in the previous draft to appease Thornton. It was a calculated risk. It was clear that a majority of the commission rejected Thornton's emphasis on private enterprise. Ginsburg likely hoped that he could satisfy Thornton by removing some of the specific goals and focusing on broad objectives.[6]

The one exception to this strategy was employment, where the draft called for a program that would create 150,000 new public service jobs in its first year and a total of 1 million over five years, while setting a similar goal for private-sector jobs. In education it advocated for aggressive steps to end segregation, hire more teachers to instruct disadvantaged students, construct better schools in urban areas, and extend opportunities for vocational and higher education. Achieving these goals, it stated, required money and a lot of it. The staff did not list figures, but they made clear the measures would not be cheap. The approach, it warned, would "entail adoption of new and costly educational policies and practices," and it placed the financial burden squarely on the back of the federal government.

The draft also suggested it was the federal government's responsibility to develop a minimum national standard for families on welfare and recommended shifting the financial burden of the welfare programs from states to Washington, while also offering job training and day-care centers for children. It called for abandoning the "absent-father rule," creating neighborhood welfare and diagnostic centers, and expanding family-planning centers. Gone were any suggestions of dormitories for welfare mothers or orphanages for their children. The welfare section concluded with a call for the establishment of a "national system of income supplementation" that would provide a "minimum standard of decent living" for all Americans.

It laid out similarly ambitious goals for housing, calling for expanding the supply of low-income units and opening suburban communities to racial minorities. This section continued to include some specific recommendations, including support for the president's existing proposal to build six million low- and moderate-income housing units in the next decade. It also endorsed LBJ's efforts to spend $1 billion on his Model Cities program "as a minimum start." The draft stated that "a much greater scale of funding will ultimately be necessary if the program proves successful."

Ginsburg sent copies of this latest draft to relevant government officials and to a few outside consultants for review. The response was very positive, perhaps raising hopes that the report might still receive a warm response from the White House. The Department of Health, Education, and Welfare found the section on education to be "in very good shape" and offered only minor points. "The recommendations are the right ones," it concluded. "The point of view is balanced and sensible; and the arguments are well presented." William Gorham, assistant secretary of the department, called the section on welfare programs "a workmanlike and thoughtful evaluation of the inadequacies of our present welfare programs," while noting that the recommendations "offer very little which is new." Housing and Urban Development called the draft housing recommendations "well directed at a number of major urban housing problems" and offered only minor points of clarification.[7]

THE REAL QUESTION WAS HOW the commissioners would respond to the most recent revision and whether Ginsburg could get all eleven commissioners to sign on to a single document. No notes survive of what was said at the commissioners' February meetings when they were voting on the report; indeed, there is no official record of what days the commission met that month. Roy Wilkins's appointment books for 1968, now housed with his papers at the Library of Congress, indicate he was scheduled to attend commission meetings on February 9–10, 15–16, and 17. Ginsburg had asked the commissioners to leave open February 27–28 in case they needed it. Each session began with Ginsburg reading the newly drafted passages before pausing, asking for discussion and changes, and then calling for a vote. Thornton, keeping the option of a dissent open, insisted that consenting votes on individual sections did not commit the commissioners to supporting the entire document. He meant it as a warning shot: even if he was outvoted on the recommendations for preventing future riots, he reserved the right to reject the whole report and write a minority opinion.[8]

Not surprisingly, Thornton continued to hammer on the section on police and community relations. He complained that even the toned-down language was too critical of the police and proposed adding language that condemned "a general erosion of respect for authority in American society and the reduced effectiveness of social standards and community restraints on violence and crime." Ginsburg, fearing that Thornton would refuse to sign the report without the additional language, pleaded with Lindsay to accept it. The negotiation continued for weeks. Finally, late in the evening of February 20, Ginsburg sent a telegram to Lindsay saying, "Staff urgently recommends acceptance." Once Lindsay agreed, Ginsburg sent telegrams to the other commissioners, asking them to accept the additional language.[9]

Except for the clash over the police, most of the discussion in the final days focused on the recommendations for new programs. While the staff did not record the votes, Lindsay's coalition, expanded by the presence of I. W. Abel and Edward Brooke, who had missed many of the commission's earlier meetings, held together on most issues. Harris often reminded his colleagues of Johnson's charge to "find the truth and express it" in the report. More than once, he followed by quoting from Lincoln, "In times like the present no man should utter anything for which he would not willingly be responsible for all time and in eternity." Lindsay's coalition even managed to strengthen some of the provisions. On housing they won support for strong, unqualified language in favor of federal open housing. Lindsay also pushed hard to expand the number of recommended low- and middle-income housing units. In the end, by a majority vote, the commission accepted Lindsay's recommendation that six hundred thousand low- and moderate-income housing units be created the next year with the goal of six million units over the next five years—double what both the latest draft and the White House supported. They also pushed back against many of the staff concessions to Thornton and reemphasized the importance of public investment to solve the nation's urban problems, calling for creating two million jobs for the unemployed and underemployed over three years, along with massive spending increases to beef up enforcement of desegregation, including the construction of new schools to overcome racial imbalance. Abel made sure that the report dropped all criticism of labor unions.[10]

Lindsay, however, once again found himself alone in his effort to force the commission to explain how it would pay for its recommendations. His objective was clear: to highlight the mistaken priorities of an administration that devoted nearly unlimited resources to the Vietnam War while pursuing cutbacks in domestic programs. The issue put Ginsburg in a tough spot. He knew that most of the commission opposed making any connection between the riots and the war in Vietnam, and he was aware that it was a nonstarter for the White House. But it was also an obvious question to ask if the commission planned to advocate for programs that could add up to $20–$30 billion in federal spending. Initially, the staff prepared a document that tried to accommodate Lindsay's demands. Using the administration's own timetable for ending the war, it suggested that the resulting savings of $15 billion could be appropriated to help pay for new domestic programs. In the end, however, Ginsburg chose to avoid the matter.[11]

In mid-February Ginsburg trimmed down the section on paying for the commission's recommendations to only a few vague paragraphs praising the healing power of economic growth. "We *will* be able to find very substantial resources," it insisted, despite the war and a budget deficit. "Moreover—thanks to the most productive economic system ever devised by man—we can do this without further new taxes."[12]

Several commissioners made last-minute concessions as the March 1 deadline approached. The commission accepted Thornton's suggestion that they endorse a tax credit for companies that employed the "hard-core" unemployed. Lindsay pushed his colleagues to support a guaranteed income, but he had to settle for language saying that the federal government would "seek to develop" a system of "income supplementation." Harris won the vote to eliminate the absent-father rule that was part of the Aid to Families with Dependent Children welfare program, but lost the fight for more community control of local schools.

Ginsburg also decided to shorten the section on conspiracy. On February 2, Kerner contacted J. Edgar Hoover to see if there was any new information on the subject. Hoover reiterated that the FBI had "received no evidence to substantiate allegations that the civil disturbances which occurred during 1967 were part of an over-all conspiracy." In response, Ginsburg asked Robert Conot, who had written the well-received first section of the report, to redraft the conspiracy chapter. He wanted the chapter to be "exceedingly brief" and instructed Conot to avoid the "where there's smoke there's fire" problem. To placate the conspiracy-minded commissioners, and likely the president, he told Conot to point out that although the commission had found no conspiracy, there was evidence of incitement and agitation that contributed to the disorders. In the end, after editing by Ginsburg, the chapter would become the shortest in the report, a single double-column page. "I remember distinctly that Ginsburg spent considerable time shaping the wording of the chapter to his exact satisfaction," David Chambers recalled in 2017. "It was, after all, addressed not only to the general public but also to LBJ."[13]

The debates, and the votes, left nearly everyone dissatisfied. Neither Lindsay and his allies nor Thornton and his minority got everything they wanted. Even after the report had been revised to align with most of LBJ's goals, Thornton, McCulloch, Peden, and Corman still opposed many of the program recommendations, and it was unclear whether they would approve the final document. After the votes on the individual program recommendations, Palmieri added language that would make the report more palatable to the minority. He took out a piece of paper and wrote in pencil: "We discuss and recommend programs, not to commit each of us to specific programs, but to illustrate the type and dimension of action needed." The gesture, however, did little to ease worries of a minority report. "At the end, we had Tex Thornton out, Kay Peden out, Bill McCulloch out," Ginsburg remembered in his oral history. Kerner had the same concerns as Ginsburg. "I had a great fear and concern that we would have minority reports," he said in 1969. "I could see some developing." He speculated that in the final days, there was the possibility of as many as seven minority reports.[14]

THE FINAL HURDLE WAS TO gain approval of a summary. As usual, it was John Lindsay driving the agenda. The final report reflected Lindsay's belief that racism and poverty were the root causes of the riots and that it fell within the purview of the commission to support a wide range of social programs to address the problem. But he was not yet ready to declare victory. He wanted to include a hard-hitting summary at the beginning of the report that would highlight many of the key findings. He believed that few people would take the time to wade through seven hundred pages of often lackluster prose. If the commissioners were going to generate media attention and have an impact on the public debate, they would need to capture the essence of the report in a summary.

Although he had won the debate on most of the major issues, Lindsay was considering voting *against* the final report. He wanted more time to study some of the problems the report addressed, and he expressed concerns that the sections had been slapped together to satisfy an artificial deadline. He planned to draw a line in the sand with the summary: if the other commissioners rejected it, he would refuse to sign the report. "The threat of Lindsay's dissent, which he never voiced explicitly, provided him with leverage in the final weeks," noted aide Peter Goldmark. "As the only mayor of a big city on the commission and a Republican, his dissent would have crippled the commission."[15]

It's unclear how much leverage Lindsay had over Ginsburg or the other commissioners. While he had reservations about the final product, Lindsay, like his colleagues, wanted a unanimous report. "If Lindsay had refused to sign (or voted against the final report), there would have been a high risk, a very high risk, that Thornton and Peden, and perhaps Corman and McCulloch, would also have refused to sign and would have written their own separate statement disavowing the social programs," Chambers reflected. Lindsay had a lot more to lose by shattering the consensus for a report that condemned white racism than he had to gain by dissenting. That is why, according to Chambers, Ginsburg "didn't fear a dissent from Lindsay," at least no more than he worried about opposition from some of the other commissioners.[16]

Still, Ginsburg tried to satisfy Lindsay's demands regarding the report's summary. The staff had prepared a summary, which Palmieri included in a February 15, 1968, draft of the report. Lindsay read it, crossing out sections while underlining others. By the time he finished, it was clear he wanted to start from scratch. The staff's draft, he felt, focused more on how the commission did its work and less on what it found. The summary was too bland, he believed, and would fail to grab the nation's attention. There was no call to arms, no sense of urgency, no great clarity about the depth of the problems the nation faced or the boldness of the proposals that would be needed to address the problem. He also felt that the staff's draft emphasized law and order so as to appease Thornton.[17]

The mayor wanted to make sure that the summary reflected his priorities, so he instructed two aides, Peter Goldmark and Jay Kriegel, to write another draft. They realized that adding new, provocative ideas to the summary would produce a war among the commissioners. "We came up with the idea that 'why don't we see what's in the report and take the strongest language we can find and string it altogether,'" recalled Goldmark. If anyone objected, there was a ready response: "It's already in the report." On the evening of February 16, Kriegel and Goldmark combed through a draft of the report during an all-night session at the Hay-Adams Hotel in Washington, DC. They faced a tough deadline: the commission would be meeting in executive session the next day, and Lindsay wanted to present his own summary. In reading the most recent draft of the report, Kriegel and Goldmark came across a sentence in the section "Future of the Cities" that resonated. It declared that aggressive efforts at integration could "reverse the already strong trend toward the development of two American societies, separate and unequal."[18]

The language about "separate and unequal" had been part of the liberal ethos since 1954 when the Supreme Court, in *Brown v. Board of Education of Topeka*, overturned "separate but equal" as the legal justification for racial segregation, one of the principal pillars of white supremacy. The *Brown* decision declared segregation in public schools to be illegal, claiming that "in the field of public education the doctrine of 'separate but equal' has no place." Ten years later, the Civil Rights Act of 1964 expanded the core notion of *Brown* to all areas of public accommodations such as transportation, restaurants, and hotels. Anthony Downs had introduced the "two societies" concept to the commission, but Jack Rosenthal, who had used the same phrase in speeches he wrote for Robert F. Kennedy, had fined-tuned the language. Kriegel and Goldmark now reworked Rosenthal's language into a powerful and haunting phrase: "This nation is at present moving toward two societies, one black, one white, separate and unequal."[19]

The summary that Kriegel and Goldmark wrote in that all-night session struck a much different tone than the staff's version. Instead of beginning with a plea for law and order, it spoke of the anger and disillusionment of those who rioted and the tough choices facing the nation. "This nation," it declared, "confronts a critical choice about the future of American society." There was no praise of Lyndon Johnson or any suggestion that his policies had made America better. Instead, it claimed that the current course the nation was on would lead to more rioting. It spoke of the "pervasive discrimination and segregation in all aspects of American life," which left blacks humiliated and bitter. It condemned the riots, but underscored that it was important to understand their roots: "We have found that in the ghettos of our country . . . a way of life totally alien to that known and taken for granted by most Americans."

Continuing the current approach would, it warned, "have the most ominous consequences for our society." It called on the president and Congress to "undertake programs of sufficient scope and daring to change drastically within the next 5 years the educational, employment and housing opportunities available to those locked in the centers of our cities." The recommendations included in the report would "require unprecedented levels of program funding and production," but that commitment was "imperative." Providing those resources, it stated in a vague reference to Lindsay's ongoing effort to get his colleagues to address the Vietnam War, would require "a reordering of our national priorities." Only then, it concluded, "can we make good our commitment to civil peace and social justice. There can be no higher priority for national action, and no higher claim to the nation's bounty."[20]

The two aides handed Lindsay their draft the following morning at breakfast. Lindsay liked it and, with their yellow legal pad in hand, made an impassioned speech to the commissioners a few hours later. "We've been together throughout this process," he said to a hushed room. "We sat in housing projects, and we have talked with policemen on the beat. I've written this summary because it reflects what we've learned together as we have traveled from one end of this torn country to another." The summary, he said, captured "what many of us would like to say. It contains what in our hearts we know we need to say to the nation. I hope we can say it together."[21]

After the mayor finished reading his summary, Corman spoke up. "I don't think I can sign this," he said. But many of the other commissioners rushed to Lindsay's defense. "It was like getting sprayed by a firehose," recalled Goldmark. "It pulled them together."[22]

On February 23, Palmieri sent a significantly revised version to the commissioners. It led with the language about two societies. "This nation is moving toward two societies, one black, one white—separate and unequal." It sustained the sense of urgency, the definition of a clear choice for the American people, and an acknowledgment that the current course was not acceptable. "To continue along the present course is to choose a future with the most ominous consequences for our society, one which will involve the continuing polarization of the American community and the destruction of values and principles to which this nation is dedicated." It included language about white racism that had not been included in the Lindsay draft. "What the American public has never fully understood—but what the Negro can never forget—is that white society is deeply implicated in his plight. White institutions created it, white institutions maintain it, and white morality condones it."[23]

Palmieri gave his draft to Rosenthal to polish. The language about "two societies" had now come full circle. Kriegel and Goldmark prepared their summary using Rosenthal's language; now Rosenthal was being asked to rework their version of his words. Rosenthal would craft three different versions of the summary. Other staff members were likely making suggestions for revision as well. In 1993 Palmieri said that he "retired to the quiet of the Georgetown Library," where he had "the draft of some material that Jay Kriegel and Peter Goldmark from Lindsay's staff had prepared," along with other versions, most likely the three versions that Rosenthal wrote. In addition, he recalled having papers that "had been written [by] academics all over the country when I put the summary together."[24]

Whatever Palmieri produced likely went to David Ginsburg for a final edit. "Ginsburg would have reviewed the [Palmieri draft] with an editor's pen," maintained David Chambers. "He was very particular about lean, precise prose." The final Palmieri-Ginsburg version kept most of the language about two societies, but it made one small change, substituting "in the ghetto" for "in his plight." "What white Americans have never fully understood—but what the Negro can never forget—is that white society is deeply implicated in the ghetto," it read. "White institutions created it, white institutions maintain it, and white society condones it."[25]

With the report finished, and all the program recommendations approved by a majority vote, it was time to vote on the entire report. Would Thornton, Peden, and Corman approve of the final document, including the summary? There was some last-minute haggling over language. Although he had signed on to it months ago, Thornton now worried that the phrase "white racism" might be too inflammatory. He and Peden suggested alternatives—"white ignorance" or "white indifference" —but the Lindsay-Harris coalition pushed back and gained approval of the draft with no significant changes. Ginsburg now called for a final vote on the entire report. The vote was unanimous, eleven to zero.[26]

Although it had not been part of the draft approved by the commissioners, Ginsburg decided to begin the report with a quotation from LBJ's July 1967 address to the nation when he announced the creation of the commission. Given the broad mandate the commission assumed, it seemed appropriate to begin with the president's acknowledgment that "ignorance, discrimination, slums, poverty, disease," and lack of jobs were the conditions that "breed despair and violence." Ginsburg knew the report would be a tough sell at the White House, so he hoped to frame their findings in the president's own words.

Although he approved the final document, Thornton staged a last-minute maneuver that almost sabotaged the carefully scripted consensus. In late February, all the commissioners gathered in a Senate caucus room for a ceremonial signing of the final report. The plan was for the commissioners to sign the document and then invite photographers into the room to record the moment. "We were ready to sign the document when Thornton announced that he had a minority report," Harris recalled. He very casually said, "I'll have a minority report." He did not say why he had changed his mind or ask for approval. "You can imagine," Harris said, "we're just shocked."[27]

It is hard to know what prompted Thornton's last-minute effort to undermine the report. He was upset with the tone and substance of the report, but Ginsburg had worked hard to address many of his objections, and Thornton had already agreed to the final carefully negotiated version. Perhaps he was focused on events outside the commission. In January Thornton had announced that Litton's profits had ended fifty-seven consecutive quarters of earnings gains. The news shocked Wall Street. Litton's stock dropped by half in the month that followed, and angry stockholders demanded answers. The revelation that Litton's financial success had been built on deceptive, but not illegal, accounting tricks produced a frenzy of bad press and tarnished Thornton's once sterling business reputation.[28]

Whatever the reason for it, Thornton's move threw the meeting into chaos. After a long silence, Lindsay spoke up. "Wait a minute," he said. "This report doesn't go nearly as far as I wanted to go. If you're going to have a conservative minority report, then I'm going to submit a liberal one." Many of the other commissioners joined in the discussion, threatening their own reports. "It began to look," Harris said in a 1994 oral history, "like we were going to have . . . as many minority reports as there were members of the commission." The standoff lasted for an hour. Ginsburg, confronted by the possibility that all their hard work would unravel at the last hour, pleaded for unity. Eventually, Thornton withdrew his report and signed the document.[29]

How DID ALL ELEVEN MEMBERS of the commission eventually sign the final document, even though a few objected strongly to its tone and a sizable minority opposed the long list of program recommendations?

Several members of the commission had already believed that the nation was in crisis at the time that the president created the commission. After their visits to riot areas and the sometimes shocking testimony at commission hearings, all the others had come to share the same belief. They also believed they could make a positive contribution to combating this crisis and potentially reduce the prospect of another "long, hot summer." But that would happen only if their report was unanimous. Even those who raised profound objections to the direction of the commission were persuaded that a unanimous report they did not entirely embrace was better than a split commission. "I think a main reason unanimity was produced at the end was because on the core issue of the treatment of African Americans in the United States, and its long roots, there was consensus," according to Fred Harris. "All the commissioners understood the importance of delivering this message as strongly as possible."[30]

That sense of crisis in the country had only intensified during the early months of 1968. In February *Newsweek* sent correspondents out to the cities deemed most susceptible to unrest to gauge the racial temperature. They found that blacks and whites had moved even further apart. In the black community, moderate leaders had been replaced by black nationalists who spoke openly about using violence to achieve their political ends. The white reaction had been just as harsh. Although *Newsweek*'s reporters could not confirm it, the rumors were that urban police forces were stocking up on "fearsome weaponry." At the same time, Gallup polling found that the "breakdown of law and order" was now the second most important issue for Americans. Only the Vietnam War topped it.[31]

Ginsburg deserves a lion share of the credit for ensuring a unanimous report. "Ginsburg was, more than anybody else, responsible for the report," Harris affirmed. The commissioners had little relationship with each other, but they all trusted Ginsburg. He emerged as the key figure in the final months, going back and forth between competing camps, tweaking language, and forging consensus. The commission likely would have imploded had it not been for his efforts.[32]

While not everyone agreed with the final language or accepted all the recommendations, Ginsburg made sure that every commissioner came away with a concession that allowed them all to support the final report. He added just enough to appease Thornton's demands for law and order while satisfying Lindsay and Harris's insistence that the report focus on the underlying sources of the riots. Many of the commissioners subsequently championed the aspect of the report they endorsed and ignored what they opposed. For example, in his speeches and talks with local leaders in Ohio, William McCulloch made no mention of the expensive social programs recommended in the report and instead emphasized the importance of acknowledging "white racism." While Harris, Lindsay, and Wilkins focused on the role the federal government needed to play in aiding the urban poor, McCulloch claimed that "the responsibility for the most direct response to the potential for urban disorder must rest with local institutions and community leadership." He acknowledged the need for better housing and education, but he also insisted that improving urban conditions did not always "involve spending more money."[33]

Chapter 11

"I'D BE A HYPOCRITE"

Having managed to produce a unanimous report, executive director David Ginsburg's next challenge would be to get the White House to embrace it. Ginsburg and many of the commissioners were hopeful. Edward Brooke later wrote that he expected LBJ to "applaud" the commission's "painstaking analysis and support our recommendations." Fred Harris anticipated a similar response from the president: "Thank you very much for your work and for telling the truth. We're going to really take this to heart and try to do something about it."[1]

There was reason for optimism. Ginsburg had steered the commission to the center, removing language that was critical of the administration while endorsing many of the Great Society's goals. The relevant cabinet officers had reviewed the report and responded favorably, noting that its recommendations aligned with policies the administration was already on record supporting.

The commissioners and the staff, however, had failed to appreciate how much the political universe had changed since the heyday of the Great Society just a few years earlier. For LBJ, the report was dead on arrival. He could not understand how the commission could think it was a good idea to recommend billions of dollars in additional social spending at a time when Congress would not fund existing Great Society programs. Initially, LBJ refused to receive a copy of the report or sign letters thanking the commissioners for their service. His tone changed only after he was nearly defeated by Senator Eugene McCarthy in the New Hampshire presidential primary and his nemesis, New York senator Robert F. Kennedy, entered the race for the Democratic nomination, using LBJ's failure to respond to the Kerner Report to attack him from the left. But it was too late. Ironically, a commission established to shore up support for LBJ's domestic agenda ended up dealing a fatal blow to his presidency.

ON FEBRUARY 13, GINSBURG REQUESTED that the president welcome the commission members to the White House, pose for pictures, and formally accept the report. The event would kick off an intensive period of public education: meetings with editors and other members of the print media, interviews on television and radio, and testimony before congressional committees. President Johnson seemed receptive to the idea. "Will the President see the members of the national advisory commission on civil disorders on Friday, March 1?" White House chief of staff Marvin Watson asked in a memo. The president checked the "yes" box, but scribbled at the bottom, "If Joe C. has seen report & says ok." Given his past hostility to the commission and his efforts to cut off its funding, LBJ's openness to holding a White House reception seems surprising. But it appears that the president had largely lost interest in the commission after December when Ginsburg informed him that they would issue a final report by March 1968. He was no longer getting briefed on the ins and outs of the commission's day-to-day work, and he was unaware of the programs that it planned to recommend in its final report.[2]

By February 1968, LBJ had bigger problems on his plate than the commission. Speechwriter Harry McPherson would later describe it as "the most dismaying month I ever remember in the White House."

On January 31, communist troops in Vietnam had launched an offensive during the lunar New Year, called Tet. The Vietcong invaded the US Embassy compound in Saigon and waged bloody battles in the capitals of most of South Vietnam's provinces. Sixty-seven thousand enemy troops invaded more than one hundred of South Vietnam's cities and towns. The communist-controlled National Liberation Front held parts of Saigon for three weeks and sections of the imperial capital of Hue for almost a month. In the push to retake these urban areas, the United States called in airpower to bomb parts of Saigon and other cities. The effort produced one of the most infamous quotes of the war, when a US military official said of the battle to regain control of one city that it had become necessary "to destroy the town to save it."[3]

From a military perspective, the Tet Offensive was a failure for the North Vietnamese. They suffered heavy casualties and failed to gain new ground or incite a popular rebellion against the United States. But the Tet Offensive represented a striking psychological victory for the communists in the North. The ferocity of the offensive belied the optimistic reports of General William Westmoreland, who had proclaimed as recently as November 1967 that he had "never been more encouraged in my four years in Vietnam." Television pictures of marines desperately defending the grounds of the American Embassy in Saigon shocked the nation. The Tet Offensive produced a seismic shift in public opinion against the war. The staid *Wall Street Journal* warned that "the American people should be getting ready to accept, if they haven't already, the prospect that the whole Vietnam effort may be doomed." Cartoonist Art Buchwald compared Westmoreland to General George Armstrong Custer, proclaiming victory in the face of utter defeat. The administration's war policy faced harsher and broader criticism than ever before.[4]

Califano recalled that following Tet, there "was a sense of siege in the White House." At some point during that time, LBJ changed his mind about having a White House reception for the commission.

Some of the liberal members of the commission later suspected that Tex Thornton had poisoned the well by secretly feeding LBJ false information, claiming that the report was critical of his administration and that it failed to give the president proper credit for his accomplishments. Fred Harris believed that Thornton was lobbying the White House behind the scenes, either directly or through Texas congressman George Mahon, who was a close confidant of the president and a friend of Thornton's. "Mahon warned Johnson," Harris asserted, that the commission "had nothing good to say about anything that Johnson had done." Journalist Andrew Kopkind similarly claimed in a 1969 report that Thornton went to Mahon "and asked him to intercede with the White House."[5]

It's impossible to confirm what messages, if any, Mahon passed on to the president, but there is a far more straightforward explanation for the White House's change of face. On February 26, before anyone in the White House had seen a copy of the report, the *Los Angeles Times* ran a long article describing some of the commission's recommendations. That article was most likely responsible for LBJ's change of heart. It certainly brought the commission back into his sights. He resented that the newspaper ran an article citing anonymous sources within the commission before the commissioners made a formal presentation to him. He was also shocked that his commission was calling for expansive new spending at such a politically delicate time for his administration. Clifford Alexander, chairman of the Equal Employment Opportunity Commission, recalled that Johnson resented "reading the headlines before he had a chance to come to his own views." What bothered him even more, according to Alexander, were reports that the commission made no effort to explain how it would pay for such expensive new programs. Most likely, LBJ viewed the leaks as another Lindsay effort to embarrass him.[6]

After reading the article while staying at his Texas ranch, LBJ fired off a telex to the White House. "I have been seeing on the wire and hearing on the radio all day long what the commission on civil disorders is going to report to me," he wrote Califano. "As you know, I would prefer to receive the report before I hear about it from news media." He went on to say that he hoped the commission would include in its report recommendations to finance the proposals. "Anyone can recommend spending," he declared, "but preparing methods to fund the cost of new programs takes more ability. It has been my experience that spenders can always spend if they can find lenders to lend or taxpayers willing to be taxed. So I hope those who are preparing the final report will be as imaginative on taxing as they are on spending."[7]

The next day, February 27, Ginsburg had breakfast with Califano. He handed Califano a copy of a seventy-eight-page summary of the report that the staff had prepared for distribution to the media. Ginsburg suspected that the report fell short of what LBJ had expected, but he saw nothing in it that would embarrass the president and likely hoped that the White House could use it to push Congress to enact much of his stalled domestic agenda. Still, he apologized to Califano for not producing a document that met all of the president's expectations. It was, he said, the best he could do for the president.

Califano took the executive summary to his office and started paging through it. As he combed through the list of recommendations, it became obvious to him that LBJ would "erupt." "The commission," he recalled later, "recommended federal spending several orders of magnitude beyond what we had proposed, and its report contained a blistering indictment of white racism." He was certain that Johnson would read the report as an attack on his administration.[8]

And that night, while Califano and his staff prepared a brief summary of the document to present to the president the next morning, the White House received more bad news. On his nightly news broadcast, Walter Cronkite, the nation's most trusted anchorman, who had just returned from a personal fact-finding tour of Vietnam, delivered his verdict on the war: "To say that we are mired in stalemate seems the only realistic, if unsatisfactory, conclusion." At that moment, Johnson turned to an aide and said, "It's all over." He knew that if he had lost Cronkite, he had lost "Mr. Average Citizen."[9]

LBJ was not in a great mood the next morning, February 28, when he met with Califano to discuss the Kerner Commission's report. Califano summarized the report for him, pointing out its indictment of white racism, its criticism of "ineffective, indifferent, backward city governments," and its many program recommendations. "In general," he told LBJ, "their direction is similar to ours, but much more ambitious, and in some cases, unrealistic in the short run." He concluded by saying that overall, the commission report suggested that the administration "is heading in the right direction, but it is moving too slowly, devoting insufficient resources to make a dramatic difference and organizationally scattering its shots." However, the report was, with a few exceptions, "completely silent on the cost of the recommendations."[10]

LBJ was pressed by problems at home and abroad. Later that same day, General Earle Wheeler, chairman of the Joint Chiefs of Staff, met with LBJ to request the deployment of 205,179 more US soldiers to Vietnam in addition to the 525,000 who were already there. Meeting the request would require mobilizing the reserves. Clark Clifford, who was replacing Robert McNamara as secretary of defense, remembered the meeting as "so somber, so discouraging, to the point where it was really shocking." The president, he recalled, was "as worried as I have ever seen him." He now had to make the biggest decision since the original commitment of troops in 1965. Either he accepted the recommendation and placed the nation on a war footing during an election year, or he rebuffed Wheeler and moved to de-escalate the conflict. The president turned to Clifford and asked him to conduct a full review of the war. "Give me the lesser evils," he said.[11]

According to Califano, the next day, February 29, proved to be "one of those days" for the president. In the morning, he and LBJ sparred for an hour about his response to the Kerner Commission report. Johnson felt angry and betrayed by the report and by the men who wrote it. He instructed Califano to inform Ginsburg that the report was "destroying the president's interest in things like this." Privately, he denounced the notion that America was moving toward two societies as "catchy but insidious slander." He later told biographer Merle Miller that he refused "to accept a diagnosis of deep racism. I can't ignore the progress we have made in a decade to write equality on our books of law." The commission, Johnson felt, had failed to recognize his efforts on race or appreciate how difficult it was to get an increasingly restless Congress to approve new domestic legislation. He could not get the House to pass a 10 percent surcharge to help pay for existing programs. "I will never understand how the commission expected me to get this same Congress to turn 180 degrees overnight and appropriate an additional $30 billion for the same programs that it was demanding I cut by $6 billion," he wrote in his memoirs. He believed that a president should not push Congress too hard. "If you're going to drink whiskey," he would say, "drink a little at a time and you can drink all night. If you drink the whole bottle right away, you'll throw it up." Dealing with Congress was the same way. "You've got to feed them legislation in easy doses," he said.[12]

That afternoon LBJ traveled to the Pentagon for a farewell ceremony for outgoing defense secretary Robert McNamara. On his way to the event, the president, McNamara, Califano, and several other aides got stuck in a White House elevator between floors for almost fifteen minutes. Once free they traveled to the ceremony, which was held outdoors in the pouring rain.

The day went further downhill from there. A few hours later, Ginsburg informed Califano that the *Washington Post* had obtained a copy of the report and planned to publish a story on it in violation of a White House embargo that barred any stories before March 1. Califano called the paper's executive editor, Ben Bradlee, and accused him of violating the embargo, but Bradlee replied that the page containing the embargo notice had been ripped off the copy of the report they had received. (According to Lawrence Stern, the paper's national news editor, the *Post* had obtained a copy from a source outside the commission.) The *Post* was not violating any agreement, Bradlee argued. Although the paper's policy was to honor embargoes on material made available by the source imposing the embargo, that did not apply when the information could be obtained from other sources. With the story out, Califano told Ginsburg to let the *New York Times* and others publish as well, so that the *Washington Post* would not have an exclusive.[13]

In 2015 Victor Palmieri settled the mystery around who had leaked the report to the *Post*, a question that has prompted a great deal of finger-pointing in the intervening decades. "My clear recollection is that David Ginsburg was the leaker," he stated. "David was afraid that the White House was going to bury the report," he said, "so he sent an anonymous copy to the *Post*." David Chambers, who served as Ginsburg's assistant on the commission, accepts Palmieri's account. Ginsburg and Palmieri, he recalled, had developed a close, mutually trusting working relationship over the previous seven months. "If anyone knew what Ginsburg was thinking or doing, it was Victor." John Koskinen, who served as Palmieri's deputy, also suspected Ginsburg. "My vote would be Ginsburg," he mused in 2016. "He knew the best way to get coverage was to give someone an exclusive so they would run a major story, forcing everyone else to run a story thereafter. You want someone to own the story and give it visibility."[14]

Ginsburg's leak to the *Post* suggests how deep the suspicion ran between the White House and the commission by February 1968 and how far Ginsburg had evolved since he was appointed executive director as a Johnson loyalist. If Ginsburg's intent, however, was to box in the president, his plan backfired. For LBJ, the leak was the last straw. The original White House plan was for the commissioners to formally hand LBJ a copy of the report at a White House ceremony where LBJ would thank the commissioners and praise their work. The president was so furious that he canceled the White House reception, refused to even accept his bound presidential copy of the report, and insisted that the commission disband. When Califano learned that Lindsay wanted to meet with the president to discuss ways of implementing the commission's recommendations, Califano fired off a handwritten note to LBJ on February 28. "I doubt whether you should reconvene the Commission to have them give you ways to raise money to implement their proposals," he wrote. "I fear many members (led by Lindsay) would get into Viet Nam and some members would recommend that we pull out of Viet Nam to pay for their programs."[15]

The two leaks—one to the *Los Angeles Times* and the other to the *Washington Post*—outraged LBJ. He tried to pretend that the commission never existed, and he doubled down on his refusal to accept the report. The president's top advisers, however, were unanimous in their belief that LBJ needed to publicly acknowledge the report. "The more I think about it, the more I fear that a cold reception to the Kerner report is bad policy for us," McPherson wrote on March 1. "I know the problems it creates," he said, but he confirmed that the commission had fulfilled the president's charge and produced a report that indicted white racism. McPherson was not worried about how "bomb throwing liberals, *New York Times* editorial writers, columnists, or militant Negroes" would respond. He cared about the response of "ordinary moderate people." A better course, he thought, would be to analyze the commission's recommendations, followed by cabinet officers briefing the press in a "*realistic*, candid way" and then a presidential speech, "weighing the possibilities for action." "Unless something like this is done—meeting the report squarely and affirmatively, rather than coldly or evasively—I think we will be in trouble."[16]

On February 29, Califano sent the president a memo reaffirming that all his domestic advisers recommended that he "do or say something about the Kerner commission report to indicate that you are taking it seriously and not ignoring it." Califano had prepared a statement in Johnson's name that called the report "essential reading for government officials" that spoke to "every American citizen concerned about the quality of life in our towns and cities." He pleaded with LBJ to issue the statement. LBJ refused."[17]

The president ignored the advice and instead organized a last-minute trip to his Texas ranch on the day the report was officially released, March 1. The report produced massive media coverage, but the man who created the commission remained mum and largely out of sight. Johnson made several speeches while away from Washington in the days that followed, but he failed to reference the report explicitly. Instead, he vigorously defended his administration's commitment to domestic issues, telling a Texas crowd that he had doubled the budget for health, education, and welfare since taking office in 1963. In a not so subtle swipe at the commission report, he said the spending increase proved wrong those who "think we are neglecting the home front while we defend freedom wherever it is attacked in the world." The only official White House response to the report in the days following its release came from press secretary George Christian, who told reporters that the report "will be evaluated very carefully by those who have responsibility in this field."[18]

LBJ's silence puzzled liberal commentators. As Max Frankel of the *New York Times* wrote, "Johnson sits silent and his official spokesmen keep weaving, ducking, and dodging. . . . Doesn't it seem strange, with all this attention focused on a report by the president's own commission, that Johnson himself has made no comment?" Journalist Drew Pearson noted the irony of a president "who has done more for race relations than any president since Abraham Lincoln" rejecting "the penetrating report of his own commission on civil disorders."[19]

The White House was also under pressure from the Democratic National Committee, which pushed Califano to have the president speak out about the report. Louis Martin, who held the unassuming position of deputy chairman for minorities, was a major power broker in the black community and a former member of Franklin Roosevelt's "Black Cabinet." He noted that the report was getting "a great reception in the liberal community." While he recognized that the administration did not get the credit it deserved for establishing the commission and that many of the proposals were unrealistic, he did not "want to lose any capital" with the liberal community by "nit-picking the report." He suggested that "the president might accept the report with praise and use the opportunity to point out that he has been moving in the right direction all along."[20]

Commission members were disappointed by the president's lack of response and stung by the suggestion that the report did not praise LBJ's efforts and initiatives. Edward Brooke later described the commission members as "shocked and disappointed." Roy Wilkins shared Brooke's displeasure. "I felt that Mister Johnson should have received the commission and receive its report and thanked the commission in person," Wilkins reflected. He contrasted Johnson's response to the way Harry Truman reacted in 1947 to a report from a similar commission that advocated new federal laws to prevent lynching and to abolish poll taxes. That report, Wilkins said, "was just as revolutionary or shocking as the Kerner commission's assertion that white racism was at the basis of the racial difficulties in this country." Truman did not ignore the report; instead, he used it to develop legislation that he submitted in a special message to Congress in February 1948.[21]

Johnson's silence also worried Tex Thornton, who called the White House to say he feared that "the riot commission report may have embarrassed" the president. "He indicated," Califano wrote LBJ, "that he is in agreement with what you have proposed to the Congress and is troubled by the fact that some of the riot commission's proposals are not realistic (particularly in the jobs and housing fields)." His comments gave Califano "the distinct impression that Thornton might well question some of the program recommendations of the report in the near future publicly." Johnson scribbled at the bottom, "I agree." The president's cryptic response may have indicated that he was already aware of Thornton's objections and had some back channel to the businessman. But it could also simply have meant that he agreed with Califano's assessment of what Thornton might do.[22]

Ginsburg responded to the White House assertion that the report failed to laud Johnson's accomplishments by instructing commission staffer Henry Taliaferro Jr. to write a memorandum that pulled together all the references to the president and his leadership in the report. After listing all the references in a nine-page single-spaced document, Taliaferro stated that the "obvious truth is that President Johnson has provided the strongest leadership in the fight against racism and poverty." He also quoted from the introduction to the report's recommendations for national action, which seemed to implicitly support LBJ's approach: "All this serves to underscore our basic conclusion: the need is not so much for the government to design new programs as it is for the nation to generate new will."[23]

Gradually, and reluctantly, LBJ began adding nuggets of faint praise for the commission into his official remarks. On March 6, addressing banking officials, Johnson called the commissioners "a very distinguished group," which had produced "one of the most thorough and exhaustive studies ever made." He made clear, however, that he would not accept all their recommendations and criticized the commission for having spent "an unprecedented amount of money—millions of dollars in a period of several months."[24]

LBJ took a similar approach a few weeks later at a cabinet meeting, where he spoke for seven minutes about the report. He said that the commission and its staff "conducted a thorough study of the riots—their causes and solutions." He told the cabinet that he had asked the budget director to examine the commission's recommendations. But he then proceeded to explain why the commission's recommendations were not feasible, pointing out that they would cost $75–$100 billion over several years. By contrast, he believed that Congress was about to cut non-Vietnam expenditures by at least $5 billion, and those cuts would be even larger if the administration's proposed tax increase was not approved. He instructed cabinet members to analyze the feasibility of the Kerner Commission recommendations as they related to their departments, but he also warned them to plan for reductions. "If you get your allowance cut from $100 a month to $50 a month," he said, "you must know where to spend what's left."[25]

The president expanded on those comments on March 15 when he met privately with African American newspaper editors and publishers. While calling the commission's findings "the most important report made to me since I have been president," adding that the report "has more good than bad," he chastised the commissioners for not explaining how they planned to pay for their proposals. "It's like saying we need sirloin steaks three nights a week, but only have the money to pay for two steaks," Johnson declared. He told the group that some of the recommendations were simply not pragmatic. "The country will not vote for $80 billion, and there is no sense holding out false hopes or expectations." As president he had to be "more practical than some of those who wrote the report and some of the staff who sent it to me."[26]

Despite words of faint praise before selected audiences, in private LBJ continued to be furious with the commission. Johnson blamed Lindsay, in particular, for steering the commission in the wrong direction. In a March 13 phone call recorded by the White House taping system, LBJ told Chicago mayor Richard Daley that he did not "realize when I appointed Kerner that this son-of-a-bitch from New York, Lindsay, would take charge. He did take charge and he recommended I hire two-and-a-half million people on the federal payroll." Johnson said he had been reluctant to publicly criticize the commission because he did not want to embarrass Kerner. "At the same time," he concluded, "I couldn't embrace it because I've got a budget."[27]

On the same day that he vented to Daley about Lindsay, LBJ refused White House speechwriter Harry McPherson's request that he sign letters thanking the commissioners for their service. McPherson was careful to note that the letters were similar to those the president had sent to other task forces and other commissions. Signing them did not mean that he endorsed any of the recommendations or even that he was praising the report. The letters simply congratulated the members for making "an exhaustive" and "historic" report to the nation. The next day, Johnson told McPherson in a phone call, "I just can't sign this group of letters. I'd be a hypocrite." However, he also did not want anyone to know that he had refused to sign the letters. "Just file them—or get rid of them," he instructed. The letters were placed into an envelope with a note from the White House chief of files: "Do not release to anyone—do not open."[28]

At a March 22 press conference, LBJ finally addressed the report publicly, in response to a question planted by his staff. In response, LBJ called it "very thorough" and "very comprehensive." In long, meandering, and defensive remarks, he said the report made many good recommendations, but that he "did not agree" with all of them. "We think it was a good report made by good men of goodwill that will have a good influence." His advisers had wanted LBJ to be a little more effusive in his praise, but they were relieved the next day when both the *New York Times* ("Johnson Praises Report on Riots") and the *Washington Post* ("Johnson Says Riot Study Has Good Points") ran headlines suggesting the president endorsed the report.[29]

Califano believed the president could have saved himself a great deal of aggravation if he had made the March 22 statement at the time the report was released. White House speechwriter Ben Wattenberg agreed with Califano's assessment. The president "could have been very gracious about it all," he admitted. He could have praised the commissioners while distancing himself from their recommendations. "Instead, he chose to smolder in silence for a while."[30]

By late March, the press had stopped asking about the report, and Johnson could have continued to ignore it with few consequences. Why, then, did he speak up? Most likely, it was a dramatically changed political universe that prodded him to change course. Johnson was facing tough criticism from the liberal wing of his party leading up to the 1968 presidential campaign. On March 12, Minnesota senator Eugene McCarthy scored a psychological victory over Johnson in the nation's first primary in New Hampshire. His victory sent shock waves through the Democratic establishment. McCarthy's voters were both hawks and doves. They were united only in their rejection of Johnson's handling of the war. McCarthy, a strong opponent of the war, not only received 42 percent of the vote, a stunning figure against an incumbent president, but also won more delegates to the Democratic National Convention that summer.

LBJ's nemesis, New York senator Robert F. Kennedy, watched these developments from the sidelines. Many of RFK's young advisers had been pushing him to enter the race, but his brother and fellow senator Edward M. Kennedy and old JFK confidants like speechwriter Ted Sorenson had urged caution. Caught in the middle, Kennedy vacillated, hinting to aides at one moment that he would run and then telling reporters that he would not oppose Johnson. The Tet Offensive, and McCarthy's "victory" in New Hampshire, increased the pressure on RFK to run. But according to biographer Arthur Schlesinger Jr., it was Johnson's refusal to embrace the Kerner Commission report that tipped the balance. "This means," Kennedy said, "that he's not going to do anything about the war and he's not going to do anything about the cities either."[31]

A few days before he announced his entry into the race on March 16, Kennedy used a Senate hearing to chastise the White House for failing to embrace the Kerner Report. Kennedy had called Kerner, Lindsay, and Harris to testify about a job-training bill that was similar to one supported by the commission. "I would like to see the executive branch of the government—the president, members of the cabinet—say this program is a valid plan of action," RFK told them. "This is the greatest crisis to face the country in 100 years," he said. He felt that the previous summer, LBJ should have done more than call for a day of prayer and set up a commission. Now that the commission report was finished, in his view the White House was failing to show leadership. "I don't see how we can go along without the direction so urgently needed. We need the executive—the president—to support a program, to make concrete suggestions." He added, "We haven't had that at all."[32]

Despite his passionate following, Kennedy faced enormous obstacles on his way to the nomination. There were only seventeen primaries that year, and many of the filing deadlines had already passed. At the time, nearly 75 percent of delegates were chosen by local Democratic political leaders, many of them loyal to the Johnson administration. Kennedy's strategy was straightforward—attack Johnson from the left and sweep the primaries, drawing such large crowds and showing such support at the polls that the party bosses would have no choice but to support his nomination.[33]

JOHNSON HAD LEGITIMATE REASONS FOR feeling frustrated with the commission's findings. The commission, rather than relieving the political pressures he had faced during the summer of 1967, instead placed him in an even more untenable position. If he rejected the commission's recommendations, he would alienate the liberal base of the party; if he accepted them, he would anger the moderates and conservatives he needed to win the election. By 1968 a majority of the public had little appetite for expansive new social programs, and Congress was enacting cuts to many existing Great Society programs. No one applauded in the 1968 State of Union address when Johnson advocated for a tax increase and additional civil rights legislation. There were enthusiastic outbursts, however, when he denounced "rising crime and lawlessness."[34]

But Johnson overreacted, seeing in the report criticism of his administration that did not exist. In truth, the report reflected the concerns of mainstream liberals and mirrored some of the president's own views on race. The language of "two societies" and "white racism" may have seemed jarring, but it expressed assumptions that had informed Johnson's own thinking about race relations in America. In his famous speech at Howard University in June 1965, Johnson had spoken with uncharacteristic eloquence about the problems facing African Americans. He talked about "the great majority of Negro Americans" who represented "another nation" and confronted a widening "gulf." Blacks living in cities, he declared, represented "a separated people," who confronted the legacy of "white hatred." He went on to say that white America had to accept responsibility "for the breakdown of the Negro family structure."[35]

Moreover, Johnson's own administration had favorably reviewed the commission recommendations. Robert Weaver, the secretary of housing and urban development and the only black member of the cabinet, wrote the president that he found the report "a comprehensive, penetrating, and perceptive analysis." Secretary of Labor Willard Wirtz found "most of the employment recommendations desirable," although he pointed out that "many of them would require additional funds." The Office of Economic Opportunity "strongly" supported almost all of the commission's recommendations in the area of private employment, education, welfare, and housing. The Department of Commerce concurred that "a Federal strategy for the cities is needed," and the Department of the Army was already implementing many of the report's recommendations for controlling civil disturbances. Unlike the other agencies, it even concluded that most of the reforms "appear feasible within the existing Army budget."[36]

In many ways, it was the introduction's language about "white racism" that made the report appear more radical than it was. The policy proposals themselves were expansive but fairly conventional. Richard Nathan, an associate director of the commission, said the final report "presented an incremental, more-of-the-same strategy for social action." John Herbers, who covered the civil rights movement and the commission report for the *New York Times*, agreed that the report was less than radical. "Mostly they were extensions of what the federal government already was doing on a broad front of social and economic assistance to the disadvantaged," he noted.[37]

It is very possible that if the commission had followed the advice of James Corman—omitting or downplaying the program recommendations while producing a hard-hitting, data-rich report that identified "white racism" as the root cause of the riots—LBJ may have reacted differently. Johnson likely could have overcome his objections to some of the provocative language in the summary and the leaks, but not the long list of expensive social programs. Califano was unequivocal on this point in a 2017 interview. "Absolutely. Absolutely," he exclaimed. "There's no question about it. Johnson would have had a much different response to the Kerner Commission if that had been true. There's no question about that."[38]

In the end, the commission's decision to include recommendations for new social programs backfired. Having studied the problems of cities so closely and witnessed conditions firsthand, the commissioners were convinced that immediate and extensive action was needed beyond what was already being done, both to make people's lives better and to prevent more unrest. In their well-intended desire to provide a clear road map for change, the commission overestimated both the public's appetite for reform and the administration's ability to achieve it. It was shocking enough to white Americans to hear a group of establishment leaders identify "white racism" as the source of the riots and warn that America was becoming two separate societies. But the commission's advocacy for specific programs alienated the man who had done more for liberal causes than any president since Franklin Roosevelt. It's possible that the findings of "white racism" and "two societies" could have provided LBJ what he had wanted all along from his commission—an endorsement of the general direction and goals of the Great Society, without the burden of explaining the need for expensive new programs during a time of fiscal austerity and public backlash.

Johnson's response to the Kerner Commission also highlighted one of the weaknesses of his leadership: his tendency to personalize problems. To a great degree, LBJ rejected the report because it hurt his feelings. Both McPherson and Califano have acknowledged as much. "He shared most of the commission's goals," Califano wrote in his memoirs. "But he felt let down by Kerner and Ginsburg for not adequately recognizing what he had already done and for failing to point out sharply that Congress would not let him do more." McPherson agreed, saying years later that he attributed Johnson's "extreme negative" response to the commission report to the fact that it "hurt his pride. There wasn't enough said about what had been done in the last few years."[39]

The report fed LBJ's belief that liberals failed to appreciate his accomplishments and his paranoia that they were plotting to remove him from office. Throughout his presidency, LBJ whined incessantly that the liberal establishment never accepted him. He lumped the commission that he had created, whose members he chose, together with elites who had loved his slain predecessor and now appeared ready to abandon him in favor of the predecessor's younger brother. Despite passing the most ambitious social agenda since the New Deal, as he saw it, LBJ could not even get a group of hand-chosen supporters to trumpet his accomplishments. "The only difference between the [John F.] Kennedy assassination and mine," he lamented a few years earlier, "is that I am alive and it has been more torturous."[40]

Finally, the Kerner Commission represented a fatal blow to Johnson's "guns and butter" strategy. Since the summer of 1967, LBJ had been convinced that his administration faced perception problems at home and abroad that could easily be fixed through a public relations campaign. Despite growing antiwar sentiment, LBJ believed the nation was winning the war in Vietnam. Thus, he brought General William Westmoreland home in the fall of 1967 to reassure a skeptical public that there was "light at the end of the tunnel." But the Tet Offensive had revealed that Vietnam would not bend to optimistic words. In March Clark Clifford, the new secretary of defense, convened several foreign policy experts, dubbed "the wise men," who had staunchly supported LBJ's Vietnam policy. Despite General

Westmoreland's optimism, the experts, faced with new evidence, now concluded that Vietnam was a "bottomless pit." Johnson was furious. "The establishment bastards have bailed out," he said. Having lost public opinion and now the foreign policy establishment, Johnson faced the high probability that the war could not be won.[41]

In a similar way, LBJ had established the Kerner Commission to change the optics at home in the wake of a summer of urban unrest, only to have its report represent a second blow to his public relations strategy. Instead of building support for his aggressive domestic agenda and making clear the United States was winning the War on Poverty, the Kerner Report only underscored the depth of urban problems in America, the limited reach of Johnson's treasured Great Society programs, and the intense and widespread anger among urban residents that would not be easily quieted by modest reforms.

On the last day of March—just a month after the Kerner Commission released its report and just days after Johnson spoke about it publicly—a beleaguered and defeated LBJ announced that he would not seek reelection. Despite popular commentary to the contrary, the decision was not based on political calculation: Johnson truly did believe that he could secure the nomination and win the general election. But with his foreign policy in shambles and his domestic agenda shattered, LBJ felt that he simply had nothing left to fight for. "I've asked Congress for too much for too long, and they're tired of me," he told McPherson. "Abdication," wrote biographer Doris Kearns Goodwin, "was thus the last remaining way to restore control, to turn rout into dignity, collapse into order."[42]

Chapter 12

"THE MOST COURAGEOUS GOVERNMENT REPORT IN THE LAST DECADE"

O NCE LBJ LIFTED THE PUBLICATION embargo on February 28, news organizations had less than twenty-four hours to write their stories about the commission and its findings. Facing crushing deadlines, most reporters did not have time to read the abbreviated executive report that the commission staff had prepared for them and instead focused on the bold language in the summary at the front of the report. The response to those stark words, and to the report as a whole, exposed the new ideological fault lines emerging in American society. Liberals, prominent newspapers, civic leaders, and big city mayors hailed it; conservative pundits and white religious leaders, especially in the South, condemned it for failing to hold rioters responsible for the unrest. Most prominent civil rights leaders embraced it, but many average African Americans expressed understandable skepticism that anything would change. Since it was released in the beginning of the presidential election season, the report produced reactions from potential candidates on both the left and the right.

In Congress its practical impact was limited, but the report did provide needed ammunition for those advocating on behalf of a stalled open-housing bill.

A FEW HOURS AFTER LBJ lifted the embargo on February 29, Fred Harris received a call from an Associated Press reporter who needed to get something on the wire in thirty minutes. "It's a madhouse around here, and I'm having to write a story without time to even read the summary fully," Harris recalled him saying. Given the truncated schedule, major newspapers focused on the language about "two societies" and "white racism." The front-page headline in the *Los Angeles Times* screamed "City Riots Laid to White Racism." Its lead sentence effectively captured the essence of the summary: "A presidential commission reported Thursday that 'white racism' rather than black agitation, is responsible for city rioting and for a deepening division within U.S. society that 'threatens the future of every American.'" The *New York Times* headline read "Panel on Civil Disorders Calls for Drastic Action to Avoid 2-Society Nation." The *Baltimore Evening Sun* editorialized that the claim of "white racism" was "calculated to shock and it does."[1]

The summary's bold declarations framed the initial stories, but over the next forty-eight hours, the report's details received extensive coverage in newspapers and magazines and on television. There were twenty separate stories in the *Boston Globe* on Friday, March 1. On Sunday, March 3, the television networks provided eight hours of coverage. *Life* devoted half of its March 4 issue to the report, and it was featured on the cover of *Newsweek*. On Sunday, March 3, Fred Harris, Roy Wilkins, and Otto Kerner appeared on an expanded one-hour edition of ABC's *Issues and Answers*. At the same time, NBC's *Meet the Press* featured interviews with mayors of cities that had experienced riots. The following morning, Harris and Edward Brooke appeared on NBC's *Today*. Both NBC and CBS also produced one-hour specials based on the report. All the major news magazines offered extensive coverage.[2]

Meanwhile, the report itself became a best seller. The commission turned to Bantam Books to publish the report after the federal government's own publisher, the Government Printing Office, said that it would take three to four weeks to print the report. Bantam put the 708-page book on sale at four o'clock on March 3 for $1.25. Their edition included an introduction by Tom Wicker, Washington bureau chief of the *New York Times*, who praised LBJ for ignoring the demands that he fill the commission with "black radicals, militant youth or even academic leftists" and instead appointing "moderate" and "responsible" establishment figures to the commission. "A commission made up of militants, or even influenced by them, could not conceivably have spoken with a voice so effective," he observed. Bantam planned a first printing of 250,000 copies, which they quickly increased to 740,000 copies. Still, demand exceeded supply. The book sold 300,000 copies in its first three days and nearly 1 million copies in the first two weeks. It became the fastest-selling book since Jacqueline Susann's *Valley of the Dolls* in 1966.[3]

Many civic and religious organizations took the report's recommendations to heart. The New York Roman Catholic diocese asked the archbishop to buy 50,000 copies and distribute them to all the schools, churches, and Catholic organizations within the diocese. The United Presbyterian Church bought 3,000 copies and sent them to all their pastors working in urban areas. The Chicago Board of Education made it required reading for teachers. In the low-income, racially mixed Bushwick neighborhood in Brooklyn, New York, priests and ministers bought 8,000 copies at wholesale prices and resold them to community residents at the same price. The National Council of Catholic Bishops used the report to develop their own draft proposals for solving urban problems. The National Council of Churches called the findings "courageous" and pledged that the federation would give "vigorous support" to implement the recommendations. The Anti-Defamation League of B'nai B'rith declared that it stood "squarely behind" the analysis and recommendations in the report.[4]

Local communities and major corporations also moved to implement some of the report's recommendations. In Seattle the mayor convened a thousand community leaders and set up a series of seminars to discuss how the city could implement the commission's ideas. On New York's Long Island, community leaders gathered to discuss ways of opening the suburbs to African Americans. Local leaders in other cities—Detroit, Newark, and Charlottesville, among others— undertook similar actions. Business groups publicized new diversity and employment initiatives, tying them to the report. Xerox announced an ambitious new program to "seek out, train and productively employ members of minority groups." The company said that it felt compelled "to accept the indictment of the National Advisory Commission on Civil Disorders," allowing that it shared "the responsibility for a color divided nation; and in all honesty, we need not look beyond our own doorstep to find out why." The National Alliance of Businessmen, headed by Henry Ford II, said that it would attempt to fulfill the commission's demand to help those out of work. They planned to find one hundred thousand permanent jobs for the hard-core unemployed and, if possible, another two hundred thousand summer jobs to help teenagers stay busy during the summer.[5]

More broadly, however, the public reaction to the report split along the geographic and cultural dividing lines that would become increasingly familiar to Americans in the years and decades to follow. The divisions highlighted the challenges Democrats faced as they tried to maintain a coalition that included liberals, African Americans, urban residents, and working-class whites. Economic distress during the 1930s had forged an uneasy alliance among these disparate groups. By the 1960s, however, many forces were driving them apart, but it was the urban unrest that began with Watts and culminated in Newark and Detroit that threatened to tear apart that coalition and unravel the consensus liberalism that it had sustained for three decades. The Kerner Report captured the belief among many liberal intellectuals, national media organizations, African Americans, and civic organizations that the federal government should play an aggressive role in combating the underlying conditions that caused the riots. Many white voters, however, complained that the commission's conclusions failed to address their fears of social disorder. Whether they were southern Protestants, working-class ethnics, or part of the masses that had fled to the suburbs, white voters rejected the assumptions that informed the commission report and increasingly viewed pleas for more federal spending on cities as an effort to reward rioters. They felt under assault from young people and antiwar protesters who questioned their deeply held assumptions about patriotism, but race and urban unrest became the vortex around which many of their social discontents revolved. Once loyal members of LBJ consensus, these voters now looked to the Republican Party to represent their interests, and GOP leaders were ready to oblige.

National news organizations, including the three television networks and major newspapers like the *New York Times* and the *Washington Post*, were sympathetic to both the diagnosis and the prescriptions for reform. The *New York Times* said that the report "offers a realistic promise of swifter advance toward a society of equal opportunity." "The report of the riot commission splits the darkness like a flash of lightning," editorialized the *Washington Post*. It called the report "a distinguished, powerful and potentially useful document" that told the truth with "stark candor." The *Christian Science Monitor* opined that "with courage and perception," the commission showed "how American society as a whole can get back onto a sane, healthy course toward a 'more perfect union.'"[6]

Big-city mayors and civic groups praised the report. The mayors of major American cities who experienced riots over the previous two summers endorsed the report. They included the mayors of Newark, Detroit, Cleveland, Atlanta, and Los Angeles. The Chicago City

Council passed a resolution calling it an "outstanding report of unparalleled importance." The National League of Cities called the report "a remarkably thorough and thoughtful probe into what has become America's foremost domestic problem."[7]

Surprisingly, only a handful of members of Congress expressed support. Liberal Republican senator Charles Percy of Illinois rose on the Senate floor, saying that the report "offers great potential in contributing to the solution of our urban problems, and perhaps its greatest value lies in the dialogue the commission hopes to stimulate among all citizens." He was joined by only a handful of Senate liberals. In the House of Representatives, only thirty-six members said they were ready to vote for its recommendations. It seems likely that even most liberals, sensitive to the growing public backlash against many Great Society initiatives, were unwilling to support expensive new social programs and to do so while the nation was spending billions in Vietnam. Others, realizing that the White House was cool to the report, did not want to alienate the president during an election year.[8]

Civil rights leaders had mixed reactions. Many were pleased with the tone of the report and with the conclusion that white racism was to blame for the conditions that produced the riots. "We're on our way to reaching the moment of truth," said Floyd McKissick, national director of the Congress of Racial Equality (CORE). "It's the first-time whites said: 'We're racists.'" Martin Luther King Jr., who was vacationing in Jamaica when the report was released, sent a telegram to Kerner, praising the commission's finding that "America is a racist society and that white racism is the root cause of today's urban disorders" and calling it "an important confession of a harsh truth." He was cautiously optimistic that "white America and our national government will heed your warnings and implement your recommendations." Whitney Young, executive director of the National Urban League, told reporters that "the answer to whether we have riots this summer depends on whether the Nation adopts the cures recommended by the commission." Walter E. Fauntroy, the Washington director of the Southern Christian Leadership Conference, believed that it was an important step for the commission to identify white racism as the heart of the problem. He was hopeful that "this will be the occasion for serious soul-searching on the part of individual Americans." H. Rap Brown, who was in jail in New Orleans for inciting a riot, released a message through his lawyer, commenting on the commission's decision to frame the report in terms of white racism. "The members of the commission," he said, "should be put in jail under $100,000 bail each because they're saying essentially what I've been saying."[9]

Not all black leaders praised the report. Some African American leaders complained that it did not go far enough in its recommendations for preventing future riots. Bayard Rustin, a pacifist and civil rights strategist, found the recommendations too timid and too bound by conventional liberalism. He said it was "silly" for the commission to call for only about a third of the new jobs that he believed were needed. The report, he claimed, "failed to declare unequivocally that the government must be the employer of first and last resort for the hard-core poor." He also argued that the report did not go far enough to condemn institutionalized racism. James Farmer, the former National Director of CORE, noted that identifying "white racism" was not enough. It was, he wrote, "much more important to empower the powerless communities." A director of the Philadelphia branch of CORE echoed the sentiment, complaining that the Kerner Report "seems to be directing us to the melting pot theory to which too many black people are already oversubscribed."[10]

At the grassroots, many African Americans viewed it as more of the same and were less hopeful than most national civil rights leaders that anything in the report would impact their lives. The *New York Amsterdam News* sent reporters out to talk to the "average man on the street" to get the reaction of local African American leaders. Ellis Douglass, a church usher, told the reporters that "the commission didn't tell us anything new, but it could be helpful if the government itself decides on the seriousness of it." Another man dismissed it as just "another one of their studies." The problem with government studies, he observed, is "they keep telling us what we know."[11]

The *Philadelphia Inquirer* found a similar reaction. Some blacks were pleased that a high-profile government commission affirmed and documented that "white racism" was at the root of the ghettos. "The trouble all along has been that white people have not been informed or have been misinformed," said Andrew Freeman, executive director of the Urban League of Philadelphia. "The best feature of the report," he said, "is that it lays bare the extent of the prejudice and racism among whites." Most, however, agreed with William Mathis, the executive director of the City Commission on Human Relations, when he called the report "a propaganda piece—the same old trick bag they've handed us before. It is full of empty promises." Others contended that the report "only says what we've been saying all along." The chairman of the "Freedom Now" organization summed up the sense of urgency among African Americans: "Black people have no more confidence whatsoever in commissions, reports or white papers that tell them things they already know. Somebody had better start coming up with some solutions, and I don't mean tanks and riot guns."[12]

Many scholars, some of whom had served as consultants to the commission, claimed that the report let white America off the hook. "Racism is a word customarily and popularly used to describe the more blatant examples of discrimination," Tommy Tomlinson, a commission consultant, told reporters. In its modern version, racism had "become exquisitely complex and subtle," so that while there was "virtually no area of American life" that was free of racism, most Americans did not think of themselves as prejudiced. He felt that the commission had not only failed to document prejudice so that whites would recognize it in themselves, but also failed to provide a strategy for addressing it. Gary T. Marx, the social scientist who helped write "The Harvest of American Racism," told the 1968 annual meeting of the American Political Science Association that the Kerner Report was "perhaps the most significant and far reaching statement of a programmatic nature ever made by a governmental unit on American race relations." But like Tomlinson, he complained that the commission did not adequately explain what it meant by the term "white racism." "Because it accuses everyone it accuses no one," he wrote, pointing out that there were "vast differences" between individual and institutional racism. He also pointed out that the final report failed to mention one of the central findings of "Harvest"—that riots can have beneficial effects by creating black solidarity in poor communities and in forcing local officials to change policies that discriminate against blacks.[13]

Social scientist Robert Fogelson, also a consultant to the commission, observed that the report made the mistake of viewing "the riots as reactions rather than protest, the rioters as victims rather than demonstrators, and racial unrest as a manifestation of problems which can be resolved within the existing institutional structure." What was necessary were not minor changes in existing programs "but drastic changes in income distribution." He also argued that the commission neglected to address the issue of institutional discrimination against African Americans. "All things considered, the Kerner Commission did a good, but not splendid job," he concluded. While he criticized the commission for being too conventional, he was aware of the practical limitations, pointing out that a more radical approach "would probably have been rejected outright by most Americans."[14]

As Lindsay had predicted, some critics scolded the commission for failing to confront the relationship between the war in Vietnam and the racial crisis at home. While claiming that the commission had produced "the most courageous government report in the last decade," *Washington Post* columnist Drew Pearson chastised the commissioners for not dealing with the reality of limited resources. "Money cannot go to the Vietnam War and the race war at the same time," he wrote. Presidential candidate Eugene McCarthy, who made opposition to the war the centerpiece of his campaign, told crowds that the nation "cannot wage the war in Vietnam and at the same time alleviate the hopelessness that leads to riots." Cleveland mayor Carl Stokes, the first African American mayor of a major city, said that Congress used Vietnam as an excuse for doing little to help urban areas. Forced to choose between the two, he said on NBC's *Meet the Press,* "you have to take care of home first."[15]

The angriest response to the report came from conservative newspapers, Republicans, southern Democrats, and disaffected whites. Some complained that the commission's recommendations were too costly and would expand an already bloated federal bureaucracy. "The answer to every problem seems to be to spend more of the taxpayers' money. There just isn't enough money to go around," complained Mississippi Democrat William Colmer. "I do not believe that the expenditures of great sums of money will solve the problem," a constituent wrote House Speaker Carl Albert. "In fact, I think it will make the situation much worse in a very short time. This creeping welfare and socialistic trend is bad for all people." Texas Democrat and LBJ loyalist George Mahon echoed LBJ's objections that the commission failed to put a price tag on its proposals or suggest how they would pay for them. He predicted that the commission's recommendation would require a 50 to 100 percent tax surcharge.[16]

Conservatives also maintained that the report's "two societies" language overlooked the great strides that had been made in recent years toward achieving a color-blind society. The *Washington Star* editorialized that the statement about "two societies" may have been true "15 years ago, when segregation was the order of the day." In the past few years, however, "there was a significant movement toward one society." The *Alexandria (VA) Gazette* complained that the report "speaks the language of class warfare." It claimed that the "natural movement of all Americans is toward cooperation and mutual assistance." Conservative columnist James J. Kilpatrick argued that for the previous three decades, "our nation has not been moving toward a separate society, but away from it."[17]

Conservative religious leaders charged that the report failed to identify the real cause of the riots—the moral decay in American society. Evangelist Billy Graham told reporters that the report "illustrates the great failures of our national leadership to understand the basic cause of all our problems from Vietnam to racial tensions." The "basic problems" are not poverty or racism, he said, but "a diseased human nature filled with lust, hate, greed and pride."[18]

Critics on the right dismissed any connection between poverty and unrest. The *Wall Street Journal* called "grossly simplistic" the suggestion that poverty and racial prejudice caused the riots. There were less poverty and less discrimination in the 1960s than at any time in the past, the paper noted. "Why then no riots a decade ago and lots of riots now?" The *Alexandria Gazette* accused the report of exaggerating the role of discrimination and segregation as a source of the riots. They were, the editorial stated, "natural factors of minor importance" that the Johnson administration emphasized "to placate the black Marxist element of the Democratic consensus."[19]

Many opponents on the right resented the suggestion that society in general, and not those who rioted, was responsible for the disorders. The *Washington Star* noted that it was "regrettable that the report does not put as much emphasis on forthrightly condemning riots and rioters as it does on offering excuses for them." The *Chicago Tribune* insisted that "the blame" for the riots "must be placed on those who have been preaching anarchy, telling people they can violate laws which they feel are wrong, and encouraging Negroes to believe that all their troubles are the fault of somebody else."[20]

Many of these detractors believed that the solution for stopping the riots was not to spend more money but to crack down on lawlessness. Virginia Democrat Watkins Abbitt told his fellow congressmen that law and order needed to be maintained to prevent more "disorder blackmail." Senator James O. Eastland from Mississippi said, "I do not believe that civil disorders and riots can be explained on the basis of some form of legitimate social expression. A return to respect for law and order must precede any meaningful social change." "No reasonable man can dispute that Negroes have legitimate grievances," a reader wrote the *Chicago Tribune*. "But to use these grievances as an excuse to riot is parallel to a college student using rejection by a fraternity as an excuse to burn down the campus."[21]

Politicians couched their dissent in concerns about expanding federal power and law and order, but many ordinary voters resorted to blatant racism. "The average Negro is lazy and without ambition," a woman wrote Governor Kerner. "By and large, the only Negroes with an average degree of intelligence are those with a fairly high percentage of white blood," opined another. "I've lived among them, and his friends, and I know whereof I speak." After reading some of the letters, Kerner remarked, in a speech shortly after the release of the report, "I need look no further than my incoming mail to note that there are Americans as fully prejudiced as our commission found them to be." A writer from South Carolina said the problem was simple. "The inherent difference between Whites and Negroes: a difference Made by God when he created the two races." Blacks, he wrote, have "reverted to human mad dogs and savages and should be treated as such. . . . Only an abject Fool would offer any objection to shooting a mad dog."[22]

Polls revealed a deep racial divide in perceptions of the report. Most whites rejected the claim that white racism was responsible for the riots; a majority of blacks supported it. While 45 percent of whites accepted the idea that the government should give cities enough aid to rehabilitate the slums, only 23 percent were willing to pay higher taxes to accomplish the goal. By contrast, 91 percent of African Americans supported additional aid for housing, and 66 percent were willing to pay higher taxes. Most African Americans believed that police brutality was a major cause of the riots. Only 10 percent of whites shared that opinion. By a two-to-one margin, whites disagreed with the commission's conclusion that the riots were not organized. By the same margin, whites disagreed that the federal government should increase welfare payments. Nevertheless, there was agreement on some issues. Large majorities of whites and blacks agreed that there should be more African American police officers in minority neighborhoods, that blacks should have a greater voice in shaping programs that affected their communities, and that most white people did not know "what the misery and poverty is like in Negro ghettos."[23]

Like the nation itself, the Johnson administration found itself deeply divided in its reaction to the report. LBJ's Commission on Civil Rights called it "a challenging and significant document which should awaken the American people to the urgency of our domestic crisis." Secretary of Labor W. Willard Wirtz told reporters that he believed "deeply that this report is right." On the day the report came out, Hubert Humphrey praised it, saying that "it pointed up the need for a tremendous, coordinated, massive program of rehabilitation and national action." Three days later, he apparently changed his mind—or, more likely, LBJ instructed him to change his mind. Humphrey now cautioned against "condemning whole societies" and claimed the charge that whites condoned slums came "dangerously close to group guilt." Wilbur Cohen, the president's choice to be the new secretary of health, education, and welfare, delivered the administration's toughest attack. Cohen said the report used "slogans" to deal with complex problems. It put too little emphasis on how the poor could lift "themselves up by their own bootstraps." Cohen's attack brought a sharp rebuke from David Ginsburg, who wrote, "No one who had read that Report, and wanted to describe it, could have said what you said."[24]

THE JOHNSON ADMINISTRATION MAY HAVE struggled to articulate a clear message about the report, but potential adversaries for the presidency did not. Former vice president Richard Nixon had launched his campaign on February 2, 1968, in New Hampshire. Just six years earlier, after losing a race for California governor, Nixon had told reporters, "You won't have Nixon to kick around anymore, because, gentlemen, this is my last press conference." But in the years following archconservative Republican senator Barry Goldwater's defeat for the presidency in 1964, Nixon had reinvented himself as a centrist and racial moderate who could appeal to both the liberal and the conservative wings of the Republican Party. In keeping with his centrist strategy, Nixon had avoided talking about the previous summer's riots during the first months of the campaign. He had been attempting to walk a fine line between appealing to angry white voters while also being presentable to northern moderates.

But in March, Nixon, picking up on the largely hostile reaction of whites to the Kerner Commission's report, began selling himself as a conservative populist rather than as a racial moderate. In doing so, he tapped into an evolving Republican critique of American liberalism. For the past few years, conservatives had been condemning the riots and criticizing liberals for being soft on crime, but the commission report provided Nixon and his allies with an obvious foil—and it conveniently did so at the beginning of the presidential election cycle. Republicans jumped on the opportunity to highlight the differences between liberal and conservative views on law and order. It was proof, they argued, that liberals coddled criminals and failed to understand the frustrations and anxiety of the white middle class. Even worse, liberals blamed the white suburban middle class for the riots. Hoping to capitalize on the growing backlash, Nixon once again reinvented himself.

Campaigning in New Hampshire in the days immediately after the report's release, he sharpened his appeal to the "silent majority." During a March 7 radio interview, Nixon complained that "the major weakness of the presidential commission is that it, in effect, blames everybody for the riots except the perpetrators of the riots." The following night, Nixon went even further, claiming that the government should meet "force with force, if necessary," and provide "retaliation against the perpetrators and planners of violence."[25]

Nixon's domestic advisers scoured the report for campaign-trail ammunition. Economist and GOP adviser Martin Anderson claimed that the report included "a fairly good description of the problems of the urban ghettos" but that its conclusion about white racism causing the riots was dead wrong. "The report clearly implies that our whole social structure is racist," he wrote, "that white people are almost solely to blame for the riots, and that we must tax ourselves so that the federal government will have enough money to pour billions into the urban ghettos." This sent the wrong message to poor blacks. "Any rational Negro who calls himself a man will revolt against such a system—by violent means if necessary," he wrote four days after the publication of the commission report. Nixon adviser Alan Greenspan agreed that the report seemed to rationalize violence. Liberals, he wrote, suggest that "the rioters had reasons—implicitly rational reasons—for their actions," which was unacceptable. "There is no conceivable moral justification for violence in a free society. This is not Nazi Germany or the Soviet Union. All citizens have the means to achieve their ends through political persuasion." Greenspan believed that the report provided Nixon with a new ideological weapon to use against the candidate the former vice president feared most— Robert F. Kennedy. Liberals needed to be asked "whether violence is unequivocally wrong," he wrote. "Does RFK consider violence in a free society morally justified or not?"[26]

Nixon aide J. Pat Rooney expressed some of the same criticisms that Robert Conot had made while the commission was debating its programmatic recommendations. He claimed that more government programs would contribute to a "psychological castration" of blacks. "The Negroes," Rooney wrote Nixon on March 8, "feel that they are not in control of their own bodies, their own lives. They feel that they must conform to the rules of the white man's society, even when the white man is trying to help them." Rooney, however, went further and took the same concept and used it to support a traditional conservative message. The commission's recommendations for expanded government programs, he argued, would exacerbate the problem by deepening black resentment and allowing them to remain beholden to Washington, and thus unable to develop the personal skills necessary for becoming productive members of society.[27]

Nixon's response stood in sharp contrast to that of one of his potential rivals for the Republican nomination: California governor Ronald Reagan. Both men appealed to white suburban voters but used different messages that reflected their contrasting personalities. The dark and brooding Nixon based his appeal on fear, while the sunny and optimistic Reagan tapped into both idealism and anxiety. Initially, the governor took a measured approach to the report. On March 30, however, Reagan told a gathering of California Republicans that they needed to take seriously the report's indictment of "white racism." "You and I know that many of today's problems are the result of the prejudice that has divided mankind from the very beginning," he said. He challenged conservatives to "take an interest" and to "make a difference" in the fight for equal rights. "We can insure equal rights and equal opportunity and equal treatment for all our citizens. We can do this by becoming involved in this great problem." Reagan's political genius was his ability to link liberal ideals with conservative policies. He managed to accept the charge of "white racism" and to embrace the goals of the report, while at the same time reaffirming his belief in small government and rejecting nearly all of the report's recommendations.[28]

Many other leading Republicans took a position like Reagan's: embrace the commission's message, reject the proposed solution. The approach offered a way of appealing to more moderate voters who opposed the report's conclusions but who also did not want to be labeled as racists. On March 7, House minority leader Gerald Ford told a gathering of public relations executives that he agreed with the commission's dire warning that "we have been moving toward a polarization of the two races, a division of the races into two war-ring camps." It was, he declared, "something that needed saying" and represented "the commission's greatest contribution." The warn-ing "should stir every American right down to his toes." He only disagreed with the commission's recommendation that the problem could be solved solely through massive federal spending. The report contained an "exaggerated emphasis on the role of the federal govern-ment," he declared, "and pays insufficient attention . . . to the private sector." The commission, he charged, advocated that "billions upon billions of federal dollars be poured on top of the billions that have failed to reach the poor under Great Society programs." Ironically, given how thoroughly the commission report angered the White House, Ford viewed it as a political document that endorsed "present and proposed Johnson administration programs."[29]

The response of leading Republican candidates for president re-vealed how the Kerner Commission report played in the evolving conservative narrative about urban unrest and the failures of consen-sus liberalism. Republican leaders adopted different tones, but they successfully conflated urban unrest with federal overreach and placed blame squarely on the Johnson administration and the consensus lib-eralism that it espoused.

ON APRIL 2, FRED HARRIS sent a letter to Otto Kerner, stating that he wanted to reconvene the commission, "to assess and discuss reaction to the report and respond to some of the mistaken criti-cism of it." The next night, Martin Luther King Jr.—who was in Memphis to support garbage workers—spoke to supporters there, saying, "I may not get there with you, but we as a people will get to the Promised Land." The following day, while King was standing on the balcony of the Lorraine Motel, an escaped convict named James Earl Ray fired a single rifle shot that ripped through King's jaw and severed an artery. "When white America killed Dr. King," declared Stokely Carmichael, "she declared war on us." Johnson knew that cities would erupt. After learning the news of King's death, Johnson remarked, "Everything we've gained in the last few years we're going to lose tonight."[30]

The debate over the Kerner Report came to a sudden and violent end, as rioting engulfed more than one hundred cities and towns across the nation. Once again, the president was forced to call out the regular army and the National Guard. Rioters burned twenty blocks in Chicago, where Mayor Daley ordered police to "shoot to kill." The worst violence occurred in Washington, DC, where seven hundred fires burned and nine people lost their lives. For the first time since the Civil War, armed soldiers guarded the steps to the Capitol. Nationally, the death toll was forty-six. "Martin's memory is being desecrated," said one black leader. General Westmoreland, in town for meetings, recalled that the capital "looked worse than Saigon did at the height of the Tet Offensive." LBJ managed to keep a sense of humor. When told that Carmichael was leading a group to burn down Georgetown—the center of the liberal establishment that LBJ resented—the president responded, "Goddamn! I've waited thirty-five years for this day!"[31]

Any hope of racial conciliation, of convincing a majority of white people to accept responsibility for the plight of poor blacks, however slim, died that night. Many whites condemned the assassination and the violence that followed, viewing both as proof of the deep racial divide that had been so well documented in the report. For most whites, however, the riots highlighted the need for tougher law enforcement. The violence that followed King's death made them less sympathetic to appeals for racial justice and less willing to endorse the kinds of social programs recommended in the Kerner Report. There would be no increase in federal spending for education, no Marshall Plan for the cities, no more discussion among prominent public leaders about "white racism." Following the April riots, two separate societies seemed desirable to most white Americans. The spasm of violence emboldened the advocates of a "get-tough" approach to rioters and smothered the report's ambitious agenda in an avalanche of white resentment and anger.

In the wake of the renewed rioting, Lindsay joined Harris in calling for an emergency meeting of the commission members to figure out ways of pushing the president and Congress to act on the recommendations in their report, which they viewed as more essential than ever. On April 9, Lindsay claimed that Kerner agreed to hold a meeting "in the next several days." But the White House moved to quash their plans. Califano instructed Ginsburg to call Kerner and tell him "to cool it off." Califano then assured the president there would be no further meetings of the commission. On April 24, Kerner issued a statement that "the commission has fulfilled its mission as outlined by the president and no further meetings are contemplated on the part of the chairman." Califano forwarded Kerner's letter to the president with a cover letter, stating, "I hope the attached closes out the Kerner commission problem."[32]

THE KERNER COMMISSION, WHICH LBJ had created to help forge consensus on how to deal with the unrest, had now issued a report that seemed to harden differences and intensify racial hostility. It widened the gap between black and white and provided fodder to Republicans, who used its recommendations as a political weapon against Democrats. Nevertheless, there were some changes that the commissioners might legitimately think of as successes.

Given White House hostility and congressional indifference, the report failed to produce a harvest of new legislation. But legislation alone cannot judge the short-term impact. The executive director of the International Association of Chiefs of Police credited the commission's recommendations for helping police departments to respond to the riots that followed the King assassination. "There is no question that the lessons learned from the report by the police and National Guard made it possible to handle the riots which sprang up" after King's death, he observed. "I believe considerable credit for the collection and dissemination of meaningful lessons belongs to the commission and the work it stimulated."[33]

The report forced the press to engage in self-examination. After King's assassination, the *Columbia Journalism Review* surveyed television coverage and concluded that broadcasters had taken to heart the commission's recommendations regarding the responsibilities of the media and passed the test "more than satisfactorily." It found that newspaper and television executives agreed that their efforts had been inadequate and that the commission's criticisms that they focused too much on violence and not enough on the underlying conditions that led to the unrest were well founded. The same survey showed that newspapers and magazines, along with radio and television stations, were making efforts to increase the hiring of African Americans and to expand and improve their coverage of black life in the cities. CBS, for example, aired a seven-part series of one-hour specials called *Black America* during the summer of 1968. New York governor Nelson Rockefeller announced the formation of a committee to help blacks and Puerto Ricans find jobs in journalism and to promote more balanced coverage of racial affairs. A few universities created courses on urban reporting. Newspapers made more serious efforts to cover black life and urban problems. The *Kansas City Star* printed a special section on black history, and the *Oakland Tribune* started running a new column called "On Being Black."[34]

The commission report also played an important role in passage of the Fair Housing Act in 1968. President Johnson had first introduced the legislation in 1966. That year Senate liberals fell 10 votes short of securing the two-thirds majority needed to end a filibuster by imposing cloture. The following year, they suffered defeat by a similar margin. Conservatives passionately opposed the bill. Louisiana senator Allen Ellender, who had led the opposition to the 1964 Civil Rights Act, declared that the bill represented "the ultimate in social extravagance in the United States." He charged that "every cherished liberty" would be "trampled underfoot" if the legislation became law.

North Carolina's senator Sam Ervin, a Bible-quoting constitutional conservative who would earn fame and admiration a few years later as chairman of the Senate Watergate Committee, claimed that the legislation was designed "to bring about equality by robbing all Americans of their basic rights of private property."[35]

Minnesota's Walter Mondale led the fight for a cloture vote in 1968. If all members voted on the motion, he needed the support of 67 of the 100 senators to end debate and move forward to a vote on the bill itself. On February 20, after five weeks of debate, the Senate showed unexpected support for the open-housing amendment, but the cloture vote still fell short. Mondale worked out a compromise with minority leader Everett Dirksen to water down the original legislation. On March 1, Mondale failed for the third time to win a cloture vote. Open housing was in grave danger and possibly doomed.[36]

The Kerner Commission report breathed new energy into the movement for passage. The *Washington Post* and other newspapers used the report's ominous warning to renew their call for fair housing. "The Commission," it editorialized, "has made the clinching argument for open housing." Senate liberals, including commission members Fred Harris and Edward Brooke, referenced the report's evidence to add weight to their appeal for passage. "Rarely," Mondale told his colleagues, "is a report as timely as this one." Mondale placed into evidence a statement signed by fourteen business leaders who supported the bill. Among those who signed was Tex Thornton, who had been an outspoken critic of open-housing legislation while on the commission. On March 4, the cloture motion won by exactly the two-thirds vote of those present and voting. On March 11, the filibuster broken, the Senate passed the open-housing bill by a vote of 70 to 20.[37]

The action then shifted to the House, where the legislation faced an uncertain future. The House had already passed its own version of the legislation. Supporters of the bill wanted the House to accept the Senate version without change, but most Republicans and conservative Democrats insisted that the bill should go to conference, which would have slowed down, if not killed, the legislation. The fate of the bill rested in the hands of the Rules Committee. On April 9, the committee met while the funeral services for Martin Luther King Jr. were taking place.

Most observers expected the committee to vote to send the bill to conference. But in a surprising move, John B. Anderson, a forty-six-year-old conservative who had supported Barry Goldwater and was on record opposing fair housing, switched his vote. By an 8–7 tally, the committee defeated a motion that would have opened the way for the bill to be sent to the Senate-House conference. "John Anderson was the real hero," said Maryland's Charles M. Mathias, who led a small bloc of Republican liberals and moderates who supported the bill. Anderson followed his vote with an eloquent speech. "I legislate not out of fear," he said, "but out of concern for the America I love."[38]

Like everyone else, Anderson had been shocked both by King's assassination and by the violence that followed. He believed that, in the wake of those events, the federal government needed to take steps to reassure African Americans that they were sympathetic to their concerns. But Anderson also credited the Kerner Commission report for swaying him to change his position on open housing. After reading the entire report, he "emerged convinced that we are living in a time of crisis today that threatens the very salvation of our democratic system." On April 10, with the motion to move to conference defeated, the House voted 250 to 171 to approve the Senate's version of the open-housing bill.[39]

These short-term victories—more effective policing, improved media coverage, and passage of the Fair Housing Act—were significant for the commission's report, but its long-term legacy is less clear. Lindsay and Harris had fought for a summary that would grab attention and generate flashy headlines. Soon they began to worry that reporters were focusing only on the report's most provocative language and ignoring its detailed descriptions of the problems facing America's cities. Harris recalled that he knew the commission had a perception problem after talking to his father, a small farmer in southwestern Oklahoma who had worked hard his whole life and had little to show for it. Based on the media reports he had seen, his father interpreted the report as saying, "You should pay more taxes to help out the black people who are rioting in Detroit." That did not make a lot of sense to his dad. "I'm already paying a lot in taxes and getting nothing for it," he responded. "Why doesn't someone pay attention to me? Is it because I'm not rioting?"[40]

Lindsay was probably right in believing it necessary to include striking language in the summary about "two societies" and "white racism" to ensure that the report would garner the attention it deserved. But the downside to this strategy was that the summary distracted attention from the heart of the report—the thoughtful narrative about the cause of the riots and the detailed, statistical evidence to support the existence of persistent discrimination. Lindsay and Harris assumed that racism persisted because most middle-class whites were unaware that it existed, and they thought that if confronted with clear evidence that discrimination imposed undue hardship on African Americans, white suburbanites would embrace new social programs, accept higher taxes, and demand more aggressive efforts to integrate their communities. "I believe that white people in America are decent people," Harris told the *New York Times* in February 1968, and that "if they can be shown the terrible conditions in which other Americans live and how this threatens our society, they will join together to try to solve these problems." The nation had mustered the political and moral will to pass groundbreaking civil rights legislation guaranteeing African Americans basic civil and political rights in the recent past. Now, he believed, it was time to finish the civil rights revolution by addressing the institutional racism that confined blacks to marginal jobs and imprisoned them in the poorest neighborhoods.[41]

But there was little reason to believe that Lindsay's strategy would work. The sensational language in the report was certainly distracting, but it also seems unlikely that evidence-based arguments would have been effective. The fact was that whites saw public policy as a zero-sum game where policies intended to help blacks would hurt them. Polls showed that whites by overwhelming majorities opposed federal efforts to integrate schools or housing. White opponents to change benefited from the very institutional racism under which blacks suffered. Furthermore, whites invoked the deeply held American values of individual rights and local control to justify their privilege. Perhaps it had been naive to believe that a government report, no matter how powerful and persuasive, was going to change minds. Roy Wilkins later mused that instead of inspiring whites, the language in the report simply made many white people uncomfortable. "They couldn't accept the report; they thought things were just fine with the colored: there we were over in our end of town, with our churches, and wasn't a colored boy captain of the basketball team? What were we yelling about?"[42]

The report overestimated the will of white suburban voters to support programs that benefited urban blacks at the same time that it underestimated their fear of racial unrest. In so doing, it further alienated a key group of voters whose power would only grow in the decades that followed. The Democratic Party would spend the next five decades trying to lure them back into the fold. White House speechwriter Harry McPherson believed that the report accelerated the unraveling of the old Roosevelt coalition. The rhetoric about white racism, he noted, "scared the be-Jesus out of a lot of [white] members of this coalition." It seemed to send a signal that "nobody really gave a damn about their concern—that the city was going to be burned down; that you could not walk in it at night anymore, and all the rest. . . . Programs were being shaped to take care of Negro needs and not to meet any of the needs of the other members of the coalition."[43]

Despite the political blowback, the report would shape the conversation about race in American for a generation. For many years, it was almost impossible for a congressional committee or a journalist dealing with subjects related to poverty and unemployment to avoid referencing the report.

Chapter 13

"THE 60s AND 70s SEEM TO HAVE LEFT US EXHAUSTED"

MOST COMMISSION MEMBERS HAD HOPED that the Kerner Report would change the debate about race and poverty in America. Although no one realized it at the time, the political universe had transformed in the months after the report's release. The assassinations of Martin Luther King Jr. in April 1968 and of Robert F. Kennedy two months later, combined with the violence and turmoil at the Democratic National Convention in August of that year, produced more polarization and doomed any possibility of making significant progress on racial issues in the near future. Over the next few decades, significant social, economic, and demographic changes further complicated discussions of race in America. In 1993 surviving commission members who gathered to mark the report's twenty-fifth anniversary found little reason to celebrate. Their prediction about American moving toward separate societies had proven far too accurate, albeit in ways they had not anticipated in 1968.

THE COMMISSION BELIEVED THAT THE nation needed to summon the "will" to improve the lives of poor blacks living in the nation's cities. "From every American it will require new attitudes, new understanding, and above all, new will," it concluded. But this "new will" never materialized. Discussions of the commission's recommendations were notably absent from the 1968 presidential campaign. Instead, extracting the nation from a now unpopular war in Vietnam dominated the public debate. When it came to race and the cities, all the candidates focused on reassuring white suburban voters—the very ones that the commission had wanted to shock into action—that they would be tough proponents of law and order.

Two candidates pursued strategies that emphasized tapping into the fears of suburban white voters: American Independence Party candidate George Wallace and Republican nominee Richard Nixon. Wallace, whose "stand in the schoolhouse door" to prevent blacks from enrolling at the University of Alabama in 1963 had made him a hero to southern whites, extended his appeal to northern white Democrats who were angry over the party's association with protest and integration. Wallace moved up in the polls by catering to the resentments of such voters, attacking the liberal elites and calling for a crackdown on lawbreakers. By contrast, Nixon campaigned as the candidate of unity, calculating that most Americans wanted an end to the civil discord. But beneath his message rested a similar appeal to white voters both north and south. His top priority, Nixon declared, was the restoration of law and order. Nixon appealed to the "forgotten Americans," those whose values of patriotism and stability had been violated by student protesters, urban riots, and so-called arrogant intellectuals.[1]

If anyone was going to champion the Kerner Commission's findings, it would have been the Democratic nominee, Vice President Hubert Humphrey. But Humphrey, already a target of voters angry at the Johnson administration's policies, distanced himself from the Kerner Commission's recommendations and instead brandished a new tough message on crime more suited to the political moment. "Rioting, sniping, mugging, traffic in narcotics and disregard for law are the advance guard of anarchy and they must and they will be stopped," he declared in his acceptance speech at the Democratic National Convention. "We do not want a police state, but we need a state of law and order." The Democratic platform that year made only passing mention of the Kerner Report, acknowledging "with concern" the findings of the commission.

On Election Day, Nixon won by a razor-thin margin, with less than seven-tenths of 1 percent of the popular vote separating him from Humphrey. Wallace carried five states, receiving forty-six electoral votes and 13.5 percent of the popular vote—the best showing for a third-party candidate in forty-four years. Combined, Nixon and Wallace won nearly 57 percent of the total vote, a massive repudiation of the Johnson administration's policies. The election also underscored the Democratic Party's close identification with the cause of racial justice. Humphrey won 97 percent of the black vote, but only 35 percent of white voters. Three of ten white voters who had supported LBJ in 1964 defected either to Nixon or to Wallace. "If not the sole cause of white defections," historian Allen Matusow has argued, "the backlash against black unrest was certainly high on the list." Despite Nixon's narrow margin and lack of a clear mandate, his election marked a watershed in American politics. Since the days of the New Deal, Democrats had used the language of economic populism to secure the loyalties of the working class, charging that a Republican economic elite was out of touch with the concerns of average voters. Nixon articulated a new lexicon of cultural populism, arguing that a cultural elite associated with the Democratic Party had lost touch with the mainstream values of average Americans.[2]

During his first year in office, Nixon proposed a few innovative policies, including a guaranteed national income, but the clear logic of his presidency was to build a new and enduring coalition of Republicans and angry working-class Democrats with appeals to cultural resentments. Nixon declared war on both antiwar protesters and civil rights activists. One of his main weapons was a phony War on Drugs. "The Nixon campaign in 1968, and the Nixon White House after that, had two enemies: the antiwar left and black people," White House domestic policy chief John Ehrlichman reflected in a 1994 interview. Since the administration could not outlaw protests or black people, Nixon staged a War on Drugs to "disrupt those communities." Employing claims of drug use as an excuse, the administration "could arrest their leaders, raid their homes, break up their meetings, and vilify them night after night on the evening news." But it was all a lie. "Did we know we were lying about the drugs?" Answering his own question, Ehrlichman confessed, "Of course we did."[3]

When campaigning for reelection in 1972, Nixon continued to play on public fear of urban violence and social disorder. The party of FDR, he told wavering Democrats, had been hijacked by antiwar protesters and New Left radicals. "The time has come," Nixon declared in a campaign speech, "to draw the line . . . for the Great Silent Majority . . . to stand up and be counted against the appeasement of the rock-throwers and the obscenity shouters in America." On Election Day, Nixon scored a resounding victory over Democrat George McGovern, winning 60.7 percent of the popular vote. Nixon carried every state except Massachusetts and the District of Columbia. Nearly one-third of registered Democrats, almost ten million voters, cast their ballots for Nixon. So did an overwhelming 70 percent of the white working class.

Two years later, Nixon was forced from office by the Watergate scandal. His resignation allowed Democrat Jimmy Carter to win a close race over Gerald Ford for the presidency in 1976. Only eight years separated the presidencies of Carter and Lyndon Johnson, but they might as well have been decades apart. Carter represented a new type of Democratic politician. Distancing himself from the party's traditional support for expanded social programs and more activist government, Carter promised to make government more efficient and responsive. Carter did, however, propose an ambitious urban policy that would provide fiscal relief to cities struggling with deficits and cash shortfalls, create a $1 billion public works program, and provide tax incentives to businesses that hired the long-term unemployed or opened offices in impoverished areas. But suburban representatives in Congress balked at the cost of Carter's proposal, and it failed to gain passage.

In 1980 former California governor Republican Ronald Reagan scored a resounding victory over Carter, winning 489 electoral votes to Carter's 49. The Democrats also lost control of the Senate for the first time since the days of Dwight Eisenhower as well as thirty-four House seats. Reagan's message of economic and cultural conservatism appealed to Americans grown tired of social experiments and cynical about government power. But like Nixon, Reagan also used racial stereotypes to tap into the resentments of white voters. One of Reagan's favorite anecdotes was about an invented Chicago "welfare queen" with "80 names, 30 addresses, and 12 Social Security cards," whose "tax-free income alone is over $150,000." The food-stamp program, he told largely white audiences, was a vehicle to let "some young fellow ahead of you buy T-bone steak," while "you were standing in a checkout line with your package of hamburger." For many conservatives, the 1980 election represented the inevitable triumph of Richard Nixon's conservative majority. "Like a great soaking wet shaggy dog, the Silent Majority—banished from the house during the Watergate storms—romped back into the nation's parlor this week and shook itself vigorously," observed columnist William Safire.[4]

In his inaugural address, Reagan declared, "Government is not the solution to our problems; government is the problem." Acting on this philosophy, Reagan pushed through Congress large tax cuts for the rich and sharp cuts in programs such as welfare, food stamps, and child nutrition. Between 1980 and 1992, the Republican-controlled White House slashed federal direct aid to cities by 60 percent. In 1987 the administration canceled federal revenue sharing, which had dispersed $85 billion over its fourteen-year existence and touched more cities than any other legislation in history.

Reagan drew inspiration from a group of neoconservative thinkers who rejected liberal proposals for helping the poor like those found in the Kerner Report. Beginning in the 1970s, conservative intellectuals dominated the public debate. With funding from wealthy individuals and foundations, conservative "think tanks" produced mounds of studies advocating the need for smaller government and a return to traditional values. They turned liberal logic on its head, claiming that programs designed to help the poor trapped them in poverty. "Our efforts to deal with distress themselves increase distress," claimed sociologist Nathan Glazer. In an influential essay titled "The Limits of Social Policy," Glazer argued that government welfare programs too often preempted the function of family, church, school, and neighborhood organizations, thus perpetuating the social dependency they sought to resolve. "I am increasingly convinced," he wrote, "that some important part of the solution to our social problems lies in traditional practices and traditional restraints."[5]

NOT ONLY DID THE CENTER of the political universe tilt in a conservative direction in the decade or so after 1968, but profound demographic changes in the years after 1968 further complicated discussions about the politics of race in America. Three years before the Kerner Commission released its report, President Lyndon Johnson signed into law the Immigration Act of 1965. The law changed the formula the United States used to allow immigrants into the country. Since 1924 the United States had allocated visas in ratios determined by the number of persons of each nationality residing in the United States in 1890. The new legislation replaced this "national origins" system with one guided by "family preference," a change that produced a dramatic upsurge in immigrants from Asia, Africa, and Latin America.

Most of these immigrants settled in large cities in a handful of states—New York, Illinois, and New Jersey, as well as Florida, Texas, and California. One of every three new immigrants entered the United States through California, making the nation's most populous state its unofficial Ellis Island. By 1990 the population of Los Angeles, the nation's second-largest city, was one-third foreign born. Los Angeles was also home to the second-largest Spanish-speaking population of any city on the North American continent (after Mexico City). New York's foreign-born population approached 35 percent of its total populace in 1990, the highest level since 1910.

The battle for scarce urban resources provoked racial tensions not only between whites and blacks, but also among groups of blacks, Hispanics, and Asians. The 1992 Los Angeles riots were the most visible demonstration of this new tension. On March 3, 1991, an intoxicated motorist named Rodney King led police on a high-speed chase through the streets of Los Angeles before eventually surrendering. When King resisted arrest, three police officers delivered fifty-six blows with their wooden batons and shocked him twice with a stun gun. A civilian caught some of the encounter on an eighty-nine-second video. The video, shown widely on national television, shocked the nation. In April 1992, however, a mostly white jury in a Los Angeles suburb acquitted the officers. Shortly after the verdicts were announced, African Americans in South Central Los Angeles erupted in the deadliest urban riot in more than a century. By the time it ended three days later, fifty-eight people lay dead, over eight hundred buildings had been destroyed, and thousands more were damaged or looted.

This riot followed a very different pattern than the disturbances during the 1960s. Instead of looting white-owned stores in their own neighborhood, African Americans attacked Asian businesses and neighborhoods. Many poor Latinos joined in the violence as well. "The riots were not carried out against Blacks or Whites, they were carried out against the Latino and Asian communities by the Blacks," asserted the Mexican American newspaper *La Prensa*. "Faced with nearly a million and a half Latinos taking over the inner city, blacks

revolted, rioted and looted." According to one African American commentator, the clash should "shatter, perhaps for good, one of the most
enduring myths of our time: The myth of black-brown solidarity."[6]

The Los Angeles riot was one flash point in a building debate
about America's growing racial and ethnic diversity, as the nation
contemplated the prospect of not just "two societies, one black, one
white," but of many different societies divided by race, culture, and
language. "The nation is rapidly moving toward a multiethnic future," *Newsweek* reported in 1992. "Asians, Hispanics, Caribbean is-
landers, and many other immigrant groups compose a diverse and
changing social mosaic that cannot be described by the old vocabulary of race relations." Many white Americans complained that the
new immigrants stole jobs from native workers, worried about the
cohesiveness of American culture, and questioned its ability to ab-
sorb and assimilate so many newcomers. These changes and fears
only hardened the resistance of many whites to measures that would
benefit racial and ethnic minorities.[7]

OTHER BROAD SOCIAL AND ECONOMIC changes complicated the
commission's warning about America moving toward "two societies." The report had blamed white racism for the problems plaguing the nation's urban core, proposed a host of expensive new social
programs to aid the cities, and expressed confidence that economic
growth would allow the nation to pay for these programs without
imposing much hardship. The commissioners had not anticipated
that the economy would instead sputter and slow or that government
policies combined with the demands of an emerging global market-
place would dramatically widen the gap between the rich and the
poor in America.

The long postwar economic boom ended abruptly in 1974, as turmoil in the Middle East led to rising oil prices at home. At the same
time, many domestic manufacturing plants moved to underdevel-
oped countries to take advantage of the cheap labor there. Between

1973 and 1980, four million jobs were lost because multinational companies moved their operations abroad. High-paying union jobs disappeared with them, replaced by nonunion service positions. By 1985 there were more people flipping hamburgers at McDonald's for minimum wage than working in steel manufacturing—one of the former cornerstones of America's industrial might. These changes, along with government policies that benefited the wealthy and cut programs for the poor, produced massive economic inequality. Increasingly, American society assumed the appearance of an hourglass: bulging on the extremes and thin in the middle.[8]

These economic transformations had a profound impact on African Americans. On the positive side, a thriving and growing black middle class emerged in the years after 1968. Many gained jobs in the public sector. African Americans were also represented in all the major professions. A much greater percentage attended law school, earned master's degrees in business administration, and became doctors. Income figures captured the progress. In 1968, 5 percent of black households had incomes exceeding $50,000 in constant 1990 dollars. By 1990 the figure, while still low, more than doubled, to 12.5 percent.

But not all the trends were positive. By 1986 the proportion of black families with incomes of less than $10,000 grew from 26.8 in 1968 to 30.2 percent. A comprehensive study by the National Research Council noted that "it is not an exaggeration to say that the two most numerically important components of the black middle-class structure have become a lower class dominated by female-headed families and a middle class largely composed of families headed by a husband and wife." Half of black families with children had only one parent. Those families were overwhelmingly poor, with 59 percent living below the poverty level in 1987.[9]

The Kerner Report had accurately predicted that white flight would lead to poorer cities, fewer resources to deal with urban ills, and a shift in political power in America. In 1960 a third of Americans lived in suburbs; by 1990 more than half did. During the 1970s,

St. Louis, Cleveland, Pittsburgh, and Detroit each lost more than 20 percent of their populations. During the same period, Philadelphia, Chicago, and New York City lost more than 10 percent. The movement of the white middle class to the suburbs accounted for much of the population loss. Although the white residents of the suburbs were far from monolithic in their political views, they tended to share a common philosophy that stressed individualism, hostility toward the federal government, and disdain for redistributive programs designed to aid cities.[10]

Many members of the new black middle class joined their white counterparts and moved to the suburbs, leaving behind decaying urban centers populated by poor blacks and recent immigrants. Abandoned by the middle class and by large manufacturers, these urban neighborhoods became even poorer and more cut off from the mainstream of American life. Businesses closed. Jobs disappeared. Rising unemployment turned mixed-income black neighborhoods into high-poverty neighborhoods. The people left behind found themselves isolated from the social and economic networks that had allowed previous generations to escape from utter poverty. While drug use expanded throughout American society, it proved especially lethal in urban areas. With few options for making a living, many urban teenagers joined gangs that ran the drug trade and terrorized many neighborhoods.[11]

Researchers agreed that overall residential segregation peaked in the late 1960s and early 1970s and then witnessed a steady decline. But the decline was concentrated in cities in the South and West with small black populations. Segregation in large industrial cities in the Rust Belt either stayed the same or grew worse. Two social scientists studying trends from the 1970s to 1990 concluded that "there are more completely black areas in our cities than there have ever been in the past." Sociologist Douglas Massey used the term "hypersegregation" to describe the profound level of racial segregation that existed in major metropolitan areas in the United States.[12]

Being trapped in the poorest areas in the cities shaped every aspect of black life. Studies showed that those living in poor neighborhoods attended underfunded schools, had less access to quality health care, and received fewer public services. They had shorter life spans, a higher incidence of heart disease and diabetes, and were more likely to be uninsured. Among women obesity levels correlated to income and education. As these declined, obesity rose. Low-income children had fewer opportunities for upward social and economic mobility, which led to a pattern of inequality over time and across generations. In 1988 the National Urban League reported that the rates of drug use, crime, and violent deaths were dramatically higher among blacks than whites. The rates of teenage pregnancy, infant mortality, and youth unemployment also skyrocketed in the two decades after the Kerner Report.[13]

While social scientists debate why segregation persisted, it is hard to ignore the central role of discrimination. Family income alone does not explain it. Black families earning more than $50,000 were just as segregated as those earning less than $2,500. The poorest Hispanic families were less segregated than the most affluent blacks. The same pattern held for education and occupation. Discrimination also followed middle-class blacks who moved to the suburbs, where many found themselves confined to the deteriorating inner suburbs adjacent to central cities. A sociologist referred to the pattern as that of "invasion-succession." Blacks would move into the aging inner suburbs, and whites would move out.[14]

Housing discrimination contributed to ongoing segregation in education. By 1990 half of all African American students in the Northeast attended schools where minorities made up 90 percent of the student body. Between 1975 and 1990, the percentage of white students in Philadelphia public schools dropped from 32 to 23 percent. The drop was more dramatic in California: Pasadena saw its white student population plummet from 40 to 19 percent, Los Angeles from 40 to 13 percent. The growth of the Hispanic and Asian communities complicated the problem of desegregation. Only the South, home of the highest proportion of blacks and site of the most ambitious school desegregation plans, showed signs of progress.[15]

IN 1993 MANY SURVIVING KERNER Commission members and staff assembled in Albany, New York, for the twenty-fifth anniversary of the report. Richard Nation, who had served as the associate director of program research, hosted the event under the auspices of the Nelson A. Rockefeller Institute of Government. Among those in attendance were James Corman, who had lost his congressional seat in 1980 and was now a Washington lobbyist; John Lindsay, who left the Republican Party and lost his bid for the Democratic presidential nomination in 1972 and was now practicing law; and Katherine Peden, who had won the Democratic nomination for a Kentucky Senate seat in 1968 but lost in the general election. Nearly half of the commissioners—Otto Kerner, Herbert Jenkins, Roy Wilkins, I. W. Abel, and Charles Thornton—had passed away.[16]

The mood was somber and the message sobering. "The pessimistic mood of the symposium was much more downbeat than I recall was the case when the Kerner Commission report came out," Nathan wrote in the introduction to an unpublished manuscript based on the conference. He noted that most of the participants "felt that the danger and bitterness of the most distressed urban areas" were even "more pronounced." The commission's executive director, David Ginsburg, was too ill to attend the conference, but he let his opinion be known to the *New York Times* a few months earlier. "The conditions now, in my view, are unquestionably worse in the inner cities," he said in 1992. "The cities have been essentially disregarded by the federal government."[17]

There had also been a noticeable shift in the national mood in the twenty-five years since the report's publication. The report had reflected the ethos of the 1960s: a sense of optimism about the future and faith that government could and should act in the public interest. All that had changed. "There is a fundamental difference in the attitude of the nation," noted economist Anthony Downs, who had helped to draft the report's long list of recommendations. "The report was written at a time of rapidly rising living standards when people believed almost anything was possible. We no longer have the optimism we had then, and the kind of commitment to improving America's domestic life is totally absent from the present leadership." John Lindsay told the assembled group that "the 60s and 70s seem to have left us exhausted." Americans, he said, seemed to believe that "if we don't think about cities, poverty and minorities, and try to avoid them, maybe, hopefully, they will go away."[18]

The Kerner Report had blamed many of the problems impacting the urban poor on white racism, but by the early 1990s many liberals were beginning to reassess that claim. Lindsay, who had aggressively pushed for the report to identify white racism as the driving force in creating two separate societies in America, now argued that a growing economic divide played a larger role in perpetuating urban poverty. In a 1987 interview, the mayor faulted the commission for not focusing enough on "the growing development in the United States of an economically depressed underclass" that was cut off from the mainstream in American society. Race still mattered, Lindsay contended, but he faulted himself, and his fellow commissioners, for not focusing enough attention on class differences.[19]

Lindsay's change of heart reflected a broader movement among liberals who claimed that class, not racial discrimination alone, was to blame for urban poverty. In 1978 African American sociologist William Julius Wilson had called for a "refocused liberal perspective" that emphasized structural changes in the economy and not racism in explaining the persistence of poverty among African Americans. He criticized the Kerner Commission for failing to account for the growing class divisions *within* the black community. He argued that blacks were now divided into three distinct groups: a black middle class that was thriving, a working class that was struggling to maintain its position, and an underclass that was slipping further and further behind the rest of society. The best way to help the "truly disadvantaged," he argued, was not with race-targeted programs but color-blind policies that promoted full employment.[20]

This debate played out at the twenty-fifth-anniversary conference. Alan Wolfe, a professor of sociology and political science at Boston University, told the group that race-based efforts had failed to solve the challenges facing the urban poor. An honest appraisal of the problems facing the country, he concluded, "would discover that a significant number of middle-class Americans, black as well as white, think that economics is the root of the problems we face, not a single-minded emphasis on white racism." Vincent Lane, the chairman of the Chicago Housing Authority, agreed. "It is not human nature," he said, "to say we ought to have racially integrated communities because it is the right thing to do. We need to develop strategies that reflect how people act and how people think." Many others, however, defended the commission's emphasis on race and integration. Peter Edelman, who had served as an aide to Senator Robert F. Kennedy, declared that "we had better be very explicit about the ugly facts of what is still going on about race in this country." He said that the nation needed to confront "plain, garden variety, ugly racial discrimination that exists." Race, he declared, "still matters."[21]

WHEN BILL CLINTON WAS ELECTED president in 1992, liberals had little reason to expect that he would embrace the sort of race-focused analysis or expansive social policies that the Kerner Commission had once recommended. During the campaign, the Arkansas governor had championed a chastened liberalism that was consciously designed to lure disaffected white voters back into the party with promises to "reform welfare as we know it" and to get tough on crime. Clinton also aggressively courted black voters, who responded enthusiastically to him, even though the 1992 Democratic Party platform was the first in almost thirty years to make no mention of racial injustice.

Even Clinton's restrained liberalism proved too much for conservative Republicans, who opposed most of his agenda and instead focused the public's attention on a series of manufactured scandals, including a failed Clinton real estate investment in Whitewater, Arkansas. After two years in office, Clinton had the lowest poll ratings of any president since Watergate. Energized Republicans, led by Georgia firebrand Newt Gingrich of the House, seized control of both houses for the first time in forty years. The ideologically pliable Clinton responded to the Republican triumph by moving to the center, professing liberal goals even as he co-opted Republican themes of small government and private initiative. "The era of big government is over," he announced in a Reaganesque moment during his 1996 State of the Union address. His strategy frustrated Republicans and angered congressional Democrats, but it won over the public. In 1996 Clinton became the first Democrat since Franklin Roosevelt to win a second term as president.

Clinton surprised liberals by launching several constructive programs designed to aid the urban poor. He directed federal grants to demolish and replace "severely distressed" public housing with mixed-use, mixed-income developments that would be integrated physically and socially into the surrounding neighborhoods. That initiative, along with the sustained economic growth of the decade, led to noticeable improvements in breaking up dense concentrations of poverty, particularly in midwestern and southern cities such as Detroit, Chicago, and San Antonio. There was still plenty of poverty, but it was more scattered at the end of the decade than it was at the beginning. The president also appointed more African Americans to high government positions and to more federal judgeships than any president before him.[22]

Not all of Clinton's actions benefited African Americans. Clinton followed through on his campaign promises to crack down on crime and "end welfare as we know it." In 1994 he signed into law a bipartisan crime bill that called for prison expansion, a federal "three strikes and you're out" policy, and an expansion of the crimes eligible for the federal death penalty. The legislation produced a massive increase in federal and state prison inmates, with the burden falling heaviest on young African American men. By 2015 there were more African Americans in prison or jail than there had been enslaved laborers in the United States in 1850. Most were swept up by a heavy-handed "War on Drugs" and then trapped in a judicial system that, sometimes reluctantly, imposed mandatory minimum sentences. Clinton also signed into a law a punitive welfare reform law that imposed a five-year lifetime limit on welfare assistance and a ban on benefits for anyone convicted of a felony drug offense. Together, the two laws led to a dramatic shift in federal money from assisting the poor to locking them up.[23]

In 1997 Clinton, looking for an initiative that would establish his legacy as a progressive president, announced the creation of a new presidential commission on race. It was clear from the beginning, however, that the administration had no intention of re-creating the Kerner Commission. Aides argued that it was necessary to adapt to the realities of race relations in the 1990s and not "try to relive the glory days of the 1960s." They pointed out that the "civil-rights landscape" was "far more complicated and politically treacherous" than it was in the 1960s, and there existed "no national consensus" on how to deal with the issue. There were now "many more claimants at the civil-rights table," and there was growing tension between blacks and Hispanics. "Navigating these treacherous currents is no easy task," wrote aide Bernie Aronson. The staff suggested that the president articulate a big idea that would be "inclusive, inspiring, and relevant." Claiming that what Americans feared most was polarization, advisers suggested the initiative emphasize the theme of national unity. "In other words," Aronson wrote, "to lead on the issue of civil-rights today the president needs to offer his own vision of America as 'a city on a hill for the 21st century.'" The best way to do that was "to build common political ground around the idea of opening up economic opportunity for disadvantaged Americans regardless of color or ethnicity."[24]

Domestic policy adviser Bruce Reed agreed, telling the president's speechwriting team that Clinton did not want his race initiative to "come across as a new departure" or as an "apology" for welfare reform or his crime bill. He wanted them to craft a speech for the president that would not blame the ongoing gap between blacks and whites on white racism or discrimination. Instead, it should place the burden on individuals to take control of their own lives. He insisted that the speech stress that "the only way for us to come together as one America is to recognize our common obligations to ourselves and one another, to stop blaming our problems on someone else and start taking responsibility for our own actions and each other."[25]

The president accepted the advice and announced his new initiative on race in a speech to the graduating class of the University of California–San Diego in July 1997. He called for the creation of "one America in the 21st century," designed to "lift the burden of race and renew the promise of America." He announced the creation of a national advisory board that he charged with conducting "a great and unprecedented conversation about race." As chairman Clinton selected the historian John Hope Franklin, who had written the chapter on African American history for the Kerner Commission. That commission had consisted of nine whites and two African Americans. Clinton's board included two blacks, one Asian American, one Latina, and three whites.

Clinton's cautious, middle-of-the-road approach to politics shaped his approach to the race initiative. Pollsters, not social scientists, led Clinton's initiative, and its goal was to emphasize what united Americans, not what divided them. There would be no finger-pointing, no bold new recommendations, just a lot of spin. The Clinton initiative downplayed the role of racism and discrimination in American life. It avoided discussions of controversial issues and refused to make specific policy recommendations. The key to achieving "racial reconciliation," it concluded, was "dialogue." The emphasis on dialogue shifted the burden from the government to private citizens. Unlike the Kerner Commission, the Clinton initiative did not ask people to make sacrifices, pay higher taxes, or approve vast new programs to improve the ghetto. They needed only to talk. The initiative paid homage to the Kerner Commission, but declared that its claim about America becoming two societies was irrelevant in today's world. "Today," it concluded, "we face a different choice: will we become not two, but many Americas, separate, unequal and isolated? Or will we draw strength from all our people and our ancient faith in the quality of human dignity, to become the world's first truly multi-racial democracy?"[26]

The White House hoped that the new initiative would start a national conversation about race. It never happened. A week before the report was issued, special prosecutor Kenneth Starr released his account of the president's relationship with Monica Lewinsky. The scandal, and the impeachment trial that followed, drowned out the president's entire agenda, including his race initiative.

Although modest in scope, the Clinton program represented one of the last serious presidential efforts to engage the nation in a conversation about race and public policy. The terrorist attacks on September 11, 2001, refocused the nation's attention away from domestic priorities. President George W. Bush presided over an expansion of federal power unseen since the days of Lyndon Johnson's Great Society, but nearly all the new spending was devoted to security at home and fighting two wars abroad. His presidency ended with a banking crisis that set off a collapse in the real estate market and resulted in a crippling recession. In December 2007, the national unemployment rate stood at 5 percent; two years later, it was approaching 10 percent.

The "Great Recession" widened the gap between rich and poor in America. "It's almost like you are looking at two different countries," said Steve Glickman, executive director of the Economic Innovation Group. A study by the Congressional Budget Office revealed that the wealthiest 10 percent of Americans emerged from the recession with three-quarters of the nation's wealth, which was greater than their share before the collapse. Poor and working-class neighborhoods, which were riddled with vacant homes, suffered most from the housing crisis. According to one study, African Americans lost half of their collective wealth during the crisis—mostly in the form of home equity. Concentrated poverty, after modest improvements in the 1990s, spiked, especially in Detroit and other midwestern manufacturing centers that lost thousands of jobs. High-poverty neighborhoods grew in the inner-ring suburbs as well as in central cities.[27]

Two members of the Kerner Commission, Fred Harris and Edward Brooke, would live long enough to see an African American elected president of the United States. Barack Obama's election in 2008 marked an important milestone in race relations. In less than a generation, the nation went from having separate black and white water fountains to having a black family living in the White House. Civil rights leaders hailed Obama's victory. John Lewis, who once marched with Martin Luther King Jr. and now represented Georgia in the House of Representatives, called the election a "non-violent revolution." Most Americans agreed with the assessment. According to Gallup, more than two-thirds of Americans viewed Obama's election as "either the most important advance for blacks in the past 100 years, or among the two or three most important such advances."[28]

Obama's election inspired great hope, but the new president inherited a steep recession. Obama spoke eloquently about the problems plaguing the middle class, and his administration followed suit, supporting policies that promised "ladders of opportunity" to help workers increase their salaries, gain access to better schools, and purchase health insurance. He said little about the poor and spoke about race only occasionally and then in muted tones. In his first two years in office, Obama spoke less about race than any Democratic president since John F. Kennedy.[29]

BEGINNING IN 2014, A SERIES of explosive racial incidents ignited an intense public debate about the role of race in American life. In November a white police officer in Ferguson, Missouri, shot and killed Michael Brown, an unarmed African American. Over the next twelve months, similar incidents took place in Baltimore, Staten Island, and Cleveland. In each case, an unarmed black man died at the hands of a police officer. And each event resulted in an outpouring of rage, millions of dollars in property damage, constant news coverage, and what the *New York Times* described as "a torrent of anguish and soul-searching about race in America."[30]

Many African Americans were engaged in their own soul-searching, questioning older tactics used to achieve racial justice while articulating a new message to promote social change. Among those who took to the streets in protest following the Michael Brown shooting were a new generation of black activists. "Black lives matter," they chanted. Within weeks the chant transformed into an influential movement. Founded by three African American women, Black Lives Matter used social media, especially Twitter, to organize large protests and to demand an end to systemic racism. "We are demanding an end to the war on black people in this country and around the world," declared cofounder Alicia Garza.

Black Lives Matter generated extensive news coverage and forced the issue of racial injustice back onto the national agenda. In the short run at least, the strategy worked. Polls revealed an important shift in public attitudes. A *Washington Post* survey taken a year after Ferguson found that 60 percent of Americans believed that the nation needed to work harder to provide equal rights for African Americans. At the same time, a Pew Research Center poll found that 50 percent of Americans viewed race relations as a "big problem." Only 33 percent felt that way five years earlier.[31]

In response to the unrest, many prominent political figures talked openly about racism and inequality. "Our problem is not all kooks and Klansmen," former secretary of state and presidential contender Hillary Clinton declared. "It's also the cruel joke that goes unchallenged. It's the offhand comment about not wanting those people in the neighborhood." President Obama now talked bluntly about his own experiences growing up as a black man and, in echoes of the Kerner Commission's report, about the need for the nation to address the underlying causes of the riots. "If you have impoverished communities that have been stripped away of opportunity, where children are born into abject poverty," he said, it was more likely that those children "end up in jail or dead, than go to college." If the nation failed to break that cycle, he warned, "we'll go through the same cycles of periodic conflicts between the police and communities and the occasional riots in the streets, and everybody will feign concern until it goes away, and then we go about our business as usual."[32]

At the same time, Obama's Justice Department moved aggressively to require local police departments to abandon practices that discriminated against blacks. It launched more than twenty investigations, issued blistering reports, and compelled officials to adopt broad reforms. The Justice Department's 163-page report on Baltimore identified "systemic deficiencies in [the police department's] policies, training, supervision, and accountability structures." Its examination of police practices in Ferguson showed that "officers routinely violate the Fourth Amendment in stopping people without reasonable suspicion, arresting them without probably cause, and using unreasonable force against them."[33]

Some states and cities that experienced unrest opened their own investigations. The state of Missouri set up a commission headed by former presidents Jimmy Carter and George W. Bush. While that commission also identified racial inequality as the underlying cause of the unrest, it intentionally avoided the hard-hitting language and bold recommendations of the Kerner Commission. "We are not pointing fingers and calling people racist," it stated. "We are not even suggesting that institutions or existing systems intend to be racist." In Chicago a task force concluded that "the police have no regard for the sanctity of life when it comes to people of color."[34]

DESPITE SIGNS OF PROGRESS, THE problem of the color line remains as real in the second decade of the twenty-first century as it was in 1900 when W. E. B. DuBois coined the phrase. Statistics reveal stubbornly persistent racial segregation in housing, education, and employment. The unemployment rate for blacks has remained twice as high as for whites, the household income gap has remained wide, and the black poverty rate continues to be triple that of whites. African American children are also more likely than whites to live in areas of concentrated poverty. School segregation decreased briefly during the 1970s, only to grow worse over the past three decades. Massive income inequality, which shifted wealth to the top 10 percent and the tax burden to the bottom 50 percent, compounded the problems of those living in poverty. By every possible measure, the poor of all races emerged from the "Great Recession" with less income, more debt, and fewer opportunities for upward mobility.

The Kerner Commission had argued for a compassionate approach to people who found themselves trapped in decaying urban neighborhoods. That plea for compassion, however, was overwhelmed by demands for "law and order" and a "get-tough" approach to crime that produced a system of mass incarceration that stigmatized its victims and savaged the social fabric of already crumbling inner-city neighborhoods. The commission called upon the United States to muster the political will to deal with its urban problems. But social and political changes over the subsequent decades conspired against ambitious plans to aid cities. The increasing power of money in the political process, a profound skepticism of government power, an electorate that skewed toward the interests of the white middle class, and a profound partisan divide made it difficult to muster much political resolve.

For all the remarkable changes over the past five decades, views of racial unrest remained unchanged. The debates carried out in public mirror the clashes that took place in commission meetings between John Lindsay and Tex Thornton. In 1968 liberals blamed the riots on discrimination, poverty, and lack of opportunity. In 2014 President Obama said, "In too many communities, too many young men of color are left behind and seen only as objects of fear." The vast majority of conservatives, however, still see urban riots as a "law-and-order" problem. "Throughout a half century of policies that have been geared towards expanding the role of government into every facet of our lives and redistributing wealth for every targeted subsidy known to man, this paradigm for liberal governance was missing one critical element," observed conservative commentator Daniel Horowitz. "The liberal politicians ignored the one aspect of government that is not only necessary, but vital to preserving liberty—robust law enforcement."[35]

Recent racial unrest serves as a reminder that many of the problems that the Kerner Commission confronted have festered in the decades since 1968. In some ways, Obama's election may have caused Americans to slip into a false sense of security. Many Americans, far from accepting their responsibility for creating and perpetuating racial division, now proudly claimed the end of racism in America. "Is America past racism against black people?" African American author John McWhorter asked in *Forbes* a few weeks after Obama's 2008 election. "I say the answer is yes," he wrote.[36]

The 2016 election of billionaire businessman Donald Trump, who led the campaign to undermine the legitimacy of the nation's first African American president by charging that he was not a US citizen, made clear that the nation has never entered a postracial era. Trump appealed to the fears of many white voters living in declining industrial towns and rural areas who worried that cultural change and the influx of new immigrants were eroding old norms and threatening their status in society. Polls showed that although Trump lost the popular tally by almost three million votes, he won over many rural white voters in key industrial states—Wisconsin, Ohio, Michigan, and Pennsylvania—who had voted for Barack Obama in 2012.

More important, the 2016 election reflected white America's ongoing unease with race and demands for racial justice. It also exposed an ugly undercurrent of intolerance that had long been a part of the American character. Trump announced his candidacy by attacking immigrants, calling them rapists and drug dealers, and moved on to Muslims, whom he wanted banned from entering the United States, before widening his reach by using well-tested racial "dog whistles" to appeal to white voters. In some ways, Trump was a nontraditional candidate, but there was nothing new about his strategy. His success was the outgrowth of five decades of Republican strategy of stoking white resentment to win elections.[37]

Ironically, during the campaign, Trump called for a federal public works program and new government policies designed to create better-paying jobs, especially in rural areas that had once been home to major manufacturing plants. In many ways, the proposals were similar to what the Kerner Commission had recommended for poor urban areas and what Republicans and conservative Democrats had opposed for five decades.

The program recommendations that preoccupied most of the commissioners' time and attention, and threatened to split the commission in half, have fallen by the political wayside. The report's most important legacy was its willingness to acknowledge the role of white racism in creating the conditions that sparked the riots, its searing account of the horrible conditions in poor urban areas, and its careful documentation of the impact of continuing discrimination. Unfortunately, despite all the progress that has been made over the past five decades, many of those same conditions still exist. In many ways, those living in urban ghettos today are even more cut off from the mainstream of American life.

Some observers have argued that the nation needs a new Kerner Commission, but it is unlikely that a new group would produce results that would be any better than the original commission. The comments that Dr. Kenneth B. Clark, whose groundbreaking study on the effects of discrimination on child development was cited by the Supreme Court in its *Brown v. Board of Education of Topeka* decision, made in his testimony before the Kerner Commission are as true now as they were fifty years ago. Referring to the reports of earlier riot commissions, he said, "I read that report . . . of the 1919 riot in Chicago, and it is as if I were reading the report of the investigating committee on the Harlem riot of '35, the report of the investigating committee on the Harlem riot of '43, the report of the McCone Commission on the Watts riot. I must again in candor say to you members of this Commission—it is a kind of Alice in Wonderland—with the same moving picture re-shown over and over again, the same analysis, the same recommendations, and the same inaction."[38]

ACKNOWLEDGMENTS

This book would not be possible were it not for the help and guidance of many colleagues, archivists, and research assistants. Archivist Allen Fisher guided me through the massive collection of materials at the Lyndon Baines Johnson Presidential Library. Debbie Hamm at the Abraham Lincoln Presidential Library provided valuable assistance in dealing with the Otto Kerner Papers. Research assistants Dustin Mack, Eric England, and Scott Russell helped gather materials.

I am especially indebted to the surviving commission members who spent many hours sharing their recollections with me. They are all listed in "A Note on Sources," but a few deserve special mention. Fred Harris, who has lost none of his passion for social and racial justice, sat down for long interviews and responded to questions by phone and email. As the only surviving commissioner, his detailed memories of the private discussions among his colleagues were invaluable. The surviving authors of the controversial report "The Harvest of American Racism"—David Boesel, Gary T. Marx, and, especially, Robert Shellow—helped me to understand the process of researching and writing the report. Both Shellow and Marx read an early draft of the "Harvest" chapter and made many valuable suggestions. I was gratified and relieved that they felt I got the story right. Peter Goldmark, who worked as an aide to John Lindsay, read the "Two Societies" chapter, while Rick Loessberg, who has studied the commission for many decades, read the entire manuscript.

My greatest debt, however, is to David Chambers, who as a young lawyer joined the staff as David Ginsberg's assistant. Chambers spent hours on the phone talking me through key moments in the commission's history. He read the entire manuscript with great care, offering background material that could not be found in official papers. I came to trust his judgment and his fair-minded assessment of the commission's strengths and weaknesses. He made this a much better book. My only regret is that, as of this writing, we have yet to meet.

I am also grateful to former White House domestic policy adviser Joseph Califano, who took the time to review documents and offer his insight into LBJ's evolving views of the commission. My mentor, James T. Patterson, read selected chapters and, as he has done for three decades, made many helpful comments. For the past two decades, I have had the privilege of working at two great institutions—the

University of Oklahoma and History. My thanks to OU president David Boren and first lady Molly Boren for their many kindnesses and to my many friends at History, especially CEO emeritus Abbe Raven and current CEO and president, Nancy Dubuc.

This is the third book that I have written for the extraordinary editor Lara Heimert at Basic Books. Lara went on maternity leave just as I finished the manuscript, so she handed it off to another talented editor, Brian Distelberg. Brian, who has a PhD in twentieth-century American race relations, combined an editor's keen eye with a scholar's deep understanding of the issues addressed in the book. Alia Massoud kept the project moving along and coordinated all the moving parts needed to turn a draft manuscript into a published book. Other members of the Basic team played key roles. Every author needs a good copy editor, and I certainly benefited from Annette Wenda's keen eye for detail. Rebecca Lown used her creative talents to design the book jacket, while Stephanie Summerhays oversaw production.

I could not have written this book without the love of my family and the support of my many friends. My siblings, Fran, Mike, and little sister Karen, have always been supportive and caring, and we are all fortunate to still have our wonderful parents, Frank and June Gillon. We grew up with the comforting knowledge that their love for us was unconditional. My dear friends, especially Jim Ryan, Ken Orkin, and Gary Ginsburg, provided moral support and on rare occasions even laughed at my jokes.

This book is dedicated to Vantuir Luiz Borges, who has been by my side for this long journey, offering his unfailing love and encouragement. He makes my life whole.

NOTES

INTRODUCTION

1. Thomas Edsall, *Chain Reaction: The Impact of Race, Rights, and Taxes on American Politics* (New York: W. W. Norton, 1992), 52.

2. There is a large body of literature on presidential commissions. See Thomas R. Wolanin, *Presidential Advisory Commissions: Truman to Nixon* (Madison: University of Wisconsin Press, 1975); Frank Popper, *The President's Commissions* (New York: Twentieth Century Fund, 1970); Hugh Davis Graham, "The Ambiguous Legacy of American Presidential Commissions," *Public Historian* (Spring 1985): 5–25; Amy Zegart, "Blue Ribbons, Black Boxes: Toward a Better Understanding of Presidential Commissions," *Presidential Studies Quarterly* (June 2004): 366–393; Martha Derthick, *On Commissionship—Presidential Variety* (Washington, DC: Brookings Institution, 1972); "Opening Statement of Senator Edward M. Kennedy at Hearings on Presidential Commissions," May 25, 1971, Otto Kerner Family Papers, Abraham Lincoln Presidential Library, Box 7; and Michael Lipsky, "Social Scientists and the Riot Commission," *Annals of the American Academy of Political and Social Science* 394 (March 1971): 72–83. On the rise of psychological explanations, see Ellen Herman, *The Romance of American Psychology: Political Culture in the Age of Experts* (Berkeley: University of California Press, 1996).

3. *Report of the National Advisory Commission on Civil Disorders* (New York: Bantam Books, 1968), 1–2.

PROLOGUE: "IT LOOKS LIKE BERLIN IN 1945"

1. There is a large body of literature on the Newark riots. The works consulted to construct this narrative include Tom Hayden, *Rebellion in Newark: Official Violence and Ghetto Response* (New York: Random House, 1967), 3–6; *Report of the National Advisory Commission on Civil Disorders* (New York: Bantam Books, 1968) (hereafter referred to as Kerner Commission), 56–69; and Allen Matusow, *The Unraveling of America: A History of Liberalism in the 1960s* (New York: Harper & Row, 1984), 362–363. The best information comes from the Kerner Commission field teams that investigated the riots. See "Newark," July 12–18, 1967, Kerner

Commission Field Report, Lyndon B. Johnson Presidential Library (LBJL), RG 220, Series E10, E56, 1–3. Local newspapers also provided extensive coverage, especially the *Newark Evening News.*

2. *Newark Evening News,* July 14–15, 1967.

3. "Newark," July 12–18, 1967, Kerner Commission Field Report, LBJL, RG 220, Series E10, E56, 1–3.

4. Hayden, *Rebellion in Newark,* 3–6; *U.S. News and World Report,* July 31, 1967; Kerner Commission, 56–69; "Races: Spark & Tinder," *Time,* July 21, 1967; Matusow, *Unraveling of America,* 362–363.

5. *Huntley Brinkley* tapes, July 26, 1967, LBJL, Series 40, Box 2.

6. Randall B. Woods, *Prisoners of Hope: Lyndon B. Johnson, the Great Society, and the Limits of Liberalism* (New York: Basic Books, 2016), 313; "The Harvest of American Racism: The Political Meaning of Violence in the Summer of 1967," November 22, 1967, Kerner Commission, Series 7, LBJL, Box 1. For the best analysis of the conditions that led to the riots, see Thomas J. Sugrue, *The Origins of the Urban Crisis: Race and Inequality in Postwar Detroit* (Princeton, NJ: Princeton University Press, 1996).

7. Kerner Commission, 84–108; Michael W. Flamm, *Law and Order: Street Crime, Civil Unrest, and the Crisis of Liberalism in the 1960s* (New York: Columbia University Press, 2005), 83–96; *Newsweek,* August 7, 1967.

8. *Time,* August 4, 1967, 14.

9. For the best account of the often overlooked Harlem riot, see Michael W. Flamm, *In the Heat of the Summer: The New York Riots of 1964 and the War on Crime* (Philadelphia: University of Pennsylvania Press, 2017).

10. Woods, *Prisoners of Hope,* 188.

11. Lindsay Lupo, *Flak-Catchers: One Hundred Years of Riot Commission Politics in America* (New York: Lexington Books, 2001), 43–66; Michael Lipsky and David Olson, *Commission Politics: The Processing of Racial Crisis in America* (New Brunswick, NJ: Transaction Books, 1977), 37–62.

12. Lipsky and Olson, *Commission Politics,* 57–59; Lupo, *Flak-Catchers,* 54–55.

13. The explanation, however, bore little resemblance to reality. Later surveys showed that as many as thirty thousand blacks had participated in the riots and another sixty thousand supported them. The typical rioters were not marginalized "riffraff" but young men with jobs and better education than the typical nonrioter. McCone concluded that the rioters were marginal people and the riots irrational outbursts. Most of the rioters were unemployed, uneducated, delinquent, and recent transplants from the South. It was the same explanation used to explain the riots in New York the previous year. The emphasis was on the personal failures of the individuals who rioted and not on the underlying conditions and grievances of the black community. See Robert M. Fogelson, "White on Black: A Critique of the McCone Commission Report on the Los Angeles Riots," *Political Science Quarterly* 82, no. 3 (1967): 337–367. For Brinkley, see *Huntley Brinkley* tapes, July 21, 1967, LBJL, Series 40, Box 2.

14. *Huntley Brinkley* tapes, July 21, 1967, LBJL, Series 40, Box 2.

15. *Time*, August 2, 1967, 15; *Huntley Brinkley* tapes, July 25, 1967, LBJL, Series 40, Box 2.

16. *Huntley Brinkley* tapes, July 25, 1967, LBJL, Series 40, Box 2.

17. Robert Weisbrot, *Freedom Bound: A History of America's Civil Rights Movement* (New York: Plume Books, 1990), 154–155.

18. Thomas J. Sugrue, *Sweet Land of Liberty: The Forgotten Struggle for Civil Rights in the North* (New York: Random House, 2008), 314–315.

19. Steven M. Gillon, *American Paradox: A History of the United States Since 1945* (Boston: Wadsworth, 2013), 179.

20. On the politics of the backlash, see Thomas Edsall, *Chain Reaction: The Impact of Race, Rights, and Taxes on American Politics* (New York: W. W. Norton, 1992), 59; James T. Patterson, *Freedom Is Not Enough: The Moynihan Report and America's Struggle over Black Family Life from LBJ to Obama* (New York: Basic Books, 2010), 70; Clay Risen, *A Nation on Fire: America in the Wake of the King Assassination* (New York: Wiley, 2009), 7; and *Time*, August 2, 1967, 17.

21. Flamm, *Law and Order*, 124–129; *New York Times*, August 15, 1967.

22. *New York Times*, July 13, 1967; *Washington Post*, June 27, 1967; *Christian Science Monitor*, August 2, 1967.

23. *Washington Post*, July 26, 1967.

CHAPTER 1: "WHAT DO THEY WANT?"

1. Rowland Evans and Robert Novak, *Lyndon B. Johnson: The Exercise of Power* (New York: New American Library, 1966), 105.

2. *Revolution in Civil Rights*, 4th ed. (Washington, DC: Congressional Quarterly Service, 1968), 54.

3. Steven M. Gillon, *The American Paradox: A History of the United States Since 1945* (Boston: Wadsworth, 2013).

4. "President Lyndon B. Johnson's Commencement Address at Howard University," June 4, 1965, www.presidency.ucsb.edu/ws/index.php?pid=27021; James T. Patterson, *Grand Expectations: The United States, 1945–1974* (New York: Oxford University Press, 1997), 531.

5. James T. Patterson, *Freedom Is Not Enough: The Moynihan Report and America's Struggle over Black Family Life from LBJ to Obama* (New York: Basic Books, 2012), 589; Eric Goldman, *The Tragedy of Lyndon Johnson* (New York: Alfred A. Knopf, 1969), 337; Randall B. Woods, *Prisoners of Hope: Lyndon B. Johnson, the Great Society, and the Limits of Liberalism* (New York: Basic Books, 2016), 189.

6. George Christian, "Notes of Meeting," July 28, 1967, Diary Backup, Lyndon B. Johnson Presidential Library (LBJL), Box 72.

7. Woods, *Prisoners of Hope*, 270–271.

8. *Los Angeles Times*, July 23, 1967.

9. Joseph A. Califano Jr., *The Triumph and Tragedy of Lyndon Johnson: The White House Years* (New York: Touchstone, 2015), 169.

10. Julian E. Zelizer, *Taxing America: Wilbur D. Mills, Congress, and the State, 1945–1975* (Cambridge: Cambridge University Press, 1998), 264–270; Califano, *Triumph and Tragedy*, 177–178.

11. *Washington Post*, August 20, 1967.

12. Steven M. Gillon, *Politics and Vision: The ADA and American Liberalism, 1947–1985* (New York: Oxford University Press, 1987), 190.

13. *Washington Post*, August 4, 1967; *New York Times*, July 15, 1967.

14. Califano, *Triumph and Tragedy*, 217; Harry McPherson Oral History, LBJL, tape 1, 6.

15. Arthur M. Schlesinger Jr., *Robert Kennedy and His Times* (Boston: Houghton Mifflin, 1978), 657; Kenneth O'Reilly, "The FBI and the Politics of the Riots, 1964–1968," *Journal of American History* (June 1988): 92–93.

16. J. Edgar Hoover to LBJ, July 26, 1967, Sherwin Markham Papers, LBJL, Box 5.

17. Markham to LBJ, July 26, 1967, ibid.

18. Graham to LBJ, May 18, 1967, ibid., Box 4.

19. Patterson, *Freedom Is Not Enough*, 80.

20. "Remarks of the President at the Ceremony Marking the 100th Anniversary of Howard University," March 2, 1967, White House Central File (WHCF), LBJL, Ex SP, Box 230.

21. Nathaniel R. Jones to Marvin Watson, July 14, 1967, Diary Backup, LBJL, Box 70.

22. *New York Times*, July 15, 1967; Califano, *Triumph and Tragedy*, 208–209.

23. Califano, *Triumph and Tragedy*, 209.

24. Ibid., 208; Woods, *Prisoners of Hope*, 311.

25. Robert Dallek, *Flawed Giant: Lyndon Johnson and His Times, 1961–1973* (New York: Oxford University Press, 1998), 443–444; Califano, *Triumph and Tragedy*, 213–217; Califano to LBJ, July 26, 1967, Diary Backup, LBJL, Box 72.

26. Califano, *Triumph and Tragedy*, 212–214; Tom Johnson meeting notes, July 24, 1967, LBJL, Box 1; Roger Wilkins, *A Man's Life: An Autobiography of Roger Wilkins* (New York: Simon and Schuster, 1982), 195–196. Polls showed that the public believed Romney. A nationwide survey showed that two-thirds of Americans thought that Johnson waited too long to send in paratroopers. See "The Cities: What Next?," *Time*, August 11, 1967.

27. *New York Times*, July 26, 1967; Tom Johnson to LBJ, July 29, 1967, Diary Backup, LBJL, Box 72; Califano to LBJ, July 26, 1967, Diary Backup, LBJL, Box 72; Woods, *Prisoners of Hope*, 314; David C. Carter, *The Music Has Gone Out of the Movement: Civil Rights and the Johnson Administration, 1965–1968* (Chapel Hill: University of North Carolina Press, 2009), 205.

28. Hoover to Clyde Tolson et al., July 25, 1967, FOIA Declassified FBI Files, Clyde Tolson, 67-9524, Series 8.

29. *New York Times*, July 25–26, 1967; *Washington Post*, July 25–26, 1967; "The Cities: What Next?" Dirksen later walked back the statement. When asked by

reporters on the CBS news show *Face the Nation* about the accusation, Dirksen responded: "Well, I have not gone quite as far as might be implied by that statement. I like to be rather cautious and careful about any allegations or accusations that I make." *Face the Nation* transcript, "Interview Transcripts," August 6, 1967, Everett M. Dirksen Papers, Dirksen Congressional Center; *Washington Star*, August 22, 1967.

30. *New York Times*, July 26, August 2, 1967; *Wall Street Journal*, August 2, 1967.

31. *Washington Post*, July 29, 1967; *Huntley Brinkley* tapes, July 24, 1967, LBJL, Series 40, Box 2.

32. *New York Times*, July 25, 1967; Michael Flamm, *Law and Order: Street Crime, Civil Unrest, and the Crisis of Liberalism in the 1960s* (New York: Columbia University Press, 2005), 96–103.

33. *Huntley Brinkley* tapes, July 26, 1967, LBJL, Series 40, Box 2; Califano, *Triumph and Tragedy*, 210–211; *Los Angeles Times*, July 23, 1967; Carter, *Music Has Gone*, 203.

34. *New York Times*, July 26, 1967.

35. A. Philip Randolph to LBJ, July 18, 1967, Ramsey Clark Papers, LBJL, Box 72; *New York Times*, July 26, 1967.

36. Fred Harris interview, May 20, 2015.

37. Harris to LBJ, July 25, 1967, WHCF, LBJL, Ex JL, Box 1; press release, July 26, 1967, Fred Harris Papers, Carl Albert Congressional Research Center, Box 94; Fred Harris, *Does People Do It?* (Norman: University of Oklahoma Press, 2008), 107; Douglass Cater to LBJ, July 25, 1967, Cater Papers, LBJL, Box 16; Harris to the author, January 6, 2016.

38. *New York Times*, August 18, 1967; *Los Angeles Times*, July 21, 1967.

39. "The Presidency," *Time*, August 25, 1967.

40. Califano, *Triumph and Tragedy*, 217; McPherson to LBJ, July 24, 1967, Harry McPherson Office Papers, LBJL, Box 32; Cater to LBJ, July 25, 1967, Cater Papers, LBJL, Box 16.

41. Christian, "Notes of Meeting," July 28, 1967, Diary Backup, LBJL, Box 72.

42. McPherson to LBJ, July 26, 1967, McPherson Office Papers, LBJL, Box 32.

43. President's Daily Diary, LBJL, July 27, 1967.

44. Califano, *Triumph and Tragedy*, 217–218.

45. The Humphrey task force continued to meet but soon fizzled out. On August 31, Humphrey said that he recommended "the cabinet group be put on ice for a while." Humphrey to LBJ, July 27, 1967; Gray to Humphrey, July 28, 1967; "Statement for Cabinet Meeting," August 2, 1967; "Verbal Report by the Vice President," August 23, 1967; Humphrey to LBJ, August 23, 1967; and Humphrey to Gray, August 31, 1967, all in Hubert Humphrey Papers, Minnesota Historical Society, 150.E.6.10F, Box 813.

46. Califano, *Triumph and Tragedy*, 217–218; Cater to LBJ, July 28, 1967, and Reedy to LBJ, August 3, 1967, WHCF, LBJL, Ex FG 686/A, Box 386.

CHAPTER 2: "LET YOUR SEARCH BE FREE"

1. Robert Dallek, *Flawed Giant: Lyndon Johnson and His Times, 1961–1973* (New York: Oxford University Press, 1998), 294; Joseph A. Califano Jr., *The Triumph and Tragedy of Lyndon Johnson: The White House Years* (New York: Touchstone, 2015), 9–22; Michael Ennis, "All the Way with LBJ," *Texas Monthly*, September 1, 2015, 64.

2. "Analysis of Proposals for Commissions to Investigate Crime and Riots," Califano Office Papers, Lyndon B. Johnson Presidential Library (LBJL), Box 11.

3. Cater to LBJ, July 27, 1967, Cater Papers, LBJL, Box 16.

4. Ramsey Clark Oral History, LBJL, 14–15.

5. Ibid.; *Washington Post*, July 30, 1967; *Chicago Tribune*, July 28, 1967; *New York Times*, July 30, 1967; *Wall Street Journal*, August 16, 1967; Bill Barnhart and Gene Schlickman, *Kerner: The Conflict of Intangible Rights* (Urbana: University of Illinois Press, 1999).

6. Richard Reeves, "The Impossible Takes a Little Longer," *New York Times Magazine*, January 28, 1968. For an excellent collection of essays about Lindsay, see Joseph P. Viteritti, ed., *Summer in the City: John Lindsay, New York, and the American Dream* (Baltimore: Johns Hopkins University Press, 2014). He was the subject of numerous profiles. See "Lindsay of New York," *Newsweek*, May 31, 1965; "The Lindsay Style," *Life*, May 24, 1968; Richard Reeves, "'A *Great* Mayor' 'That Bum?,'" *New York Times Magazine*, January 1, 1967; and "Rx for a Long, Hot Summer: A Long, Cool Mayor," *Newsweek*, August 28, 1967.

7. Califano, *Triumph and Tragedy*, 110–111; Joseph Califano interview, January 17, 2017; *New York Times*, July 26, 28, 1967.

8. Clark Oral History, 14–15; Cater to LBJ, July 27, 1967, Cater Papers, LBJL, Box 16; Diary Backup, LBJL, Box 72.

9. President's Daily Diary, LBJL, July 27, 1967.

10. Yvonne Ryan, *Roy Wilkins: The Quiet Revolutionary and the NAACP* (Lexington: University Press of Kentucky, 2014), 138–140; Roy Wilkins, *Standing Fast: The Autobiography of Roy Wilkins* (New York: Viking, 1982), 313–319; Martin Arnold, "There Is No Rest for Roy Wilkins," *New York Times Magazine*, September 28, 1969.

11. Roy Wilkins Oral History, LBJL, 208–209; *New York Times*, March 30, 1967; "The Roy Wilkins Column," August 19–20, 1967, Roy Wilkins Papers, Library of Congress (LOC), Box 44.

12. "The Senate: An Individual Who Happens to Be a Negro," *Time*, February 17, 1968; *New York Times*, March 24, 1967; Edward W. Brooke, *Bridging the Divide: My Life* (Brunswick, NJ: Rutgers University Press, 2007), 170.

13. Fred Harris, *Does People Do It?* (Norman: University of Oklahoma Press, 2008), 1–94.

14. *New York Times*, March 2, 1968; Richard Lowitt, *Fred Harris: His Journey from Liberalism to Populism* (New York: Rowman & Littlefield, 2002).

15. Jenkey to Fred Harris, September 4, 1967; Underwood to Harris, September 4, 1967; Foster-Harris to Harris, July 16, 1967; and "Race Riots Are Part of the

Communist Plan to Take over America," all in Fred Harris Papers, Carl Albert Congressional Research Center, Box 94.

16. *Dayton Journal*, July 28, 1967; *New York Times*, January 5, 2001.

17. "An Appetite for the Future," *Time*, October 4, 1963, 104–111.

18. Ibid.; John A. Byrne, *The Whiz Kids: Ten Founding Fathers of American Business—and the Legacy They Left Us* (New York: Doubleday, 1993), 23–30.

19. Byrne, *Whiz Kids*, 32–36.

20. President's Daily Diary, LBJL, July 27, 1967.

21. Herbert Jenkins, *Keeping the Peace: A Police Chief Looks at His Job* (New York: Harper & Row, 1970), 1–6, 71–77.

22. Katherine Peden Oral History, LBJL, 2–11; *Los Angeles Times*, August 4, 1968; Califano to LBJ, September 16, 1967, David Ginsburg Papers, LOC, Box 96.

23. *Time*, August 11, 1987.

24. President's Daily Diary, LBJL, July 27, 1967.

25. Flores to Marvin, August 2, 1967, LBJL, Ex FG 690, Box 387.

26. Frank Stanton, president of CBS News, offered LBJ a critique of his performance, saying that his performance was "many times better" than his last televised address. He complained that "the leather head-rest showing at the sides of your head was distracting." Jim Hagerty, who served as Dwight Eisenhower's press secretary, congratulated him on the "demonstration of dignity and strength," but also complained about the chair. Fleming to LBJ, July 27, 1967, Diary Backup, LBJL, Box 72; Califano, *Triumph and Tragedy*, 216. The speech did impress LBJ's national security adviser, Walt W. Rostow, who sent the president a memorandum the next day that highlighted what he perceived to be "parallels" in the White House approach to the riots and its policy in Vietnam. "At home," he wrote, "your appeal is for law and order as the framework for economic and social progress. Abroad we fight in Vietnam to make aggression unprofitable while helping the people of Vietnam and all of Free Asia build a future of economic and social progress." Rostow to LBJ, July 28, 1967, Harry McPherson Office Papers, LBJL, Box 32.

27. Fred Harris interview, September 17, 2015.

28. United Press International, July 29, 1967, Diary Backup, LBJL, Box 72.

29. LBJ's remarks and the discussion that followed were pieced together by using four sets of notes: "Notes of Meeting," James Gaither Papers, LBJL, Box 189; Tom Johnson to LBJ, July 29, 1967, Diary Backup, LBJL, Box 72; "Minutes of Meeting," July 29, 1967, LBJL, Series 47, Box 6; and Califano to LBJ, July 28, 1967, Diary Backup, LBJL, Box 72.

30. Executive Order 11365, July 29, 1967, Otto Kerner Office Papers, Abraham Lincoln Presidential Library, Box 1392.

31. George Christian to LBJ, July 29, 1967, White House Central File, LBJL, Ex FG 686/A, Box 386; Harris interview, May 20, 2015.

32. Peden Oral History, 20. The *New York Times* agreed with Peden that the president took the guests to lunch. *New York Times*, July 30, 1967. Fred Harris, however, recalled it differently. "We scattered for lunch," he reflected in 2015. "There was no organized lunch. A few people may have gone to the White House

mess, but everyone else scattered." Most, he said, went in search of a phone to find out what messages they may have missed that morning.

33. The conversation that follows is from the following sources: "Transcript of the Proceedings Before the National Advisory Commission on Civil Disorders," August 8, 1967, LBJL, Series 1, Box 1; "Minutes of Meeting," July 29, 1967, LBJL, Series 47, Box 6; and Harris, *Does People Do It?*, 110.

34. Harris interviews, May 20, September 17, 2015.

35. David Chambers interview, February 28, 2016.

36. *Long Island Press*, August 11, 1967.

37. The comments were part of a summary provided to Ginsburg. Spivak to Ginsburg, September 5, 1967, LBJL, Series 46, Box 9. See also Taliaferro to Commission, August 21, 1967, LBJL, Series 47, Box 6.

38. McPherson to LBJ, August 14, 1967, McPherson Office Papers, LBJL, Box 32; *New York Times*, March 8, 1968.

39. *New York Times*, July 30, 1967.

40. Buchanan to RN, July 30, 1967, 1968 Campaign Research Files, Richard Nixon Presidential Library, Box 14.

CHAPTER 3: "I'LL TAKE OUT MY POCKETKNIFE AND CUT YOUR PETER OFF"

1. *Wall Street Journal*, August 16, 1967; Joseph A. Califano Jr., *The Triumph and Tragedy of Lyndon Johnson: The White House Years* (New York: Touchstone, 2015), 218; Joseph Califano interview, January 17, 2017.

2. The main source for the Ginsburg background are two *Washington Post* articles: "FDR's Living Memorial; David Ginsburg Came to Washington When the Deal Was New," April 26, 1997; and his obituary, "Led U.S. Panel on Race," May 24, 2010.

3. Califano interview, January 17, 2017.

4. Fred Harris interview, February 2, 2016.

5. President's Daily Diary, Lyndon B. Johnson Presidential Library (LBJL), July 31, 1967; David Ginsburg Oral History, LBJL, 1–6.

6. Ginsburg Oral History, 3.

7. Ibid., 7.

8. Ibid., 7–9.

9. Ibid., 8.

10. In his oral history, Ginsburg claimed that he rejected Jones and never officially hired him. But the paper trail suggests otherwise. Ibid.; news conference, August 1, 1967, Harry McPherson Office Papers, LBJL, Box 32; Jones to Kerner, August 7, 1967, Otto Kerner Office Papers, Abraham Lincoln Presidential Library (ALPL), Box 1329.

11. Victor Palmieri interview, September 28, 2015.

12. Califano to LBJ, August 7, 1967, Joseph Califano Office Papers, LBJL, Box 11.

13. David Chambers to author, December 15, 2016.

14. John A. Koskinen interview.

15. David Chambers interview, October 11, 2016. Nimitz and Chambers were both editors of the *Harvard Law Review*. Jay Kriegel, a third classmate of Nimitz and Chambers, also an editor of the *Harvard Law Review*, worked as Lindsay's liaison with the commission.

16. Stephen Kurzman interview; Charles Nelson interview, October 17, 2016.

17. *New York Times*, May 7, 1968; Nathaniel R. Jones, *Answering the Call: An Autobiography of the Modern Struggle to End Racial Discrimination in America* (New York: New Press, 2016), 84–96.

18. Chambers to the author, December 31, 2016.

19. Ginsburg Oral History, 10–11.

20. Arnold Sagalyn interview.

21. Arnold Sagalyn, *A Promise Fulfilled: The Memoir of Arnold Sagalyn* (Washington, DC: International Arts and Artists, 2010), 266–270; Sagalyn interview.

22. Sagalyn interview.

23. "Memorandum for the Commission: Research Programs," October 28, 1967, LBJL, RG 282, Series 49, Box 1; Richard Nathan interview.

24. Palmieri to Lindsay, September 1967, John Lindsay Papers, Yale University Manuscript Archive, Series 592, Box 2.

25. "Proceedings," NACCD, August 1, 1967, LBJL, Series 1, Box 1, 21; Al Spivak to Ginsburg, August 29, 1967, Kerner Office Papers, ALPL, Box 1393.

26. J. Edgar Hoover, "Memorandum for Personal Files," July 31, 1967, FOIA Declassified FBI Files, Clyde Tolson, 67-9524, Series 8.

27. "Proceedings," NACCD, August 1, 1967, LBJL, Series 1, Box 1, 6–8.

28. Ibid., 84–85.

29. Ibid., 87–90.

30. Hoover to Tolson and Sullivan, August 2, 1967, FOIA Declassified FBI Files, Tolson, 67-9524, Series 8.

31. This discussion was re-created from "Proceedings," NACCD, August 1, 1967, LBJL, Series 1, Box 1.

32. Chambers interview, March 15, 2015. In his autobiography, Wilkins confessed that he saw little difference between use of the words "black" and "Negroes." "The black power movement declared 'Negroes' a dirty word because it was considered a 'white man's word,'" he wrote. "That, of course, was true, but I could never see how the word black was much of an improvement. . . . There's not a word in the English language that couldn't be considered a white man's word." Roy Wilkins, *Standing Fast: The Autobiography of Roy Wilkins* (New York: Viking, 1982), 320.

33. "Proceedings," NACCD, August 1, 1967, LBJL, Series 1, Box 1, 42. Attorney General Ramsey Clark was also highly critical of the National Guard's performance. He told the president a few days after the Newark riot had ended that sending a nearly all-white military force "heightened the tension and anger in the Newark riot area." He also pointed out that the National Guard was not well trained in riot control. "At Newark," he wrote, "there appeared to have been serious instances of overreaction and poor judgment by the Guard." See Clark to LBJ, July 21, 1967, Ramsey Clark Papers, LBJL, Box 72.

34. Califano to LBJ, August 7, 1967, Califano Office Papers, LBJL, Box 11.

35. *New York Times*, August 11, 1967; *Washington Post*, August 11, 1967.

36. Fred Harris, *Does People Do It?* (Norman: University of Oklahoma Press, 2008), 108–109; Harris interview, May 20, 2015.

37. *New York Post*, August 24, 1967; Dolan to Harris, August 11, 1967, Fred Harris Papers, Carl Albert Congressional Research Center, Box 94; Byrd to Kerner, September 13, 1967, Kerner Office Papers, ALPL, Box 1392.

38. *New York Post*, August 24, 1967; *Nashville Banner*, September 23, 1967; *Washington Post*, August 14, 1967; *New York Times*, August 11, 1967; *Chicago Tribune*, August 11, 1967.

CHAPTER 4: "I THINK WE SHOULD AVOID OVERSTATEMENT"

1. "Trips by Commissioners," n.d., Otto Kerner Office Papers, Abraham Lincoln Presidential Library (ALPL), Box 1392; *Newark News*, August 16, 1967.

2. John Roche to LBJ, August 22, 1967, Joseph Califano Office Papers, Lyndon B. Johnson Presidential Library (LBJL), Box 11.

3. John Lindsay speech, Nelson A. Rockefeller Institute of Government, May 17, 1993, Richard Nathan Papers (private).

4. *Newark Star-Ledger*, August 24, 1967.

5. Mallett to David Chambers, September 7, 1967, LBJL, Series E10, Box E46.

6. Craig Brandon interview of James Corman, January 12, 1994, Nathan Papers.

7. Maier would repeat many of these comments in his October testimony before the commission. *Milwaukee Journal*, October 5, 1967.

8. Fred Harris, *Alarms and Hopes: A Personal Journey, a Personal View* (New York: Harper & Row, 1968), 6–16.

9. David Llorens, "Miracle in Milwaukee," *Ebony*, November 1967; Taliaferro to Staff, September 26, 1967, LBJL, RG 282, Series 47, Box 9.

10. Harris, *Alarms and Hopes*, 6–16.

11. Ibid., 10–16; Taliaferro to Staff, September 19, 1967, LBJL, RG 220, Series E10, Box E43.

12. Harris, *Alarm and Hopes*, 6–16; Taliaferro to Staff, September 19, 1967, LBJL, RG 220, Series E10, Box E43.

13. Taliaferro to Staff, September 19, 1967, LBJL, RG 220, Series E10, Box E43.

14. Harris, *Alarms and Hopes*, 6–16.

15. Taliaferro to Staff, September 19, 1967, LBJL, RG 220, Series E10, Box E43.

16. Edward W. Brooke, *Bridging the Gap: My Life* (New Brunswick, NJ: Rutgers University Press, 2007), 174–175.

17. Hunt to Staff, October 17, 1967, LBJL, RG 282, Series 47, Box 9.

18. Draft speech, n.d., Otto Kerner Family Papers, ALPL, Box 7.

19. Ibid.; *New York Times*, December 19, 1967; *Cincinnati Enquirer*, October 17, 1967.

20. *Rockford (IL) Register-Republic*, September 25, 1967.

21. Fred Harris interview, May 20, 2015; "Senator Fred Harris Reports," August 20, October 29, and November 19, 1967, Fred Harris Papers, Carl Albert Congressional Research Center, Box 94.

22. Harris, *Alarms and Hopes*, 6–16; Harris interview.

23. Draft speech, n.d., Kerner Family Papers, ALPL, Box 7; *Chicago Daily News*, March 2, 1968; *New York Times*, December 19, 1967; *Chicago Daily Defender*, October 11, 1967; *Cincinnati Enquirer*, October 17, 1967.

24. Chambers to the author, December 31, 2016.

25. Between August 1 and November 9, the commission would call 167 witnesses during nineteen days of hearings. They included cabinet and administration officers, defense and National Guard officials, governors, mayors, judges, police chiefs, professional law enforcement organizations, national civil rights leaders, ghetto representatives, economists, historians, educators, and leaders of industry, banking, commerce, and housing. McCurdy to Koskinen, February 13, 1968, LBJL, Series 46, Box 5.

26. *Washington Star*, August 22, 1967; *Trenton Times*, August 23, 1967; *Newark Star-Ledger*, August 23–24, 1967.

27. Randall B. Woods, *Prisoners of Hope: Lyndon B. Johnson, the Great Society, and the Limits of Liberalism* (New York: Basic Books, 2016), 200–201.

28. *Baltimore Sun*, December 17, 1967.

29. Bohen to Califano, August 24, 1967, David Ginsburg Papers, LOC, Box 96. Califano forwarded Bohen's memo to the president with a cover note: "I thought you might be interested in the attached report on the last meeting of the Kerner Commission." Califano to LBJ, August 24, 1967, Califano Office Papers, LBJL, Box 11.

30. Palmieri to Ginsburg, August 31, 1967, LBJL, Series 49, Box 3.

31. Ginsburg to Kerner, September 28, 1967, Kerner Office Papers, ALPL, Box 1392.

32. *Washington Post*, October 7, 1967.

33. Victor Palmieri speech at the Nelson A. Rockefeller Institute of Government, May 17, 1993, Nathan Papers.

34. David Ginsburg Oral History, 20.

35. Joseph A. Califano Jr., *The Triumph and Tragedy of Lyndon Johnson: The White House Years* (New York: Touchstone, 2015), 260.

36. Victor Palmieri interview; Harris interview.

37. Fred Harris, *Does People Do It?* (Norman: University of Oklahoma Press, 2008), 108–112; Harris interview.

CHAPTER 5: "A STRAITJACKET OF FACTS"

1. Jay Kriegel interview; Fred Harris interview, January 5, 2016.

2. "Selection of Cities for Intensive Study," n.d., Lyndon B. Johnson Presidential Library (LBJL), Series 49, Box 1.

3. Bruce Thomas interview, December 21, 2015.

4. Ibid.

5. Isaac Hunt interview.

6. Victor Palmieri to Commission, "Draft: Research Programs"; "Memorandum for the Commission: Research Programs," October 28, 1967; "Team Leader's

Check List," n.d.; and Nelson to "All Team Leaders and Members," September 29, 1967, all in LBJL, Series 49, Box 1; Thomas interview; Hunt interview; "Team Operations," n.d., Series 49, LBJL, Box 1.

7. Thomas interview, December 21, 2015.

8. *Louisville (KY) Courier-Journal*, November 8, 1967; Andrew Kopkind, "White on Black: The Riot Commission and the Rhetoric of Reform," *Hard Times* 44 (September 15–22, 1969): 1–4.

9. "Field Research Report," Newark, Vol. 3, LBJL, RG 220, Series E10, Box E55, 1–52; "Analysis of Phoenix, Arizona, Disturbances," Staff Paper #8, November 7, 1967, LBJL, RG 220, Series E12, Box 67.

10. "Field Research Report," 1–43; "Detroit," LBJL, RG 220, Series E10, Box E40, 1–12, 83; "Section 3: Atlanta," RG 220, LBJL, Series E10, Box E40.

11. "Field Research Report," 1–52.

12. "Detroit," 1–80.

13. "Team Evaluation: Atlanta," LBJL, RG 220, Series E10, Box E40.

14. "Detroit," 1–80.

15. "Field Research Report," 1, 23–27; "Detroit," 1–77.

16. "Detroit," 84; "Team Evaluation: Atlanta"; "Analysis of Plainfield, New Jersey, Disturbance," Staff Paper #3, October 27, 1967, LBJL, RG 220, Series E12, Box E66.

17. "Analysis of Dayton, Ohio, Disturbance," Staff Paper #6, rough draft, November 4, 1967, LBJL, RG 220, Series E12, Box 67; "Section 3: Atlanta."

18. "Analysis of Plainfield, New Jersey, Disturbance"; "Analysis of Dayton, Ohio, Disturbance"; "Analysis of Phoenix, Arizona, Disturbances."

19. "Detroit," 1–29; "Field Research Report," 3–85; "Detroit," 180–182; "Analysis of Dayton, Ohio, Disturbance."

20. Shellow to Ginsburg et al., "Plainfield and Cambridge Analyses," October 19, 1967, LBJL, RG 220, Series E12, Box E66; "Analysis of Dayton, Ohio, Disturbance."

21. "Detroit," 1-9; "Field Research Report," 3–6; "Analysis of Phoenix, Arizona, Disturbances."

22. "Analysis of Dayton, Ohio, Disturbance"; Gary Marx, "Analyses of Dayton," LBJL, RG 220, Series E12, Box E67; "Analysis of Plainfield, New Jersey, Disturbance."

23. "Thoughts Toward an Analysis of Cincinnati," n.d., LBJL, RG 220, Series E12, Box 67; "Section 3: Atlanta."

24. "Thoughts Toward an Analysis of Cincinnati"; "Field Research Report," 2–3.

25. Shellow to Ginsburg et al., "Plainfield and Cambridge Analyses."

26. "Milwaukee"; "Detroit," 89; "Team Evaluation: Atlanta"; "Analysis of Phoenix, Arizona, Disturbances."

27. The conversation that follows was re-created using "Official Transcript, Executive Confidential," October 27, 1967, LBJL, Series 1, Box 5; and "Attitude Survey Meeting," November 7, 1967, James Gaither Papers, LBJL, Box 244.

28. Hopkins to Watson, October 2, 1967, LBJL, Ex FG 686/A, 386; Ginsburg to Commission, October 23, 1967, LBJL, Series 5, Box 1.

29. Ginsburg to Watson, September 25, 1967, LBJL, RG 282, Series 47, Box 8; McGrath to Kerner, October 13, 1967, Otto Kerner Office Papers, ALPL, Box 1392. Not all the thinkers moved to the new building. The social scientists, for example, stayed behind. Chambers to the author, December 31, 2016.

30. McGrath to Kerner, September 29, October 13, 1967, Kerner Office Papers, ALPL, Box 1392.

31. Ibid., October 20, 1967.

32. Robert Shellow, "Social Scientists and Social Action from Within the Establishment," *Journal of Social Issues* (Winter 1970): 207–215; Robert Shellow interview.

33. Victor Palmieri interview.

CHAPTER 6: "WHITE RACISM"

1. Jenkins to Ginsburg, October 31, 1967, and Corman to Ginsburg, October 17, 1967, Lyndon B. Johnson Presidential Library (LBJL), Series 46, Box 9; McGrath to Ginsburg and Palmieri, "November 10th Meeting of the Commissioners," November 16, 1967, LBJL, Series 48, Box 3; Califano to LBJ, September 16, 1967, David Ginsburg Papers, Library of Congress (LOC), Box 96; Jones to Ginsburg, December 6, 1967, LBJL, Series 47, Box 4; Roy Wilkins Oral History, 12.

2. Speech draft, n.d., Otto Kerner Family Papers, Abraham Lincoln Presidential Library (ALPL), Box 7; Fred Harris interview, May 20. 2015.

3. Chambers to Campbell, November 20, 1970, David Chambers Papers (private).

4. "Report Draft—Part II: "Why Did It Happen?" January 1, 1968, LBJL, Series 6, Box 1.

5. Jenkins to Ginsburg, October 31, 1967, Series 46, Box 9. In a questionnaire completed in 1992, Lindsay lumped himself, Harris, and Wilkins as the liberals and labeled McCulloch, Peden, and Thornton as conservative. The others, including Kerner and Jenkins, he listed as moderates. Lindsay said that the top priority of the commission initially was to determine the facts behind the urban disorders to see if there was a conspiracy. Lindsay to Schlickman, December 7, 1992, John Lindsay Papers, Yale University Manuscript Archive, Group 592, Box 2; David Chambers interview, October 12, 2016.

6. Kurzman to All Department Heads, November 25, 1967, LBJL, Series 49, Box 3; "Final Report Options," November 20, 1967, James Gaither Papers, LBJL, Box 188.

7. Corman to Ginsburg, October 17, 1967, and Corman to Kerner, December 5, 1967, LBJL, Series 46, Box 9.

8. McGrath notes, "Meeting of Commissioners," December 8, 1967, Otto Kerner Office Papers, ALPL, Box 1329.

9. Ibid.

10. Victor Palmieri interview.

11. Bruce Thomas interview.

12. In his cover letter to Ginsburg, Thornton said that he drew on the expertise of scholars in the field. Thornton to Ginsburg, December 14, 1967, LBJL, Series 46, Box 3.

13. Ibid.

14. Franklin to Ginsburg, November 17, 1967, Ginsburg Papers, LOC, Box 129; Thornton to Ginsburg, December 14, 1967, LBJL, Series 46, Box 3.

15. McGrath to Ginsburg and Palmieri, "November 10th Meeting of Commissioners."

16. Ibid.

17. Arnold Sagalyn, *A Promise Fulfilled: The Memoir of Arnold Sagalyn* (Washington, DC: International Arts and Artists, 2010), 270–272; Arnold Sagalyn interview.

18. McGrath notes, "Meeting of Commissioners," November 20, December 8, 1967.

19. Ibid., December 8, 1967.

20. Ibid.; Michael W. Flamm, *In the Heat of the Summer: The New York Riots of 1964 and the War on Crime* (Philadelphia: University of Pennsylvania Press, 2017), 271–273.

21. McGrath notes, "Meeting of Commissioners," November 20, 1967.

22. McGrath to Ginsburg and Palmieri, "November 10 Meeting of Commissioners"; McGrath notes, "Meeting of Commissioners," November 20, 1967.

23. McGrath notes, "Meeting of Commissioners," November 20, 1967.

CHAPTER 7: "CAN YOU REALLY SAY THIS
IN A GOVERNMENT REPORT?"

1. Robert Shellow interview.

2. Ellen Herman, *The Romance of American Psychology: Political Culture in the Age of Experts* (Berkeley: University of California Press, 1996); "Memo to the Commission," October 31, 1967, Lyndon B. Johnson Presidential Library (LBJL), Series 47, Box 6.

3. Robert Shellow, "Social Scientists and Social Action from Within the Establishment," *Journal of Social Issues* (Winter 1970): 207–215; Stephen Kurzman interview.

4. Shellow interview; David Sears interview, July 28, 2016; Gary Marx interview.

5. David Boesel interview; Marx interview.

6. Shellow, "Social Scientists and Social Action"; "Plainfield Riot Scenarios," LBJL, RG 220, Series E10, Box E58.

7. Boesel interview; Shellow interview, October 18, 2016.

8. The following discussion comes from "The Harvest of American Racism: The Political Meaning of Violence in the Summer of 1967," LBJL, Series 7, Box 1, 1–176.

9. Boesel interview. There was disagreement among the authors about just how rational the riots were. "I was at odds with Boesel and Goldberg about just how

rational it all could be painted and who defined rational," Marx wrote the author in January 2017.

10. Marx developed his ideas into an article, "Civil Disorder and the Agents of Social Control," *Journal of Social Issues* 26, no. 1 (1970).

11. There is some confusion about who wrote this report. "This sounds like what I had written about the varied after the fact outcomes as part of my work," Gary Marx reflected in a January 2017 note to the author.

12. Boesel interview.

13. Ibid.

14. Shellow interview; Boesel interview; Marx interview.

15. Journalist Andrew Kopkind claimed that after reading the report, Palmieri threw it across the room at Shellow. Asked about the scene in 2015, both Palmieri and Shellow said it never happened. Andrew Kopkind, "White on Black: The Riot Commission and the Rhetoric of Reform," *Hard Times* 44 (September 15–22, 1969): 1–4; Chambers interview, March 16, 2016; Kurzman interview.

16. Victor Palmieri interview.

17. Charles Nelson to Palmieri et al., December 5, 1967, LBJL, Series 49, Box 3, Box 1.

18. Minutes for Meeting of Department Heads, November 13, 1967, and Meeting of Department Heads, November 22, 1967, LBJL, Series 49, Box 3; David Ginsburg interview, January 12, 1994, Richard Nathan Papers (private).

19. Shellow to the author, January 12, 2017.

20. It appears that Palmieri asked Shellow to rewrite the last chapter. The new version toned down many of the claims in the original version. It pointed out that violence as a political struggle was just one of many ways violence impacted cities. "The picture then is a mixed one," he concluded. "Taking the cities in their entirety, there is not much evidence that a bloody reign of terror or white repression is as yet upon us," the revised version read, "nor is there much evidence that fundamental and deep-lying changes will soon be made in the structure of our local communities." The new version brought the report in line with the commission's thinking, emphasizing the role of racism, and not powerlessness, in explaining the riots. "Shellow Redraft of Last Section," David Ginsburg Papers, Library of Congress, Box 128. When asked in 2016, Shellow said he had no recollection of rewriting the last section. But in 2017, after reading the document, he admitted that it was possible he wrote it.

21. Kurzman interview; Charles Nelson interview.

22. Martin Theodor Jaeckel, "The Use of Social Science Knowledge and Research in a Presidential Commission: A Case Study in Utilization" (PhD diss., University of Pittsburgh, 1989), 92–93.

23. "Draft Report," January 1, 1968, John Lindsay Papers, Yale University Manuscript Archive, Group 592, Box 2.

24. Jaeckel, "Use of Social Science Knowledge and Research," 92–93.

25. Ibid.; Hans W. Mattick, "The Form and Content of Recent Riots," *University of Chicago Law Review* 35, no. 4 (1968): 660–685.

26. Isaac Hunt interview.

27. Palmieri interview; Elizabeth Drew, "A Fink Operation," *Atlantic*, November 1967.

CHAPTER 8: "THAT'S GOOD AND TELL HIM
I APPRECIATE THAT"

1. News conference, August 1, 1967, Harry McPherson Office Papers, Lyndon B. Johnson Presidential Library (LBJL), Box 32.

2. Schultze to LBJ, August 17, 1967, James Gaither Papers, LBJL, Box 189.

3. David Chambers interview, April 28, 2015.

4. David Ginsburg Oral History, LBJL, 12; Schultze to LBJ, October 5, 1967, LBJL, Ex FI 4, Box 24; "Budget of the Advisory Commission on Civil Disorders," September 29, 1967, Gaither Papers, LBJL, 188.

5. Schultze to LBJ, October 5, 1967, LBJL, Ex FI 4, Box 24. Schultze was following the advice of his staff. "In view of the current congressional attitudes, we do not recommend a supplemental appropriation at this time. The only alternative way of getting staff expenses is through the inter-agency committee route." See "Budget of the Advisory Commission on Civil Disorders," 188. The Defense Department was asked to contribute $275,000 and Justice $150,000. The Departments of Labor, Commerce, Housing and Urban Development, and Health, Education, and Welfare as well as the Office of Economic Opportunity were asked to give $125,000.

6. Califano to LBJ, October 13, 1967, LBJL, Ex DF 14, Box 24; "Explanation of Breakdown of Personnel and Expenses by Office," October 13, 1967, Gaither Papers, LBJL, 189.

7. Schultze to LBJ, October 19, 1967, LBJL, Ex FI 4, Box 24. Califano included Schultze's memo as part of the president's reading that evening. Califano to LBJ, October 19, 1967, Ex FI 4, LBJL, Box 24.

8. Chambers interview; Victor Palmieri interview; Ginsburg to Bundy, October 29, 1967, John Lindsay Papers, Yale University Manuscript Archive, Group 592, Box 2; *Akron (OH) Beacon Journal*, November 15, 1967.

9. Ginsburg to William Carey, November 28, 1967, LBJL, Ex FI 4, Box 24.

10. Califano to LBJ, December 4, 1967, 2:55 p.m., ibid.

11. Ibid.

12. President's Daily Diary, LBJL, December 4, 1967.

13. Califano to LBJ, December 4, 1967, 7:30 p.m., LBJL, Ex FI 4, Box 24; Joseph Califano interview, January 17, 2017.

14. John A. Koskinen interview.

15. Joseph A. Califano Jr., *The Triumph and Tragedy of Lyndon Johnson: The White House Years* (New York: Touchstone, 2015), 245–246; Palmieri interview; Fred Harris interview.

16. "Procedure," n.d., Gaither Papers, LBJL, Box 3. The document referred to discussing the issue with the commissioners when they met in Washington on

Thursday, Friday, and Saturday. The Thursday meeting was December 7, which meant the document was likely written on Monday or Tuesday, December 4 or 5.

17. Chambers interview, October 11, 2016.

18. McGrath notes, "Meeting of Commissioners," December 9, 1967, Otto Kerner Office Papers, Abraham Lincoln Presidential Library (ALPL), Box 1329.

19. Stephen Kurzman interview.

20. McGrath notes, "Meeting of Commissioners," December 9, 1967; Chambers interview.

21. Califano to LBJ, December 9, 1967, David Ginsburg Papers, Library of Congress (LOC), Box 96.

22. Lindsay to Kerner, December 26, 1967, and Ginsburg to Califano, December 28, 1967, ibid.

23. Schultze to Ginsburg, December 29, 1967, Gaither Papers, LBJL, Box 188; Ginsburg, "N.A.C.C.D. Budget," January 6, 1968, Ex FG 686/A, LBJL, Box 386. The memo is dated January 6, 1967, but clearly that was a mistake. Since the commission managed to publish both supplemental reports, it appears that they received the extra money.

24. "For Release AM of Monday, December 11," December 10, 1967, LBJL, Series 5, Box 2.

25. "Staff," n.d., Kerner Office Papers, ALPL, Box 1392.

26. Koskinen interview; Kurzman interview.

27. David Boesel interview; Gary Marx interview.

28. Spivak to Ginsburg, "News Leaks," Ginsburg Papers, LOC, Box 96.

29. *Washington Post*, December 14, 1967; *Washington Star*, December 14, 1967.

30. Spivak to Ginsburg, January 17, 1968, LBJL, Series 47, Box 2; *Washington Star*, December 14, 1967; Spivak to Ginsburg, December 29, 1967, LBJL, Series 47, Box 2.

31. *New York Times*, December 19, 1967.

32. Ibid.; *Washington Post*, January 10, 1968.

33. "Riot Panel: High Aims, Low Budget," *Newsweek*, December 25, 1967.

CHAPTER 9: "LINDSAY HAS TAKEN EFFECTIVE
CONTROL OF THE COMMISSION"

1. Victor Palmieri interview, June 22, 2015; David Ginsburg, "Memorandum to the Commission," December 22, 1967, Lyndon B. Johnson Presidential Library (LBJL), Series 49, Box 1.

2. Jacob Rosenthal interview, July 20, 2016.

3. Palmieri to Ginsburg, August 20, 1967, David Ginsburg Papers, Library of Congress (LOC), Box 134. Downs's testimony, "The Future of American Ghettos," was presented to the Senate Subcommittee on Executive Reorganization, April 21, 1967, ibid.

4. Anthony Downs, "The Future of American Ghettos," American Academy of Arts and Sciences Conference on Urbanism, October 27–28, 1967, ibid., Box 131.

5. Palmieri to Ginsburg, August 20, 1967, ibid., Box 134; Downs testimony, "Future of American Ghettos."

6. Downs testimony, "Future of American Ghettos."

7. Downs, "Future of American Ghettos," Ginsburg Papers, LOC, Box 131.

8. "The Fundamental Issue of Whether Policies Should Focus upon Negroes Specifically," n.d., LBJL, Series 49, Box 1; R. Lowry and R. Moss to Kurzman, December 15, 1967, LBJL, Series 46, Box 7.

9. Ginsburg, "Memorandum to the Commission."

10. John A. Koskinen interview.

11. The discussion that follows is based on "Preliminary Program Recommendations Concerning Jobs and Employment, Welfare and Income Maintenance, Housing, and Education," Ginsburg Papers, LOC, Box 132.

12. Chambers interview, December 7, 2016.

13. "Long Term Programs," October 18, 1967, LBJL, RG 282, Series 47, Box 6.

14. Bergheim to Palmieri, January 16, 1968, LBJL, Series 46, Box 1.

15. Lowry to Palmieri, January 17, 1968, LBJL, Series 46, Box 1.

16. Bergheim to Palmieri, January 16, 1968, LBJL, Series 46, Box 1.

17. McGrath notes, "Meeting of Commissioners," January 9, 1968, Otto Kerner Office Papers, Abraham Lincoln Presidential Library (ALPL), Box 1329.

18. Ibid.

19. Ibid., January 11, 1968.

20. Lindsay to Commission, January 9, 1968, Kerner Office Papers, LBJL, Series 46, Box 3.

21. McGrath notes, "Meeting of Commissioners," January 20, 1968.

22. McGrath to Kerner, January 2, 1968, Kerner Office Papers, ALPL, Box 1329.

23. Ibid.

24. McGrath notes, "Meeting of Commissioners," January 9, 1968.

25. Ibid., January 19, 1968.

26. Ibid., January 9, 1967, January 18, 1968.

27. Ibid., January 18, 20, 1968.

28. Ibid., January 20, 1968.

29. Ibid.

30. Staff Davis and Whitt Schultz, "Riot Coverage: Cool It?," *Quill* (October 1967): 1620; *Lebanon Valley (PA) News*, November 7, 1967.

31. A. M. Rosenthal to Lindsay, October 30, 1967, and Palmieri to Ginsburg, October 13, 1967, LBJL, Series 48, Box 3.

32. McGrath notes, "Meeting of Commissioners," January 19, 1968.

33. Ibid.

34. Ibid., January 20, 1968.

35. Kurzman interview.

36. Corman to Kerner, January 13, 1968, LBJL, Series 46, Box 9.

37. Irv Sprague to Barefoot Sanders, January 15, 1968, Ginsburg Papers, LOC, Box 96.

38. McGrath notes, "Meeting of Commissioners," January 19, 1968.

39. Ibid.

40. Ibid.

41. McGrath to Kerner, February 1, 1968, Kerner Office Papers, ALPL, Box 1392.

42. Robert Conot, "Profiling the Riots: Conflict, but No Conspiracy," *Newsday*, March 6, 1988.

43. Kriegel to Lindsay, January 15, 1968, John Lindsay Papers, Yale University Manuscript Archive, Group 592, Box 2.

44. Rosenthal to Ginsburg and Palmieri, January 12, 1968, Jack Rosenthal Papers, John F. Kennedy Library, Box 2.

CHAPTER 10: "TWO SOCIETIES"

1. Program Recommendations, David Ginsburg Papers, Library of Congress (LOC), Box 133.

2. President's Commission on Law Enforcement and the Administration of Justice, *The Challenge of Crime in a Free Society* (Washington, DC: US Government Printing Office, 1967).

3. Schwartz to Bower, February 17, 1968, Lyndon B. Johnson Presidential Library (LBJL), Series 21, Box 1.

4. Robert Conot, "Profiling the Riots: Conflict, but No Conspiracy," *Newsday*, March 6, 1988.

5. McGrath to Kerner, February 1, 2, 1968, Otto Kerner Office Papers, Abraham Lincoln Presidential Library (ALPL), Box 1392.

6. "Draft," February 1, 1968, and "Chapter 19: Recommendations for National Action," February draft, John Lindsay Papers, Yale University Manuscript Archive (YUL), Group 592, Box 2. Some of the background documents that went into rewriting the new draft can be found at "Background Reports," Ginsburg Papers, LOC, Boxes 133–134.

7. "Memorandum to Commission," February 12, 1968, Kerner Office Papers, ALPL, Box 1394; Gorham to David, February 8, 1968, LBJL, Series 47, Box 4.

8. Appointment books, Roy Wilkins Papers, LOC, Box 73.

9. Rush telegrams, February 20, 1968, Lindsay Papers, YUL, Group 592, Box 2.

10. Fred Harris interview, May 20, 2015.

11. Ginsburg to Lindsay, February 3, 1968, LBJL, Series 47, Box 2. Attached to the letter was a January 24, 1967, draft titled "Financing Possibilities for New and Expanded Ghetto-Oriented Federal Programs."

12. "The Budget Deficit and the Social Deficit for the Urban Poor," draft, February 5, 1968, Ginsburg Papers, Box 132; "Draft," February 15, 1968, Kerner Office Papers, ALPL, Box 1400; David Ginsburg Oral History, LBJL, 28; Nathaniel R. Jones, *Answering the Call: An Autobiography of the Modern Struggle to End Racial Discrimination in America* (New York: New Press, 2016), 95.

13. Kerner to Hoover, February 22, 1968, and Hoover to Kerner, February 27, 1968, Kerner Office Papers, ALPL, Box 1392; Ginsburg to Commission, February 22, 1968, ibid., Box 1394; Chambers to the author, January 27, 2017.

14. Ginsburg Oral History, 27; Otto Kerner Oral History, LBJL, 19–20.

15. Peter Goldmark interview, March 3, 2015.

16. Chambers to the author, January 27, 2017.

17. "Preface," n.d., Lindsay Papers, YUL, Group 592, Box 2.

18. Goldmark interview; Jay Kriegel interview.

19. "Summary Draft, Mayor Lindsay," Lindsay Papers, YUL, Group 592, Box 2. In an October 1967 conference on urbanism, Downs said that pursuing the current strategy in the city "would involve mainly nonwhite, mainly poor, and fiscally bankrupt central cities on the one hand, and mainly white, much wealthier, but high-taxed suburbs on the other hand." Anthony Downs, "The Future of American Ghettos," American Academy of Arts and Sciences Conference on Urbanism, October 27–28, 1967, Ginsburg Papers, LOC, Box 131. On the evolution of the language, see "The Future of the Cities," Rosenthal master, February 8, 1968, Jack Rosenthal Papers, John F. Kennedy Library (JFKL), Box 2; Rosenthal to Ginsburg and Palmieri, February 9, 1968, Ginsburg Papers, LOC, Box 131.

20. Lindsay, "Summary Draft," n.d., Lindsay Papers, YUL, Group 592, Box 2.

21. There are no dates on most drafts of the summary, but it is possible to identify the date of the Lindsay draft by piecing together information from a few sources. On February 22, Ginsburg sent a copy of Lindsay's draft to the commissioners with a cover letter stating that the mayor "asked that the summary he read at the last meeting be sent to each Commissioner." See Ginsburg, "Mayor Lindsay's Summary," February 22, 1968, LBJL, RG 282, Series 5, Box 3. There is no official schedule of commission meetings in February, but Roy Wilkins's appointment book offers a clue. The meeting immediately preceding the date of Ginsburg's letter was February 17. See appointment books, Wilkins Papers, LOC, Box 73.

22. Goldmark interview.

23. Palmieri to Commission, February 23, 1968, LBJL, Series 5, Box 3. Peter Goldmark has a clear recollection of writing similar words during the all-night session with Jay Kriegel. "We had it a little different," he wrote the author in 2016. "White institutions created it, white society maintains it, and white morality condones it." The language, however, does not appear either in the copy of the summary in Lindsay's official papers or in the version of Lindsay's summary that Ginsburg sent to the commissioners on February 23. It's hard to reconcile the documentary evidence with Goldmark's detailed recollection. One possibility is that Goldmark and Kriegel wrote the sentence, but it was not added to the official summary until the editing process. Goldmark to the author, December 25, 2016.

24. Rosenthal, "Summary of the Report: Introduction," February 24, 1968, and "Summary of the Report: Introduction," draft 3, February 25, 1968, Rosenthal Papers, JFKL, Box 2; Palmieri presentation at the Nelson A. Rockefeller Institute of Government, May 17, 1993, Richard Nathan Papers (private); Victor Palmieri interview. For the best and most detailed analysis of the evolution of the summary, see Rick Loessberg, "Two Societies: The Writing of the Summary of the *Report of the National Advisory Commission on Civil Disorders,*" *Journal of Urban History* (2017).

25. Palmieri to the author, June 5, 2015; Chambers interview, March 8, 2016.

26. Fred Harris interview.

27. Ibid. Harris recalled Thornton holding up a document, suggesting that he had written a minority report. No such document exists in the commission papers or in the Ginsburg Papers, both at the Library of Congress. Thornton's son, who controls his father's personal papers, said he searched the papers and did not find such a document.

28. John A. Byrne, *The Whiz Kids: The Founding Fathers of American Business—and the Legacy They Left Us* (New York: Doubleday, 1993), 483–491.

29. Harris interview.

30. Ibid.

31. "Roots of Riot—Call to Battle," *Newsweek*, March 11, 1968, 39–46.

32. Harris interview.

33. William McCulloch, "Speech Before the City Club, Cleveland, Ohio," March 8, 1968, William McCulloch Papers, Ohio Congressional Archives, Series 2, Box 34; Mark Bernstein, *McCulloch of Ohio: For the Republic* (New Bremen, OH: Crown Equipment, 2014), 200–201.

CHAPTER 11: "I'D BE A HYPOCRITE"

1. Edward W. Brooke, *Bridging the Divide: My Life* (New Brunswick, NJ: Rutgers University Press, 2007), 173; *Los Angeles Times*, April 7, 1968.

2. Watson to LBJ, Tuesday, February 13, 1968, 9:15 p.m., David Ginsburg Papers, Library of Congress (LOC), Box 96.

3. George C. Herring, *LBJ and Vietnam: A Different Kind of War* (Austin: University of Texas Press, 1994), 154.

4. Terry H. Anderson, *The Movement and the Sixties: Protest in America from Greensboro to Wounded Knee* (New York: Oxford University Press, 1995), 183–186.

5. Andrew Kopkind, "White on Black: The Riot Commission and the Rhetoric of Reform," *Hard Times* 44 (September 15–22, 1969): 1–4; Fred Harris Oral History, Richard Nathan Papers (private). The oral history, conducted by the Nelson A. Rockefeller Institute of Government, most likely took place on January 12, 1994.

6. Clifford Alexander Oral History, Lyndon B. Johnson Presidential Library (LBJL), 30.

7. LBJ to Califano, February 26, 1968, LBJL, Ex FG, Box 387.

8. Joseph A. Califano Jr., *The Triumph and Tragedy of Lyndon Johnson: The White House Years* (New York: Touchstone, 2015), 261.

9. Stanley Karnow, *Vietnam: A History* (New York: Viking, 1983), 547; Taylor Branch, *At Canaan's Edge: America in the King Years, 1965–68* (New York: Simon and Schuster, 2006), 706.

10. Califano to LBJ, February 28, 1968, Ginsburg Papers, LOC, Box 96.

11. Karnow, *Vietnam: A History*, 551–552.

12. Califano, *Triumph and Tragedy*, 263; Merle Miller, *Lyndon: An Oral Biography* (New York: G. P. Putnam's Sons, 1980), 515–516.

13. Califano, *Triumph and Tragedy*, 262; *New York Times*, March 11, 1968.

14. Victor Palmieri interview; David Chambers interview, April 28, 2015; John A. Koskinen interview. Fred Harris was deeply skeptical that Ginsburg would leak the report. "I have no idea why Victor would say that Ginsburg leaked the report," he said. Harris to the author, February 2, 2016.

15. Califano, *Triumph and Tragedy*, 262; Califano to LBJ, February 28, 1968, Ginsburg Papers, LOC, Box 96.

16. McPherson to Califano, March 1, 1968, Ginsburg Papers, LOC, Box 96.

17. Califano to LBJ, March 2, 1968, ibid.; draft statement for LBJ, February 28, 1968, James Gaither Papers, LBJL, Box 188.

18. *New York Daily News*, March 5, 1968.

19. *Louisville (KY) Courier-Journal*, March 6, 1968; *Washington Post*, March 11, 1968; Califano, *Triumph and Tragedy*, 262.

20. Martin to Califano, March 5, 1968, LBJL, Ex FG 690, Box 387. Califano included the memorandum in LBJ's nightly reading. Califano to LBJ, March 5, 1968, LBJL, EXS FG 690, Box 387.

21. Roy Wilkins Oral History, LBJL, 11; Roy Wilkins, *Standing Fast: The Autobiography of Roy Wilkins* (New York: Viking, 1982), 328; Brooke, *Bridging the Divide*, 173.

22. Califano to LBJ, Friday, March 8, 1968, 7:45 p.m., Ginsburg Papers, LOC, Box 96.

23. Taliaferro to Ginsburg, March 11, 1968, Gaither Papers, LBJL, Box 188.

24. "Remarks of the President at the Meeting with the Joint Committee on Urban Problems of the Savings Bank and Loan Industries," March 6, 1968, White House Central File (WHCF), LBJL, Ex SP, Box 5.

25. Jones to Watson, March 15, 1968, WHCF, LBJL, Ex FG 690, Box 387.

26. "Notes on the President's Meeting with Negro Editors and Publishers," March 15, 1968, WHCF, LBJL, Ex FG 690.

27. LBJ and Daley, March 13, 1968, Miller Center, tape WH6803.02. Apparently, LBJ did not hold a grudge against Kerner. On March 8, just one week after the commission issued its report, the president nominated Kerner to the US Court of Appeals for the Seventh Circuit in Chicago.

28. McPherson to LBJ, March 13, 1968, and "LBJ/mf, 3-13-68, 4:20p," Ginsburg Papers, LOC, Box 96.

29. Press conference, LBJL, Series 47, Box 6; *New York Times*, March 23, 1968; *Washington Post*, March 23, 1968.

30. Califano, *Triumph and Tragedy*, 262; Ben Wattenberg Oral History, LBJL, 33.

31. Arthur Schlesinger Jr., *Robert Kennedy and His Times* (New York: Ballantine, 1978), 904–908.

32. *New York Times*, March 14, 1968.

33. Rick Perlstein, *Nixonland: The Rise of a President and the Fracturing of America* (New York: Scribner, 2008), 246–247.

34. Miller, *Lyndon: An Oral Biography*, 516; Califano, *Triumph and Tragedy*, 256–257.

35. *Public Papers of the Presidents of the United States: Lyndon B. Johnson, 1965*, vol. 2, entry 301 (Washington, DC: US Government Printing Office, 1966), 635–640.

36. "Memorandum for the President," March 15, 1968, LBJL, Ex FG 690, Box 387.

37. Nathan, "The Role and Impact of the Kerner Commission Report," January 1988, Nathan Papers (private).

38. Califano interview, January 17, 2017.

39. Califano, *Triumph and Tragedy*, 262–263; Harry McPherson Oral History, LBJL, 2, 20.

40. Robert Dallek, *Flawed Giant: Lyndon Johnson and His Times, 1961–1973* (New York: Oxford University Press, 1998), 413; Allen Matusow, *The Unraveling of America: A History of Liberalism in the 1960s* (New York: Harper & Row, 1984), 394.

41. Randall B. Woods, *Prisoners of Hope: Lyndon B. Johnson, the Great Society, and the Limits of Liberalism* (New York: Basic Books, 2016), 354.

42. Clay Risen, *A Nation on Fire: America in the Wake of the King Assassination* (New York: Wiley, 2009), 25; Doris Kearns Goodwin, *Lyndon Johnson and the American Dream* (New York: St. Martins, 1991), 347.

CHAPTER 12: "THE MOST COURAGEOUS GOVERNMENT REPORT IN THE LAST DECADE"

1. "A Draft Proposal for National and Local Conferences on the First Anniversary of the Report of the President's National Advisory Commission on Civil Disorders," Fred Harris Papers, December 16, 1968, Carl Albert Congressional Research Center (CACRC), Box 101; Fred Harris interview, May 20, 2015; *Los Angeles Times*, March 1, 1968; *New York Times*, March 1, 1968; *Baltimore Evening Sun*, March 1, 1968.

2. Rosenthal to Ginsburg, March 20, 1968, David Ginsburg Papers, Library of Congress (LOC), Box 135; *New York Times*, March 5, 1968; Spivak to Ginsburg, February 21, 1968, James Gaither Papers, Lyndon B. Johnson Presidential Library (LBJL), Box 188.

3. *New York Times*, March 2, 1968; *Washington Daily News*, March 7, 1968; "Paperback," March 22, 1968, Harry McPherson Office Papers, LBJL, Box 32.

4. "Paperback"; *New York Times*, March 2, 1968.

5. "To All Xerox People," May 16, 1968, Ginsburg Papers, LOC, Box 123; *Christian Science Monitor*, March 6, 1968.

6. *New York Times*, April 10, 1968; *Washington Post*, March 1, 1968; *Christian Science Monitor*, March 4, 1968.

7. "Cities: Studying the Study," *Time*, March 15, 1968, 16–17; *Washington Evening Star*, March 4, 1968; "The Riot Report's Prescriptions," *Nation's Cities*, April 1968, 4.

8. Percy comments from the Senate floor, March 7, 1968, John Lindsay Papers, Yale University Manuscript Archive, Group 592, Box 2; *Washington Post*, March 6, 1968.

9. King to Kerner, March 7, 1968, Otto Kerner Family Papers, Abraham Lincoln Presidential Library (ALPL), Box 34; *Philadelphia Inquirer*, March 2, 1968; *Washington Evening Star*, March 12, 1968; *New York Times*, March 2, 1968.

10. *Chicago Tribune*, March 12, 1968; *Philadelphia Bulletin*, March 3, 1968; Bayard Rustin, "The Lessons of the Long Hot Summer," *Commentary* (October 1967): 1–8; Bayard Rustin, "*The Report of the National Advisory Commission on Civil Disorders*: An Analysis," Ginsburg Papers, LOC, Box 121; *New York Times*, April 28, 1968.

11. *New York Amsterdam News*, March 23, 1968.

12. *Philadelphia Inquirer*, March 2, 1968.

13. *Los Angeles Times*, April 11, 1968; Gary T. Marx, "Report of the National Advisory Commission: The Analysis of Disorder or Disorderly Analysis?," Harris Papers, CACRC, Box 101.

14. Robert Fogelson, "Review Symposium," *American Political Science Review* 63, no. 4 (1969): 1269–1281.

15. *Chicago Daily News*, March 2, 1968; *Washington Daily News*, March 14, 1968.

16. *Washington Evening Star*, March 2, 1968; Litton to Albert, March 9, 1968; and Kelso to Albert, March 6, 1968, all in Carl Albert Papers, CACRC, Box 103; *Washington Post*, March 2, 1968.

17. The *Washington Star* editorial was republished in the *New York Times*, March 10, 1968. See also *Alexandria (VA) Gazette*, March 7, 1968.

18. *Raleigh News and Observer*, March 2, 1968.

19. *Wall Street Journal*, March 4, 1968; *Alexandria (VA) Gazette*, March 7, 1968.

20. *Washington Star*, March 7, 1968; *Chicago Tribune*, March 2, 1968.

21. *Richmond (VA) Times-Dispatch*, March 1, 1968; *Philadelphia Inquirer*, March 2, 1968; *Chicago Tribune*, March 6, 1968.

22. Hamilton to NACCD, March 6, 1968; Buter to Kerner, January 11, 1968; Nimitz to NACCD, March 10, 1968, all in LBJL, Series 30, Box 1. For Kerner's comments, see "Speech Draft," n.d., Kerner Family Papers, ALPL, Box 7.

23. *Washington Post*, April 16, 1968; Panzer to Jones, May 13, 1968, LBJL, Ex FG 690, Box 387.

24. Press release, "U.S. Commission on Civil Rights," March 15, 1968, LBJL, Series 47, Box 6; *Washington Post*, March 22, 26, 1968; Ginsburg to Cohen, March 29, 1968, LBJL, Series 47, Box 4. Later that month, Humphrey changed his mind again, calling the report "a comprehensive, in-depth analysis of social, economic and psychological problems facing the American people today." "Speech to the Legislative Conference of the Building Construction Trades Department, AFL-CIO," March 28, 1968, LBJL, Series 47, Box 6.

25. "An Address by Richard Nixon," March 7, 1968, 1968 Campaign Research Files, Richard Nixon Presidential Library (RNPL), Box 1; Evan Thomas, *Being*

Nixon: A Man Divided (New York: Random House, 2015), 142–159; *New York Times*, March 7, 1968; Stephen Lesher, *George Wallace: American Populist* (New York: Da Capo, 1995), 402–403.

26. Anderson to DC, March 4, 1968; AG to DC, April 8, 1968, 1968 Campaign Research Files, RNPL, Box 17. "DC" referred to Dwight Chapin, who was Nixon's "body man." According to Nixon speechwriter Patrick Buchanan, the staff always addressed their memos to Chapin. In the event something controversial in the memos ever leaked to the press, Nixon could deny having read it. Buchanan interview, September 14, 2015.

27. J. Pat Rooney, "Report of Commission on Civil Disorders, March 8, 1968," 1968 Campaign Research Files, RNPL, Box 1.

28. "Press Conference of Governor Ronald Reagan," March 5, 1968, Ronald Reagan Gubernatorial Papers, 1966–1975, Ronald Reagan Presidential Library (RRPL), Box P2; "Excerpts from Speech by Governor Ronald Reagan, California Republican Assembly," March 30, 1968, RRPL, P52.

29. Ford address to the Virginia Public Relations Conference, Gerald Ford Congressional Papers, Gerald Ford Presidential Library, Box D12.

30. Harris to Kerner, April 2, 1968, Otto Kerner Office Papers, ALPL, Box 1392; Randall B. Woods, *Prisoners of Hope: Lyndon B. Johnson, the Great Society, and the Limits of Liberalism* (New York: Basic Books, 2016), 359.

31. Woods, *Prisoners of Hope*, 360.

32. *New York Times*, April 11, 1968; Califano to LBJ, April 10, 1968; Kerner to Califano, April 25, 1968; and Califano to LBJ, April 30, 1968, all in LBJL, Ex FG 690, Box 387.

33. Quoted in "Draft Proposal for National and Local Conferences."

34. "A Failure to Communicate," *Columbia Journalism Review* (Spring 1968): 4; "A Time of Assassins," *Columbia Journalism Review* (Summer 1968): 5–9; "News Media and Race Relations: A Self-Portrait," *Columbia Journalism Review* (Fall 1968): 42–49; Harris, "First Rough Draft: The Kerner Commission Report One Year Later," Harris Papers, CACRC, Box 101.

35. "Congress Enacts Open Housing Legislation," in *CQ Almanac*, 24th ed. (Washington, DC: Congressional Quarterly, 1969), 14–152.

36. Cong. Rec., 90th Cong., 2nd Sess. (February 6, 1968): 2533, (February 15, 1968): 3134–3135.

37. Ibid. (March 2, 1968): 4898–4899; "Congress Enacts Open Housing Legislation," 14–152.

38. *Washington Post*, April 15, 1968; *Chicago Tribune*, April 10, 1968.

39. Clay Risen, *A Nation on Fire: America in the Wake of the King Assassination* (New York: Wiley, 2009), 214–215; *New York Post*, April 15, 1968.

40. Harris interview.

41. *New York Times*, February 18, 1968.

42. Roy Wilkins, *Standing Fast: The Autobiography of Roy Wilkins* (New York: Viking, 1982), 328.

43. Harry McPherson Oral History, LBJL, tape 2, 20.

CHAPTER 13: "THE 60S AND 70S SEEM TO HAVE LEFT US
EXHAUSTED"

1. Michael W. Flamm, *Law and Order: Street Crime, Civil Unrest, and the Crisis of Liberalism in the 1960s* (New York: Columbia University Press, 2005), 161.

2. Allen J. Matusow, *The Unraveling of America: A History of Liberalism in the 1960s* (New York: Harper & Row, 1984), 437–439.

3. Dan Baum, "Legalize It All," *Harper's Magazine*, April 26, 2016. In October 1970, Nixon signed into law the bipartisan Comprehensive Drug Abuse and Control Act, which toughened mandatory sentence guidelines for "dope pushers." In signing the bill, Nixon called heroin "America's Public Enemy Number One." See Michael J. Flamm, *In the Heat of the Summer: The New York Riots of 1964 and the War on Crime* (Philadelphia: University of Pennsylvania Press, 2017), 288.

4. Thomas Byrne Edsall with Mary D. Edsall, "Race," *Atlantic*, May 1991.

5. Samuel Lubell, *The Future of American Politics* (New York: Doubleday, 1956); Nathan Glaser, "The Limits of Social Policy," *Commentary* 52 (September 1971): 51.

6. Thomas Muller, *Immigrants and the American City* (New York: New York University Press, 1993), 260; Jack Miles, "Blacks vs. Browns," *Atlantic*, October 1992, 51; Robin D. G. Kelley and Earl Lewis, eds., *To Make Our World Anew: A History of African Americans* (New York: Oxford University Press, 2000), 608–609.

7. "Beyond Black and White," *Newsweek*, April–June 1992, 24.

8. Gerald David Jaynes and Robin M. Williams, eds., *A Common Destiny: Blacks and American Society* (Washington, DC: National Academy Press, 1989), 8; Kelley and Lewis, *To Make Our World Anew*, 558–564.

9. Jaynes and Williams, *Common Destiny*, 275–276.

10. For an excellent discussion of the impact of suburbanization in Atlanta, see Kevin M. Kruse, *White Flight: Atlanta and the Making of Modern Conservatism* (Princeton, NJ: Princeton University Press, 2005).

11. William Julius Wilson, *When Work Disappears: The World of the New Urban Poor* (New York: Alfred A. Knopf, 1996); Kelley and Lewis, *To Make Our World Anew*, 576–577.

12. Reynolds Farley and William H. Frey, "Changes in the Segregation of Whites from Blacks During the 1980s: Small Steps Toward a More Integrated Society," *American Sociological Review* (February 1994): 23–45; Douglas S. Massey and Nancy A. Denton, *American Apartheid: Segregation and the Making of the Underclass* (Cambridge, MA: Harvard University Press, 1993); David Cutler, Edward Glaeser, and Jacob Vigdor, "The Rise and Decline of the America City," *Journal of Political Economy* (1999): 455–506; Gary Orfield, "Segregated Housing and School Resegregation," in *Dismantling Desegregation: The Quiet Reversal of "Brown v. Board of Education,"* by Gary Orfield, Susan E. Eaton, and the Harvard Project on School Desegregation (New York: New Press, 1996), 318–320; Paul A. Jargowsky, "Take the Money and Run: Economic Segregation in U.S. Metropolitan Areas," *American Sociological Review* 61 (1996): 984–998.

13. Sean F. Reardon and Kendra Bischoff, "Growth in the Residential Segregation of Families by Income, 1970–2009," Russell Sage Foundation, November

2011, https://s4.ad.brown.edu/Projects/Diversity/Data/Report/report1111111.pdf, 1–32; Greg J. Duncan and Jeanne Brooks-Gunn, *The Consequences of Growing Up Poor* (New York: Russell Sage Foundation, 1997).

14. Mark Schneider and Thomas Phelan, "Black Suburbanization in the 1980s," *Demography* (May 1993): 269–279; John M. Stahura, "Changing Patterns of Suburban Racial Composition, 1970–1980," *Urban Affairs Quarterly* (1988): 448–460.

15. Orfield, "Segregated Housing and School Resegregation," 53–57.

16. A few days after the commission finished its work, LBJ nominated Otto Kerner for a federal judgeship. In 1974, however, he became the first sitting federal judge to be convicted of a felony. The charges stemmed from bribes he accepted during his first term as governor. He died in May 1976.

17. Richard Nathan, "Riots in Slow Motion: The Kerner Commission Revisited Twenty-Five Years Later," unpublished manuscript, Richard Nathan Papers (private); *New York Times*, May 26, 1992.

18. Lindsay to Curtis, April 7, 1993, John Lindsay Papers, Yale University Manuscript Archive, Group 592, Box 2.

19. Lindsay to Johnson, January 5, 1988, ibid.; Fred Harris interview, May 20, 2015.

20. William Julius Wilson, *The Declining Significance of Race: Blacks and Changing American Institutions* (Chicago: University of Chicago Press, 1978). Critics pointed out that he painted too optimistic a portrait of middle-class blacks, failed to acknowledge how discrimination prevented their upward mobility, and ignored the persistence of housing segregation. In response, Wilson revised his views, saying that a class-based approach was not sufficient and that he now supported race-specific policies such as affirmative action. For his revised views, see William Julius Wilson, "*The Declining Significance of Race*: Revisited and Revised," *Daedalus* 140, no. 2 (2001): 55–69.

21. Nathan, "Riots in Slow Motion," 88–96.

22. *New York Times*, February 6, 2015; James T. Patterson, *Restless Giant: The United States from Watergate to "Bush v. Gore"* (New York: Oxford University Press, 2005), 308.

23. Michelle Alexander, *The New Jim Crow: Mass Incarceration in the Age of Colorblindness* (New York: New Press, 2012), 56–57; Michelle Alexander, "A System of Racial and Social Control," *Frontline*, April 29, 2014; Heather Ann Thompson, "Why Mass Incarceration Matters: Rethinking Crisis, Decline, and Transformation in Postwar American History," *Journal of American History* (December 2010): 708.

24. Aronson to Emanuel, April 18, 1997, Office of Speechwriting and Michael Waldman, Race Initiative, Clinton Digital Library, https://clinton.presidentiallibraries.us/items/show/45700.

25. Reed to Waldman, "Race Speech," June 12, 1997, ibid., https://clinton.presidentiallibraries.us/items/show/46128.

26. Claire Jean Kim, "Clinton's Race Initiative: Recasting the American Dilemma," *Polity* 33, no. 2 (2000): 175–197.

27. *New York Times*, February 24, 2016; Ned Resnikoff, "Race Is the Elephant in the Room When It Comes to Inequality," MSNBC, May 23, 2014.

28. Frank Newport, "America Sees Obama Election as Race Relations Milestone," *Gallup*, November 7, 2008.

29. *Christian Science Monitor*, June 29, 2014.

30. *New York Times*, June 21, 2015.

31. *Washington Post*, August 5, 2015.

32. *New York Times*, May 12, 2015.

33. *Los Angeles Times*, August 10, 2016; Office of Public Affairs, Department of Justice, "Justice Department Announces Findings of Two Civil Rights Investigations in Ferguson, Missouri," March 4, 2015, www.justice.gov/opa/pr/justice-department-announces-findings-two-civil-rights-investigations-ferguson-missouri.

34. *New York Times*, June 21, 2015, and August 10, 2016.

35. *Daily Telegraph*, August 24, 2014; Daniel Horowitz, "Baltimore Riots: Mob Rule and the Role of Local Government," *Conservative Review* (April 28, 2015).

36. John McWhorter, "Racism in America Is Over," *Forbes*, December 30, 2008.

37. Jamelle Bouie, "How Trump Happened," *Slate*, March 13, 2016.

38. *Report of the National Advisory Commission on Civil Disorders* (New York: E. P. Dutton, 1968), 483.

A NOTE ON SOURCES

The Lyndon B. Johnson Presidential Library in Austin, Texas, is the starting point for any book about the Kerner Commission. The library houses the commission's official papers, along with most of the relevant collections of administration officials who were involved with the commission's work. Especially useful are the papers of White House domestic policy adviser Joseph Califano. The library also houses a rich oral history collection that includes interviews with many key players.

There are other valuable manuscript collections that shed light on the internal workings of the commission. David Ginsburg's papers at the Library of Congress contain important materials not found in the official papers. Also useful are the John Lindsay Papers at Yale University and Fred Harris's collection at the Carl Albert Congressional Research Center at the University of Oklahoma. Otto Kerner's papers at the Abraham Lincoln Presidential Library contain insightful memos from Kerner's assistant Kyran McGrath that are not included in the official collection at the LBJ Library.

While there are no book-length treatments of the commission, there are several useful articles and book chapters: Michael Lipsky, "Social Scientists and the Riot Commission," *Annals of the American Academy of Political and Social Science* 394 (March 1971); Lindsay Lupo, *Flak-Catchers: One Hundred Years of Riot Commission Politics in America* (New York: Lexington Books, 2001); Michael Lipsky and David Olson, *Commission Politics: The Processing of Racial Crisis in America* (New Brunswick, NJ: Transaction Books, 1977); Andrew Kopkind, "White on Black: The Riot Commission and the Rhetoric of Reform," *Hard Times* 44 (September 15–22, 1969); and David C. Carter, *The Music Has Gone Out of the Movement: Civil Rights and the Johnson Administration, 1965–1968* (Chapel Hill: University of North Carolina Press, 2009).

Many of the commissioners later penned autobiographies that included coverage of their role on the commission. By far the best is Fred Harris, *Alarms and Hopes: A Personal Journey, a Personal View* (New York: Harper & Row, 1968). Harris started writing the book while the commission was still active. Another Harris memoir, *Does People Do It?* (Norman: University of Oklahoma Press, 2008), also contains a chapter on his commission work. Other autobiographies include Roy

Wilkins, *Standing Fast: The Autobiography of Roy Wilkins* (New York: Viking, 1982); Edward W. Brooke, *Bridging the Divide: My Life* (Brunswick, NJ: Rutgers University Press, 2007); and Herbert Jenkins, *Keeping the Peace: A Police Chief Looks at His Job* (New York: Harper & Row, 1970). Two staff members also wrote books: Arnold Sagalyn, *A Promise Fulfilled: The Memoir of Arnold Sagalyn* (Washington, DC: International Arts and Artists, 2010); and Nathaniel R. Jones, *Answering the Call: An Autobiography of the Modern Struggle to End Racial Discrimination in America* (New York: New Press, 2016).

Many of the commissioners have also been the subject of biographies. John A. Byrne sheds light on the life of Charles "Tex" Thornton in *The Whiz Kids: Ten Founding Fathers of American Business—and the Legacy They Left Us* (New York: Bantam Books, 1993). Other biographies include Richard Lowitt, *Fred Harris: His Journey from Liberalism to Populism* (New York: Rowman & Littlefield, 2002); Yvonne Ryan, *Roy Wilkins: The Quiet Revolutionary and the NAACP* (Lexington: University Press of Kentucky, 2014); Joseph P. Viteritti, ed., *Summer in the City: John Lindsay, New York, and the American Dream* (Baltimore: Johns Hopkins University Press, 2014); Bill Barnhart and Gene Schlickman, *Kerner: The Conflict of Intangible Rights* (Urbana: University of Illinois Press, 1999); and Mark Bernstein, *McCulloch of Ohio: For the Republic* (New Bremen, OH: Crown Equipment, 2014).

There is a large body of literature on presidential commissions. See Thomas R. Wolanin, *Presidential Advisory Commissions: Truman to Nixon* (Madison: University of Wisconsin Press, 1975); Frank Popper, *The President's Commissions* (New York: Twentieth Century Fund, 1970); Hugh Davis Graham, "The Ambiguous Legacy of American Presidential Commissions," *Public Historian* (Spring 1985): 5–25; Amy Zegart, "Blue Ribbons, Black Boxes: Toward a Better Understanding of Presidential Commissions, *Presidential Studies Quarterly* (June 2004); and Martha Derthick, *On Commissionship—Presidential Variety* (Washington, DC: Brookings Institution, 1972).

A handful of books by the historian James T. Patterson provide context and perspective for understanding race relations in American since the end of World War II: *Grand Expectations: The United States, 1945–1974* (New York: Oxford University Press, 1997), *Restless Giant: The United States from Watergate to "Bush v. Gore"* (New York: Oxford University Press, 2007), and *The Moynihan Report and America's Struggle over Black Family Life from LBJ to Obama* (New York: Basic Books, 2012).

Joseph Califano has written the best insider account of life in the Johnson White House: *The Triumph and Tragedy of Lyndon Johnson: The White House Years* (New York: Touchstone, 2015). Other useful accounts include Robert Dallek, *Flawed Giant: Lyndon Johnson and His Times, 1961–1973* (New York: Oxford University Press, 1998); Doris Kearns Goodwin, *Lyndon Johnson and the American Dream* (New York: St. Martins, 1991); Randall B. Woods, *Prisoners of Hope: Lyndon B. Johnson, the Great Society, and the Limits of Liberalism* (New York: Basic Books, 2016); Allen Matusow, *The Unraveling of America: A History of Liberalism in the 1960s* (New York: Harper and Row, 1984); Merle Miller, *Lyndon: An Oral Biography* (New York: G. P. Putnam's Sons, 1980); and Eric Goldman, *The Tragedy of Lyndon Johnson* (New York: Alfred A. Knopf, 1969). LBJ tells his own story in *The Vantage Point: Perspectives of the Presidency, 1963–1969* (New York: Holt, Rinehart, and Winston, 1971).

Two books by Thomas Sugrue set the standard for understanding race relations in the North after World War II: *The Origins of the Urban Crisis: Race and Inequality in Postwar Detroit* (Princeton, NJ: Princeton University Press, 1996) and *Sweet Land of Liberty: The Forgotten Struggle for Civil Rights in the North* (New York: Random House, 2008). The best account of the impact of riots on American politics is Michael W. Flamm, *Law and Order: Street Crime, Civil Unrest, and the Crisis of Liberalism in the 1960s* (New York: Columbia University Press, 2005). Dan T. Carter's *The Politics of Rage: George Wallace, the Origins of the New Conservatism, and the Transformation of American Politics* (New York: Simon & Schuster, 1995) highlights the role George Wallace played in the emergence of the modern Republican Party.

There are several general books on American politics in the late 1960s that place the commission in its proper historical context. Among the best are Terry Anderson, *The Movement and the Sixties: Protest in America from Greensboro to Wounded Knee* (New York: Oxford University Press, 1995); Clay Risen, *A Nation on Fire: America in the Wake of the King Assassination* (New York: Wiley, 2009); Arthur M. Schlesinger Jr., *Robert F. Kennedy and His Times* (Boston: Houghton Mifflin, 1978); Todd Gitlin, *The Sixties: Years of Hope, Days of Rage* (New York: Bantam Books, 1987); George C. Herring, *LBJ and Vietnam: A Different Kind of War* (Austin: University of Texas Press, 1994); Taylor Branch, *At Canaan's Edge: America in the King Years, 1965–68* (New York: Simon and Schuster, 2006); Stanley Karnow, *Vietnam: A History* (New York: Viking, 1983); and Rick Perlstein, *Nixonland: The Rise of a President and the Fracturing of America* (New York: Scribner, 2008). David Farber has collected insightful essays for his book *The Sixties: From Memory to History* (Chapel Hill: University of North Carolina Press, 1994).

A couple of studies sponsored by the Russell Sage Foundation, based on census data, are helpful in assessing the commission's legacy and its prediction of America becoming two separate societies. The most relevant for this study are John R. Logan and Wenquan Zhang, "Global Neighborhoods: New Evidence from the Census 2010" (November 2011); and Sean F. Reardon, "Growth in the Residential Segregation of Families by Income, 1970–2009" (November 2011). Other relevant articles include John R. Logan and Charles Zhang, "Global Neighborhoods: New Pathways to Diversity and Separation," *American Journal of Sociology* (2010). On why until recently there have been few riots, see Michael Katz, "Why Don't American Cities Burn Very Often?" *Journal of Urban History* 34, no. 2 (2008).

Gerald David Jaynes and Robin M. Williams, eds., *A Common Destiny: Blacks and American Society* (Washington, DC: National Academy Press, 1989), offers a wide-ranging analysis of trends in black life over the past seventy-five years. Michelle Alexander has written the definitive account of how changes in the criminal justice system have led to the mass incarceration of African Americans: *The New Jim Crow: Mass Incarceration in the Age of Colorblindness* (New York: New Press, 2012). Also useful is Heather Ann Thompson, "Why Mass Incarceration Matters: Rethinking Crisis, Decline, and Transformation in Postwar American History," *Journal of American History* (December 2010).

On trends in segregation, see Reynolds Farley and William H. Frey, "Changes in the Segregation of Whites from Blacks During the 1980s: Small Steps Toward a More Integrated Society," *American Sociological Review* (February 1994); Douglas S. Massey and Nancy A. Denton, *American Apartheid: Segregation and the Making of the Underclass* (Cambridge, MA: Harvard University Press, 1993); David Cutler, Edward Glaeser, and Jacob Vigdor, "The Rise and Decline of the America City," *Journal of Political Economy* (1999); Gary Orfield, "Segregated Housing and School Resegregation," in *Dismantling Desegregation: The Quiet Reversal of "Brown v. Board of Education,"* by Gary Orfield, Susan E. Eaton, and the Harvard Project on School Desegregation (New York: New Press, 1996); and Paul A. Jargowsky, "Take the Money and Run: Economic Segregation in U.S. Metropolitan Areas," *American Sociological Review* 61 (1996).

On the politics of suburbanization, see Peter Applebome, *Dixie Rising: How the South Is Shaping American Values, Politics, and Culture* (New York: Harvest, 1997); Mark Schneider and Thomas Phelan, "Black Suburbanization in the 1980s," *Demography* (May 1993); and John M. Stahura, "Changing Patterns of Suburban Racial Composition, 1970–1980," *Urban Affairs Quarterly* (1988). Two of the best books on the subject are Kevin M. Kruse, *White Flight: Atlanta and the Making of Modern Conservatism* (Princeton, NJ: Princeton University Press, 2005); and Thomas and Mary Edsall, *Chain Reaction: The Impact of Race, Rights, and Taxes on American Politics* (New York: W. W. Norton, 1992).

MANUSCRIPT COLLECTIONS

Abraham Lincoln Presidential Library, Springfield, IL
 Kerner, Otto, Family Papers
 Kerner, Otto, Office Papers

American University, Washington, DC
 Sagalyn, Arnold

Carl Albert Congressional Research Center, Norman, OK
 Albert, Carl
 Harris, Fred

Dirksen Congressional Center, Pekin, IL
 Dirksen, Everett M.

Federal Bureau of Investigation
 FOIA Declassified FBI Files

Gerald Ford Presidential Library, Ann Arbor, MI
Ford, Gerald, Congressional Papers

John F. Kennedy Library, Boston
Rosenthal, Jack

Library of Congress, Washington, DC
Ginsburg, David
Wilkins, Roy

Lyndon B. Johnson Presidential Library, Austin, TX
Bohen, Fred
Califano, Joseph, Office Papers
Califano, Joseph, Personal Papers
Cater, Douglass
Christian, George
Clark, Ramsey
Diary Backup
Executive Federal Government Ex FG
Gaither, James
Levinson, Lawrence
Markham, Sherwin
McPherson, Harry, Office Papers
McPherson, Harry, Personal Papers
National Advisory Commission on Civil Disorders
Nimetz, Martin
Panzer, Fred
Temple, Larry
White House Central File

Minnesota Historical Society, Minneapolis
Humphrey, Hubert

Ohio Congressional Archives, Columbus
McCulloch, William

Private Collections
Chambers, David
Nathan, Richard

Richard Nixon Presidential Library, Yorba Linda, CA
1968 Campaign Research Files
Pre-Presidential Speech Files
White House Central Files

Ronald Reagan Presidential Library, Simi Valley, CA
Reagan, Ronald, Gubernatorial Papers, 1966–1975

William Jefferson Clinton Digital Library
Office of Speechwriting and Michael Waldman

Yale University Manuscript Archive, New Haven, CT
Lindsay, John

INTERVIEWS

Boesel, David	August 3, 2016
Buchanan, Patrick	September 14, 2015
Califano, Joseph	June 12, 2015; January 17, 2017
Chambers, David L.	February 28, 2015; March 15, 2015; April 28, 2015; June 21, 2015; December 29, 2015; March 8, 2016; March 16, 2016; October 11, 2016; December 7, 2016
Goldmark, Peter	March 3, 2015; December 25, 2016.
Harris, Fred	May 20, 2015; September 17, 2015; January 6, 2016; February 2, 2016; March 8, 2016; December 10, 2016
Hunt, Isaac	July 18, 2016
Koskinen, John A.	August 1, 2016
Kriegel, Jay	February 25, 2015
Kurzman, Stephen	September 8, 2016
Marx, Gary	August 10, 2016
Nathan, Richard	January 23, 2015
Nelson, Charles	September 23, 2016; October 17, 2016
Palmieri, Victor	June 5, 2015; June 22, 2015; September 28, 2015
Rosenthal, Jacob	July 27, 2015; July 20, 2016
Sagalyn, Arnold	September 8, 2016
Sagalyn, Louise	September 8, 2016
Sears, David	July 28, 2016
Shellow, Robert	June 19, 2015; October 18, 2016
Thomas, Bruce	December 21, 2015; July 18, 2016

ORAL HISTORIES
Lyndon B. Johnson Presidential Library, Austin, TX

Abel, I. W.	Tape 1, July 29, 1969
Alexander, Clifford	November 1, 1971
Clark, Ramsey	April 16, 1969
Ginsburg, David	Tape 3, September 19, 1988
Jenkins, Herbert	Tape 1, May 14, 1969
Kerner, Otto	July 24, 1990
McPherson, Harry	Tape 1, April 9, 1969; Tapes 2 and 4, March 24, 1969

Peden, Katherine	December 15, 1978
Wattenberg, Ben	November 29, 1968
Wilkins, Roy	Tape 1, April 1, 1969

Richard Nathan Collection (Private)

Brooke, Edward	June 1, 1994
Corman, James	January 12, 1994
Ginsburg, David	January 12, 1994
Harris, Fred	Circa 1994
Peden, Katherine	Circa 1994

INDEX

Abbitt, Watkins, 277–278
Abel, I. W., 61, 134, 139
   background of, 53
   death of, 304
   final revisions and approval process,
      235, 236
   policy recommendations and, 210, 213
   visits to riot-ravaged cities, 93
"absent-father" rule (welfare), 201, 233,
   237
Addonizio, Hugh, 2, 92, 103–104, 105,
   106, 121
African Americans. *See* Black Lives
   Matter movement; black militant
   groups; black nationalism; Black
   Power movement; civil rights
   movement; Kerner Commission;
   Kerner Report; riots; white
   racism; *specific social issues
   affecting*
Agnew, Spiro, 9
Aid to Families with Dependent
   Children, 237
Alarms and Hopes (Harris), 149
Albert, Carl, 35, 276
Alexander, Clifford, 250
Alexandria (VA) Gazette, 276, 277
American Federation of Labor
   and Congress of Industrial
   Organizations (AFL-CIO), 47
American Independence Party, 294
American Political Science Association,
   274
American Veterans Committee, 90
Anderson, John B., 288

Anderson, Martin, 281
Anti-Defamation League of B'nai
      B'rith, 270
"antighetto" strategies, 197, 199
Army, Department of, 263
Aronson, Bernie, 308
Asians, 299, 303–304
Associated Press, 31, 208, 268
Atlanta, GA
      field teams in, 117, 118, 119, 122, 124
      riot, 271
Atlantic, 174

Baltimore, MD, riot, 312, 313
Baltimore Evening Sun, 268
Bantam Books, 269
Bedford-Stuyvesant, NY, riot, 5, 27
Bergheim, Mel, 205
Birenbaum, David, 203
Black America (television program), 286
Black Lives Matter movement, 312
black militant groups, 97, 142, 203–204,
      206, 217
Black Muslims, 10, 125
black nationalism, 10–11, 26, 246
Black Power movement, 11, 27, 142, 161
      Brooke on, 99
      coining of term, 8
      Harris on, 85
      Wilkins on, 30, 48
Boesel, David, 157–159, 161, 163–164, 169
      background of, 154
      firing of, 189–190
      section of "Harvest" written by, 156
Bohen, Fred, 106

"Bonus Army," 24
Boston Globe, 268
Boston University, 306
Bradlee, Ben, 253–254
Brinkley, David, 4
Brooke, Edward, 48–49, 53, 61, 63, 80
    background of, 48
    (H. Rap) Brown's meeting with,
      98–99
    death of, 311
    Fair Housing Act and, 287
    final revisions and approval process,
      235
    interim report reviews and, 147
    Johnson's reaction to Kerner Report
      and, 247, 257
    policy recommendations and, 139, 210
    visits to riot-ravaged cities, 91, 102
Brookings Institution, 78, 195
Brooklyn, NY
    Kerner commissioners' visit to, 93
    riot, 55
Brown, H. Rap, 7–9, 11, 26, 86, 121, 141,
    148, 157, 158, 217
    Brooke's meeting with, 98–99
    Hoover on, 81, 84
    on Kerner Report, 273
    media coverage of, 123–124
Brown, Michael, 312
Brown, Pat, 7
Brown v. Board of Education of Topeka,
    47, 144, 240–241, 317
Brownsville, NY (Kerner
    commissioners' visit to), 93
Buchanan, Patrick, 64
Buchwald, Art, 249
Budget Bureau, 181, 205
Bullock, Paul, 105
Bush, George W., 310, 313
busing, 202
Byrd, Robert, 33

cabinet task force on riots, 29–31, 40, 41
Cairo, IL, riot, 3
Califano, Joseph, 29–30, 31, 32, 55, 67,
    73–74, 75, 88, 106, 127, 186–187,
    285
    background of, 44

on conspiracy theory argument, 25
    on "Harvest," 190
    on Johnson-Lindsay animosity, 46,
      108, 109
    on Johnson's reaction to riots, 20
    on Kerner Commission funding,
      179–180, 181–183, 184–185
    Kerner Commission set up by, 44
    on Kerner Report, 249–258, 260,
      264, 265
    on special commission plan, 39, 40
Cambridge, MD
    field teams in, 121, 123
    riot, 8–9, 155, 157
Campbell, Angus, 124
Cantwell, James, 89
Carey, Hugh, 92
Carmichael, Stokely, 7–8, 9, 11, 26, 85,
    121, 141, 158, 286
    background of, 8
    Hoover on, 81, 84
    on King assassination, 283
    Wilkins's criticism of, 48, 217
Carson, Johnny, 60
Carter, Jimmy, 296–297, 313
Case, Clifford, 13
Cater, Douglass, 36–37, 38, 40–41, 45,
    47
Cedar Rapids, IA, riot, 3
Cermak, Anton, 45
Chambers, David, 76, 87, 103, 136, 238,
    239, 243
    background of, 75
    on "Harvest," 165
    Kerner Report edited by, 199
    on Kerner Report leak, 254
    on Lindsay, 185
Charlottesville, NC (community leader
    meeting), 270
Chicago, IL
    Clinton-era antipoverty measures
      in, 307
    population decline in, 302
    riots, 6, 27, 284
Chicago Board of Education, 269
Chicago City Council, 271–272
Chicago Tribune, 90, 277, 278
Christian, George, 58, 256

Christian Science Monitor, 62, 271

Christopher, Warren, 32, 73, 80, 88

Cincinnati, OH
  field teams in, 122, 123
  Kerner commissioners' visit to, 96–98
  riot, 8, 157

Civil Rights Act of 1964, 18, 50, 76, 118, 240–241, 286

civil rights movement, 10
  Johnson and, 17–20, 28
  whites' opinions of, 12

civilian review boards, 146, 147–148

Clark, Jim, 19

Clark, Kenneth B., 317

Clark, Ramsey, 32, 45, 47, 54, 55

class, 305–306

Clay, Lucius, 68

Cleveland, OH
  Kerner commissioners' visit to, 100
  population decline in, 302
  riots, 27, 125, 271, 312

Clifford, Clark, 252, 265

Clinton, Hillary, 313

Clinton, William (Bill), 306–310

Cohen, Wilbur, 279

Colmer, William, 276

Columbia Journalism Review, 286

Columbia University, 105

Commerce, Department of, 263

Commission on Civil Rights, 279

Congress of Racial Equality (CORE), 272, 273

Congressional Budget Office, 311

Congressional Quarterly, 18

Conot, Robert, 142, 167, 230, 281
  commissioners' policy recommendations and, 222–223
  conspiracy chapter redrafted by, 237
  field team reports and, 112
  Rivers of Blood, Years of Darkness, 78

conservatives
  conspiracy theory argument and, 34, 83
  Johnson administration and, 18
  Kerner Commission and, 63
  Kerner Report and, 207, 219, 267, 276–278

conspiracy theory argument, 36
  Hoover on, 25–27, 33, 66, 81–83, 84, 101, 237
  Kerner Commission on, 70, 71, 78, 81–86, 148
  Kerner Report on, 171–172, 217, 237–238
  legislators' belief in, 33–34
  meaning for advocates and detractors of, 83

CORE. *See* Congress of Racial Equality

Corman, James, 50, 53, 74–75, 80, 124, 134, 230, 264
  final revisions and approval process, 231, 238, 242, 243
  Ginsburg's private meeting with, 128–129
  interim report reviews and, 146, 147, 149
  modest expectations of, 139–140
  policy recommendations and, 194, 199, 213, 215, 217–225
  twenty-fifth anniversary of Kerner Report and, 304
  visits to riot-ravaged cities, 91, 93–95

Cornell University, 154

"credibility gap," 22

crime, 24, 34, 35, 306, 307–308, 309, 314.
  See also law-and-order platform

criminal justice system, 228–229

Cronkite, Walter, 251–252

Custer, George Armstrong, 249

Daley, Richard, 45, 105, 259, 284

Dayton, OH
  dissatisfaction index on, 126
  field teams in, 119, 120, 121–122
  riot, 8

de facto discrimination, 9–10

de jure discrimination, 9

deaths
  poverty-related, 117
  riot-related, 3, 4, 5, 6, 95, 96, 171, 284, 299

Defense, Department of, 179, 180, 210

DeLoach, Cartha D., 84

Democratic National Committee, 256–257

Democratic National Convention, 261,
    293, 295
Democrats
    Clinton administration and, 306,
        307
    conspiracy theory argument and,
        33, 34
    divisions within, 270
    Johnson administration and, 15, 23,
        24, 35
    Kerner Report and, 276
    Nixon administration and, 295, 296
    presidential election of 1968 and,
        294, 295
    presidential election of 1972 and, 296
    presidential election of 1980 and,
        297
    special commission proposed by, 36
    whites' defection from, 290
Des Moines, IA, riot, 3
Detroit, MI
    Clinton-era antipoverty measures
        in, 307
    community leader meeting in, 270
    field teams in, 112, 116, 117, 118–119,
        120, 121, 124, 154–155
    "Great Recession" and, 311
    historical racial tensions in, 11
    Kerner commissioners' visit to,
        94–95, 100, 102
    population decline in, 302
    riots, 3–5, 6–7, 8, 12, 15, 24, 26,
        31–33, 36, 39, 46, 57, 62, 81–82, 88,
        157, 159, 169, 171, 270, 271
Dirksen, Everett, 33, 34–36, 53, 287
"dispersal strategy" (antighetto
    strategy), 197, 217
"dissatisfaction index," 126
Douglas, William O., 68
Douglass, Ellis, 273–274
doves, 21, 61, 261
Downs, Anthony, 193–200, 203, 204,
    205, 217–218, 241, 305
    background of, 195–196
    on Great Society programs, 196–197
    influence of ideas, 193, 195
    key elements of plan disregarded,
        199–200
Drew, Elizabeth, 174

drug abuse, 117, 302, 303
Drummond, Roscoe, 62
DuBois, W. E. B., 10, 314
Durham, NC, riot, 3

East St. Louis, MO, riot, 6
Eastland, James O., 34, 278
economic inequality, 300–301, 310–311.
    See also poverty
Economic Innovation Group, 311
Economic Opportunity Act of 1964, 16
Edelman, Peter, 306
education and schools
    Brown decision on, 47, 144,
        240–241, 317
    continuing segregation in, 303–304,
        314
    employment of African Americans
        in, 118–119
    field teams' findings on, 117–119
    policy recommendations on,
        202–203, 204, 211–212, 231, 232,
        233, 236, 237
    whites' attitudes on, 290
Ehrlichman, John, 296
Eisenhower, Dwight, 297
Elizabeth, NJ, riot, 3
Ellender, Allen, 286
Emancipation Proclamation, 19
employment
    business initiatives in, 270
    field teams' findings on, 116, 118–120
    increase of in African Americans,
        301
    outsourcing of, 300–301
    policy recommendations on,
        200–201, 204, 207–208, 228,
        230–231, 232, 233, 237
    See also unemployment
Englewood, NJ, riot, 3
Equal Employment Opportunity
    Commission, 250
Erie, PA, riot, 3
Ervin, Sam, 34, 287
Executive Order 11365, 58

Fair Housing Act of 1968, 286–288
Fairlie, Henry, 215–216
family income levels, 10, 301, 303, 314

Farmer, James, 273
Fauntroy, Walter E., 272–273
Federal Bureau of Investigation (FBI),
    25–27, 33, 66, 82–83, 84, 85, 101,
    112, 237
female-headed households, 160, 201,
    212–213, 231, 232
Ferguson, MO, riot, 312, 313
field teams, 111–124, 135, 138, 142, 151,
    154–155, 165, 172
    African Americans in, 113, 115–116
    characteristics of members, 112–113
    checklist for, 113–114
    findings of, 116–124
    firing of members, 188–189
    importance of findings, 112
    informal presentation to
        commission, 129–131
    senior staff and, 115–116, 173–175
Fisk University, 8
Flint, MI, riot, 5
Fogelson, Robert, 275
Forbes, 315
Ford, Gerald, 24, 33, 282–283, 296
Ford, Henry, II, 270
Ford Foundation, 181, 195
Ford Motor Company, 52
Fortas, Abe, 32, 38–39, 69–70
Fowler, Henry, 184
Frankel, Max, 256
Frankfurter, Felix, 68
Franklin, John Hope, 143–144, 228, 309
Freedom Now, 274
Freeman, Andrew, 274
From Slavery to Freedom (Franklin), 143
Fulbright, J. William, 22

Gallup polls, 246, 311
Gans, Herbert, 105, 228
Gardner, John, 40
Garvey, Marcus, 10
Garza, Alicia, 312
ghetto-improvement strategy
    (antighetto strategy), 197, 217
Gingrich, Newt, 307
Ginsburg, David, 65, 67–79, 87, 90, 91,
    108, 111, 112, 127–131, 133–137, 139,
    140, 141, 169–170, 175, 279, 285
    background of, 67–69

commissioners' approval process
    and, 227, 229–230, 233, 234–235,
    236–239, 243, 244, 245, 246
commissioners' policy discussions
    and, 193, 194–195, 196, 197, 199,
    203, 206, 207, 210, 213–214, 215,
    222–223, 225
Corman's private meeting with,
    128–129
field teams and, 115, 116, 129
funding of Kerner Commission and,
    178–181, 183, 184, 185–188
"Harvest" and, 151–152, 156, 165, 166,
    167, 168, 169, 173, 190
hearings and, 79, 107
interim report cancellation and, 189
interim report reviews and, 142, 143,
    144
Johnson's reaction to Kerner Report
    and, 247, 248, 251, 253, 258, 265
leaking of Kerner Report by, 254
on the media, 216–217
on National Guard integration, 88
social scientists and, 124, 153, 155
twenty-fifth anniversary of Kerner
    Report and, 304
as unheralded leader of commission,
    69
visits to riot-ravaged cities, 92–93,
    102–103
on white racism, 135–137, 203
Ginsburg, Feldman, and Bress (law
    firm), 72
Ginzberg, Eli, 105
Glazer, Nathan, 298
Glickman, Steve, 311
Goldberg, Lou, 154, 156, 161–165, 168,
    169
Goldfarb, Ronald, 78
Goldmark, Peter, 239, 240–243
Goldwater, Barry, 15, 16, 280, 288
Goodwin, Doris Kearns, 266
Gordon, Kermit, 195
Gorham, William, 234
Government Printing Office, 269
gradualism, 11, 162
Graham, Billy, 277
Grand Rapids, MI, riot, 5
"Great Recession," 310–311, 314

Great Society programs, 16–21, 22–25,
    30, 31, 66, 70, 114, 175, 184, 310
  backlash against, 24, 272
  Brooke's support for, 48
  Corman's support for, 50
  expectations vs. reality of, 124,
    196–197
  (Gerald) Ford on, 283
  funding cuts in, 248, 262
  "Harvest" on, 162
  interracial support for, 12
  Johnson's diminished hopes for, 21
  Kerner Report and, 200, 206, 247,
    248, 264, 266
  limited reach of, 101, 105, 106, 138,
    266
  Lindsay on, 167
  major initiatives of, 16
  Palmieri's support for, 73
  Thornton's support for, 52
  ultimate goal of, 16
  Vietnam War and, 22–24
Greenspan, Alan, 281
Groppi, James, 96
guaranteed minimum income
    (proposed), 37, 209, 237, 295
"guns and butter" strategy, 265–266

Haley, James, 35
Harlem, NY
  field teams in, 112
  Lindsay's visits to, 46
  riots, 5, 6, 8, 317
Harper & Row, 149
Harris, Fred, 44, 49–50, 53, 54, 55, 61,
    69, 80, 82, 92, 107, 109, 125, 168,
    191, 192
  agenda for Kerner Commission, 59,
    60
  Alarms and Hopes, 149
  background of, 49
  conspiracy theory argument and, 85
  death of, 311
  dominance of in Kerner
    Commission, 60, 90
  downside of strategy encouraged by,
    288–289

emergency meeting called for by,
    285
  Fair Housing Act and, 287
  final revisions and approval process,
    235–236, 237, 243, 244, 245, 246
  funding of Kerner Commission and,
    181, 184
  "Harvest" and, 190
  independence of commission urged
    by, 65–66, 87
  interim report reviews and, 146
  Johnson demands loyalty from, 89
  Johnson's reaction to Kerner Report
    and, 247, 250
  (Robert) Kennedy's call to, 261
  media and, 268
  on National Guard integration, 88
  policy recommendations and,
    138–139, 199, 209, 210, 213, 221
  special commission proposed by,
    36–37
  suggests reconvening of Kerner
    Commission, 283
  visits to riot-ravaged cities, 95,
    96–98, 100, 101–102
  on white racism, 135, 243, 268
Harvard Business School, 51
Harvard Law School, 65, 74
Harvard University, 154
"Harvest of American Racism, The"
    (report), 151–170, 172–174,
    203–204, 214, 230, 274
  consequences of discarding, 169
  conventional narrative challenged
    by, 157–158
  destruction of copies, 190
  senior staff reaction to, 165–169,
    173–174, 189–190
Hastie, William, 47
hawks, 21, 61, 261
Hayden, Tom, 2–3
Hayes Homes, 1
Head Start, 16, 202
Health, Education, and Welfare,
    Department of, 234
Health and Human Services,
    Department of, 179

Herbers, John, 62, 263
Herbert, F. Edward, 89
Hispanics, 54, 228, 299–300, 303–304, 308
Hoover, J. Edgar, 25–27, 32, 33, 66, 81–83, 84, 101, 108, 237
Horowitz, Daniel, 315
housing, 10, 11–12, 228, 290, 302–303
    field teams' findings on, 116–117
    policy recommendations on, 197, 202, 204, 205, 210–211, 220, 228, 234, 236
    See also open housing; public housing projects
Housing and Urban Development, Department of, 234
Houston, TX (integration survey of), 126
Howard University, 19, 28, 55, 263
Hughes, Richard J., 2–3, 29, 31
Humphrey, Hubert, 49, 55, 58
    cabinet task force headed by, 29–31, 40, 41
    on the "Johnson Treatment," 18
    on Kerner Report, 279
    presidential campaign of, 294–295
Hunt, Isaac, 113, 114, 174
Huntley Brinkley Report (television program), 4
"hypersegregation," 302

immigrants, 10, 228, 298–300, 316
Immigration Act of 1965, 298
incarceration rates, 308, 314
infant mortality rates, 117, 303
integration
    African Americans' lack of interest in, 125–126
    Kerner Report on, 197, 202, 204, 212
    school, 202, 212, 290
interim report, 107–108, 109, 127, 130, 169–175
    cancellation of, 185–189
    lack of consensus on, 148–149
    review of draft chapters, 141–149
    See also "Harvest of American Racism, The"

International Association of Chiefs of Police, 285
Issues and Answers (television program), 268

Janss Corporation, 73
Javitz, Jacob, 76
Jenkins, Herbert, 134, 147, 168
    background of, 52
    death of, 304
    policy recommendations and, 138–139, 210–211, 217, 221
    visits to riot-ravaged cities, 91, 93, 95
Jersey City, NJ, riot, 3
Job Corps, 16
John Birch Society, 50
Johns Hopkins, 154
Johnson, Lady Bird, 52
Johnson, Lyndon B., 15–41, 43–59, 104–105, 106, 137, 142, 143, 154, 174, 175, 206, 224, 238, 241, 269, 298
    bewilderment over riots, 19–21
    broad mandate for Kerner Commission, 56, 57, 66, 235–236
    (H. Rap) Brown on, 9
    Carter compared with, 296
    civil rights movement and, 17–20, 28
    conspiracy theory argument, 25–27, 33, 83–84
    containment measures for riots, 4, 31–33
    control of Kerner Commission and, 65–67, 72, 189–192
    Fair Housing Act and, 286
    field teams' attitude toward, 115
    first meeting with Kerner Commission, 55–59
    funding of Kerner Commission and, 177–185, 187, 192, 248
    Ginsburg and, 65, 67, 69–74
    Great Society of (see Great Society programs)
    "guns and butter" strategy of, 265–266
    "Harvest" on, 164, 165
    "Johnson Treatment," 18, 73

Johnson, Lyndon B. (*continued*)
  King assassination and, 283–284
  lifts publication embargo on Kerner
    Report, 267, 268
  Lindsay and, 46, 108–109, 178, 250,
    255, 259
  Model Cities program and, 234
  National Guard integration proposal
    and, 88–89
  quoted in Kerner Report, 243–244
  reaction to Kerner Report, 247–266,
    276
  reelection bid dropped, 266
  secret missions to riot-affected areas,
    27–28
  televised announcement of Kerner
    Commission, 38–39, 41, 44–45,
    54–55, 177
  three questions for Kerner
    Commission, 43, 56–57, 71–72,
    107, 108, 130, 169, 194
  Vietnam War and, 15, 21–24, 27, 31,
    45, 182–183, 210, 249, 251–252, 255,
    265–266
  voters' repudiation of policies, 294,
    295
Jones, James H., 134, 139
Jones, Nathaniel R., 76
Jones, Theodore, 72–73
Justice, Department of, 313

Kalamazoo, MI, riot, 5
Kansas City Star, 286
Kennedy, Edward M., 261
Kennedy, John F., 30, 46, 64, 67, 76, 77,
    261, 312
  assassination of, 15–16, 265
  civil rights movement and, 17–18
  Vietnam War and, 21
Kennedy, Robert F., 30, 49, 241, 306
  assassination of, 293
  Kerner Report praised by, 261–262
  presidential candidacy of, 248, 261,
    281
  on riots, 24
Kerner, Otto, 53, 58–59, 61, 62, 72, 80,
    89, 107–108, 128, 192, 206, 259,
    283, 285

  background of, 45
  Corman's complaints to, 218–220,
    222
  death of, 304
  final revisions and approval process,
    232, 237, 238
  funding of Kerner Commission and,
    178, 180, 187
  interim report cancellation and, 188
  interim report reviews and, 148
  Johnson's reaction to Kerner Report
    and, 265
  (Robert) Kennedy's call to, 261
  King's telegram to, 272
  limited involvement in Kerner
    Commission, 45, 108
  media and, 216, 268
  policy recommendations and, 210
  public reaction to Kerner Report
    and, 278
  reasons for appointing as chairman,
    66–67
  Shellow and, 152
  visits to riot-ravaged cities, 99–100,
    101, 102
  on white racism, 134–135
Kerner Commission, 43–64, 308, 309,
    310, 314–315, 316, 317
  African American appointees, 43,
    47–49
  African American skepticism about,
    62–63
  biggest challenge facing, 63
  call for emergency meeting of, 285
  commissioners of, 43, 45–54
  commissioners' visits to riot-ravaged
    cities, 91–103, 106
  crisis in, 175
  Executive Order 11365 on, 58
  female appointee to, 43, 52
  field teams' informal presentation
    to, 129–131
  firings of workforce in, 188–190
  funding of, 70–71, 76–77, 177–192,
    193, 248
  genesis of, 35–41
  groups not represented in, 54
  hearings of, 79–87, 100, 103–107

ideological views of members, 59–61
independence asserted by, 65–66,
    87, 184
Johnson's broad mandate for, 56, 57,
    66, 235–236
Johnson's first meeting with, 55–59
Johnson's intent to control, 65–67,
    72, 189–192
Johnson's litmus test for members,
    45
Johnson's three questions for, 43,
    56–57, 71–72, 107, 108, 130, 169,
    194
media and (*see under* media)
offices of, 71, 127–128
payment and reimbursement of
    members, 58
people not selected for, 47
reception for suggested and denied,
    248, 249–250, 254
reconvening of suggested, 283
senior staff of (*see* senior staff of
    Kerner Commission)
social scientists in (*see* social
    scientists)
televised announcement of creation,
    38–39, 41, 44–45, 54–55, 177
Wilson's criticism of, 305
Kerner Report, 293–295, 298, 303, 313
African Americans' responses to,
    267, 273–274, 278–279
ceremonial signing of, 244
civic and religious organizations on,
    269–270
civil rights leaders on, 272–273
commissioners' dissatisfaction with,
    238
commissioners' shared goal for, 87
commissioners' unanimous
    acceptance of, 243–246
congressional reaction to, 272
cost estimates in, 101–102, 198, 232,
    233–234, 236–237, 248, 250–251,
    252, 256, 258–259
on criminal justice system, 228–229
deadline for, 186–187, 188, 194, 227,
    237
drafting of final version, 193–225

editorial limits suggested for, 227,
    231
"Final Report Options," 139
final revisions and approval process,
    227–245
on the future of the city, 217–218
interim (*see* interim report)
Johnson administration responses
    to, 263, 279
Johnson's reaction to, 247–266, 276
"kitchen cabinet" for, 195
mayors and civic groups on, 271–273
media and (*see under* media)
minority reports considered, 219,
    220, 222, 225, 235, 238, 244–245
most important chapter in, 136–137
most important legacy of, 316
national responses to, 267–291
paternalism charge, 205–206
policy recommendations of (*see*
    policy recommendations)
publication of, 269
race relations history chapter,
    143–144, 228
racial divide in responses to,
    278–279
reviews of by officials and
    consultants, 234
on rural area improvement, 231
scholars on, 274–275
successes stemming from, 285–289
summary of, 227, 238–243, 251,
    288–289
twenty-fifth anniversary of, 293,
    304–306
"two societies" concept in, 240–241,
    242, 243, 253, 262–263, 264, 268,
    276, 289, 300, 310
Kilpatrick, James J., 276–277
King, Martin Luther, Jr., 9, 10, 25, 146,
    311
assassination of, 283–286, 288, 293
Hoover on, 26, 81
Johnson and, 18, 19
on Kerner Report, 272
on Vietnam War, 22
Wilkins's criticism of, 48
King, Rodney, 299

Knight newspapers, 181
Kopkind, Andrew, 250
Koskinen, John, 74–75, 254
    background of, 74
    funding of Kerner Commission and,
        178, 183, 189
    Kerner Report edited by, 199, 203
Kriegel, Jay, 111, 223, 240–243
Ku Klux Klan, 52, 143–144, 147
Kurzman, Stephen, 75–76, 139, 169–174,
        186, 189, 203, 214, 218

La Prensa, 299
labor unions, 10, 230–231, 236, 301
Laitin, Joseph, 181
Lane, Vincent, 306
law-and-order platform, 24, 33, 45, 86,
        124, 240, 246, 277–278, 295, 314,
        315
LBJ Presidential Library, 47
Lewinsky, Monica, 310
Lewis, John, 311
liberals
    Clinton and, 306, 307
    conspiracy theory argument and, 83
    "Harvest" on, 164, 165
    Johnson and, 24–25, 30, 36–37,
        260–261, 265
    Kerner Commission and, 63,
        137–138, 149, 204
    Kerner Report and, 219, 267, 271,
        272
    Vietnam War and, 21
Life, 5, 268
"Limits of Social Policy, The" (Glazer),
        298
Lincoln, Abraham, 19, 144, 236, 256
Lindsay, John, 53, 58, 61, 76, 80, 85, 102,
        107, 111, 115, 124–125, 126, 134, 315
    agenda for Kerner Commission,
        59–60
    background of, 46
    conspiracy theory argument and,
        81–82, 84
    Corman's distrust of, 219–222
    dominance of in Kerner
        Commission, 60, 90, 108–109,
        178, 193–195, 220, 239, 259
    downside of strategy encouraged by,
        288–290
    emergency meeting called for by,
        285
    final revisions and approval process,
        227, 232, 235–237, 238–240,
        241–242, 243, 244–245, 246
    funding of Kerner Commission and,
        180, 185, 187
    "Harvest" and, 167–168
    independence of commission urged
        by, 65–66, 87
    interim report cancellation and, 186,
        188
    interim report reviews and, 147–148
    Johnson's reaction to Kerner Report
        and, 250, 255, 259
    (Robert) Kennedy's call to, 261
    policy recommendations and,
        138–139, 193–195, 199, 200,
        208–210, 211–212, 213, 215, 218,
        219–222
    presidential ambitions of, 109, 304
    reasons for Kerner Commission
        appointment, 45–46
    Shellow and, 152
    twenty-fifth anniversary of Kerner
        Report and, 304, 305
    on Vietnam War, 209–210, 236, 241,
        255, 275
    visits to riot-ravaged cities, 92–93,
        96–98
Lippmann, Walter, 23
Litton, Charles, 47, 50
Litton Industries, 47, 52, 244
Los Angeles, CA
    immigrant population of, 299
    riots, 271, 299–300
    school system of, 303
Los Angeles Times, 22, 62, 250, 268
Lowry, Roye, 205–206

Maddox, Lester, 12
Mahon, George, 180, 250, 276
Maier, Henry, 95, 96
Malcolm X, 10–11
"man-in-the-house" rule (welfare), 201
Mansfield, Mike, 24, 35, 36, 37

Markham, Sherwin, 27
Marshall, Thurgood, 7
Marshall Plan for cities, 102, 104,
    138–139, 284
Martin, Louis, 256–257
Marx, Gary T., 158, 164, 169
    firing of, 190
    Protest and Prejudice, 154
    reaction to Kerner Report, 274–275
    section of "Harvest" written by, 156
Massey, Douglas, 302
maternal mortality rates, 117
Mathias, Charles M., 288
Mathis, William, 274
Mattick, Hans, 173
Matusow, Allen, 295
McCarthy, Eugene, 248, 261, 275–276
McClellan, John L., 34
McCone, John, 7
McCone Commission, 7, 80, 125, 317
McCulloch, William, 53, 61, 134,
    139–140, 220, 222, 230
    background of, 50
    final revisions and approval process,
        238, 239, 246
    interim report reviews and, 144, 149
    policy recommendations and, 221
    visits to riot-ravaged cities, 91, 93,
        100–101
    on white racism, 136
McCurdy, Merle, 76, 115–116, 127
McGovern, George, 296
McGrath, Kyran, 128, 129, 206, 210,
    222, 232
McKenzie, Norman, 78
McKissick, Floyd, 272
McNamara, Robert, 32, 44, 51, 89, 252,
    253
McPherson, Harry, 28, 29, 55, 62–63,
    248, 255, 265, 266, 290
    on citizen distrust of Johnson, 22
    on conspiracy theory argument, 25
    letter of thanks suggested to
        Johnson by, 259–260
    televised presidential address
        suggested by, 38–39
McWhorter, John, 315
Meany, George, 47, 53

media
    African Americans hired by, 286
    field teams' findings on, 123–124
    "Harvest" on, 158
    Kerner Commission covered by, 62,
        80–81, 190–191
    Kerner Report covered by, 250–251,
        253–255, 256, 260, 267–269, 271,
        276–277
    Kerner Report leaked to, 250–251,
        253–255
    Kerner Report on, 57, 215–217, 229,
        286
    race relations covered by, 245–246
    riots covered by, 4, 5, 7
    Vietnam War covered by, 249,
        251–252
Meet the Press (television program), 268,
    276
Memphis, TN, 56
Metropolitan Service Organization,
    201, 206
Meyer, Philip, 181
Middle East, 300
Miller, Merle, 253
Mills, Wilbur, 23, 183–184
Milwaukee, WI
    field teams in, 112, 120, 124
    Kerner commissioners' visit to, 95–96
Milwaukee Commission on
    Community Relations, 95
Minneapolis, MN
    field teams in, 112
    riot, 3
minority reports (considered), 219, 220,
    222, 225, 235, 238, 244–245
Miskovsky, Milan, 78, 127, 217
Model Cities program, 234
Mondale, Walter, 36, 44, 287
Montgomery, AL
    bus boycott, 9
    march to, 18–19
Moss, Frank, 36
Moyers, Bill, 73, 105
Moynihan, Daniel Patrick, 12, 160, 205,
    212
Muskegon, MI, riot, 5
Muslims, 10, 125, 316

NAACP. *See* National Association for the Advancement of Colored People
Nashville, TN (field teams in), 112
Nathan, Richard, 78, 263, 304
Nation, Richard, 304
National Advisory Commission on Civil Disorders. *See* Kerner Commission
National Alliance of Businessmen, 270
National Association for the Advancement of Colored People (NAACP), 7, 20, 29–30, 47, 123, 142
National Council of Catholic Bishops, 269
National Council of Churches, 269–270
National Guard, 45, 67, 86, 87–90, 284
   Michigan, 4
   New Jersey, 2–3
   New York, 5–6
   proposed racial integration of, 88–90
   proposed reform of, 57–58, 59, 66, 174
   Tennessee, 56
National Guard Association of the United States, 89
National League of Cities, 272
National Research Council, 301
Negro Factories Corporation, 10
"Negro Family, The: The Case for National Action" (Moynihan), 160
Neighborhood Youth Corps, 201
Nelson, Charles, 76, 165–166, 169
Nelson A. Rockefeller Institute of Government, 304
Ness, Eliot, 77
New Brunswick, NJ, riot, 3, 169
New Deal, 15, 65, 67, 68, 265, 295
New Haven, CT
   bomb threat in, 217
   field teams in, 121
New York Amsterdam News, 273–274
New York City (population decline), 302
New York City Housing Authority, 93

New York Roman Catholic diocese, 269
New York Times, 25, 33, 46, 62, 63–64, 90, 103, 108, 109, 207, 216, 254, 255, 256, 260, 263, 268, 269, 271, 289, 304, 312
Newark, NJ
   community leader meeting in, 270
   field teams in, 112, 116, 117, 118, 120, 121, 122
   Kerner commissioners' visit to, 92, 93, 99–100, 103, 106
   riot, 1–3, 8, 12, 15, 24, 26, 27, 29–30, 33, 35, 39, 46, 62, 81–82, 157, 171, 270, 271
Newsweek, 4, 5, 12, 192, 245–246, 268, 300
Nimitz, Matt, 75
Nixon, Richard, 64, 213, 279–282, 294, 295–296, 297
Nyack, NY, riot, 3

Oakland Tribune, 286
Obama, Barack, 311–313, 315, 316
Office of Economic Opportunity (OEO), 16, 104, 179, 263
Office of Price Administration (OPA), 68
oil prices, 300
"On Being Black" (newspaper column), 286
open housing, 96, 145
   Kerner Report on, 202, 211, 232, 236
   legislation passed for, 268, 286–288

Palmer, A. Mitchell, 26, 76
Palmieri, Victor, 65, 73–74, 75, 77, 90, 91, 106, 108, 109, 111, 112, 127–130, 142, 151–153, 173–175
   backgroud of, 73
   on challenges facing Kerner Commission, 78–79
   commissioners' approval process and, 238, 239, 242–243
   commissioners' policy discussions and, 194–195, 196, 199, 206, 213, 225
   field teams and, 115, 116, 129

firing of commission's workforce,
189
funding of Kerner Commission and,
183, 184
"Harvest" and, 151–152, 155, 156–157,
165, 166–167, 168–169, 173, 190
hearings and, 79, 80
on leaking of Kerner Report, 254
media coverage study, 216
meeting with commissioners'
assistants, 128
Shellow and, 152–153, 155
social scientists and, 124
Pasadena, CA (school system of), 303
Pearson, Drew, 256, 275
Peden, Katherine, 52–53, 59, 61, 134, 145,
149, 220, 230
background of, 52
final revisions and approval process,
231, 238, 239, 243
on the media, 216
policy recommendations and, 141,
199, 208, 210, 211, 222, 225
twenty-fifth anniversary of Kerner
Report and, 304
visits to riot-ravaged cities, 91, 93,
95, 100
Percy, Charles, 272
Pew Research Center polls, 312
Philadelphia, PA
population decline in, 302
riot, 5, 28
school system of, 303
Philadelphia Inquirer, 274
Phoenix, AZ (field teams in), 122, 124
Pittsburgh, PA (population decline),
302
Plainfield, NJ
field teams in, 119, 122
riot, 3, 155, 169
police
African American officers in, 120,
122, 215, 279
civilian review board
recommendation, 146, 147–148
"Harvest" on, 158–159, 163, 168, 169,
172, 173, 214

improved response during riots,
285–286
interim report on, 145–148, 170–171
investigations and recommendations
for, 313–314
murder of, 8
policy recommendations for,
214–215, 229–230, 235
shootings by, 312
as symbols of white oppression, 137
See also police brutality
police brutality, 18–19, 99, 100, 126,
145–148
field teams' findings on, 114, 120–121
racial divide on belief in, 278–279
policy recommendations, 193–215,
217–225
approval process for, 227
backfiring of, 264
Downs's input (*see* Downs,
Anthony)
early discussions and debates on,
137–141, 144–145
on education and schools, 202–203,
204, 211–212, 231, 232, 233, 236,
237
on employment, 200–201, 204,
207–208, 228, 230–231, 232, 233,
237
on housing, 197, 202, 204, 205,
210–211, 220, 228, 234, 236
on police, 214–215, 229–230, 235
Republicans on, 281–283
on welfare, 201–202, 205, 209,
212–213, 231, 232, 233–234, 237
Pontiac, MI, riot, 5
Poughkeepsie, NY, riot, 56
poverty, 301–303, 314
Clinton administration policies and,
307
"Great Recession" and, 311
percentage of blacks living in, 10, 301
riots' relationship with, 125–126, 138,
139, 141, 159, 221, 238, 277
social class and, 305–306
See also War on Poverty
Powers, Francis Gary, 78

presidential commission on race,
308–310
presidential elections
1964, 15, 16–17
1968, 248, 261, 279–283, 294–295
1972, 296
1980, 297
2016, 315–316
president's emergency fund, 178, 183
private enterprise, 207–208, 230–231
Proposition 14, 12, 50
Protest and Prejudice (Marx), 154
Providence, RI, riot, 6
public housing projects, 93, 97, 99, 106,
116, 307

racism. *See* white racism
Randolph, A. Philip, 36
Rankin, Lee, 80–81
Rat Extermination Act (proposed), 35,
55
Ray, James Earl, 283
Reagan, Ronald, 282, 297–298
Reed, Bruce, 309
Reedy, George, 40
Republican Coordinating Committee,
34, 35, 46
Republicans
Clinton administration and, 307
conspiracy theory argument and,
33, 83
federal aid cut by, 297–298
increase in voters turning to, 271
Johnson administration and, 15, 23,
24, 34–36
in Kerner Commission, 45–46
Kerner Report and, 276
Nixon administration and, 295
presidential election of 1968 and,
279–283, 294
special commission proposed by,
35–36
Ribicoff, Abraham, 37
riots, 1–13, 24–41, 315
African Americans' approval of, 125
Atlanta, 271
Baltimore, 312, 313

Bedford-Stuyvesant, 5, 27
Brooklyn, 55
cabinet task force on, 29–31, 40, 41
Cairo, 3
Cambridge, 8–9, 155, 157
Cedar Rapids, 3
Chicago, 6, 27, 284
Cincinnati, 8, 157
Cleveland, 27, 125, 271, 312
commissioners' visits to cities
ravaged by, 91–103, 106
concerns about "rewarding," 20–21,
29, 271
conspiracy theory of (*see* conspiracy
theory argument)
Dayton, 8
deaths in, 3, 4, 5, 6, 95, 96, 171, 284,
299
Des Moines, 3
Detroit (*see under* Detroit, MI)
Durham, 3
Elizabeth, 3
Englewood, 3
Erie, 3
Ferguson, 312, 313
Flint, 5
Grand Rapids, 5
Harlem, 5, 6, 8, 317
Jersey City, 3
Johnson's bewilderment over, 19–21
Kalamazoo, 5
Kerner Commission on (*see* Kerner
Commission; Kerner Report)
King assassination and, 284–286
liberals' view of, 24–25
Los Angeles, 271, 299–300
McCone Commission on, 7, 80, 125,
317
Minneapolis, 3
Muskegon, 5
New Brunswick, 3, 169
Newark (*see under* Newark, NJ)
Nyack, 3
Philadelphia, 5, 28
Plainfield, 3, 155, 169
political conflict resulting from, 33–38
Pontiac, 5

Poughkeepsie, 56
poverty related to, 125–126, 138, 139,
    141, 159, 221, 238, 277
profile of rioters, 57, 85, 125–126,
    160, 171
Providence, 6
Rochester, 5
root cause of (*see* white racism)
San Francisco, 6
secret missions to affected areas,
    27–28
South Bend, 56
St. Louis, 6
Staten Island, 312
Tampa, 229
Tulsa, 6
Washington, DC, 284
Watts (*see under* Watts, Los Angeles,
    CA)
West Fresno, 3
West Michigan City, 5
World War I and II era, 6
Rivers of Blood, Years of Darkness
    (Conot), 78
Rochester, NY, riot, 5
Rockefeller, Nelson, 5, 78, 286
Romney, George, 4, 31–33, 45, 57
Rooney, J. Pat, 281–282
Roosevelt, Franklin D., 15, 20, 45, 51, 65,
    68, 256, 264, 290, 296, 307
Rosenthal, Jack, 195, 217, 223–224, 241,
    242–243
rural areas, 231, 316
Russell, Richard, 18
Rustin, Bayard, 10, 205, 273

Safire, William, 297
Sagalyn, Arnold, 77–78, 145–147, 214
San Antonio, TX (antipoverty measures
    in), 307
San Francisco, CA
    integration survey of, 126
    riot, 6
Schlesinger, Arthur, Jr., 261
schools. *See* education and schools
Schultze, Charles, 178, 179, 180, 181–182,
    183, 185, 187–188

Schwartz, Herman, 230
Sears, David, 154, 159–161, 169
Seattle, WA (mayors' meeting), 270
segregation. *See* education and schools;
    housing; integration
Selma, AL, march, 18–19
Senate Watergate Committee, 287
senior staff of Kerner Commission, 65
    African Americans in, 76
    field teams' distrust of, 115–116,
        173–175
    "Harvest" rejected by, 165–169,
        173–174, 189–190
    personnel of, 72–78
    tension between commissioners and,
        127–129
September 11 terrorist attacks, 310
Shellow, Robert, 78, 129, 152–158,
    166–169, 170, 172–173, 190
    background of, 152
    concerns about mission, 153
    ostracism of, 166
    reaction to last chapter of "Harvest,"
        164–165
"silent majority," 280, 296, 297
Simulmatics Corporation, 216
single mothers. *See* female-headed
    households
Smith, John, 1–2, 121
social class, 305–306
social media, 312
social scientists, 91
    firings of, 189–190
    reactions to Kerner Report, 274–275
    Statler Hilton meeting of, 124–126
    See also "Harvest of American
        Racism, The"
Sorenson, Ted, 261
South Bend, IN, riot, 56
Southern Christian Leadership
    Conference, 273
Spina, Dominick, 2
Spivak, Al, 80, 191
St. Louis, MO
    population decline in, 302
    riot, 6
St. Louis Post-Dispatch, 62

Starr, Kenneth, 310
State of the Union addresses
    Clinton's, 307
    Johnson's, 22, 23, 262
State University of New York at
    Buffalo, 230
Staten Island, NY, riot, 312
status quo approach (antighetto
    strategy), 197, 198, 217, 218
Stern, Lawrence, 253–254
Stewart, Julia, 47
Stokes, Carl, 276
Students for a Democratic Society, 2,
    154
suburbs, 60, 104, 111–112, 117, 137, 197,
    200, 202, 228, 234, 270, 271
    African Americans in, 302, 303
    "invasion-succession" in, 303
    population increase in, 196, 301–302
    poverty in, 311
    See also white flight
Sugrue, Thomas J., 11
Supreme Court, 34, 47, 240, 317
Susann, Jacqueline, 269
Svirdoff, Mitchell, 195

Taliaferro, Henry, 95–96, 97, 98, 258
Tampa, FL, riot, 229
taxes, 23, 237, 278, 314
Taylor, William, 105
teenage pregnancy, 303
Tet Offensive, 249, 261, 265, 284
Thomas, Bruce, 112–113, 114, 173–174
Thornton, Charles "Tex," 50–52, 66, 80,
    84–87, 88, 90, 115, 124, 126, 134,
    137, 145, 168, 220, 225, 315
    agenda for Kerner Commission,
        60–61
    background of, 51–52
    conspiracy theory argument and, 82,
        84–86, 148
    death of, 304
    Fair Housing Act and, 287
    final revisions and approval process,
        228, 230–231, 232, 233, 235, 236,
        237, 238, 239, 240, 243, 244–245,
        246

interim report reviews and, 143–144,
    146, 147, 148, 149
Johnson's reaction to Kerner Report
    and, 250, 257–258
on the media, 216
policy recommendations and,
    140–141, 193, 195, 207–208, 210,
    211, 212–213, 215, 217–218, 222
private enterprise favored by,
    207–208, 230–231
racially insensitive language used
    by, 87
visits to riot-ravaged cities, 93, 100,
    101
white racism claim and, 136, 140
"three strikes and you're out" policy,
    307–308
Thurmond, Strom, 34
Time, 5, 49, 51
Tobin, James, 195
Tomlinson, Tommy, 274, 275
Tonight Show, The (television program),
    60
TransCentury Associates, 112
Truman, Harry, 257
Trump, Donald, 315–316
tuberculosis, 117
Tulsa, OK, riot, 6
Twitter, 312
"two societies" concept. *See under*
    Kerner Report
Tydings, Joseph, 35

unemployment, 10, 93, 106, 116, 172,
    302, 303, 310, 314. *See also*
    employment
unions. *See* labor unions
United Afro-American Association, 99
United Nations General Assembly, 53
United Presbyterian Church, 269
United Press International, 31
United States Civil Rights
    Commission, 105
United Steelworkers of America, 53
University of Alabama, 294
University of California-Los Angeles
    (UCLA), 105, 154

University of California-San Diego, 309
University of Chicago, 143
University of Chicago Law School, 173
University of Michigan, 16, 124
urban areas, 59, 60, 105, 111, 113, 114, 115,
    116, 133, 141, 160, 167, 198, 200,
    202, 207, 209, 217, 219, 231–232,
    266, 270, 276, 286, 299, 304, 305,
    306
    Carter administration and, 297
    Clinton administration and, 307
    current conditions in, 316–317
    Marshall Plan suggested for, 102,
        104, 138–139, 284
    Model Cities program, 234
    See also riots; white flight; *specific
        cities*
Urban Coalition, 209
Urban League, 29, 102, 120, 272, 274, 303

Valenti, Jack, 73
Valley of the Dolls (Susann), 269
Vance, Cyrus, 32, 55, 57–58, 59, 87–88
Vietnam War, 15, 21–24, 27, 31, 45,
    61, 105, 246, 251–252, 265–266,
    275–276, 294
    Brooke's support for, 48
    escalation of, 21
    Lindsay on, 209–210, 236, 241, 255,
        275
    protests against, 22, 81, 296
    spending on, 11, 22–23, 37, 94, 101,
        182–183, 209, 272
    Tet Offensive, 249, 261, 265, 284
    Wilkins's support for, 48
Voting Rights Act of 1965, 19

Waldman, Roger, 203
Wall Street Journal, 249, 277
Wallace, George, 294, 295
War on Drugs, 296, 308
War on Poverty, 92, 104–105, 163, 205,
    266
    field teams' findings on, 124
    funding for refused, 35
    spending on programs, 16
Warren Commission, 71, 80–81

Washington, DC, riots, 284
Washington Daily News, 190
Washington Post, 13, 62, 68, 89, 103,
    253–255, 260, 271, 275, 287, 312
Washington Star, 190–191, 276, 277
Watergate scandal, 296, 297, 307
Watson, Marvin, 29, 84
Wattenberg, Ben, 260–261
Watts, Los Angeles, CA
    integration survey of, 126
    riots, 5–6, 7, 19–21, 78, 80, 154, 157,
        159, 216, 270, 317
Weaver, Robert, 263
welfare
    "absent-father" rule, 201, 233, 237
    Clinton administration and, 306,
        307, 308, 309
    "man-in-the-house" rule, 201
    policy recommendations on,
        201–202, 205, 209, 212–213, 231,
        232, 233–234, 237
    Reagan administration and, 297, 298
West Fresno, CA, riot, 3
West Michigan City, MI, riot, 5
Westmoreland, William, 249, 265–266,
    284
Wheeler, Earle, 252
white flight, 112, 117, 137, 196, 301–302
White House Conference on Civil
    Rights, 62
White House Task Force on Urban
    Employment Opportunities, 200
white racism, 103, 134–137, 139, 140, 148,
    151, 170, 172, 194, 224, 242, 246,
    251, 252, 255, 257, 272–275, 278,
    284, 316
    civil rights leaders on, 272–273
    Clinton administration and, 309
    Corman on, 219, 221, 264
    Democrats divided on issue, 290
    Ginsburg on, 135–137, 203
    Harris on, 135, 243, 268
    Johnson on, 262–263
    Kerner on, 134–135
    Lindsay on, 134, 209, 243, 289
    McCulloch on, 136
    media on, 268

white racism (*continued*)
Reagan on, 282
reassessment of claim, 305
Republicans on, 281
suggested alternative terms for, 243
Thornton on, 136, 140
See also "Harvest of American
Racism, The"
whites
black neighborhoods attacked by,
6, 55–56
field teams' interviews of, 121
Great Society programs and, 12, 24
housing desegregation resisted by,
11–12, 290
immigrants and, 300
Johnson's concern for, 20–21, 28, 29
Kerner Report and, 198–199, 200,
232, 271, 276, 278–279, 290
New York Times editorial on, 63–64
presidential election of 1968 and,
294, 295
presidential election of 1972 and, 296
presidential election of 1980 and,
297
presidential election of 2016 and,
315–316
riots condemned by, 12, 13, 24, 28,
29, 33, 284–285
See also white flight; white racism
Whitewater scandal, 307
Wicker, Tom, 269
Wilkins, Roger, 32

Wilkins, Roy, 20, 29–30, 53, 61, 63, 87,
134, 168, 222, 235, 290
background of, 47–48
Black Power advocates and, 30, 48
conspiracy theory argument and, 85,
148, 217
death of, 304
final revisions and approval process,
246
interim report reviews and, 142, 144,
146–147, 148
Johnson's reaction to Kerner Report
and, 257
media and, 216, 268
policy recommendations and, 138,
145, 210, 211, 212, 213, 218, 220,
221, 225
visits to riot-ravaged cities, 93, 95
Wilkinson, Bud, 49
Wilmington, DE (white mob in), 55–56
Wilson, William Julius, 305–306
Winnich, Louis, 195
Wirtz, W. Willard, 263, 279
Wolfe, Alan, 306
World War I era riots, 6
World War II era riots, 6
Wright, Isaac, 7
Wright, Willie, 99

Xerox, 270

Yale University, 195
Young, Whitney, 29–30, 39, 47, 102, 272

Credit: © Andrew Weir

Steven M. Gillon is a scholar-in-residence at History and a professor of history at the University of Oklahoma. The author of several books on American history, he lives in Miami Beach.